Chef
White

Introduction to Psychology

Second Edition

Print ISBN 978-1-934920-94-7

For permission to use material from this text or for general questions about permissions, submit a request on line to http://www.wordsofwisdombooks.com/contact.asp

Publisher: Words of Wisdom, LLC
Book Title: Introduction to Psychology
Author: Editorial Board
Rights: Words of Wisdom, LLC
Publication Date: 2014
Edition: 2

VS 12

Acknowledgments

We would like to thank the Editorial Board for their time
and dedication to the creation of this book.

TABLE OF CONTENTS

Foundational Principles of Psychology

"Like all science, psychology is knowledge; and like science again, it is knowledge of a definite thing, the mind."

—James M. Baldwin

WHAT IS PSYCHOLOGY?

Psychology is a science that focuses on studying the mind, mental processes, and human behavior. It is a science because research psychologists use **empirical** research methods to observe, explain, and predict behavioral and mental processes. For example, a psychologist might conduct research to explain the phenomenon of racism, that is, how individuals perceive certain groups and what factors predict racist behaviors. Psychological research methods range from descriptive studies to tightly controlled laboratory experiments. In descriptive studies, researchers describe behavior as it occurs naturally, without manipulation of the environment. In the laboratory, experimental psychologists create artificial situations for the purpose of isolating and measuring participants' responses. For example, a psychologist might examine how individuals respond to attractive people versus people who are perceived to be less attractive. These responses would be examined by manipulating various conditions of "attractiveness." The results of psychological research are carefully reviewed by other scientists before they are published.

EMPIRICAL Relating to the direct observation and collection of data.

WHY SHOULD YOU STUDY PSYCHOLOGY?

It is natural to want to understand your own thoughts and behaviors and the thoughts and behaviors of those around you. The study of psychology will complement your curiosity about yourself and others by describing the scientific basis of what is known about human nature. The following sections provide brief discussions of how psychology will help you to better understand

- the biological foundations of behavior;
- how people sense, perceive, learn, and think about the world;
- the sources of change and stability in behavior across the lifespan;
- how psychological factors affect physical and emotional health;
- how social networks affect behavior; and
- how psychology will serve humanity in the future.

The Biological Foundations of Behavior

This introduction to psychology will help you understand the biological systems that underlie your thoughts, emotions, and behaviors. Your thoughts, feelings, and behaviors and the functions of your body originate in your brain. The brain is a three-pound mass of gray tissue composed of more than one billion neurons, or nerve cells, that communicate with each other. Nerve impulses travel from your brain down your spinal cord, where they intersect with nerves that control your internal organs and muscles.

1. Psychology is the study of thought, behavior, and emotion. See page 3.

2. Psychology is a broad and diverse field, including basic research and practical applications of research findings. See page 5.

3. An introduction to psychology is good preparation for any career. See page 7.

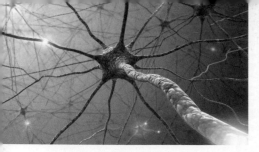

How People Sense, Perceive, Learn, and Think about the World

Sensation refers to the processes by which your sense organs (eyes, ears, nose, mouth, and skin) detect external stimuli and transform them into signals that are transmitted to the brain. Inside the brain, these sensory signals are organized into meaningful units, such as an image of a familiar face or the taste of a favorite food. **Perception** refers to the brain's processes of transforming raw sensory signals into recognizable information (for example, knowing the "tiny" cars you see on the ground from an airplane window are actually larger than they appear).

Psychologists define **learning** as any enduring change in behavior that occurs as the result of experience. Individuals learn by

- getting feedback from people and objects in their environment;
- observation; and
- **thinking**, which involves making mental associations between ideas and concepts.

The study of psychology will help you understand how you respond to and transform outside stimuli into meaningful perceptions and knowledge.

SENSATION The processes by which your sense organs (eyes, ears, nose, mouth, and skin) detect external stimuli and transform them into signals that are transmitted to the brain.

PERCEPTION The brain's process of transforming sensory signals into recognizable information.

LEARNING The process of making mental associations between ideas and concepts.

THINKING The process of making mental associations between ideas for a specific goal or purpose.

Sources of Change and Stability in Behavior across the Lifespan

Developmental psychology investigates how thoughts, feelings, and behaviors develop and change throughout the human lifespan, from birth to death. Understanding the predictable stages in human development can help you appreciate the personal changes you have experienced in your life and prepare for those that lie ahead.

DEVELOPMENTAL PSYCHOLOGY The branch of psychology that investigates how thoughts, feelings, and behaviors develop and change throughout the lifespan, from birth to death.

How Psychological Factors Affect Physical and Mental Health

Chronic **stress** is a psychological state that affects physical and mental health. It occurs whenever humans must adapt to changing conditions. When you are under too much stress, your endocrine system secretes stress hormones directly into your bloodstream.

Other psychological factors that can affect physical and mental health are adverse behaviors, such as smoking and excessive alcohol or drug consumption. An important benefit of studying psychology is learning how psychological factors contribute to your mental and physical health.

STRESS A pattern of behavioral and physiological responses to events that matches or exceeds your ability to respond.

How Social Networks Affect Behavior

Humans are innately social creatures. Social psychology examines how social relationships work. Studying social psychology involves understanding how humans develop prejudices and make judgments about others. It teaches why people's behavior when they are part of a group may be different than when they are acting alone. Social psychology explores the qualities that make someone a leader and explains what attracts people to their significant others.

How Psychology Will Serve Humanity in the Future

Many new developments in psychology cross disciplinary boundaries. One area of rapid growth is *neuroscience*, a branch of research that uses medical imaging tools to watch the brain at work. Neuroscience research can help psychologists better understand how the brain affects emotion, thought, and behavior. Health psychology investigates how biology, psychology, and social factors interact to affect health. Health psychologists help people change unhealthy behaviors; they also create education programs targeted to at-risk groups. *Cross-cultural psychology* considers how cultural differences interact with other psychological factors to affect an individual's values and goals. Practitioners who are trained in cross-cultural methods are particularly well-suited to serve people from diverse backgrounds.

FIELDS OF PSYCHOLOGY

In the broadest sense, the field of psychology includes two types of practitioners: those who engage in basic scientific research and those who apply scientific research findings to improve the function of people, organizations, and communities. Research psychologists investigate everything from the mechanics of perception to the causes of abnormal psychological conditions. Some research psychologists teach in universities and colleges. In general, working in the field of research psychology requires doctoral-level training.

Following are some major areas of basic research in psychology:

■ Biopsychology (sometimes called physiological psychology) investigates the physiological basis of psychological phenomena, including thought, emotion, and stress. For example, a biopsychologist may research the chemistry of stress hormones or drug addiction. Increasingly, biopsychologists are using neuroscience techniques in their research.

■ Cognitive psychology investigates processes related to thinking, including memory, reasoning, and decision making. Cognitive psychologists also research perceptual and learning processes.

■ Developmental psychology investigates how thought, feeling, and behavior develop and change throughout the lifespan, from birth to death.

■ Personality psychology studies differences in thoughts, emotional responses, and behaviors that are relatively stable in an individual over time and across circumstances.

■ Social psychology examines the dynamics and interactions of individuals and groups.

The practical applications of psychology are surprisingly varied. Most people are familiar with clinical psychology, the branch of psychology that focuses on the treatment of emotional and mental problems. Other practical applications of psychology include human factors psychology, industrial/organizational psychology, and sports psychology.

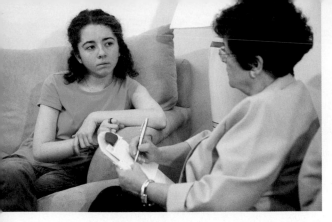

The training required for a professional field can include masters' and doctoral-level certification and requires knowledge of the basic topics in psychology research.

Major fields of professional psychology include:

■ Clinical psychology, which involves diagnosing and treating people with emotional and mental disorders. Training includes education in all areas of basic psychology research. Knowledge of developmental, personality, motivational, and abnormal psychology is particularly important.

■ Health psychology, which focuses on improving individual and community health by applying research from biology, psychology, and social psychology. Health psychologists need solid training in all areas of basic psychology research.

■ Human factors psychology, which focuses on improving interactions between humans and their work environment. Human factors psychologists deal with a range of topics, including human–computer interaction, workplace safety, sources and prevention of human error, and product design. Knowledge of perception and cognitive psychology is important.

■ Industrial/organizational (I/O) psychology, which prepares psychologists to help organizations, including businesses, nonprofits, and educational institutions, solve personnel and organizational problems. An I/O psychologist may help a business recruit new employees or develop more effective training. An I/O psychologist needs a strong background in cognitive, personality, and social psychology.

■ School psychology, which involves diagnosing and treating behavioral and learning problems in children and adolescents. Training in cognitive, clinical, developmental, motivational, personality, and social psychology is emphasized.

■ Sports psychology, which involves helping recreational and professional athletes understand how psychological factors affect their performance. Sports psychologists need a strong background in cognitive, motivational, personality, and social psychology.

As psychology evolves, new applications of basic scientific research emerge. The American Psychological Association is the largest association of psychologists worldwide, and its website (www.apa.org) is an excellent resource for learning more about any field of psychology.

TRY IT! AN INTERVAL SCALE FOR SELF-ESTEEM

INTERVAL SCALES A scientific measurement tool with equal distances among the units on the scale.

SELF-ESTEEM A person's evaluation of his or her own self-worth.

Psychologists sometimes use scientific measurement tools, such as interval scales, to measure people's attitudes and beliefs. **Interval scales** have equal distances between each unit on the scale. The results of interval scales can be used for research or for diagnosis of emotional problems in clinical psychology. The following self-test items are taken from an interval scale that measures **self-esteem**, which is a person's evaluation of his or her own self-worth.

DISAGREE STRONGLY	DISAGREE	AGREE	AGREE STRONGLY
1	2	3	4

For each of the following statements, use the following scale to indicate your agreement or disagreement.

- I feel that I am a person of worth, at least on an equal scale with others.
- I feel that I have a number of good qualities.
- I am able to do things as well as most people.
- I take a positive attitude toward myself.
- On the whole, I am satisfied with myself.

Source: Rosenberg, M. (1965). *Society and the adolescent self-image.* Princeton, NJ: Princeton University Press.

Why Is Psychology Important in All Careers and Other Realms of Life?

Learning about psychology will increase your self-knowledge, which can help you to reach your goals. Developing an understanding of the psychological factors that affect all human beings will help you develop more empathy for others and a better understanding of how people behave in groups. Studying psychology will help you prepare for careers in which you interact with other people. In other words, the study of psychology will help you prepare for any career.

PSYCHOLOGY & CAREERS: HOW DOES UNDERSTANDING PSYCHOLOGY LEAD TO SUCCESS IN NURSING?

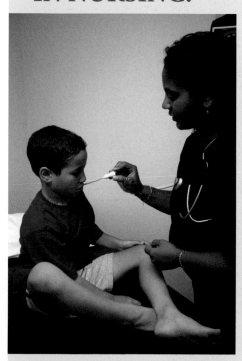

Psychology and nursing share similar goals: the improvement of physical and mental health for individuals and society. They also share similar perspectives because both fields are related to the biological sciences and are interdisciplinary. While both fields consider the biology of human beings, psychology adds an understanding of how emotional and mental factors contribute to the uniqueness of each individual. Both psychology and nursing rely on scientific methodology and codes of ethics to investigate new topics and to set the standards for the fair and equitable treatment of individuals who seek their care.

A basic familiarity with the range of topics addressed in psychology can help nurses treat their patients. Nurses must understand the biology of behavior in order to appreciate how psychological factors, such as anxiety, depression, and stress, affect health. They must be able to differentiate between normal and abnormal behaviors, including taking into account an individual's background. Nurses

(Continued on next page)

(Continued from previous page)

need to understand the predictable changes that occur during every stage of life in order to appreciate the context in which behaviors are presented. Understanding the dynamics of human motivation can help nurses inspire a reluctant individual to follow health guidelines. Appreciating how social and cultural differences can affect an individual's perception of pain is a valuable skill.

Both nursing and psychology use scientific methods to conduct research. An exposure to the research methods of psychology can help nurses understand how new treatment protocols are developed. In addition, nurses who have experience collecting and analyzing data and reading research reports will be well-prepared to perform these tasks in a health care setting. Nursing and psychology both have strict codes of ethics for their practices. Nurses who are already familiar with the ethical standards of practice in psychology will be able to understand the logic and necessity underlying similar practices in nursing.

THE HISTORY AND EVOLUTION OF PSYCHOLOGY

Throughout recorded history, humans have pondered the nature of the mind. One long-standing debate, called the **mind-body controversy**, questions if and how the physical body and the mind are connected. In the fifth century BC, the Greek philosopher Plato argued that the mind was separate from the body and that it continued to exist after death. Plato also argued that humans were born with all the knowledge they would ever have. He viewed education as a process of discovering what you already knew.

Aristotle, another Greek philosopher of the same period, opposed Plato's point of view. He argued that mind and body were intertwined and made of roughly the same substance. Knowledge was not innate, according to Aristotle; instead, it was derived from experience in the world.

Another classic debate was about the nature of physical matter. Philosophers questioned: *What is the smallest unit of matter? What makes objects move and stop moving?* Many early philosophers believed that all matter, including the human body, was animated by special "vital forces." Aristotle believed that all matter, including the human body, was composed of four elements: earth, water, air, and fire.

Eventually, the use of scientific investigation was extended to the study of the mind. In 1879, a medical doctor named Wilhelm Wundt (1832–1920) opened the first scientific laboratory in Leipzig, Germany. Wundt wanted to discover the smallest unit of thought. He used a method he called **introspection**, which is the process of looking inward and examining oneself and one's actions in order to understand oneself better. Wundt asked volunteers to report verbally every thought that passed through their minds when they were presented with a particular task. Because he was interested in studying the structure of consciousness, his approach to understanding the mind was known as **structuralism**.

Functionalism, which focuses on the role or function of psychological processes, is another school of thought that dominated early psychology. The philosopher William James (1842–1910) was one of the leaders of the functionalism movement and wrote the first psychology textbook in 1890. James argued that knowledge about the mind could come not only from experimentation, but also from the study of children, other animals, and the mentally ill.

MIND-BODY CONTROVERSY The debate in psychology and philosophy about if and how the physical body and the mind are connected.

INTROSPECTION The process of looking inward and examining oneself and one's actions in order to understand oneself better.

STRUCTURALISM The school of psychology that studies the structure of consciousness.

FUNCTIONALISM The school of psychology that studies the purpose of psychological processes.

KEY THINKERS IN PSYCHOLOGY: SIGMUND FREUD

Sigmund Freud (1856–1939) is perhaps the most recognizable figure in the history of psychology. Freud was a medical doctor in late 19th-century Vienna. Many of his patients had ailments for which he could find no physical cause. After unsuccessful attempts using hypnosis to cure his patients, Freud encouraged them to talk freely about their problems, a therapeutic practice known as psychoanalysis. Through psychoanalysis, Freud's patients often remembered painful events that had been hidden from their awareness. By understanding the connections between past trauma and present discomfort, Freud's patients were often relieved of their symptoms.

Based on his experience with patients, Freud compared the structure of the human mind to an iceberg. The tip of the iceberg represents the conscious mind. Below the surface are hidden events and emotions. Freud's perspective is called the psychodynamic approach because it emphasizes the active role of hidden, unconscious forces in mental life.

Freud also proposed theories about personality structure and development and revolutionized the way physicians viewed mental problems. Many adopted his psychoanalytic approach. Freud proposed his theories without conducting scientific experiments, relying instead upon his observations to formulate his theories. For this reason, his work is sometimes criticized for its lack of empirical evidence. In the face of this criticism, Freud's recognition of the power of the unconscious mind remains one of the most significant contributions to the history of psychology.

THE FOUR MAJOR PERSPECTIVES IN PSYCHOLOGY

The field of psychology has been in an almost constant state of growth, change, and debate, and it appears this happens in psychology more so than in other disciplines. This chapter briefly go through a few exciting times in the history of psychology with a review of four perspectives in psychology, highlighting along the way key figures in psychology whose passion ignited new theories or changed a working theory. This chapter will also address the development of these major theories that are debated and developed today. Each theory is considered a perspective in psychology and has been generated to give everyone a better understanding of highly complex human behavior. The field has been through times of heated debate and conflict over the best way to capture the essence of a person. Keep in mind the time period in history when the theory was developed, the level of technology (or perhaps the lack thereof), and consider that these individuals dedicated much of their life on working to unlock the human mind. Research is always open to criticism, questioning, rebuff, and debate, and there has been plenty of this in the history of psychology. The ultimate goal of psychology is to understand the human mind and this will be shown through the history of psychological perspectives and how they have moved society closer to unlocking the mind. This chapter will also show how past perspectives paved the way for psychologists today.

As the scientific study of psychology evolved, other perspectives on the mind and behavior emerged. Several important approaches have made major contributions to psychology, as follows:

- Psychodynamic
- Behaviorism
- Humanistic
- Cognitive

Psychodynamic

Sigmund Freud is the well-known founder of the psychodynamic perspective in psychology. His first theory—in the late 19th Century—was based upon his believe that the conflict between one's conscious and unconscious was the basis for his or her mental functioning. His theory further included the strong sexual drive that he described as being located in the unconscious and demanded expression. The conscious had a repressing force that was the counterbalance for the sexual drive. Sigmund Freud believed that the ultimate source of human behavior was the quest to satisfy innate biological drives, particularly the drive for sexual satisfaction. The conscious and unconscious were central to his original theory. Conscious refers to the state of one's mind where one is aware of what is currently being thought. Unconscious thus refers to an area of one's mind that cannot be directly monitored, reached, understood, or known to the individual without the input of another.

Freud suggested the personality was formed from the interplay of three forces: the id, the ego, and the superego. Freud's book, *The Ego and Id* (1923), illustrated his theory and attempted to explain the human mind in a way that had never been done before. Freud believed that neurosis, a kind of mental disorder involving emotional problems in everyday living, stemmed from an individual's inability to negotiate the drives of the id with the demands of the superego. The **id**, is without regard for consequences, wants immediate gratification and is driven by the pleasure principal. Sounds like the perfect recipe for trouble, right? Perhaps the id would be more suited to be labeled as fun? If an individual only functions from the id, things like hyper sexual behaviors, over eating, and physically dangerous activities are seen. The opposite of the id is the superego. The **superego** is another powerful force on the personality. The superego is both conscious and unconscious. Largely, the unconscious portion of the superego is similar to that of a parental force. This unconscious portion of the superego is the driving force in self-control, boundary setting, rule following, and even guilt. Surely, the id would label this part of the human mind as boring, and see the superego as limiting the desire for fun. With the id and the superego set firmly in opposite seats, the third force is left to be the moderator. The **ego** is considered to be the middle and balancing force between the id and the superego. The ego is the part of one's personality that considers the situation and circumstances in decision making. In a way, the ego becomes the peacemaker between the two other super forces; the id and superego. With the stage set with these three components—the id, ego, and superego—Freud theorized that the mind is in a complex power struggle. Freud's revolutionary theories attracted many students, some of whom modified the psychodynamic approach.

The psychodynamic perspective largely came from psychoanalytic therapy, Freud's method of treatment. His development of psychoanalysis was derived from a combination of his belief that one had to help a patient bring up their unconscious and the Oedipus Complex hidden inside. The process of psychoanalysis was to get the patient to remember the things they had repressed. Repression is more than simply forgetting a memory. Freud distinguished **repression** as the intentional act of forgetting. He made a connection between his own adoration for his mother and jealous feelings he had towards father, and saw a resemblance to this in the Oedipus Rex play. He labeled this conflict between the two as the *Oedipus Complex*. Furthermore, he not only saw that he had these conflicting feelings between his parents, but generalized the conflict to everyone else. He theorized that these conflicting feelings become repressed, but could resurface to the conscious due to the unconscious still grappling with the conflict. The Oedipus Complex was an essential ingredient to his development of psychoanalysis that eventually led to a psychodynamic perspective. Although, this is not a generalized belief today, it laid the foundation for the future development of the psychodynamic perspective.

Freud is further known for his work on interpreting dreams. He wrote *The Interpretation of Dreams* (1900), where he made the analogy that dreams were like a picture-puzzle. He used psychoanalysis with his patients in an effort to solve the puzzle that was the patient's dream. His book asserted that the meaning of dreams was hidden in the unconscious, and that was in essence, repressed. Matalon (2011) wrote "On Freud's psychogenic model, dreaming constitutes an indirect channel by which disagreeable and/or distressing materials can bypass the psyche's defense and rise from the dreamer's unconscious toward her conscious awareness." In essence, Freud is saying that dreams are a puzzle meant to be solved, because the dream can only express a portion of the *truth* (or repression) behind the dream.

Neo-Freudians, such as Karen Horney (1885–1952) and D. W. Winnicott (1896–1971), downplayed Freud's emphasis on the role of sexuality in the unconscious mind, and made significant contributions to psychodynamic theory. In contrast with Freud, Horney proposed that neurotic patterns resulted from an individual's thwarted attempts to establish secure relationships with others. To develop a healthy, secure sense of self, Horney argued that infants and young children required trusting relationships with reliable parents to meet their needs for security. Horney is also known as one of the first psychologists to explore psychology from a female's perspective. Winnicott is known for his contribution to the attachment theory and object-relations theory that emphasizes the importance of a nurturing parental relationship to a young child's developing personality. Winnicott's theory of object relations is relevant to many types of close relationships, including those between therapist and client.

NEO-FREUDIANS They are psychologists who downplayed Freud's emphasis on the role of sexuality in the unconscious mind, but furthered the cause of psychodynamic theory.

Behaviorism

Behaviorism is the study of understanding human behaviors that are both measurable and observable. From 1920 to 1960, psychology in the United States was heavily oriented toward behaviorism. Behaviorism conducted scientific research, using experiments to give more validity to their claims on human behavior. Many of the concepts learned from these experiments have been used with great success—even in present times—throughout classrooms, families, and businesses.

John B. Watson (1878–1958) is well-known for being the father of behaviorism, a field that began with his publication of *Psychology as the Behaviorist Views It* in 1913. People of the late 19th Century were looking at science as the way of the future. If mankind was to progress, society believed it would be because of science. It was a natural move for psychologists to adopt the methods of science. In fact, Watson started his publication in 1913 by stating that psychology is a natural science. He felt that if the concept could not be directly observed, then it could not be measured, and thus it could not be scientifically studied. Critics of behaviorism at the time argued that there was more to science than what Watson believed.

Associative Learning

According to behavioral psychologists, human behavior is anything that is measureable and observable, and is a result of one's environment. Understanding how people learn is an age old curiosity. Behaviorists identified one theory of learning as associative learning. **Associative learning** is when people learn from making a connection between two events. Associate learning can be further broken down into two categories: classical conditioning and operant conditioning.

Classical Conditioning

Ivan Pavlov (1849–1936) was a Russian physiologist investigating digestion in dogs. Pavlov rang a bell before each feeding. He noticed that the dogs began to salivate when they heard the bell, even before the food was presented. He further explored and found that they would salivate with the bell ringing and no food present. Pavlov proposed that the animals' association of the bell with food was a type of learning. The bell ringing at the beginning was paired with the food and then identified as the neutral stimulus (NS). A neutral stimulus means that a dog would not have a prior response to a bell ringing. The smell of food was identified as the unconditioned stimulus (US). A dog's involuntary response to the smell of food is salivating, and thus labeled as an unconditioned response. Pavlov then repeatedly paired the smell of food and the ringing of the bell together. He then only presented the ringing bell without the smell of food. He found that the bell became a condition stimulus (CS), because the dogs began to salivate when the bell rang; the salivation with just the ringing bell is a conditioned response (CR). Pavlov's discovery of learning through association proposes that learning results from stimuli that are associated with specific involuntary response behaviors. This is now known as **classical conditioning**.

Watson embraced the concept of classical conditioning when the idea came to America and began to experiment with the concept. While at John Hopkins University, he conducted what is now known at the Little Albert experiment. Watson used a 9-month-old boy named Albert to study his theory of translating classical conditioning to human behavior. Albert had no previous fear of rats. He did, however, become startled and upset when a loud noise occurred. The loud noise became the US and the white rat was the CS. When Watson and his graduate student, Rosalie Rayner, paired the noise with the rat repeatedly, Albert began showing fear with just the presence of the rat (without the noise). The fear response to the rat became the CR. It is said that Watson planned on extinguishing the conditioned fear response, but Albert's mother removed him from the experiment before this could be done.

Operant Conditioning

Behaviorism was revived in the late 1930s and 1940s by researcher B.F. Skinner. Skinner supported Watson's prior working in omitting language about thinking, the mind, or consciousness in the pursuit of behaviorism. In fact, he theorized that "behavior is the learned result of consequences" (Rholetter, 2013). The foundation of his theory was based upon the idea that humans respond to rewards and punishments. He termed the phrases positive reinforcement, negative reinforcement, and punishments from the three types of consequences that can result from human behavior. Skinner presented his theory in his book *The Behavior of Organisms: An Experimental Analysis* (1938). His book first presented the term **operant conditioning,** and identified it as the association between a behavior and its consequence when utilizing reinforcement and punishment.

Skinner presented that both positive reinforcement and negative reinforcement are used to increase a desired behavior. **Positive reinforcement** is when a favorable stimulus is given following the desired behavior. For example, an employee is given verbal praise for effectively managing a situation with an upset customer. **Negative reinforcement** is when an unfavorable stimulus is removed following the desired behavior. If the same employee was on probationary status, the supervisor removes the probation status after their demonstration of effective customer services skills. **Punishment** is a technique used to decrease undesirable behavior. Punishment is giving an unfavorable stimulus after the undesirable behavior. If an employee arrives late to work (undesirable behavior) the supervisor notifies the employee upon arrival that the time missed from work will be deducted from his or her paycheck. Remember, reinforcement (either positive or negative) is the tool used to increase a desirable behavior, while punishment is a tool used to decrease or eliminate an undesirable behavior. One important key with both reinforcement and punishment is that the stimulus is most effective when closely followed by the behavior.

Skinner's findings on operant conditioning have had far reaching impacts for many decades. Behavior modification using reinforcement has been widely used in treating many psychological disorders and conditions. It has even moved beyond just the field of psychology, going into the areas of training animals, management techniques in the workforce, and even in sales and marketing. These applications are seen when animals perform for food, and when work absenteeism decreases when bonuses are given for attendance, and when customers return to a store after given a coupon at the checkout. A major implementation of this has been seen in education. Operant conditioning has transformed behavior modification in the school systems. Skinner's assertions that positive reinforcement is most effective at creating and sustaining desirable behavior in students has heavily influenced the schools' decreased use of punishment. Token economy has been found in many classrooms around the nation. **Token economy** is rooted in positive reinforcement for desirable behaviors. For example, students are given stickers after a desirable behavior is demonstrated. Perhaps there is also a treasure box the children can choose from once a predetermined amount of stickers are earned.

Behaviorism had many great contributions to the field of psychology. Behaviorism was the subject of great critique for many decades, and the theorists' firm rejection of inclusion of thoughts and cognition into the theory may have been the crux of its downfall. Although the perspective has run its course as the main theory in present day psychology, many of its concepts can still be used. In fact, one author made the analogy that behaviorism is like a sugar cube dissolved into tea. It is everywhere, without being in a specific place in present psychology.

Humanistic

Humanistic psychology was developed in the mid-1900s and the concept of the self was at the foundation of this perspective. Humanistic psychology was made popular by Carl Rogers and Abraham Maslow. The two defined and identified the difference between the actual-self and the self-concept as elements of humanism. The **self-concept** is how a person understands who they are within the framework of society and, or loved ones. The self-concept almost has an element of containment about it, because people's self-concepts stay where they perceived are to be in relation to society and, or relationships. For example, a student in high school has a self-concept they he is not part of the in-crowd and is not popular. He is more likely

NEGATIVE REINFORCEMENT It is when an unfavorable stimulus is removed following the desired behavior.

POSITIVE REINFORCEMENT It is when a favorable stimulus is given following the desired behavior.

PUNISHMENT It is giving an unfavorable stimulus after the undesirable behavior

SELF-CONCEPT It is how a person understands who they are within the framework of society and, or loved ones.

ACTUAL-SELF It is how a
person understands who they are
without the social expectations
and influences of those around
them.

to maintain that self-concept when he moves on from high school. In contrast, the **actual-self** is who people are without the social expectations and influences of those around them. Taking the same high school student and delving deeper into his own idea of self without the influence of his peers at school, he might see that his actual-self is a loyal friend who enjoys photography. The actual-self allows for more adaptability and the power for people to define who they are, based on their own authentic values. There is less demand to be who others want an individual to be, perceive this individual to be or expect the individual to be. This freedom allows the individual to have greater acceptance, autonomy, and individuality.

Abraham Maslow (1908–1970) was dissatisfied with the behaviorism and psychodynamic perspectives due to their lack of inclusion of human potential. He believed that people have the ability to advance to their full potential, and that these earlier perspectives did not embrace this concept. In fact, he felt both perspectives focused on psychopathology. Maslow's response was to create a psychological perspective that includes the higher levels of human function. He investigated processes related to human motivation. Maslow's hierarchy of needs proposed that all humans must satisfy basic needs, such as the physiological necessity of food, water, and shelter, before they can realize their talents to the fullest. The result of his work was to form the humanistic approach to psychology, also referred to as the *Third Force*. His organization of the hierarchy of needs showed that there is a dependence upon the lower levels for the upper levels to be reached. His visualization of a pyramid indicates that the higher levels are not obtained as often. Maslow did emphasize that some of the needs can be only partially obtained. He made further exceptions to allow for some individuals to obtain the needs in a different order than he created. With a hierarchy, he also theorizes that human thoughts and actions are dominated by meeting those needs or having them met. When a level is satisfied, the individual moves on to the next level. Again, the individual is consumed with the desire to satisfy those needs. Maslow further asserted that these needs are universal to all humans. Therefore, his model is unique in that it "crosses geographic, racial, gender, social, ethnic, and religious boundaries" (Zalenski & Raspa, 2006).

The needs, as Maslow outlined, fall into 5 basic categories: (in order of the bottom to the top) physiological, safety, love and, or belonging, esteem, and self-actualization. The first human need is in the physiological level. This level includes basic biological needs, including but not limited to food, water, air, shelter, sleep, and sex. The next level is safety, and this addresses the human needs of security, protection, stability, and law. The third level is love and belonging. This leve is sometimes referred to as social. This level is encompassed by the concept of both giving and receiving affection. This can be met with things such as family, relationships, and even work. The fourth level is esteem, a level rooted in obtaining achievement, responsibility, status, and reputation. Societal recognition is the crux of this level, and can come after mastery of the environement. As an adult, this can be related to the accomplishments in one's career. The fifth level is self-actualization. **Self-actualization** is obtaining self-fullfilment, the full potential one has as an individual with unique gifts, talents, and beliefs. Maslow's theory indicates that this level is the ultimate experience in existance, where one can have deep connections with others, a profound faith and, or true meaning in life. He believed these experiences motivate and create feelings of being enlightened.

The humanistic perspective values the integrity of each individual. Carl Rogers (1902–1987) was a pioneer in the field of humanistic psychology. Rogers' concepts came from observing his patients as a psychotherapist. He proposed that each individual has an internal core, or true self, that can become distorted if an

SELF-ACTUALIZATION It is the
desire of a person to achieve his
or her full potential.

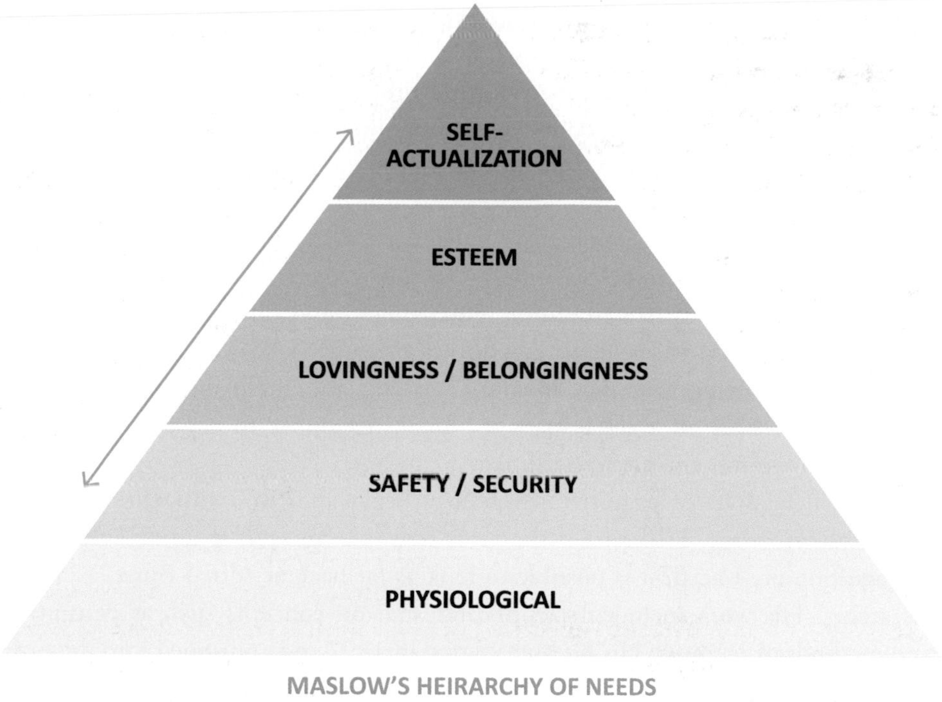

FIGURE 1.1 Maslow's Hierarchy of Needs

individual is preoccupied with gaining the approval of others. Rogers championed a therapeutic technique called client-centered therapy. His therapeutic approach came from his clients and what he saw as them being inhibited by trying to fit in to society's assigned roles to be accepted, loved, and respected. The therapist expresses unconditional empathy, or acceptance and understanding, of the client's subjective experience. He theorized that individuals have a natural desire to seek authenticity and embrace personal values and beliefs. He used his client-centered therapy to encourage his clients to discover elements of their true self that had been buried while trying to be someone else under the eyes of the world. These elements of the self could be different beliefs, values, interests, passions, or talents. Additionally, client—centered therapy also strived to "enhance self-regard, openness to experience and emotions, which are thought to result in greater autonomy and mastery of life" (McDonald & Wearing, 2013). Rogers believed for the self to grow into its full potential, the client needed a supportive and nurturing environment.

Although humanistic psychology began to lose ground in the 1970s, the field still has some champions trying to urge it along with current trends in the field. Theories propose some adaptations and changes to help negate the arguments of its detractors. It's been considered possible by lowering the focus on previously defined self-actualization, and focusing on a reconceptualization of the self from the humanistic view by Martin Heidegger. Only time and continued publications from psychological research will unravel humanistic psychology and see if it can stay relevant in the mainstream world of psychology.

Cognitive

Cognitive psychology was born out of dissatisfaction and rejection of the behavioral perspective. As mentioned previously, the behaviorist created a hot topic of debate when it came to the concept of thinking. Other researchers wanted a scientific study of psychology that included the mystery of cognition (internal processes); these concepts that cannot be seen, touched, felt, or measured. Cognitive psychologists wanted to further explore the concepts within the mind, beyond unconscious and conscious. The scientific method for researching these concepts of the mind would continue to be embraced and expanded to secure the validity of the research outcomes. As cognitive psychology came together, it had two basic goals. The first was to explore real human experiences and understand the cognitive functions that are paired with those activities. The second goal was to created solutions to problems that are faced in fields like education, government, and business. Cognitive psychology is expanded to include many topics of study, such as sensation, perception, problem-solving, attention, memory, learning, and intelligence to name a few. These subtopics are all a global part of humanity's ability to use higher levels of cognitive functions, and are referred to as cognition.

The official start of cognitive psychology began in 1967 with Ulric Neisser's *Cognitive Psychology*. However, if the roots that have grown up around the study of cognition are traced, it is possible to look as far back at Alfred Binet, a French researcher. His work included scientific research on concepts such as perception and methods of memory. His research started in 1892 and continued into the early 1900s. Binet paired up with Theophile Simone, and together they created cognitive testing for children and introduced the idea of a mental age. Intelligence testing has naturally evolved over the years, but is still used in educational settings to this day. Much of the early pioneers in cognitive psychology were European researchers, including Ebbinhaus, who was also researching cognitive abilities in children, and specifically researched tasks such as memorization. The questions of cognitive functions are timeless and have been of great intrigue throughout history.

Historical time periods and other fields of academia greatly influenced the development of cognitive psychology. During World War I, there was a need to have a better selection process for pilots. In the 1950s and 60s the growth of computer technology paved the way for the cognitive perspective to grow. Computers allowed for even greater amount of research in the field. This is when the analogy of the human brain to a computer processor was created. Researchers were able to discover greater understanding of how the human mind processes information.

Ulric Neisser is most often seen as the first to identify cognitive psychology. His work included the research of at least the two previous decades, and when he published *Cognitive Psychology* (1967), cognitive psychology was already well on its way. It is important to note that the cognitive perspective has been critical in moving people from very little understanding of the complexities of the human mind to greater insight into internal processes, such as memory, learning, thinking, problem-solving, emotions, and language.

Jean Piaget (1896–1980) is an important cognitive psychologist whose theory of stages of cognitive development laid the groundwork for understanding how human's cognitive abilities develop throughout childhood. His studies focused specifically on children as learners and developmental sequences that he identified in specific order. Piaget introduced the idea of a schema. A schema is how humans organize information into smaller units and relate them to the world around them. Piaget identified schemas as the basic building blocks of intelligence. Piaget saw "intelligence as a mental adaptation to new circumstances" (McGuire & Rowland, 1966). The four stages of intelligence according to Piaget are in chronological order. The first stage is sensorimotor, the second stage is pre-operational, the third stage is concrete operational, and the fourth is formal operational.

PIAGET'S STAGES OF COGNITIVE DEVELOPMENT

STAGE NAME	AGE GUIDELINES	KEY ELEMENTS OF THE STAGE
Sensorimotor	Birth to 2 years	■ Ability to perceive objects and stimuli from the environment. ■ Lacks internal representation of the world. ■ Acquisition of object permanence (ability to know that an object continues to exist outside of yourself).
Preoperational	2 to 7 years	■ Uses of language to interact with the world. ■ Ability to think in images and can draw images to represent thought. ■ Is still egocentric (cannot see beyond own perspective) and intuitive (answers questions based on own experience rather than logic)
Concrete Operational	7 to 11 years	■ The start of using logical reasoning (moving beyond their own experiences). ■ Ability to think in multiple dimensions (height, width, length, etc.) ■ Beginning conservation skills (a cup of water remains a cup of water regardless of the size of container you pour it into).
Formal Operational	11 to adulthood	■ Increased ability to have abstract, idealistic and logical thoughts. ■ Begin to be able to see from another person's perspective. ■ Ability to create novel ideas and thoughts.

FIGURE 1.2 Four Stages of Development (McGuire & Rowland, 1966).

Two key beliefs of cognitive psychology are that it is a science, and that behavior is explained and controlled by various mental processes. The perspective of cognitive psychology is far reaching in day-to-day application. It is seen in daily decision making, attention, child development, aging, memory, language skills, learning styles, and moral development. With these applications, it is possible to see its other possible applications to other academia fields or professions. Use of these concepts can be made in government systems (prisons, welfare, child protection service), businesses (marketing, effectiveness, motivation), education (special education, remediation, teaching styles, effective strategies), and even family life (raising children, marital satisfaction, loss).

The four major schools of thought in psychology are compared in Figure 1.3.

MAJOR PERSPECTIVE	PSYCHODYNAMIC	BEHAVIORISM	HUMANISTIC	COGNITIVE
Key Concepts	Unresolved internal conflicts are the source of mental problems. Behavior is shaped by internal forces.	Rejects the study of subjective mental states. Behavior is shaped by external forces, particularly reward and punishment.	Every person has a true inner core, or self. Maladaptive behaviors, thoughts, and emotions are learned, and can be replaced with healthier alternatives.	Scientific study of cognition. Behavior is explained and controlled by various mental processes.
Key Figures	Sigmund Freud Karen Horney David Winnicott	John Watson B.F. Skinner Ivan Pavlov	Carl Rogers Abraham Maslow	Ulric Neisser Jean Piaget Alfred Binet

FIGURE 1.3 A Comparison of the Four Major Schools of Thought in Psychology

SUMMARY

This brief glimpse at the journey through these four psychological perspectives is intended to summarize where the field of psychology has been over the years. In any attempt to move forward, it's important to glance back to get a better framework of where the field stands now, and most importantly, where it can go from here. Just imagine how knowledge will continue to grow and support the goal of psychology. With neuroscience, biology, and psychology all working together, it's exciting to see what future psychologists will bring to the world. As the field moves forward, it will be filled with more passionate debate and collaboration! History clearly demonstrates that growth will be the end result.

The primary goals of psychology are to describe, explain, and predict human behavior in the interest of improving the quality of life of all individuals and communities. Research psychologists use experimental methods to investigate basic psychological processes, such as perception, cognition, and motivation. Professional psychologists apply basic research findings to practical endeavors.

A solid foundation in psychology helps students understand their own behavior, emotions, and thoughts, as well as the behavior of others. An introduction to psychology can improve the quality of people's lives simply by making them aware of how they and others operate. An introduction to psychology is essential for anyone thinking about pursuing a career in one of the helping professions, such as nursing or the other branches of health care.

Psychology's roots can be traced to philosophical questions about the nature of the human mind. As a contemporary discipline, psychology bridges the biological and social sciences. Experimental psychology is less than 150 years old. A number of approaches, or perspectives, on human personality have evolved during that time. Freud's psychodynamic approach revolutionized the discipline by emphasizing the importance of the unconscious mind. In contrast, the behaviorist movement negated the importance of internal mental processes, and built its theories exclusively on observable behavior. Humanistic psychology emphasizes the integrity of the individual and arose partly in reaction to behaviorism's neglect of internal mental states. The cognitive perspective is the scientific study of mental processes.

Psychology is a growing multidisciplinary field. New subdisciplines, such as health psychology and cross-cultural psychology, recognize the complex factors that shape the human experience. Advances in neuroscience contribute to a greater understanding of the connection between mind and body. What students learn in the study of psychology will serve them for the rest of their lives.

REFERENCES

Barker, S. (2007). *Psychology*. Malden, MA: Blackwell Publishing.

Bergman, M. S. (2010). The Oedipus Complex and psychoanalytic technique. *Psychoanalytic Inquiry*, 306(6), 535–540.

Hall, G. (2009). Watson: The thinking man's behaviourist. *British Journal of Psychology*, 100(1a), 185–187.

Harzem, P. (2004). Behaviorism for new psychology: What was wrong with behaviorism and what is wrong with it now. *Behavior & Philosophy*, 32(1), 5–12.

Hoffman, R. R., & Deffenbacher, K.A. (1991). A brief history of Applied Cognitive Psychology. *Applied Cognitive Psychology*, 6 (1), 1–48.

Leichsenring, F., Hiller, W., Weissberg, M., & Leibing, E. (2006). Cognitive-behavioral therapy and psychodynamic psychotherapy: techniques, efficacy, and indications. *American Journal of Psychotherapy*, 60(3), 233–259.

Macmillan, M. (2009). *Psychodynamic theories of the unconscious*. Retrieved from http://search. credoreference.com/content/entry/estcon/psychodynamic_theories_of_the_unconscious/0.

Matalon, N. (2011). The riddle of dreams. *Philosophical Psychology*, 24(4), 517–536.

McDonald, M., & Wearing, S. (2013). A reconceptualization of the self in humanistic psychology: Heidegger, Foucault and the sociocultural turn. *Journal of Phenomenological Psychology*, 44(1), 37–59.

McGuire, C., Rowland, T. (1966). *An introduction to Jean Piaget*. Texas University.

McLeod, S. A. (2009). *Jean Piaget*. Retrieved from http://simplypsychology.org/piaget.html.

Pieces of the mind, in conflict. (2004). *Secrets of Genius*, 29.

Rholetter, W. (2013). Operant conditioning. *Salem Press Encyclopedia*.

Rosenberg, M. (1965). *Society and the adolescent self-image*. Princeton, NJ: Princeton University Press.

Watson, J. B. (2009) Is thinking merely the action of language mechanisms? *British Journal of Psychology*, 100(1a), 169–180.

Zalenski, R. J., & Raspa, R. (2006). Maslow's hierarchy of needs: A framework in achieving human potential in hospice. *Journal of Palliative Medicine*, 9(5), 1120–1127.

Understanding Research

"Research is formalized curiosity. It is poking and prying with a purpose."

—Zora Neale Hurston

THE PURPOSE OF CONDUCTING RESEARCH

Do eating disorders come from struggles with our parents, from our genetics, or from both? Are bystanders more likely to help someone in need if no one else is around, or are they more likely to intervene if many others are around? These questions could be answered by relying on common sense or intuition, but to bring these issues into the realm of science requires scientific research, a methodical approach, and accurate experiments. Research allows people to put ideas to the test and to organize and predict human behavior. As a science, psychology relies on research evidence to provide answers to questions about human behavior.

Check out the What Do You Think? box. As you read the box, you might think, *Drivers have more control over the steering wheel with hands-free phones. More control results in quicker reaction times.* Perhaps you might think that hands-free phones are safer because it is legal in many states to use them while driving. Devices that are legal are likely to be safe … aren't they?

It is normal to use common sense, logic, intuition, and knowledge derived from your own experiences to explain the behavior of others. However, these

1. Psychology uses the scientific method to investigate human thought and behavior. See page 22.

2. Types of research in psychology include descriptive and experimental. See page 23.

3. Experimental research investigates whether one variable causes another. See page 28.

4. Human and nonhuman participants of research studies must be treated ethically. See page 31.

WHAT DO YOU THINK?

Which is more likely to slow a driver's reaction time?

- Talking on a handheld cell phone
- Talking on a hands-free cell phone

How did you determine your answer to this question? Perhaps you applied common sense and logic. In a 2007 study, researchers Joy Hendrick and Jamie Switzer measured the time it took for participants in three different sets of experimental conditions to apply the brakes in a driving simulation:

- *First set of conditions:* The participants were not talking on a cell phone.
- *Second set of conditions:* The participants were talking on a handheld cell phone.
- *Third set of conditions:* The participants were talking on a hands-free cell phone.

Twenty-five undergraduate students (13 males and 12 females) participated in the study and were randomly assigned to one of the three conditions. Participants who were not conducting a telephone call took significantly less time to apply the brakes compared with the participants who were either talking on the handheld phone or the hands-free phone. However, when looking at the response time of participants who either used the handheld phone or the hands-free cell phone, researchers found they both applied the brakes in the same amount of time.

are highly subjective, so to investigate the questions raised in psychology, researchers instead use the scientific method, a systematic and objective methodology, to answer research questions.

THE SCIENTIFIC METHOD, HYPOTHESIS, AND THEORY

THEORY A systematic set of interrelated statements with the goal of explaining, understanding, or predicting some social or psychological phenomenon.

A **theory** is a systematic set of interrelated statements with the goal of explaining, understanding, or predicting some social or psychological phenomenon. Examples of psychological theories include behavioral theory, cognitive theory, humanistic theory, and psychoanalytical theory. A theory is developed or generated when observations are made. Consider cognitive theory, which offers a set of explanations about human behavior by understanding thought processes and belief systems. Sigmund Freud developed a psychodynamic theory about human behavior. He observed how "talking therapy" helped his patients release powerful unconscious emotional energies.

Freud also conducted the famous case study of Anna O., a patient of Josef Breuer. Anna O. had partial paralysis, blurred vision, and hallucinations. Breuer noticed how talking helped Anna O. alleviate the symptoms. Freud used these observations to formulate his theory about how behavior is influenced by the unconscious.

SCIENTIFIC METHOD A method of obtaining objective knowledge about the world through systematic, empirical, and replicable observations.

HYPOTHESIS A proposed explanation for an observation or scientific problem.

VARIABLES Measurable phenomena that have more than one value.

After a theory is developed, it needs to be tested for validity. The **scientific method** is a system of testing a **hypothesis**, a proposed explanation for an observation or scientific problem. The research to test the hypothesis will examine the relationship between two or more **variables** (measurable phenomena that have more than one value) by using different research methods. If a hypothesis is supported by convincing experimental evidence, a theory is said to be validated.

Consider another example of cognitive theory. A researcher wants to test the effectiveness of a type of cognitive intervention, which is based on cognitive theory. The intervention focuses on clients spending 30 minutes identifying false beliefs about themselves and substituting these thoughts with more positive beliefs. The researcher sets up an experiment in which 30 clients are randomly assigned to the group that receives the cognitive-based intervention and 30 other clients are assigned to the control group, in which they do not receive any intervention. The researcher formulates the following hypothesis: Clients who receive the cognitive intervention are more likely to reduce the number of negative thoughts about themselves and score higher on the self-esteem measure compared with those clients who did not receive any intervention. If the findings from the study confirm the hypothesis, the findings from the study help to validate cognitive theory.

The hands-free versus handheld cell phone study was motivated by theories that propose a limit to the amount of information a person can process at any given time. These theories of attention inspired Hendrick and Switzer to propose this hypothesis: Participants who are *not* talking on phones will have shorter braking times than participants who are talking on either hands-free or handheld phones. The results of their study supported their hypothesis.

There are many theories to explain psychological and social phenomena. Consequently, how does one evaluate theories? A sound theory should:
- predict
- explain a phenomenon accurately
- be parsimonious; that is, it should explain as much with as little as possible
- have heuristic value; that is, it should generate more research and should motivate new research on the same or related topics

Types of Research

Psychology is a science that addresses physical and social phenomena. It examines emotions, thoughts, and behaviors that originate in the brain and the nervous system. It is also a social science, because psychology investigates how human beings develop into individuals and form relationships with others. Because psychology bridges the biological and social sciences, psychological research is conducted at different **levels of analysis**.

At the biological level, psychological researchers investigate brain function, the chemistry of neurons, and the contribution of genetics to human development. At the individual and social levels, psychologists study personality, perception, cognition, interpersonal relationships, and behavior. Psychologists also study how culture affects thought, behavior, and well-being, and they use descriptive and experimental methods to investigate research questions in the biological and social arenas.

LEVELS OF ANALYSIS A variety of viewpoints from which researchers investigate a problem, such as biological, individual, group, community, and societal.

DESCRIPTIVE RESEARCH

Descriptive research methods are used to observe and record **psychological phenomena** (thoughts, behaviors, attitudes, or beliefs) as they occur naturally, *without manipulating any aspect of an environment or situation.* For example, a study that examines international college students' attitudes toward women is descriptive research. Descriptive research methods include archival research, surveys, naturalistic observation, case studies, and correlational studies. Experimental research, on the other hand, requires a *deliberate manipulation,* or change in procedure. Researchers observe how this change affects participants' performance. You will read more about experimental research later in the chapter.

An archive is any collection of records or documents that is made available for research. **Archival research** uses such materials to investigate behavior or events that occurred in the past. Physical documents, such as historic newspapers and photographs, are held in archives. Data collected for a research purpose in the past may be archived for future research.

Longitudinal studies are a type of observational research that examines archival data collected on the same group of individuals over an extended period of time. The benefit of longitudinal research is that researchers can examine changes over time. Longitudinal methods are helpful for studying development and lifespan issues.

The Michigan Panel Study of Income Dynamics (PSID) is a database of information about a representative sample of U.S. residents and their families. The data collection began in 1968 and has been updated annually ever since. This archive of longitudinal data includes information such as birth weight, levels of education, family composition, employment status, marital status, and health on more than 9,000 individuals. The PSID has been extensively used by psychologists, sociologists, and other social scientists to investigate the long-term effects of these variables on the health and welfare of individuals and their families.

The following Try It! box features an introduction to the **Big Five personality test**, a test widely used in personality research. The Big Five personality traits are openness, conscientiousness, extraversion, agreeableness, and neuroticism (to remember these five traits, use the acronym OCEAN). Personality tests like the Big Five are sometimes included in **surveys**, which are collections of questions used to gather information about participants. Researchers use surveys to ask people about

PSYCHOLOGICAL PHENOMENA Thoughts, behaviors, attitudes, emotions, or beliefs.

ARCHIVAL RESEARCH Research that uses materials collected in the past to investigate behavior or events that occurred in the past.

LONGITUDINAL Data collected on the same group of individuals over an extended period of time with the benefit of examining changes over time.

BIG FIVE PERSONALITY TEST A test to measure five broad domains or dimensions of personality.

SURVEYS Collections of questions used to gather information about participants.

TRY IT! TAKE A SURVEY

In the following list are pairs of adjectives that may or may not apply to you. Please write a number next to each statement to indicate the degree to which you agree or disagree with that statement, even if one characteristic applies more strongly than the other.

DISAGREE STRONGLY	DISAGREE MODERATELY	DISAGREE A LITTLE	NEITHER AGREE NOR DISAGREE	AGREE A LITTLE	AGREE MODERATELY	AGREE STRONGLY
1	2	3	4	5	6	7

_____ 1. Extroverted, enthusiastic

_____ 2. Critical, quarrelsome

_____ 3. Dependable, self-disciplined

_____ 4. Anxious, easily upset

_____ 5. Open to new experiences, complex

Source: Excerpted from Gosling, S. D., Rentfrow, P. J., & Swann, W. B., Jr. (2003). A very brief measure of the Big Five personality domains. *Journal of Research in Psychology, 37(6)*, 525, (Appendix A).

their attitudes, beliefs, and values and to collect factual information, such as gender, marital status, birthdates, or income.

Survey data can be collected from individuals or groups in several ways, including face to face, over the telephone, through the mail, and online or via e-mail. Surveys are useful when researchers need to collect information from large numbers of people, such as in market research. Although surveys are commonly used, they have disadvantages. First, they produce self-reported data, and some participants might answer in a way that makes them look good. Second, surveys, particularly mail or e-mail surveys, have low response rates. Third, surveys may not always capture the context of the phenomenon being studied.

Different types of questions are used in surveys, such as the following:

- Binary questions have two possible answers. *Example:* "Did you vote in the presidential election? ___Yes ___No"
- Multiple-choice questions offer more than two options from which you should choose the best possible answer. *Example:* "Indicate your undergraduate major: (a) nursing, (b) business, (c) computer science, (d) psychology."
- Open-ended questions ask the participant to provide a description or explanation. *Example:* "Describe your careergoals._____"

- Scale questions have the participant answer questions with graded responses, such as in the Big Five test. Scale questions transform nonnumerical **qualitative data**, such as a person's rating of his or her attitudes or feelings, into **quantitative data**, or numerical data. When a qualitative response is changed into a number, it can be used in statistical analysis. *Example:* "On a scale of 1 to 5, 1 being not at all likely and 5 being very likely, how likely are you to recommend this resource to a friend? 1 2 3 4 5"

Naturalistic Observation

Jane Goodall, an anthropologist and primatologist, is known for her observational studies of wild chimpanzees in Tanzania. She began her research in the 1960s and continued for 45 years. She quietly watched the animals without disturbing them and documented chimpanzee behaviors that had never been seen by researchers. **Naturalistic observation** like Jane Goodall's involves observing and recording behaviors in the real world, not in a laboratory or other controlled environment. Naturalistic researchers remain inconspicuous and make no attempts to modify the behavior of the individuals they observe.

Naturalistic observation is used to study human behavior for the same reasons it is used to study animal behavior. Participants are more likely to behave naturally when they do not know that they are being observed. However, there are limitations to this method of studying human behavior and social phenomena. One of the concerns has to do with reliability. How does one ensure that what one researcher observes will be reliable—that is, consistent with what another researcher observes?

Ethical issues also come into play in naturalistic observation. In some observational research, such as unobtrusive observational research, individuals under study do not know that they are being observed. This raises ethical issues about privacy and informed consent. In research, it is required that participants give their permission or consent to participate in a study. But how does a researcher obtain the consent of those who do not realize they are being studied or observed?

Naturalistic observation can be useful when working with people who feel uncomfortable in laboratory situations (infants, homebound individuals, or people with developmental disorders, for instance). It also is a useful way to observe situations that are impossible to simulate in a laboratory.

Case Study

A **case study** is an in-depth investigation, perhaps of a single individual, a group of people, a business, or a phenomenon. Case studies enable psychologists to learn how rare conditions affect human thinking, behavior, and emotions. One concern with case studies is the lack of generalizability of the findings produced. Because the sample size is very small, the extent to which the findings and conclusions can be applied to other populations or settings is questioned.

A patient usually referred to only by his initials, H.M., was the subject of a well-known 1957 case study in psychology. H.M. suffered from

QUALITATIVE DATA Nonnumerical information, such as people rating their observations, interpretations, attitudes, or feelings.

QUANTITATIVE DATA Numerical data.

NATURALISTIC OBSERVATION The observation and recording of behaviors in real-world environments.

CASE STUDY An in-depth investigation of a single individual, a group of people, a business, or a phenomenon.

epilepsy. To control his seizures, surgeons removed most of H.M.'s hippocampus, amygdala, and surrounding cortex—critical areas of the brain. After his surgery, H.M. experienced an unusual pattern of memory loss. He could remember events that happened long before his operation, but he could not retain new information. H.M. had not lost his memories, but he had lost the ability to form new, long-lasting memories.

Prior to H.M.'s surgery, the role of the hippocampus in memory was not clearly understood. By observing H.M.'s pattern of memory loss, psychologists learned about the role of the hippocampus in the formation of new memories.

PSYCHOLOGY & CAREERS: HOW RESEARCH AIDS MARKETING

Research methods used in psychology are also used by marketing professionals to understand how customers think and behave. Businesses use surveys to investigate their customers' (or potential customers') **demographics**—characteristics that are typical of a particular population, such as age, sex, income, and level of education. Another research method used in marketing is **focus groups**, in which a group of people who represent a target population meet and answer questions about products and services.

Focus groups are frequently used in **health psychology**, an emerging field that investigates the relationship between people's beliefs, social environment, family, and culture and their health. For example, researchers used focus groups to find out what young women knew and how they felt about the relationship between secondhand smoke and premenopausal breast cancer. The target population consisted of female smokers and nonsmokers aged 15 to 24. From these focus groups, the researchers learned how to best craft a public health campaign that alerted young female smokers and nonsmokers alike to the potential dangers of secondhand smoke.

Successful marketing professionals use many skills that are used in psychology research, such as choosing a sample to represent a population, writing survey questions, and conducting focus groups.

DEMOGRAPHICS Characteristics that are typical of a particular population, such as age, sex, income, and level of education.

FOCUS GROUPS Events at which a group of individuals who represent a target population are invited to meet and answer questions about new products and services.

HEALTH PSYCHOLOGY A science that investigates the relationship between an individual's beliefs and social environment, including genetics, family, culture, and individual differences, and his or her health.

Correlational Research

Suppose you are investigating the relationship between extraversion, the personality trait of being outgoing and seeking social contact, and risky behavior, such as binge drinking. You predict that people with high scores on an extraversion scale will also have high scores on a scale that measures attitudes about engaging in risky behavior. The method you will use to investigate your prediction is called **correlation**, a process of measuring the direction and strength of the relationship between two variables. A correlational analysis will tell you if scores on the extraversion scale increase in the same direction, and at the same rate, as scores on the risk-taking scale.

Correlation can be visualized in a **scatterplot**, a graph that shows the association between two variables. See Figure 2.1 for an example. For the risky behavior study, each diamond in the graph would represent one person's scores on two scales: one that measures extraversion and one that measures attitude toward risky

CORRELATION A process of measuring the direction and strength of the relationship between two variables.

SCATTERPLOT A graph that shows the association between two variables' positive or negative correlation.

behavior. In this example, people who have low scores on the extraversion have low scores on risk-taking. Those who have high scores on extraversion have high scores on risk-taking. This scatterplot illustrates a **positive correlation** between extraversion and risk-taking because the two scores change in the same direction—as extraversion increases, so does risk-taking. The scatterplot also suggests a strong correlation between the two variables because they change direction at similar rates.

On the other hand, a **negative correlation** shows an association where one variable increases while the other variable decreases. For example, if there is a negative relationship between age and level of pessimism, when age goes down, the level of pessimism goes up. In other words, younger individuals tend to be more pessimistic.

A **correlational study** is a descriptive research method because it investigates the relationship between two variables as they *occur naturally*, without manipulation by the experimenter.

POSITIVE CORRELATION
A correlation in which both variables change in the same direction.

NEGATIVE CORRELATION
A correlation in which one variable goes up and the other variable goes down.

CORRELATIONAL STUDY
A descriptive research method that investigates the relationship between two variables as they occur naturally, without manipulation by the experimenter.

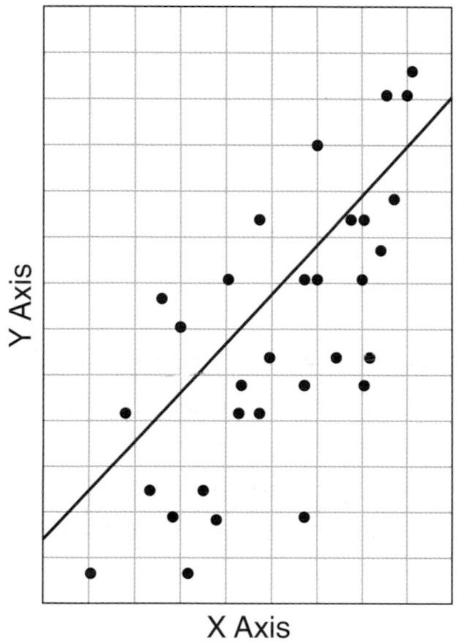

Source: NASA.gov
FIGURE 2.1 Example of a Scatterplot

Correlation versus Causation

When interpreting a correlational study, it is easy to fall into the trap of thinking that correlation equals causation. **Causation** demonstrates how one variable influences or affects other variables. When one variable affects another, you can say that you have causation. On the other hand, a correlation is merely a trend or a relationship between two variables. For example, imagine a friend told you, "You should take this new medication for your headaches—a study has found a relationship between those who took this drug and decreased levels of pain." How confident would you be about taking this drug, knowing you would be basing your decision on a trend? It is important to remember that *correlation does not imply causation.*

What if someone told you that there is a correlation between socioeconomic status and crime? It would be wrong to conclude that high socioeconomic bracket (or low socioeconomic bracket) causes crime. If a study found a relationship between age and amount of cheating, it would be wrong to conclude that age does not cause cheating.

CAUSATION Demonstrates how one variable influences other variables.

EXPERIMENTAL RESEARCH

In contrast to descriptive research, experimental research requires a deliberate **manipulation**, or change in procedure, in some aspect of the study in order to observe how this change affects participants' performance.

An experiment is a specific research strategy that emphasizes controlled observation. It includes (1) an experimental group, (2) a control group, and (3) randomization of participants to either the experimental group or control group. An **experimental group** is the group in which the participants are exposed to the experimental stimulus or intervention. A **control group** is the group in which participants do not receive the experimental stimulus or intervention. **Randomization of subjects** refers to randomly assigning participants to either the experimental group or the control group. Participants have an equal chance of being assigned to one of the two groups; the purpose of randomization is to ensure that both groups are similar.

Quasiexperimental research is another specific research strategy that is commonly used when it is not practical to conduct an experiment. It resembles an experimental method; however, it is missing either the element of a control group or a randomization of participants to either the experimental or control group.

For example, if a psychologist wants to empirically evaluate the effectiveness of a clinical intervention targeted to help those who are depressed, it may not be practical to conduct a true experimental study. It would not be ethical to have a control group where research participants are randomly assigned to the control group that does not receive any intervention. As a result, the psychologist might design a simple quasiexperimental study whereby two groups (one that receives the targeted intervention and one that is on a waiting list) are compared in terms of their outcomes before and after the implementation of the intervention. Note that the research participants are not randomly assigned to the groups.

Independent and Dependent Variables

The **independent variable** is the concept that is being manipulated. The **dependent variable** is the concept that is being measured or the outcome. A 2007 experiment by researcher Andrew Elliot and colleagues involved changing the ink color on tests that sets of individuals took. Green, black, and red inks were used. The study's objective was to manipulate an independent variable (in this case, the color of ink, which in Elliot's hypothesis created feelings of anxiety) to observe its effect on a dependent variable (the participants' performance on the test). The researchers were investigating whether the independent variable had a significant effect on the dependent variable—whether a **causal relationship** existed between the variables (did red ink cause lower performance?). A true experiment tests whether an independent variable has a significant effect on a dependent variable.

Intervening, Confounding, and Moderator Variables

An intervening variable refers to some variable or factor that enters the picture between the independent and dependent variable. For example, imagine that a researcher finds out that there is a correlation between adolescents' level of coping with peer pressure and good grades. However, another variable may enter this picture, such as self-esteem. Adolescents who have the ability to cope with peer pressure also have a healthy, positive self-esteem, which has an effect on their academic outcomes.

A confounding variable is an extraneous factor or variable that is not the focus of the study that ends up correlating with the independent and dependent variables. Let's take the above example again—there is a positive correlation between adolescents' ability to cope with peer pressure and good grades. However, if the researcher does not take into account self-esteem, it may be that self-esteem is the variable that is correlated with coping and good grades and the researcher concludes a correlation that actually does not exist.

A moderating variable is a variable that affects the strength or the direction of the relationship. Many studies, for example, have shown that there is a relationship between race and use of mammography among women. In other words, there seems to be a correlation between not being a racial or ethnic minority and mammography usage. However, if a researcher introduces age as a moderating variable, this correlation may be shown to be stronger or weaker because of a potentially stronger correlation between race and mammography usage among older women.

Populations and Samples

A **population** is the entire set of units, groups, or individuals with the characteristics or attributes that a researcher wants to investigate. In Elliot's red ink study, the population would include any human being raised in a culture in which the color red is associated with danger or anxiety. Contacting every member of a population of interest is almost impossible, so researchers use a subset of a population, called a **sample**, to represent the population. The sample must share the same key characteristics as the population so that the results of the study can be **generalized**, or extended, to the population of interest to assure validity.

The extent to which the results of a study can be generalized from a sample to a population depends on how closely the sample resembles the population. **Participant selection** is the process of choosing participants from a sample that represents the population of interest to the study. The two major sampling designs are probability sampling and nonprobability sampling. In **probability sampling**, everyone in the population under study has an equal chance of getting selected to participate in the study. For example, **simple random sampling** involves selecting an individual by chance; therefore, everyone has the same chance of being chosen.

Systematic sampling consists of drawing the kth interval; for example, every 10th person is randomly selected, and the researcher has to ensure that there is no pattern to the interval.

With **nonprobability sampling**, not everyone in the population of interest has an equal chance of being selected for the study. In the red ink study, university students participated in return for partial course credit or a small payment. When participants who are easily available to the researcher are recruited for a study, the sample is called a **convenience sample**. Another nonrandom sampling method is **snowball sampling**, in which participants who meet the eligibility criteria for the study are recruited, then those participants refer another individual who might fit the criteria for the study. The referral process continues.

The participants in the red ink study were randomly assigned to one of three conditions—one experimental condition and two control conditions. In **random assignment**, participants are assigned to experimental and control

POPULATION The entire set of units, groups, or individuals with the characteristics that the researcher wishes to study.

SAMPLE A subset of the population.

GENERALIZED Expanded to the population.

PARTICIPANT SELECTION The process of choosing participants from a sample that represents the population of interest to the study.

PROBABILITY SAMPLING A category of sampling methods where everyone or every unit in the population under study has an equal chance of getting selected to participate in the study.

SIMPLE RANDOM SAMPLING A probability sampling method where an individual is selected by chance.

NONPROBABILITY SAMPLING A category of sampling strategies where not everyone or every unit in the population under study has an equal chance of getting selected to participate in the study.

CONVENIENCE SAMPLE A nonprobability sampling method where participants are easily available to the researcher are recruited for a study.

SNOWBALL SAMPLING A nonprobability sampling method where participants who meet the criteria of the study refer others.

RANDOM ASSIGNMENT A study design in which participants are assigned to experimental and control conditions by chance, minimizing preexisting differences among those assigned to the various groups.

conditions by chance; this minimizes preexisting differences between those assigned to the different groups. Each participant has an equal chance of being assigned to any condition. Random assignment is a requirement of a true experiment in which researchers test predictions about causal relationships between independent and dependent variables.

Experimental and Control Groups

EXPERIMENTAL CONDITION This condition exposes participants to the treatment (to one version of the independent variable).

CONTROL CONDITION This condition contrasts with the experimental condition and serves as a comparison for evaluating the effect of the treatment.

In Elliot's study, the participant's code number was written in red ink on a packet of test materials. This part of the study is the **experimental condition**, which exposes participants to the treatment. The experimenters made sure that the participants read their code before opening the packet. The red ink condition was the experimental condition because the researchers assumed that the color red would affect participants' performance. In the two control conditions, the participant codes were presented in exactly the same fashion, but in green or black ink. **Control conditions** serve as a comparison for evaluating the effect of the treatment. The green and black ink groups were control conditions because there was no evidence that green or black ink would cause anxiety. The color of ink was the manipulation in this experiment because it was the variable that changed among the three experimental conditions.

The participants' task was to solve anagram (scrambled word) problems in a five-minute period. The researchers' hypothesis was that participants in the red ink condition would solve fewer anagrams than participants in the two control conditions (green or black ink). The researchers were testing the prediction that red ink would cause participants to be anxious, while green and black ink would not. After taking into account factors that might affect performance, such as verbal ability and gender, the researchers discovered that their prediction was supported by their results. Participants in the red ink condition solved fewer problems than participants in the green or black ink conditions. This finding supported the researchers' theory and motivated further research on the effect of color on performance.

ETHICS AND RESEARCH

ETHICS A branch of philosophy that considers questions of morality.

RESEARCH ETHICS The obligation of researchers to treat participants with honesty, fairness, respect, and responsibility.

Ethics is a branch of philosophy that considers questions of morality. **Research ethics** in psychology concern the obligation of researchers to treat participants with honesty, fairness, respect, responsibility, and concern for their welfare.

Volunteer Bias and Researcher Bias

BIAS The tendency to show favoritism to one side of an argument, or to a particular individual or group of individuals.

One ethical issue in research is **bias**, the tendency to show favoritism to one side of an argument or to a particular individual or group of individuals. **Volunteer bias** refers to the possibility that sample populations may not truly represent a population of interest because people who volunteer for experiments may differ from the general population. Some research evidence suggests that individuals who volunteer for experiments tend to be more educated, intelligent, and sociable than those who do not. Investigators take the widespread use of convenience samples into consideration when they evaluate the work of their peers.

Researcher bias refers to the possibility that a researcher will influence the results of a study, either intentionally or unintentionally. For example, a researcher may unintentionally be warmer and more welcoming to members of an experimental group than to members of a control group. In laboratory studies, researchers take care to be impartial to all participants and to use the same tone of voice, instructions, and body language with all.

The Ethical Treatment of Participants

Researchers must consider how their studies will affect the well-being of the participants. Following are some common questions researchers address when planning an experiment:

- Does the experiment require that the participants do anything unusual?
- Could the participants suffer physical harm?
- What are the benefits and risks of study participation, and do the benefits outweigh the risks?
- Do potential participants receive enough information about the study before they decide to participate, and do they understand the information well enough to make an informed decision about whether to participate?

The guidelines that protect the rights of participants in any government-funded research are maintained by the U.S. Department of Health and Human Services (HHS). In the late 1970s, HHS formed the National Commission for the Protection of Human Subjects of Biomedical and Behavioral Research to formulate regulations for the protection of human subjects in research. In 1978, the Belmont Report was written and identified three major principles to guide the protection of human subjects in research: (1) respect for persons, (2) beneficence, and (3) justice. Respect for persons refers to the fact that human beings are autonomous agents and those who are limited in their autonomy require protection. Beneficence refers to the research participants' well-being and ethical research implements mechanisms to mitigate any risks and promote well-being. Finally, justice refers to how the benefits and the risks are equally distributed.

The HHS requires any agency that receives government funding for experimental work to undergo review by an **institutional review board (IRB)** to ensure that they conform to ethical codes. An IRB is a committee that is organized to oversee and approve any research on human beings. IRB members are not personally associated with the research project. IRBs are independent committees comprised of scientists and researchers who review, monitor, and approve both biomedical and behavioral research to ensure that human participants' rights are protected. The three principles of the Belmont Report now guide IRB reviewers in their evaluation of research studies, coupled with the specific rules governing the conduct of research in psychology as established by the American Psychological Association (APA), which established its first code of ethics in 1953.

Institutional animal care and use committees (IACUC) oversee the ethical treatment of animals at universities and research institutions. Animals have been used in experimental psychology research for more than 100 years, and all institutions that conduct research on animals are required by federal law to establish such a committee. The use of animals in research raises serious ethical questions but has yielded important findings in many studies. An increasing number of doctors,

VOLUNTEER BIAS The possibility that sample populations may not truly represent a population of interest because people who volunteer for experiments may differ from the general population.

RESEARCHER BIAS The possibility that a researcher will influence the results of a study, either intentionally or unintentionally.

INSTITUTIONAL REVIEW BOARD (IRB) A committee at a research institution that reviews the ethics and methodology of all research involving human participants.

INSTITUTIONAL ANIMAL CARE AND USE COMMITTEE (IACUC) A committee at a research institution that reviews the ethics and methodology of every experiment involving animals.

Source: U.S. Public Health Service.

scientists, and concerned citizens are opposed to using animals for research experiments. They oppose animal cruelty involved in experiments, and some people claim that results from animal experimentation actually yield few medical benefits to humans.

The ethical codes and practices that currently govern experimental research were formally established after World War II. This was due in part to the Nuremberg Trials, which occurred from 1945 to 1949 and made public the barbarous practices of Nazi doctors and prison guards. These trials resulted in the formation of the Nuremberg Code, a set of 10 guidelines for the ethical treatment of human participants in research. The Nuremberg Code laid the groundwork for ethical standards that currently govern research with human participants.

Codes of research ethics do not guarantee that the rights of participants will always be protected. For example, the Tuskegee Syphilis Study (see photo at left) was conducted by the U.S. Public Health Service to monitor the effects of untreated syphilis. The study began in 1932 and was headquartered at the Tuskegee Institute, a historically black university in Alabama. The study was initially intended to be a six-month-long project to compare the outcomes of 400 men with syphilis to 200 control participants without the disease. None of the participants were told the true nature of the study. Instead, they were told that the government was studying the causes of "bad blood," a term used to describe a variety of ailments.

None of the study participants with syphilis were ever told that they had the disease, nor were they given any treatment. (When penicillin became the standard treatment for syphilis, study participants were not given access to it, nor were they told about its availability.) This deception allowed researchers to continue to monitor the progression of their disease in its untreated state.

The study continued until 1972, when it was exposed by an Associated Press reporter. It took more than 25 years more before a public apology was made to the participants: In 1997, President Clinton issued a formal apology to the surviving men and families of those who had died, calling the government's conduct during the study "shameful."

KEY THINKERS IN PSYCHOLOGY: STANLEY MILGRAM

In the early 1960s, American psychologist Stanley Milgram, along with the rest of the world, struggled to understand how ordinary people committed unspeakable acts of cruelty during World War II. Milgram decided to conduct laboratory experiments to investigate whether people would comply with the orders of an authority figure even if they believed that their actions would harm others.

Milgram concealed the true nature of his research from participants. Recruitment ads asked for male volunteers for a study on "learning and memory." The participant was greeted at the laboratory door by an experimenter dressed in a white coat, and then introduced to another "volunteer," who was actually an associate, or **confederate**, of the experimenter. A lottery was held to assign the roles of learner and teacher—but the lottery was rigged. The participant always received the assignment of "teacher," and the confederate the role of "learner." In an adjacent room, the learner was connected to "electrical wires" in the presence of the teacher. In another room, the teacher was seated

CONFEDERATE An actor who participates in a psychological experiment who pretends to be a subject but is working for the researcher.

in front of what appeared to be an electric shock generator facing a console of switches labeled from 15 to 450 volts. Switches at the lower voltages were marked "slight." Those at higher voltages were labeled "danger—severe shock," and finally "XXX."

The experimenter instructed the teacher to read word pairs to the learner. The learner was expected to memorize the pairs and later supply the missing word when only one word from the pair was given. The experimenter instructed the teacher to administer an electric shock each time the learner made an error and to increase the voltage each time the learner made another mistake. In reality, no electric shocks were administered.

Most teacher–participants argued to stop the experiment, particularly when they heard cries of pain (in actuality, recorded sound effects) coming from the learner. Whenever the teacher hesitated to give a shock, the experimenter told the teacher, "The experiment requires that you go on" and other scripted verbal prods that emphasized compliance. More than 65 percent of the participants gave what they thought was the maximum level of electrical shock—450 volts.

Milgram was concerned with the welfare of his participants after the experiments. He debriefed each participant, explaining the true nature of the studies. He also introduced them to the learners, who were obviously unharmed. Many participants expressed satisfaction at having participated in the studies because they felt they contributed to the investigation of an important topic. The publication of Milgram's obedience studies ignited fierce debate over the ethics of experimental research methods. Many researchers felt that his methods were unnecessarily harsh. Others criticized his use of deception.

The APA's Ethics Code as amended in 2010 includes five general principles intended to inspire psychologists to the highest ethical standards of their profession. These principles are listed in Figure 2.2.

Principle A: Beneficence and Nonmaleficence
Psychologists strive to benefit those with whom they work and take care to do no harm.

Principle B: Fidelity and Responsibility
Psychologists establish relationships of trust with those with whom they work.

Principle C: Integrity
Psychologists seek to promote accuracy, honesty, and truthfulness in the science, teaching, and practice of psychology.

Principle D: Justice
Psychologists recognize that fairness and justice entitle all persons to access to and benefit from the contributions of psychology and to equal quality in the processes, procedures, and services being conducted by psychologists.

Principle E: Respect for People's Rights and Dignity
Psychologists respect the dignity and worth of all people, and the rights of individuals to privacy, confidentiality, and self-determination.

FIGURE 2.2 General Principles in the APA Ethics Code

SUMMARY

Research in psychology uses the scientific method—a process of observation, prediction, experimentation, and analysis—to investigate questions about human thought and behavior. Descriptive research methods include archival studies, naturalistic studies, case studies, surveys, and correlational studies. Descriptive studies involve observation and recording of behaviors that occur in natural settings. In descriptive studies, researchers try to remain inconspicuous and make no attempt to change the observed environment or situation.

Experiments investigate whether one variable causes another. Experiments always involve a manipulation, or change in procedure, in order to investigate the effect of an independent variable on a dependent variable. Participants in the experimental group experience the manipulation that is predicted to change their behavior. Participants in the control group are exposed to a neutral condition. Experimenters select samples of a population to participate in their studies. In a true experiment, participants are randomly assigned to experimental and control groups to avoid bias in the composition of either group.

Research ethics concerns the rights and welfare of human and nonhuman participants. Any institution that receives research funding from the U.S. government must have special committees to review the ethics of research proposals. Proposals for research using human participants are reviewed by institutional review boards. Proposals for research using nonhuman participants are reviewed by institutional animal care and use committees (IACUC).

Research on human and nonhuman participants is governed by formalized ethical principles and overseen by institutional research boards. Many issues in psychological research ethics and integrity are debatable and merit intelligent dialogue and discussion. There are no easy rights or wrongs; students of psychology should familiarize themselves with these issues in order to weigh in on what defines ethical research practices. The APA, the primary professional organization for psychology, has established a code of ethics that includes principles and guidelines for conducting research.

REFERENCES

American Psychological Association. (2010). Ethical principles of psychologists and code of conduct, 2010 Amendments. Retrieved from http://www.apa.org/ethics

Benjamin, L. T., Jr., & Simpson, J. A. (2009). The power of the situation: The impact of Milgram's obedience studies on personality and social psychology. *American Psychologist, 64* (1), 12–19.

Bottorff, J. L., McKeown, S., Carey, J., Haines, R., Okoli, C., Johnson, K. C., & Ptolemy, E. (2010). Young women's responses to smoking and breast cancer risk information. *Health Education Research, 25*(4), 668–677.

Centers for Disease Control and Prevention. (2009). *US public health service syphilis study at Tuskegee.* Retrieved from http://www.cdc.gov/tuskegee/timeline.htm

Elliot, A. J., Maier, M. A., Binser, M. J., Friedman, R., & Pekrun, R. (2009). The effect of red on avoidance behavior in achievement contexts. *Personality and Social Psychology Bulletin, 35*(3), 365–375.

Elliot, A. J., Maier, M. A., Moller, A. C., Friedman, R., & Meinhardt, J. (2007). Color and psychological functioning: The effect of red on performance attainment. *Journal of Experimental Psychology: General, 136*(1), 154–168.

Gazzaniga, M., Heatherton, T. & Halpern, D. (2010). *Psychological science.* New York: W. W. Norton.

Gosling, S. D., Rentfrow, P. J., & Swann, W. B., Jr. (2003). A very brief measure of the Big Five personality domains. *Journal of Research in Personality, 37*(6), 504–528.

Gravetter, F. J., & Forzano, L. (2009). *Research methods for the behavioral sciences*. Belmont, CA: Cengage.

Hendrick, J. L., & Switzer, J. R. (2007). Hands-free versus hand held cell phone conversation on a braking response by young drivers, *Perceptual and Motor Skills, 105*(2), 514–522.

Louw, J. (1997). Regulating professional conduct. Part I: Codes of ethics of national psychology associations in South Africa. *South African Journal of Psychology, 27,* 183–188.

Miller, A. G., Collins, B. E., & Brief, D. E. (1995). Perspectives on obedience to authority: The legacy of the Milgram experiments. *Journal of Social Issues, 51*(3), 1–19.

Monette, D. R., Sullivan, T. J., & DeJong, C. R. (1998). Applied social research: Tool for the human services. Orlando, FL: Harcourt Brace and Company.

Nagy, T. F. (2011). A brief history and overview of the APA Ethics Code. In T. F. Nagy (Ed.), *Essential ethics for psychologists: A primer for understanding and mastering core issues* (pp. 29–48). Washington, DC: American Psychological Association.

Neuman, W. L. (2003). *Social research methods: Qualitative and quantitative approaches.* Boston: Pearson Education, Inc.

Scoville, W., & Milner, B. (1957). Loss of recent memory after bilateral hippocampal lesions. *Journal of Neurology, Neurosurgery & Psychiatry, 20,* 11–21.

Sulloway, F. J., & Zweigenhaft, R. L. (2010). Birth order and risk taking in athletics: A meta-analysis and study of major league baseball. *Personality and Social Psychology Review, 14*(4), 402–416.

University of Michigan Institute for Social Research. (2011). *Panel study of income dynamics.* Retrieved from http://psidonline.isr.umich.edu/

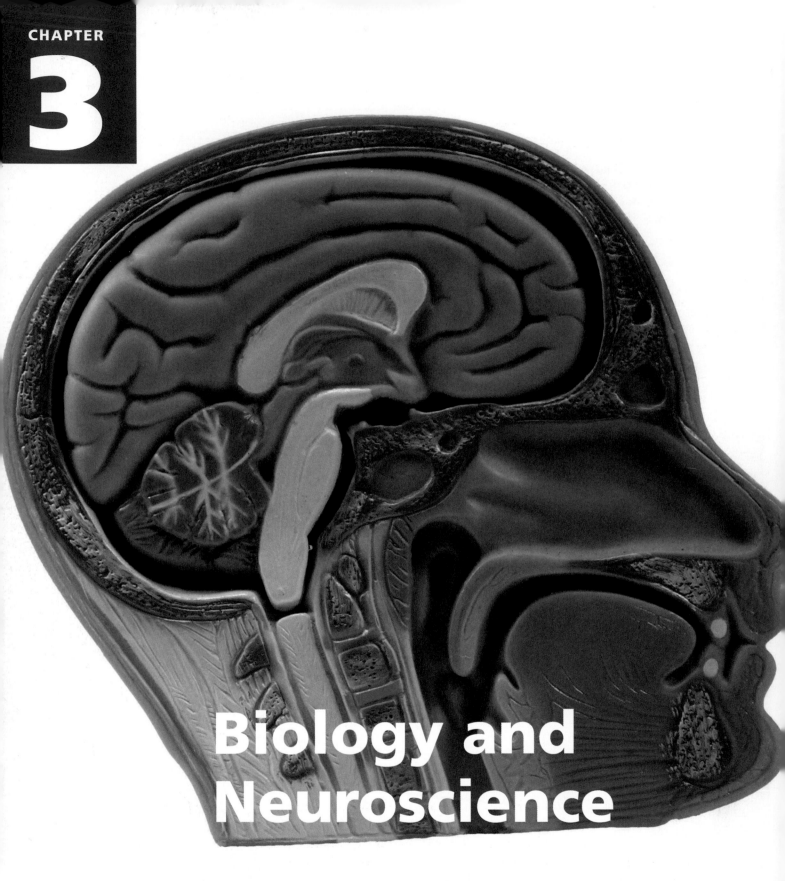

Biology and Neuroscience

"Between stimulus and response there is a space. In that space is our power to choose our response. In our response lies our growth and our freedom."

—Viktor E. Frankl

NEUROLOGY

Psychology examines behavior and mental processes such as thoughts and feelings. To more fully understand mental processes and behavior requires learning about the workings of the brain and nervous system. Neuroscience is the study of these physiological and biological underpinnings. In this chapter, you will learn how your brain and nervous system affect your thoughts, feelings, and behavior. You will explore the components of the nervous system, from molecules to brain structures, and how these various elements contribute to psychology and behavior.

NEUROSCIENCE The study of the physiological aspects of psychology and behavior.

NEUROLOGY The study of disorders of the nervous system.

COGNITIVE NEUROLOGY The study of the effects of nervous-system disorders on cognition.

NEUROLOGIST A physician who specializes in treating the nervous system.

Neuroscience is the study of the brain and nervous system. **Neurology** is the study of disorders of the nervous system. One specialty in neurology is **cognitive neurology**, which examines the effects of nervous system disorders on cognition, or thought. For example, strokes, seizures, and diseases such as Alzheimer's may lead to cognitive impairments.

Neurologists study people with neurological disorders. The well-known writer Oliver Sacks (see the "Key Figures in Psychology" box) is also a practicing neurologist.

Everyone has opportunities and constraints in learning ability. That is why it is helpful, especially for psychologists, to understand the biological limits of the brain, and the many, and often unexpected, opportunities that are illuminated by neuroscience as well. Neuroscience is not just the study of how people's talents are enabled; rather, it is the study of the physiological underpinnings of psychology, starting at the cellular level.

NEURONS: THE SMALLEST UNIT OF THE BRAIN

One of the smallest units in the brain is a nerve cell, or neuron. Neurons communicate with other nerve cells and with muscles and other organs in the body. They communicate by sending chemical or electrical impulses, or both, to other neurons.

Structure of a Neuron

NEURON A nerve cell; the smallest unit of the nervous system.

The smallest unit of the nervous system is a cell: specifically, a nerve cell, which is more commonly called a **neuron**. There are different types of neurons, each of which has a different shape, size, and function. Neurons are structured like other cells of the body. Each is surrounded by a membrane, which is a semipermeable skin that encloses the rest of the cellular body.

As with other types of cells, the neuron's body is called a soma. Within the soma is a nucleus, which contains cytoplasm (cell fluid) and the genetic material of a neuron (DNA and RNA). Also within the neuron, as with other cells, there are systems for synthesizing and transporting proteins, fats, and other materials.

KEY CONCEPTS

1. Neurons exchange information through electrical and chemical signals. See page 38.

2. Neurotransmitters and hormones are chemical substances that influence thinking and behavior. See page 40.

3. Different parts of the brain are associated with different types of thought and emotion. See page 41.

4. The brain, the central nervous system, and the rest of the body are interconnected. See page 42.

5. Technological methods are used to gather information about the brain. See page 46.

6. Experience and learning affect the brain's physiology. See page 47.

KEY FIGURES IN PSYCHOLOGY: OLIVER SACKS AND HOW THE BRAIN INTERPRETS REALITY

Oliver Sacks, a professor at Columbia University, is a renowned neurologist and the author of many bestselling books. He has investigated and written about people with unusual neurological disorders. Sacks also has a genetic neurological disorder.

Sacks's illness, which is caused by an abnormality in his genes or chromosomes, directly affects the functioning of his brain. Sacks cannot recognize familiar faces. He can see and register the patterns of light that define a face and can describe eyes, emotions, and attitude. But he is unable to look at a picture of a person—perhaps someone famous, such as President Obama, or someone he knows well—and recognize or name the person in the photograph. Sacks has used his own disorder to better understand other neurological disorders firsthand, help people who suffer with them, and write about these disorders.

Neurons are different from the other cells of the body because of the way they make connections and exchange information. Axons and dendrites project from the somas of neurons. **Dendrites** are short structures that receive electrochemical information from other cells. **Axons** are structures that send electrochemical information to other cells. The part of the axon nearest to the cell body is called the **axon hillock**. The **terminal bouton** is the part of the neuron that is farthest away from the soma. It is the part of the neuron that releases, or sends, electrochemical information to other neurons.

One way of classifying neurons is by describing how many axons and dendrites emerge from the cell body. Some neurons have only one extension from their bodies (unipolar); some have two extensions (bipolar); some have more; and some cells, called interneurons, have short axons or no axons at all. Interneurons convey information between neurons. For example, an interneuron might carry information among neurons that receive sensory information and send motor information.

The nervous system has about ten times as many glial cells as neurons. **Glial cells** are cells in the nervous system that do not directly send information to other cells. Instead, glial cells remove waste, fill empty space, and help other neurons communicate, in part by synthesizing chemicals that help electrochemical signals travel through the body. They also wrap themselves around parts of neurons to form a fatty sheath, which may aid the conduction of information between neurons.

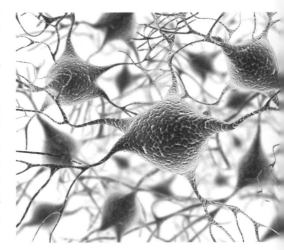

Neural Impulse

Neurons send and receive electrical and chemical signals via electrically charged particles called ions. Information flows in the brain between negatively charged and positively charged neurons. Neurons change from a resting state to a firing, or active, state. Three physical factors affect the **action potential**, or likelihood, that a neuron will fire: the cell membrane, the relative electric charges of the ions, and the relative concentrations of molecules inside and outside the cell membrane.

DENDRITES Short structures that receive electrochemical information from other cells.

AXONS Structures emerging from the neuron that send electrochemical information to other cells.

AXON HILLOCK The part of the axon nearest to the cell body.

TERMINAL BOUTON The part of the axon farthest away from the cell body.

GLIAL CELLS Cells in the nervous system that do not directly send information to other cells.

ACTION POTENTIAL A rapid rise and fall in the membrane potential of a cell.

The membrane that surrounds the neuron controls the exchange of ions. The membrane is semipermeable, which means that it allows some substances, but not others, to pass freely through it. The semipermeable membrane allows potassium, oxygen, carbon dioxide, and water to pass through relatively freely. Positively charged protein molecules are trapped inside the cell. With some difficulty, sodium and chloride can cross the membrane. In this manner, the membrane effectively has "gates" that can let molecules through.

The movement of ions occurs because neurons at rest have an electrical imbalance. The movement of molecules occurs because the relative concentration of molecules is out of balance. Molecules migrate from areas of greater concentration to lesser concentrations. Ions migrate from greater electrical charges to lesser ones, and vice versa. Ions correct the lack of balance inside and outside of the membrane, when the membrane allows.

A system that is imbalanced at rest is advantageous, because when it is stimulated, parts of the brain can respond quickly and decisively. When a neuron reaches its threshold, the neuron will fire. The process is all or nothing—a neuron will fire rapidly or not at all. When the electrical charge of the neuron reaches its threshold, the gates of the membrane open and ions rapidly move inside the neuron through the gates.

The **membrane potential**, which is the difference between the voltage of the interior and exterior portions of a cell, effectively permits a cell to power molecular devices in the membrane. A membrane potential with a stable value is known as a **resting potential**.

The neuron's electrical polarity changes so rapidly because of its semipermeability. When the neuron's membrane becomes selectively permeable to sodium, the membrane allows sodium inside the cell. When these gates open, sodium rushes into the cell, the sodium concentration balances out, and the electrical gradient weakens. The positively charged sodium raises the electric charge of the inside of the neuron relative to the outside of the neuron.

As the electrical gradient, which was holding the positively charged potassium in, weakens, the potassium inside the cell leaves the cell. Because the potassium does not leave as quickly, the sodium rushes in, creating an action potential. When the potential is positive, sodium is no longer attracted into the cell, and the potassium exits the cell. This returns the cell to a negative charge and returns the membrane to a semipermeable state. The membrane then pumps the sodium out, which returns the neuron to its resting potential. This shift of polarity and exchange of molecules constitutes the firing of a neuron.

MEMBRANE POTENTIAL
The difference between the voltage of the interior and exterior portions of a cell.

RESTING POTENTIAL
A membrane potential with a stable value.

TRY IT!

Sit in a circle with a group of at least seven friends. Each person except one should place his or her right hand on the ankle of the person to his or her right. When a signal is given, the person in the group without a hand on his or her ankle (Person A) should squeeze the ankle of the person to his or her right (Person B). Then, Person B should squeeze the ankle of Person C, who is on his or her right. Each person should do this in turn. When the ankle of the last person in the circle—Person G—is squeezed, Person G should raise his or her hand. Repeat the cycle three times, and keep track of how long it takes to complete the circle. Next, repeat the same exercise, this time squeezing shoulders instead of ankles. Why do you think that it takes longer to complete the circle when the ankle is squeezed instead of the shoulder?

Neurotransmitters

NEUROTRANSMITTERS The chemicals that are transmitted from one neuron to another.

SYNAPTIC VESICLES Sacs of chemicals in the terminal button.

SYNAPSES Junctions between neurons characterized by a small gap over which neurotransmitters can flow.

POSTSYNAPTIC MEMBRANE The membrane of a neuron on the other side of the synapse.

REUPTAKE The process by which neurons reabsorb neurotransmitters floating freely in the synapse.

NEUROMODULATORS Neurotransmitters that act indirectly, altering the effect of other neurotransmitters by making their effects either short- or long-lived.

AMINO ACIDS The major excitatory and inhibitory neurotransmitters in the nervous system.

Action potentials travel down the axon to the terminal buttons, or end feet, of the neuron. Then a change occurs in the synapse, the space between the end foot and other neurons. Located near the synapse is the neuron's terminal button, where **neurotransmitters**—the chemicals that are transmitted from one neuron to another—are stored in sacs. These sacs of chemicals in the terminal button are called **synaptic vesicles**. The electric charges that action potentials bring about make the vesicles release neurotransmitters into **synapses**.

Once the neurotransmitters are released, they may drift across the synapse and attach to receptor sites on the **postsynaptic membrane**, which is the membrane of a neuron on the other side of the synapse. Alternatively, the neurotransmitters may not find a target and float in the synapse, and reuptake may occur. **Reuptake** is the process by which neurons reabsorb neurotransmitters floating freely in the synapse.

Neurotransmitters can be divided into five classes: amino acids, monoamines, soluble gases, acetylcholine, and neuropeptides. These five classes have different characteristics, and each performs a different function related to neuron activity. Some neurotransmitters, called **neuromodulators**, act indirectly, altering the effect of other neurotransmitters by making their effects either short- or long-lived.

Amino acids are the major excitatory and inhibitory neurotransmitters in the nervous system. Glutamate, aspartate, GABA, and glycine are four of the most important amino acids. Receptors for these substances are found in all organisms, including the simplest life forms. Receptors for amino acids work by raising or lowering the threshold of excitation on axons.

Glutamate is the principal excitatory transmitter substance in the brain. It is found throughout the brain. Many foods contain glutamate in the form of the additive monosodium glutamate (MSG). Glutamate's excitatory property is why after eating food with MSG, some people experience such symptoms as dizziness or numbness.

Monoamines are a type of neurotransmitter. Most people have heard of the monoamine epinephrine, which is more popularly called adrenaline. This hormone is released into the bloodstream in response to stress, such as fear or injury. Epinephrine may increase heart rate, blood pressure, lung capacity, and blood glucose.

Norepinephrine, which is also called noradrenaline, is a monoamine with significant influence on brain activity. It can cause increases in heart rate, blood pressure, and blood sugar level. It is both a hormone and a neurotransmitter. The difference between a hormone and neurotransmitter is that a hormone is released directly into the bloodstream by glands, while neurotransmitters are released by neurotransmitters. Receptors for norepinephrine, which are called noradrenergic, are involved in control of alertness.

Another monoamine, dopamine, is inhibitory. It affects movement, attention, and learning. Degeneration of the neurons that produce dopamine can cause Parkinson's disease, a neurological illness with symptoms including tremors, rigid limbs, poor balance, and difficulty in starting movement. Imbalances of dopamine also seem to be involved in schizophrenia.

Serotonin is also a monoamine. It is a neurotransmitter involved in regulating mood, eating, sleeping, arousal, pain, and dreaming. The hallucination-inducing drug LSD (lysergic acid diethylamide) appears to work by stimulating serotonin receptors. Major classes of antidepressants work by making more serotonin available to the brain. One of these classes of antidepressants is a group of medications called selective serotonin reuptake inhibitors (SSRIs). SSRIs increase the level of serotonin by making it more available, thus inhibiting reuptake.

THE BRAIN: ITS STRUCTURE AND FUNCTION

The brain is the center of the nervous system. Brain size and complexity vary greatly between species. For example, fish and birds have smaller and less complex brains than dogs and cats. Although dolphins and whales have larger brains than humans, human brains are larger in proportion to a human's body size. The human brain is perhaps the most complex system known to man. In fact, the number of connections among the synapses in a single human brain is estimated to be approximately 1,000 trillion—more than the number of stars in the universe. The billions of neurons in our brains control thoughts, feelings and actions.

Starting at the base of the brain and moving upward to the top of the skull, brain processes change from basic (life sustaining) to more complex (higher mental processes).

The **central nervous system (CNS)** consists of the brain and spinal cord. The spinal cord is responsible for sending and receiving information between the brain and the rest of the body. It is also responsible for simple reflexes.

CENTRAL NERVOUS SYSTEM (CNS) The majority of the nervous system, including the brain and spinal cord.

At the base of the brain is the brainstem. It is responsible for physical survival functions, such as heartbeat and respiration. The brainstem, along with the autonomic nervous system, is also responsible for the fight-or-flight response induced by stress (see image of woman being mugged). When faced with physical or psychological stress, the body and brain prepare the individual to either stay and fight, or run (flight).

The Hindbrain

Above the brainstem lies the hindbrain; it consists of the medulla, pons, and cerebellum. These structures are also considered lower-level and evolutionarily old when compared to higher brain structures. The medulla is responsible for vital automatic functions (like breathing, blood pressure, digestion, swallowing, and heart rate). Humans could not live without the medulla, due to the important processes it regulates. The pons (Latin for "bridge") contains axons that cross from one side of the brain to the other. It is involved in sleeping, waking, and dreaming, as well as respiration and movement. The cerebellum (Latin for "little brain") is a cauliflower-shaped structure that controls movement and some simple learned responses, such as classically-conditioned fears.

The Midbrain

Moving upward, the midbrain coordinates eye and body movement, and works with the pons to regulate arousal and sleep. The reticular formation runs through the center of the brain stem, hindbrain, and midbrain. It screens incoming sensory information, and lets higher brain structures know whether that information is relevant or whether the information should be ignored. For example, a person might be able to block out surrounding conversations in a noisy coffee shop, but when this person hears his or her name called, the individual is alerted immediately and looks up.

The Forebrain

The forebrain contains structures that evolved more recently, including the limbic system and the evolutionarily youngest structure, the **cerebral cortex**. The limbic system contains the thalamus, hypothalamus, hippocampus, and amygdala. The thalamus is often thought of as the brain's relay station or sensory switchboard. It integrates input

CEREBRAL CORTEX The upper part of the brain.

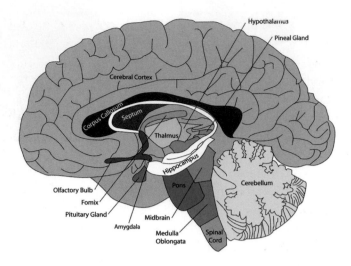

Hypothalamus
Pineal Gland
Cerebral Cortex
Corpus Callosum
Septum
Thalamus
Hippocampus
Olfactory Bulb
Fomix
Pituitary Gland
Amygdala
Midbrain
Medulla Oblongata
Pons
Cerebellum
Spinal Cord

from the senses (except smell) and directs sensory information to appropriate areas of the cortex for processing. Because it is a relay center, damage to the thalamus can affect the cortices' ability to interpret sensory information, such as visual information. For example, thalamus irregularities are linked to schizophrenia, a condition where people have problems with sensory perception. The hypothalamus (under the thalamus) regulates drives, such as sex, hunger, and thirst. It also regulates the endocrine system to control body temperature, and is involved in reward, emotion, hormone release, eating, and drinking. A major area of importance within the limbic system is the amygdala. The amygdala influences emotion, particularly fear and aggression. The hippocampus (this part looks like a sea horse) is involved in the formation of different types of memories, such as forming new memories and long-term episodic memories. If the hippocampus is damaged, a person may not be able to form new memories, as was the case with the famous case-study patient H.M. (see the section Methods for Studying the Brain later in this chapter).

The cerebral cortex is the newest structure to evolve in the human brain, and it governs higher mental processes and complex behaviors. It distinguishes humans from most other animals. It is so vital that a person can be declared legally dead if the cortex dies, even if lower-level structures are still intact and functioning. Think of the cortex as a newspaper crumpled up into a ball. It has a large surface area when spread out, but can fit into the small space of the skull when folded up. The folds, or "wrinkles," in the cortex are called sulci, and the ridges ("bumps") between them are called gyri. If the human brain was unfolded and stretched out, its total surface area would measure around 2.5 ft, or about the size of a pillow case.

The cerebral cortex is divided down the center by a fissure that marks the left and right hemispheres of the brain. Each hemisphere controls the opposite side of the body. The primary connection between the two hemispheres is a ribbon-like band of nerve fibers called the **corpus callosum**. The corpus callosum allows for communication between the two cerebral hemispheres. The hemispheres are further divided into eight distinct lobes—four in each hemisphere. Like all other brain structures, each lobe specializes in specific tasks; this is an example of localization of function. However, many functions overlap between lobes.

Starting at the front of the brain—behind the eyes—are the frontal lobes of the brain. The frontal lobes are responsible for speech production, motor control, and higher brain functions, such as thinking, emotion, and personality. These higher functions distinguish humans from other animals. One of the ways scientists learn about localization of function is from instances where the brain is not functioning normally, as from damage or disease. For example, in 1848, Phineas Gage, 25, was working as a railroad foreman in Vermont. When he was using a tamping iron to pack explosive powder into a hole, the powder detonated. The metal rod (13.25 pounds, 3.6 feet long, 1.25 inches in diameter) shot upward through his left cheek and left frontal lobe, mostly destroying it. Gage did not die, however, and he remained coherent enough to tell a doctor that day (1.5 hours later), "Here is business enough for you." Although he seemed to have healed, he was later described as "fitful, impatient, and lacking in deference to his fellows." His temperament changed, indicating that the frontal lobe is involved in personality. Along with other

CORPUS CALLOSUM A bundle of neural fibers that connects the two halves of the brain.

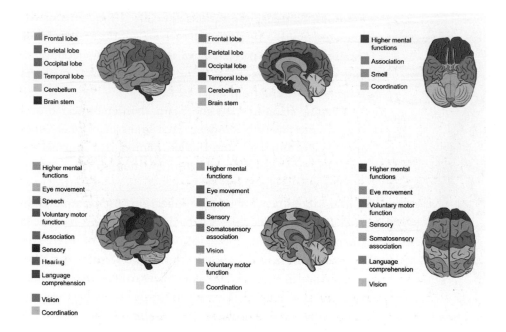

FIGURE 3.1 Human Brain Structure and Function

evidence, researchers have learned that the frontal lobe is important for motivation, creativity, initiative, reasoning, and self-awareness.

At the back of the frontal lobe lies the **motor cortex**. The motor cortex guides the body's motor movement by interpreting information it receives from the senses (like first seeing an apple before reaching for it).

The parietal lobes begin behind the frontal lobes, and receive and interpret bodily sensations, including pressure, pain, touch, and temperature. At the front of the parietal lobe, near the motor cortex, lies the **somatosensory cortex** that processes the body's senses. Areas of the body with more somatosensory and motor cortex devoted to them (like the hands and face) are most sensitive to touch, and have the most precise motor control. If the areas of the human body were proportional to the amount of tissue on the motor and somatosensory cortices, humans would have huge heads and hands!

The temporal lobes (in between the ears) are important for speech, visual object recognition, and the formation of long-term memories. Damage to the temporal lobes can affect language comprehension or facial recognition. For example, German neurologist Karl Wernicke noted that patients with damage to a specific region of the temporal lobe could not understand what they read or heard, but they could speak quickly and easily. However, their speech was often unintelligible because it contained made-up words, sound, and word substitutions. This brain region is referred to as Wernicke's area.

The occipital lobes of the brain that contain the visual cortex are involved in receiving and processing visual information. Patterns of light and color are processed here, as is information about the shapes of objects, their relative distances, and their motion. Damage to the occipital lobe can lead to blindness, even when the eyes and their connections to the brain are functioning normally.

Brain Lateralization

The brain is divided into the left and right hemispheres, each hemisphere controlling the opposite side of the body. The hemispheres are connected by the corpus

MOTOR CORTEX The part of the cortex where movement is guided by information that it gets from the senses.

SOMATOSENSORY CORTEX Processes input from systems in the body that are sensitive to touch, including pain, pressure, and temperature.

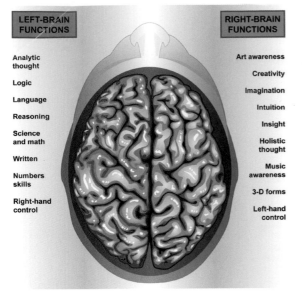

LEFT-BRAIN FUNCTIONS

Analytic thought

Logic

Language

Reasoning

Science and math

Written

Numbers skills

Right-hand control

RIGHT-BRAIN FUNCTIONS

Art awareness

Creativity

Imagination

Intuition

Insight

Holistic thought

Music awareness

3-D forms

Left-hand control

callosum. Consider the various specialized functions of the brain discussed so far. Although each area of the brain exhibits localized function, everything in the brain is interconnected and works together. Each brain area depends on messages transmitted to and from other areas.

Keeping in mind that the brain is interconnected and that all areas work in tandem, each brain hemisphere does specialize in function, and the left hemisphere controls the right side of the body, while the right hemisphere controls the left side of the body. As discussed above, scientists have learned about hemispheric specialization (for example brain lateralization) from cases where the hemispheres have been disconnected. For example, in some rare cases of severe epilepsy, surgeons cut the corpus callosum to stop the spread of epileptic seizures from one hemisphere to the other. Because this operation cuts the communication bridge between the two hemispheres, it reveals what the hemispheres do in isolation.

The right hemisphere not only controls movement of the left side of the body, it also is dominant at nonverbal, visual, and spatial tasks. The left hemisphere, in addition to controlling movement of the right side of the body, is dominant in language and symbolic reasoning tasks.

Patients who have had their corpus callosum severed are referred to as being split-brained. Even when meeting and speaking with a split-brain patient, it is hard to know he or she had the operation. The subtle changes in split-brain patients normally appear only with specialized testing. Research with these patients has aided scientists' understanding of how the two halves of the brain function.

NEUROPLASTICITY The ability of neurons in the brain to change connections when given new information or stimulation.

Neuroplasticity and Neurogenesis

Until recently, neuroscientists believed that the neurons in the brain were hardwired and could not change. Now, scientific research shows that the brain exhibits **neuroplasticity**; this means that neurons in the brain change their connections when they receive new information or stimulation. Thus, the human brain is more malleable than previously thought. This "rewiring" is what makes human brains so adaptive. For example, it makes it possible for humans to learn a new sport or a foreign language.

Remarkably, this rewiring has even helped "remodel" the brain following strokes. For example, psychologist Edward Taub and his colleagues have had success working with stroke patients. Because the left half of the brain controls the right half of the body, a stroke in the left hemisphere would affect movement in the right side of the body. By constraining the unaffected (left, in this case) arm or leg, and requiring rigorous and repetitive exercise of the affected (right) limb, Taub "recruits" stroke patients' intact brain cells to take over for damaged cells. The therapy, called Constraint Induced Movement Therapy (CI Therapy), has restored function in some patients up to 21 years after their strokes. Neuroplasticity exists throughout the lifespan and persists into old age.

NEUROGENESIS The brain's ability to produce new cells that can become part of its circuitry.

In addition to being plastic and malleable, the brain is also capable of producing new brain cells (neurons) through a process called **neurogenesis**. The brain is constantly replacing lost cells with new cells that originate deep within the brain, and migrate to become part of its circuitry. These new cells come from stem cells that are like "blank slates"—they have the potential to develop into many different cell types in the body. Their fate depends on the chemical signals they receive. They can be induced to become tissue or organ-specific cells with special functions. Stem cells have been used for bone marrow transplants, and clinical trials using stem cells to repopulate or replace cells devastated by injury or disease have helped patients suffering from strokes, Alzheimer's, Parkinson's, epilepsy, stress, and depression.

Researchers at the Mayo Clinic Developmental and Regenerative Neurobiology Laboratory in Rochester, Minn., have developed a laboratory therapy for zebrafish with spinal cord injuries. After treatment, the injured fish demonstrated dramatic functional recovery. "After injury, the fish don't swim very well or very far. After treatment, they have recovered," says John R. Henley, Ph.D., a molecular neuroscientist who directs the lab. The ultimate goal is to translate discoveries in fish and other animals into treatments that can help people recover from spinal cord injury.

Returning to the case of Phineas Gage, he did experience several dramatic changes in his personality after frontal lobe damage, but the extent and perpetuity of the changes are debated. Most accounts of Gage after the injury reported him as impulsive and unreliable until his death. However, later and more reliable evidence showed that Gage recovered appreciably, and spent many years driving stagecoaches, a skill that required demanding motor, cognitive, and interpersonal skills. In Gage's time, scientists were not aware of the amazing capabilities of the human brain to rewire and replace damaged cells. Today's knowledge of neuroplasticity and neurogenesis explains this previously ignored evidence of Gage's recovery later in life.

Methods for Studying the Brain

Knowing about which areas of the brain control which functions is critical to helping patients with brain disorders. If a person has a severe speech disorder, it is important to first examine whether there is damage to the part of the person's brain that is involved in speech. People with seizure or attention disorders must undergo tests to discover how electrical patterns in their brains respond to stimuli, including which areas specifically respond. As has been demonstrated throughout the chapter, researchers often learn best how the brain and mind function by studying living people who have suffered brain injuries. Many patients are unable to recover from brain damage, because of the location of the lesion and extent of the lesion. For example, to decrease his epileptic seizures, in 1953 a patient known as H.M. had most of his hippocampus and surrounding areas surgically removed. H.M. suffered from a severe form of amnesia as a result: he was unable to form new memories. By studying H.M. throughout his life, scientists learned that the hippocampal area was crucial for the formation of new memories.

Recovery from brain damage is more likely in younger patients than in older people. Children who have an entire hemisphere of the brain removed (called a hemispherectomy) are sometimes able to live normal lives because the remaining brain is able to take over the functions of its missing half.

Many types of X-rays, scans, and tests are used to examine and diagnose injury and problems with brain function. Each type has its own advantages, disadvantages, costs, and benefits.

Although brain research has become much more sophisticated in recent years, there is still a great deal left to understand. New imaging and sensing techniques will continue to be developed, along with new research into behavior and brain activity. This should yield a far more incisive understanding of the links between human physiology and psychology.

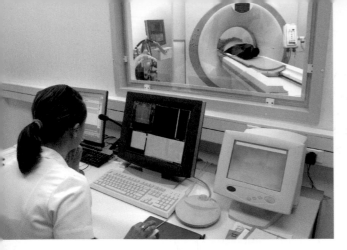

CT Scan

A sophisticated imaging method called X-ray computed tomography (known generally as a CT scan) compiles a three-dimensional view of the brain by taking many X-rays from many points of view. CT scans may be useful for examining traumatic brain injury because the scans are brief, relatively inexpensive, widely available, and can quickly reveal brain lesions or swelling that needs to be addressed immediately. The X-rays generated by a CT scan yield a static picture of the brain (what the brain looks like at one point in time).

PET and MRI

Another type of technology, positron emission tomography (PET), involves using nuclear medicine to produce a three-dimensional image of the inner workings of the body. PET is usually used in conjunction with CT scans or with magnetic resonance imaging (MRI), which provides higher resolution images than CT scans. MRI provides a three-dimensional picture using radio frequency waves in a magnetic field. A functional MRI applies specifically to brain activity; this technique shows when and where oxygen (via imagery of the blood flow) increases in certain parts of the brain. MRI provides structural and functional information and gives high-quality visual results.

More Invasive Methods for Studying the Brain

The methods described in the previous section are noninvasive, which means that they do not require probing or cutting beneath the skin in order to see inside the body. Invasive physiological research methods allow researchers to look directly inside the body. For example, physicians may surgically open the skull to locate lesions or hemorrhaging in the brain. Radiation may be used to penetrate the skin and skull and administer therapy.

If, after a part of the brain is incapacitated through either an invasive injury or other incident, a particular behavior is changed or absent, physicians can conclude

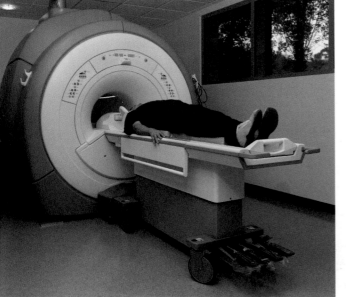

that the part of the brain that was incapacitated must have been involved in that particular behavior. For example, in 2001, researchers A. K. Anderson and E. A. Phelps found a connection between lesions on the amygdala and an inability to perceive important emotional events.

Another invasive form of research involves the use of drugs and observations of the resulting behavior. Researchers can assess the effects of neurotransmitters on behavior by altering the neurotransmitters via drugs. A lack of serotonin, which comes specifically from an area in the brain stem, can cause depression. As a result, drugs that affect serotonin levels in the brain can help treat depression.

How Neurotransmitters Affect the Brain

Neurons release dozens of different neurotransmitters, and different combinations of these chemicals may affect postsynaptic cells differently. Most neurotransmitters either excite or inhibit neurons. Exciting a neuron makes that neuron more likely to fire. Inhibiting a neuron makes the neuron less likely to fire. Consider the following characteristics of various neurotransmitters:

- Some neurotransmitters both excite neurons when they bind to some receptor subtypes and inhibit neurons when they bind to other receptor subtypes. For example, acetylcholine is a neurotransmitter that can excite skeletal muscles and inhibit the heart muscle.

- Some neurotransmitters have a direct, immediate effect on the neurons they encounter. For example, epinephrine (also known as adrenaline), a neurotransmitter that affects attention systems and other systems, may make postsynaptic neurons more likely to fire.

- Neurotransmitters may also inhibit a postsynaptic cell. For example, a neurotransmitter called **GABA** is inhibitory. GABA, in fact, is the major inhibitory neurotransmitter, preventing overstimulation in the brain.

- Neuromodulators act indirectly, altering the effect of other neurotransmitters by making their effects short- or long-lived.

Four classes of neurotransmitters—amino acids, monoamines, soluble gases, and acetylcholine—have small molecules. The fifth class of neurotransmitter, neuropeptides, has large molecules. These five classes have different characteristics, and each performs a different function related to neuron activity.

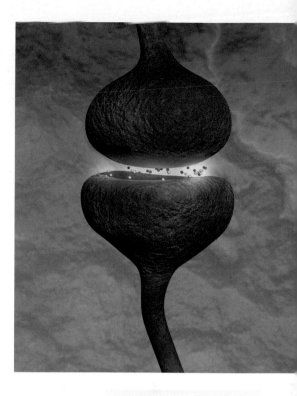

GABA An inhibitory transmitter found throughout the brain. GABA malfunctions may be involved in seizure disorders, as the lack of inhibitory chemicals may lead to uncontrolled firing patterns.

How Hormones Affect the Brain

One significant area of brain research is the interaction between the nervous system and the endocrine system. The endocrine system controls the body's glands, which are organs that secrete chemicals called hormones. These hormones influence other parts of the body and can affect human capabilities and behavior. Glands secrete these chemicals through ducts, which may travel to the skin or directly into the circulatory system. The primary purpose of glands is to release hormones, but other organs release hormones as well. The pituitary gland, which is often called the master gland, releases tropic hormones, which are chemicals that influence the release of hormones from other glands.

Hormones tend to exert their effect by binding to receptors in cell membranes. There are three general classes of hormones. First are amino acid derivatives, which are hormones that are synthesized from amino acids, such as epinephrine. Second are peptides and proteins. Peptides are short chains of amino acids, and protein hormones are long chains of amino acids. The third class of hormones is steroids, which are chemicals synthesized from cholesterol; steroids play a major role in sexual development and behavior. Hormones can bind to receptors within the cell. They can pass through cell membranes, which gives them the ability to influence gene expression, which is the biologic process that converts the information encoded in DNA (such as the DNA sequence) into proteins. Gene expression can lead to long-lasting effects on cellular function.

Gonads—the testes in males and the ovaries in females—are glands that produce hormones called androgens (such as testosterone), estrogens (such as estradiol), and progestins (such as progesterone). All three are produced in each gender, but the testes produce more testosterone and the ovaries produce more estradiol. The other glands that produce these hormones are the adrenal glands, which are located on top of the kidneys.

Hormones affect human development. Sexual differentiation begins at conception: Zygotes with XX chromosomes will be female and XY zygotes will be male. At about six weeks, male zygotes trigger the production of an antigen that causes the gonads to develop into testes. Female zygotes do not, so their gonads continue to develop into ovaries. Following this, the male and female reproductive systems begin to develop. They continue to develop, constantly affected by hormones, until adulthood.

Hormones also affect adults as they interact with the nervous system. For example, primate females (including humans, of course) have menstrual cycles and other species of mammals have estrous cycles. The major difference between the endocrine function of males and females is that female hormones cycle and male hormones do not.

The effect of hormones on behavior is a continuing subject of study. Epinephrine is associated with fear; norepinephrine is associated with anger. Steroids contribute to excitability. Women who receive estrogen replacement therapy perform better on verbal learning and memory tests than women who do not. Hormones also affect the way that attention, motivation, empathy, and decision making work together to affect nurturing and caregiving in parents.

SUMMARY

Neurons are the smallest units of the nervous system. They make connections and exchange information. Electrical information and chemical signals flow freely among the brain's neurons. Neurotransmitters are chemicals transmitted from one neuron to another.

The brain is slightly larger than a person's fist. The base of the brain contains the brain stem, medulla, pons, and cerebellum. The cerebellum is attached to the brainstem and mediates motor movement. The limbic system is above the brainstem and is involved in sensory processing, drives, emotion, learning, and memory. The cerebral cortex is the upper part of the brain and is divided into two hemispheres connected by the corpus callosum. The cerebral cortex is involved in everything from memory to perception.

Human brains are divided into eight lobes—four in each hemisphere. The lobes perform specialized functions, although functions overlap between lobes. In general, the left side of the brain controls motor movements of the right side of the body, and the right side of the brain controls the left side of the body. The right hemisphere is dominant at nonverbal, visual, and spatial tasks. The left hemisphere is dominant in language and symbolic reasoning tasks.

The brain exhibits both neuroplasticity and neurogenesis. Neuroplasticity is the brain's ability to change its connections when it receives new stimulation, making it very malleable and adaptable. Neurogenesis is the production of new brain cells that can replace lost or damaged cells and take over their function.

Methods for studying the brain include a variety of types of X-rays, such as CT scans and MRI.

Neurotransmitters and hormones affect the function of brain. Neurotransmitters send chemical information to neighboring neurons, either exciting or inhibiting their action. The effect of hormones on behavior is a continuing subject of research. The brain is more malleable than formerly thought. Neurons adapt and change depending on the stimulus. The nervous system responds to and organizes incoming stimuli from sights, sounds, scents, and sensations from the outside world.

REFERENCES

Anderson, A. K., & Phelps, E. A. (2001). Lesions of the human amygdala impair enhanced perception of emotionally salient events. *Nature*, 411, 305–309.

Banissy, M. J., Sauter, D. A., Ward, J., Warren, J. E., Walsh, V., & Scott, S. K. (2010). Suppressing sensorimotor activity modulates the discrimination of auditory emotions but not speaker identity. *Journal of Neuroscience*, 30(41), 13552–13557.

Bor, J., Brunelin, J., Sappey-Marinier, D., Ibarrola, D., d'Amato, T., Suaud-Chagny, M. F., & Saoud, M. (2011). Thalamus abnormalities during working memory in schizophrenia. An FMRI study. *Schizophr Res.*, 125(1), 49–53.

Caine, R. N., & Caine, G. (1990). *Making Connections: Teaching and the Human Brain*. Nashville, TN: Incentive Publications.

Carpenter, S., & Huffman, K. (2013). *Visualizing psychology* (3rd ed.). Upper Saddle River, NJ: John Wiley & Sons.

Cavanagh, J. F., Cohen, M. X., & Allen, J. J. B. (2009). Prelude to and resolution of an error: EEG phase synchrony reveals cognitive control dynamics during action monitoring. *Journal of Neuroscience*, 29(1), 98–105.

Desimone, R. (1991). Face-selective cells in the temporal cortex of monkeys. *Journal of Cognitive Neuroscience*, 3(1), 1–8.

Egashira, N., Tanoue, A., Matsuda, T., Koushi, E., Harad, S., Takano, Y., . . . Fuiwara, M. (2007). Impaired social interaction and reduced anxiety-related behavior in vasopressin V1 a receptor knockout mice. *Behavioural Brain Research*, 178(1), 123–127.

Gholipour, B. (2014, February 3). A brain surgery decades ago is getting a new look and raising questions about memory. *Washington Post*.

Grohol, J. M. (2008, September 21). It's alright: Teens playing video games. Retrieved from http://psychcentral.com/blog/archives/2008/09/21/its-alright-teens-playing-video-games/

Gross, C. G., Rocha-Miranda, C. E., & Bender, D. B. (1972). Visual properties of neurons in inferotemporal cortex of the macaque. *Journal of Neurophysiology*, 35, 96–111.

Jonkman, L. M., Kenemans, J. L., Kemner, C., Verbaten, M. N., & van Engeland, J. (2004). Dipole source localization of event-related brain activity indicative of an early visual selective attention deficit in ADHD children. *Clinical Neurophysiology*, 115(7), 1537–1549.

Kilner, J. M., Neal, A., Weiskopf, N., Fristin, K. J., & Frith, C. D. (2009). Evidence of mirror neurons in human inferior frontal gyrus. *Journal of Neuroscience*, 29(32), 10153–10159.

Lagorio, C. (2006, June 14). This is your brain online: How video games, multitasking and blogging are shaping the GenTech brain. Retrieved from http://www.cbsnews.com/stories/2006/06/11/gentech/main1699513.shtml

Levin, H. S., Wilde, E. A., Chu, Z., Yallampalli, R., Hanten, G. R., Li, X., . . . Hunter, J. V. (2008). Diffusion tensor imaging in relation to cognitive and functional outcome of traumatic brain injury in children. *Journal of Head Trauma Rehabilitation*, 23(4), 197–208.

Ley, R. G., & Bryden, M. P. (1979). Hemispheric differences in processing emotions and faces. *Brain and Language*, 7(1), 127–138.

Macmillan, M. (2000). *An odd kind of fame: Stories of Phineas Gage*. MIT Press.

Macmillan, M., & Lena, M. L. (2010). Rehabilitating Phineas Gage. *Neuropsychological Rehabilitation*, 20(5), 641–58.

Maki, P. M., Zonderman, A. B., & Resnick, S. M. (2001). Enhanced verbal memory in nondemented elderly women receiving hormone-replacement therapy. *American Journal of Psychiatry*, 158, 227–233.

Murre, J. M., & Sturdy, D. P. (1995). The connectivity of the brain: Multi-level quantitative analysis. *Biological Cybernetics*, 73(6), 529–545.

Narr, K. L., Woods, R. P., Thompson, P. M., Szeszko, P., Robinson, D., Dimtcheva, T., . . . Bilder, R. M. (2007). Relationships between IQ and regional cortical gray matter thickness in healthy adults. *Cerebral Cortex*, 17(9), 2163–2171.

National Institutes of Health, U.S. Department of Health and Human Services. (2009). Stem cell basics. In *Stem Cell Information*. Bethesda, MD: Author.

Nestler, E. J. & Self, D. W. (2010). Neuropsychiatric aspects of ethanol and other chemical dependencies. In S. Yudofsky & R. E. Hales (Eds.), *Essentials of neuropsychiatry and behavioral neuroscience*. Arlington, VA: American Psychiatric Publishing.

Oberman, L. M., Hubbard, E. M., McCleery, J. P., Altschuler, E. L., Ramachandran, V. S., & Pineda, J. A. (2005). EEG evidence for mirror neuron dysfunction in autism spectrum disorders. *Cognitive Brain Research*, 24(2), 190–198.

Peters, & Jones, E. G. (1984). *Cerebral cortex.*

Ramachandran, V. S. (2006). Mirror neurons and imitation learning as the driving force behind the great leap forward in human evolution. Retrieved from http://www.edge.org/3rd_culture/ramachandran/ramachandran_p1.html

Reiss, A. L., Abrams, M. T., Singer, H. S., Ross, J. L., & Denckla, M. B. (1996). Brain development, gender and IQ in children: A volumetric imaging study. *Brain*, 119(5), 1763–1774.

Reuter-Lorenz, P., & Davidson, R. J. (1981). Differential contributions of the two cerebral hemispheres to the perception of happy and sad faces. *Neuropsychologia*, 19(4), 609–613.

Sergerie, K., Chochoi, C., & Armony, J. L. (2008). The role of the amygdala in emotional processing: A quantitative meta-analysis of functional neuroimaging studies. *Neuroscience and Biobehavioral Reviews*, 32(4), 811–830.

Soliman, F., Glatt, C. E., Bath, K. G., Levita, L., Jones, R. M., Pattwell, S. S., . . . Casey, B. J. (2010). A genetic variant BDNF polymorphism alters extinction learning in both mouse and human. *Science*, 327(12), 863–866.

Sperry, R. W. (1964). The great cerebral commissure. *Scientific American*, 210, 42–52.

Sperry, R. W. (1968). Hemisphere disconnection and unity in conscious awareness. *American Psychologist*, 23, 723–33.

Sperry, R. W. (1970). Perception in the absence of neocortical commissures. In *Perception and its disorders* (Res. Publ. A.R.N.M.D., 48). New York: The Association for Research in Nervous and Mental Disease.

Squire, L. R., & Zola-Morgan, S. (1991). The medial temporal lobe memory system. *Science*, 253(5026), 1380–1386.

Swain, J. E., Lorberbaum, J. P., Kose, S., & Strathearn, L. (2007). Brain basis of early parent–infant interactions: Psychology, physiology, and in vivo functional neuroimaging studies. *Journal of Child Psychology and Psychiatry*, 48(3), 262–287.

Taub, E. (2004). Harnessing brain plasticity through behavioral techniques to produce new treatments in neurorehabilitation. *American Psychologist*, 59(8), 692–704.

Taub, E., Uswatte, G., King, D. K., Morris, D. M., Crago, J. E., & Chatterjee, A (2006). A placebo controlled trial of constraint-induced movement therapy for upper extremity after stroke. *Stroke*, 37, 1045–1049.

Toman, B. (2014). *Neuroregenerative medicine booklet.* Retrieved from http://www.mayo.edu/research/documents/neuroregenerative-medicine-booklet/doc-20092381

Tucker, D. M., & Williamson, P. A. (1984). Asymmetric neural control systems in human self-regulation. *Psychological Review*, 91(2), 182–215.

Weinstein, A., Brickner, O., Lerman, H., Greenland, M., Bloch, M., Lester, H....Freeman, N. (2008). Brain imaging study of the acute effects of THC on attention and motor coordination in regular users of marijuana. *Psychopharmacology*, 196(1), 119–131.

Wernicke K. (1995). The aphasia symptom-complex: A psychological study on an anatomical basis (1875). In *Paul Eling, reader in the history of aphasia: From sasi* (*Franz Gall to*) (pp. 69–89). Amsterdam: John Benjamins.

Wolf, U., Rapoport M. J., & Schweizer T. A. (2009). Evaluating the affective component of the cerebellar cognitive affective syndrome. *J. Neuropsychiatry Clin. Neurosci.*, 21(3), 245–53.

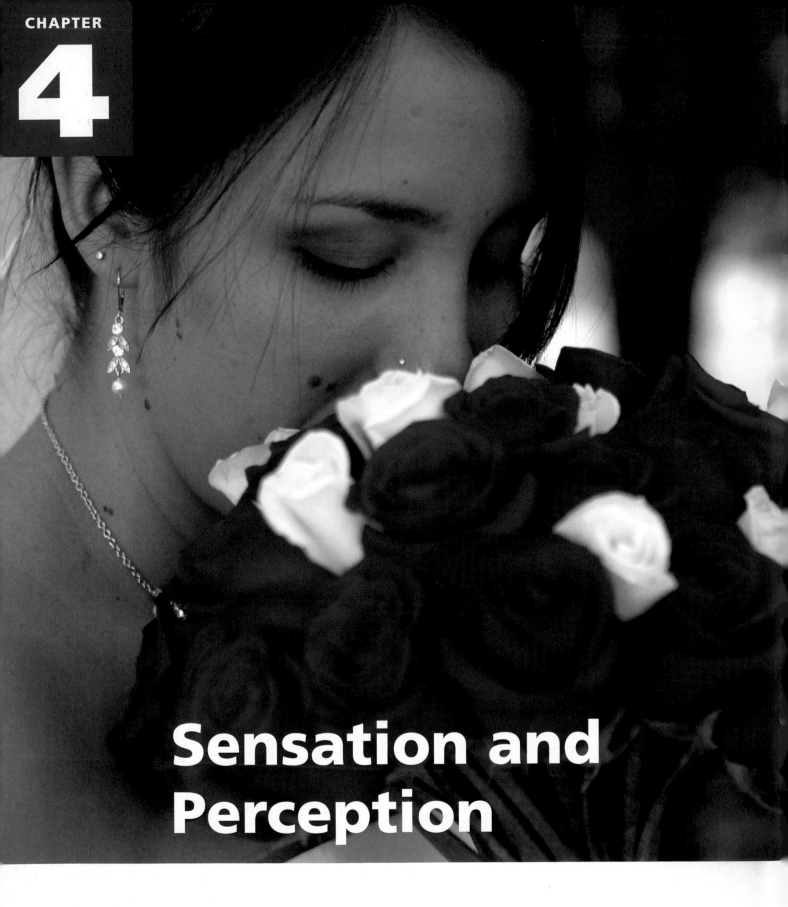

Sensation and Perception

"All our knowledge has its origins in our perceptions."

—Leonardo da Vinci

WHAT ARE SENSATION AND PERCEPTION?

Sensation and perception are the link between your body and the outside world. Without them, people would be unable to experience or comprehend any information about the world around them. They could not taste the crisp tartness of an apple, feel a cool breeze, or recognize a familiar face. All those inputs that make up our interactions with the world are received, transmitted, and interpreted by our nervous system, making up our experiences of sensation and perception. **Sensation** is the way that physical energy affects the sensory receptors and organs. **Perception** is the organization of the various inputs of sensation.

Throughout history, scientists have debated whether certain knowledge and abilities are learned or innate. **Empiricists**, beginning with the Greek philosopher Aristotle, have suggested that an understanding of the world is developed through experience. Qualities such as distance, size, and shape are learned through one's experiences with them. For example, a person could understand the category of a circle by touching or seeing one. **Nativists**, such as Aristotle's teacher Plato, proposed that people are born with categories, such as circles, and experience helps uncover those innate categories. To a nativist, these categories are *found* in the mind, whereas empiricists believe the mind *creates* them through experience. For both nativists and empiricists, there is a chain of events:

- *A distal stimulus*—the stimulus outside of the body, such as a sound wave or a pattern of light
- *A proximal stimulus*—the physical stimulation of sensory receptors, like the receptors in back of the eye
- *Transduction*—the transformation of one type of energy to another (for example, light converted to electrical signals within the brain)
- *Neural processing*—operations in systems of neurons in the brain
- *Interpretation*—an understanding of stimuli
- *Action*—taking action on that understanding of stimuli

Perception always occurs in relation to something else. People comprehend and recognize the world because experience activates neural circuits and mental categories, and because the mind and nervous system enable them to recognize the categories.

Perception is studied in three basic ways:

- *The relationship between stimuli and perception.* For example, a perceptual scientist may study how converging lines can convey a sense of depth to an individual.
- *The relationship between stimuli and physiology.* For example, in a 1981 study, researchers Charles Bruce, Robert Desimone, and Charles Gross found that some cells in the brain of a monkey respond to faces.

SENSATION The way that physical energy affects the sensory receptors and organs.

PERCEPTION The organization of the various inputs of sensation, which may involve understanding neural processing, understanding how to organize the physics of sensations, and understanding how to behave in response to these sensations, or a combination of all of those understandings.

EMPIRICISTS Scientists who believe that all knowledge comes from experience.

NATIVISTS Scientists who believe that people are born with certain knowledge and abilities.

1. Understanding sensation and perception involves understanding how the nervous system takes in the physical world. See page 53.

2. Sensory thresholds are measured in more than one way to determine the smallest amount of stimulus necessary to be detected by the body. See page 54.

3. Perception organizes sensory information and is a complex process in the brain. See page 61.

4. Sensory adaptation involves responses to stimuli that can change depending on variables such as the amount of time of exposure to the stimulus. See page 56.

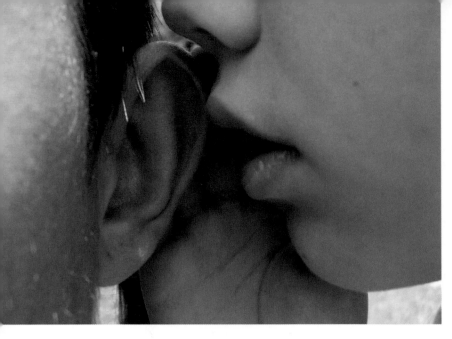

■ *The relationship between perception and physiology.* For example, neurosurgeons Wilder Penfield and Herbert Jasper were working on developing treatments for epilepsy and found that when they stimulated certain parts of their patients' brains, the patients would report "seeing" or "hearing" certain sights, sounds, or memories, such as songs.

Another way the mind and perception are often studied is by closely examining patterns in patients who have suffered brain damage. Consider the example of Kallman syndrome, a disease in which an anomaly occurs in the neuronal migration of cells that normally produce sex hormones in the pituitary gland. As a result, the patient's sense of smell is affected.

The various ways that brain lesions affect behavior can reveal much about the mind and the way it perceives stimuli. In 2009, researcher Jan Gläscher and his colleagues examined 241 patients with brain damage and found that a pattern of damage in the frontal and parietal cortex was highly correlated with lower general intelligence scores.

SENSORY THRESHOLDS

How loud does a sound have to be before someone can detect it? You do not have an on/off switch that tells your brain when there is a sound in the world. Instead, your sensory receptors and brain work in terms of probabilities. The **absolute threshold** is the smallest amount of stimulus energy necessary for an observer to detect a stimulus. As energy levels, such as the magnitude of a sound wave, increase, the probability of perceiving the sound also increases.

Usually when a person detects stimulus energy, such as sound, more than 50 percent of the time, scientists consider that the person can detect that stimulus. The change from one state (such as not hearing a sound) to another (such as hearing a sound 50 percent of the time or more) is the crossing of the threshold. The development of psychophysics by Gustav Fechner in the 1800s introduced a way of measuring thresholds, or how brain activity responds to the environment, in a noninvasive manner. His techniques are still in use today.

ABSOLUTE THRESHOLD The smallest amount of stimulus energy necessary for an observer to detect a stimulus.

ABSOLUTE THRESHOLDS FOR THE FIVE SENSES

Vision—A candle flame approximately 30 miles away on a clear, dark night.

Hearing—A ticking watch placed about 20 feet away from a person in a quiet room.

Taste—One teaspoon of sugar in two gallons of water.

Smell—One drop of perfume in a six-room house.

Touch—Dropping the wing of a bee onto someone's cheek from a distance of 1/2 inch (1 centimeter).

One group of perceptual psychologists, most famously J. J. Gibson, pioneered an approach to perception called **ecological perception**. Instead of looking at stimuli, such as light, independently of its environment, these psychologists looked at stimuli as they occurred in the environment. Perception, they argued, should be seen as an active process—a process for obtaining information and acting on that information, rather than a process in which a passive observer has energy impinging upon them.

There are four main principles of ecological perception. First, stimuli should be described as arrays in the environment, not as light impressing itself on the retina. Second, the movement of the observer should be taken into account when studying perception. Third, the invariant movement of the perceiver indicates what information is relevant. For example, the ratio of an object's height to the distance between its base and the horizon can indicate what size an object is and can be the basis for size constancy. Size constancy refers to perceiving an object of a certain size, such as a six-foot-tall man, as being six feet tall regardless of whether he is close to the viewer or far away from the viewer.

Another invariant is time-to-contact. People and animals can accurately judge when they will have contact with another, but they are not always accurate at predicting speed. According to a 1981 study by researchers Davis Lee and Paul Reddish, birds fold their wings at a precise time just before reaching the water. However, in a 1990 study, William Schiff and Rivka Oldak found that men and women judge time to arrival differently—findings few people would likely dispute.

A **difference threshold** examines how different two stimuli must be before an animal can detect that they are different at least 50 percent of the time. For example, a person might feel two weights and be asked to indicate whether they are the same or different. The minimum amount of weight necessary in order to perceive a difference 50 percent of the time is known as the difference threshold or the just noticeable difference (JND).

In the nineteenth century, psychologist Ernst Weber developed a law for all stimuli relating physical intensity to magnitude perception. It stated that the change in the intensity of a stimulus (for example, from a quieter to louder sound) divided by the intensity of the stimulus (the loudness of a sound) equals a constant. Later, Gustav Fechner modified Weber's law slightly by expressing the relationships in terms of logarithms. As a result, the law is sometimes called the Weber–Fechner law.

$$dp = k\frac{dS}{S}$$

In the equation, dp refers to the differential change in perception, dS refers to the differential increase in stimulus, S refers to the stimulus, and k is the constant factor.

Experiments have shown that as stimulus intensity increases (i.e., as a sound gets louder or a light gets brighter), it takes a greater difference in stimulus to reach the difference threshold. In other words, you are less likely to notice a change in the brightness of a bright light than a dim light, and you are less likely to notice a comparable change in loudness in a soft sound than in a loud sound. For pain, on the other hand, the more intense the stimulus, the more easily people detect small differences. Each sense has its own mathematical function. For each sense, both the

ECOLOGICAL PERCEPTION A theory that sees perception as an active process that is affected by the environment in which it occurs.

DIFFERENCE THRESHOLD The minimum difference required between two stimuli before an animal can detect that they are different.

absolute and difference thresholds are similar. For both thresholds, the stimulus usually must be detected at least 50 percent of the time; remember, however, that there will always be "noise" in the environment and in your body that will affect your perception.

The physical basis for perception is in your brain and your physiology. Different stimuli affect different parts of the brain. Neurobiologists David Hubel and Torsten Wiesel, who won the Nobel Prize in 1981 for research on the visual system, found that certain cells in the visual system respond to very specific stimuli in the environment. For example, some cells respond to lines of very specific spatial orientation and are inhibited by lines of other orientation. Hubel and Wiesel's Nobel Prize was awarded for their work linking neural physiology with visual stimulus.

Sensory Adaptation

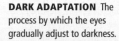

Sensory adaptation is the process by which senses become less responsive to particular stimuli. Consider the enjoyment of flowers in a garden at dusk. When the surroundings are brightly lit, the red of a rose or geranium will appear bright against the greens and blues of their leaves. As darkness falls, however, the greens and blues appear brighter, and the red of the flower becomes harder to see. Some people take advantage of this phenomenon by planting "moon gardens," which are gardens filled with whites, greens, and blues. All of these elements reflect the capability of the visual system.

What are the physical and physiological properties of sensory adaptation? The retina contains cells called rods and cones. Cones are receptive to color and adapt to darkness more quickly than rods. Rods, which are more sensitive to light than the cones, do not sense differences in colors. Rods are better able to see at low light levels. This provides some adaptive benefits, like the ability to see vividly in the dark (with rods) and in the light (with cones), through **dark adaptation**. In the process of dark adaptation, the cone receptors are the first to adapt to the dark. Then the rods adapt slowly, giving people the ability to see vividly in the dark.

Adaptation affects taste. Consider tasting orange juice in the morning, just after brushing your teeth. The orange juice tastes sour because of your tongue's adaptation to the sweetness of the toothpaste. Receptors that are sensitive to sweetness stop responding, but the receptors responding to the sourness of the orange juice continue responding. As a result, the sweetness of the orange juice will not be processed, but the sourness will be processed.

Human enjoyment of food is predicated on this principle. If people ate nothing but chocolate, for example, the chocolate would taste less and less chocolatey over time. If different flavors are mixed with the chocolate, then the taste of the chocolate is accentuated. This is why for many people, an assorted box of chocolate, with many different subtastes, is more appealing than a simple chocolate bar.

Olfactory systems adapt rapidly and completely. Consider walking into a house in which someone is cooking apple pie. When you first walk in, the smell is probably overwhelming, but after a few moments, the smell is gone unless you sniff deeply in order to raise the intensity of the molecules. You no longer smell the apple pie, because your system has adapted. This is one reason that it is hard to smell your own body odor—you adapt to your own odor and thus find it difficult to detect.

VISION

Most people rely on vision to navigate the world. The stimulus for vision is light: energy radiated as waves, produced by electric charges. Light is described by wavelength, which is the distance between peaks of electromagnetic waves. Different wavelengths are perceived as different colors. Light also is described by photons, or packets of light.

Light travels first through the **cornea** (the clear outside membrane in the eye), which does most of the focusing for distance and clarity. The **lens** then bends the rays to focus on near and far objects. Then light travels through a gap, called the **pupil**, which regulates how much light gets into the eye. Light is gathered by **photoreceptors**, which are on the back of the **retina**.

We do not see wavelengths or packets of lights, but patterns and objects, in depth. Light reflects off objects and creates a structured pattern that reaches the photoreceptors—rods and cones—at the back of the eye. The structured array is what you respond to. **Rods** and **cones** are distributed differently in different parts of the eye. Cones are primarily present in the **fovea**, which is in the center of the eye. Rods are found in the eye's periphery, around the edges. Cones are able to transmit fine information about shape and color. Rods transmit information about subtle changes in brightness and motion. This is why one can often catch subtle changes in light and motion, like shooting stars, from the periphery, but not when looking straight at them. Both of these receptors are embedded into the back of the eye in order to get nutrients. From there, information travels through the nervous system.

CORNEA Clear outer membrane of the eye.

LENS Clear structure in the eye that focuses images.

PUPIL Gap in the center of the eye that light passes through.

PHOTORECEPTOR Cell that gathers light in the eye.

RETINA Light-sensitive tissue within the eye.

RODS Light-sensitive cells within the eye that are more sensitive than their counterparts, cones, but do not sense color.

CONES Light-sensitive cells within the eye that sense color but are less light-sensitive than their counterparts, rods.

FOVEA Central area within the eye where cones are prevalent.

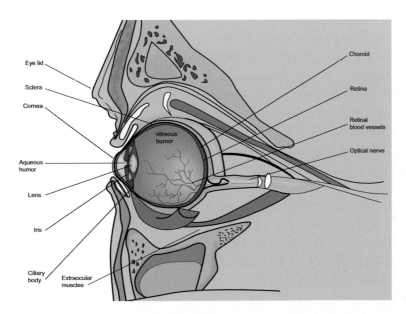

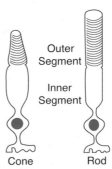

Rods and cones transmit signals through specific cells that leave the eye via the optic nerve. The space required for the optic nerve to leave the eye results in a gap in the receptors. This gap creates a blind spot—an area out of which a person cannot see.

Most axons from the eye travel to the thalamus. From there, the axons go to the visual cortex. As neurons in the eye are excited, they inhibit neighboring neurons. This means that when patches of light and dark are next to each other, the neurons responding to the edge will be the most excited—the neurons straddling the edge between light and dark will not be as inhibited as the neurons that are completely in the light, because they will not suffer the increased inhibition. At the same time, these neurons will be more excited than the neurons in the dark because they are excited by the light. This characteristic of the visual system heightens the perception of edges.

To bind several distinct characteristics of a perceived object, the cortex uses its ability to focus attention on the object. Attention involves orienting, often with eye movements that focus on something specific. Different parts of the cortex process color, motion, and depth. Attention serves, for example, to bind these attributes of perception together. Imagine a group of children sliding down a snowy hill on blue, green, and red sleds. The colors of the sleds, the motion of the sleds, and the shapes of the children and their sleds do not seem separate.

Different wavelengths of light that correspond to the colors of the spectrum are processed by different types of cones. Animals have varying combinations of these cones, depending on their environments, which makes them responsive to different wavelengths. Bees, for example, do not process reds, and fish, which live in low light, respond very little to color. People and primates have three different kinds of cones, each of which has its own spectral sensitivity. The cones are called short-, medium-, and long-wavelength cones. Short-wavelength cones, for example, are triggered by short-wavelength colors, such as violet, at the low end of the visible spectrum. The color of an object is encoded within the brain when it assesses the relative activity of the different classes of cones. Cells also respond to whether colors are complementary colors, as well as how light or dark the various wavelengths are in relation to each other.

COLOR CONSTANCY The ability to sense the same color under different light levels and in different contexts.

These processes, working together, enable people to have **color constancy**, which is the ability to see a color even when different predominant hues are present. For example, a red sled appears red whether it is in the store, on a computer screen, in a house, or outside—even though in each of those circumstances, it is likely to be lit by sources with differing intensities and differing wavelengths. At the same time, even though colors remain constant, one's perception of them can change, because the perception of color rests on a foundation of cells that respond to different wavelengths and the relative strength of that wavelength with respect to its neighbors. When colors are placed beside other colors, one may perceive the colors differently. The same red will look different when it is surrounded by a field of green, a field of gray, or a field of deeper or lighter red. Many artists, such as Vincent van Gogh and Claude Monet, use juxtaposition of colors to convey form, emotion, and meaning to great effect.

Context also affects a person's sense of motion. On some occasions, you may be sitting in a car, subway, or train and feel movement even when the vehicle is stopped. This illusion may occur because a large object, such as another train or truck, is moving in the periphery of your eye. Usually when you are moving, motion is happening in your peripheral field of vision. In this case, your brain would mistakenly interpret the difference between the motion you perceive in the periphery of your eye and the lack of motion you perceive in the center of your eye as a signal that you are moving.

The sense of motion is useful; it has helped people survive since antiquity. Motion can attract one's attention to approaching dangers or opportunities. Motion also helps you identify what you see. You can recognize people or objects by their motion alone. Finally, the sense of motion helps people to navigate the world; it helps a football quarterback know where to throw the ball and helps the receiver catch the ball.

Motion is first detected on the retina, when adjacent receptors are stimulated. Neurons in the visual cortex then respond to motion in a particular direction. In order to detect motion, eye movements also are evaluated by the nervous system. Consider watching a sled travel down the hill—your eyes are moving, but the shape in your fovea remains the same. You know, however, that the object is moving. The nervous system takes in the motion of your eyes and the motion on the retina and compares them.

Motion also provides information about the size and distance of objects. Close objects travel faster across the retina than objects that are farther away. If an object such as a train travels laterally across the retina, that object is not changing in depth. As a ball travels away from one's hand, it appears smaller and seems to speed up as it goes. This visual sense of motion provides information about depth.

Depth can also be perceived without motion, with just one eye. Simple lines can create the illusion of depth—for example, when straight lines converge on a point. Cues perceived with one eye are called **monocular cues**. Monocular cues are also called pictorial depth cues; one example is **occlusion**, which is when one object covers, or occludes, another object. This suggests to a perceiver that the object being covered is farther away in depth than the object doing the covering. The relative height of objects gives viewers greater perception of depth—objects with bases that are farther away, in the lower half of the visual field, appear farther away in depth. The relative size of objects also affects depth perception. Objects that are bigger seem closer. All of these cues can contribute to depth perception. No single cue creates the perception of depth alone. Cues need to be combined. The more sources the nervous system uses to perceive a quality, the more accurate its perception will be.

One source that is particularly good for judging depth at close distances is the information the brain receives from both eyes (**binocular** vision). Because of their positions, the eyes see two slightly different scenes. The images from the two eyes are fused perceptually.

Visual Illusions

An **optical illusion** is a perception that differs from reality. One compelling optical illusion is the illusion of depth where none exists. In one experiment, psychologist Bela Julesz shifted two random-dot patterns only slightly and presented them separately to the eyes. The pattern appeared to pop out in depth. The impression of depth that is perceived, based on the slightly different position of the scene, is called

MONOCULAR CUES Visual cues that are perceived with one eye.

OCCLUSION Visual cue that occurs when one object covers another, suggesting to the observer that the covered object is farther away than the covering object.

BINOCULAR A stimulus that is perceived with two eyes.

OPTICAL ILLUSION A perception that differs from reality.

STEREOPSIS An impression of depth that is perceived based on the slightly different position of the scene.

STEREOGRAM An image that uses shifting patterns to create the illusion of depth.

HORIZONTAL–VERTICAL ILLUSION Optical illusion that leads observers to overestimate the length of a vertical line in comparison to a horizontal line.

VISUAL DRIFT ILLUSION Optical illusion in which motion is incorrectly perceived in the periphery of the viewer's eye.

stereopsis, and the image Julesz created is known as a **stereogram**. Different neurons in the visual system respond to different angles of disparity. Some neurons respond when the shift is small, and some when the shift is large.

Stereopsis is the basis for 3-D movies and games. In order for stereopsis to work, there must be some overlap in the scene. To create 3-D movies, for example, cameras record the same scene from two different perspectives. Then the images are superimposed on the movie (or television) screen. Specially made glasses block the light differently in the two eyes, so that the scenes are seen from a slightly different perspective from each eye. Special depth-detecting neurons in the brain respond to the same scene shifted to two separate parts of the retina as signaling depth.

This, in turn, leads to vivid perceptions of depth. Predatory animals with eyes in the front of their heads have overlapping visual fields. Animals with eyes on the sides of their heads, like rabbits and horses, do not have overlapping fields and have no process for stereopsis.

Research on visual illusions has helped clarify the mechanisms that underlie visual perception; this clarification guides interface design. For example, in a 2009 study, researcher David Elliot and his colleagues used the **horizontal–vertical illusion** to create the illusion that stairs were higher than their actual height. This illusion led to people lifting their feet higher and decreased the number of times that people tripped on that set of stairs. The horizontal–vertical illusion is that people tend to overestimate how long a vertical line is, relative to a horizontal line. For example, if two lines of the same length are presented in a T-shaped configuration, people judge that the T's vertical line is longer than the horizontal line.

Another study used the **visual drift illusion** to understand how micromovements of the eye stabilize perception. In the visual drift illusion, motion is perceived in the periphery of the eye when no motion exists.

To understand how eye movements affect perception, try the following exercise. Close one eye and push very gently on the inside corner of the other eye (near your nose). When you push, the world appears to move. The reason for the moving world is that your brain takes into account two factors. First, a scene travels across

your retina. Second, you do not command your eyes to move, which signals to your brain that the world is moving, but you are not. Consider looking out a car window—the scene is moving; your eyes are not. Your brain interprets these cues together as motion of the world around you.

Conversely, if you move your eyes, a scene also moves across your retina. Your brain interprets this as a stationary world; the world appears stationary because your brain takes into account the movement of your eyes.

Perceptual Organization

People, like all other animals, see scenes and patterns. In order to perceive a scene, the brain needs to organize it. This process feels effortless, yet it is extremely complex—as robotics researchers have discovered when trying to build a machine that "sees."

Consider how objects seen from different viewpoints appear different. The front and sides of a horse when seen from two different angles look very different from each other. Then consider the ways in which the objects seem to change as the person viewing them changes direction. Sometimes objects have the same color and brightness but may be very different from each other. (This explains why camouflage is effective.) Other times, the brightness and color of an object change as you see it from another view, yet you still recognize that object as coherent. It may be hard for a machine to know where one object starts or stops based on color or brightness—yet it is easy for a perceiver. When an object is partially hidden, it does not look damaged. You still perceive the whole object.

In the early 1900s, psychologists developed a theory of **perceptual organization** that suggested that the whole is different from the sum of the parts. This idea formed the basis for **gestalt psychology**. Gestalt psychology was a departure from a previous psychological theory of perception, structuralism, which hypothesized that people perceived each element of an object separately and developed a sense of the world piece by piece. Gestalt psychologists demonstrated that perception of a scene is not the sum of perception of the elements in that scene. For example, if a series of lights are flashed in a row, from left to right, at a reasonably fast tempo, the lights are not perceived separately. Instead, a motion is perceived—a single light moving across a line.

Gestalt psychologists also proposed other observations about the perception of wholes, such as the rule of proximity. Things that are near each other appear to be grouped together. For example, look at the following two lines of text. How many things do you see?

XXXX XXXX

XX XX XX XX

In both lines, your visual system sees eight objects—eight letter Xs. But your natural tendency is to group them perceptually—to perceive two entities in the top line and four in the line below it. The degree to which the grouping is dominant depends on how the XXs are spaced—for example, how close they are to each other.

The theory of perceptual organization has led to additional insights into how people perceive the world. Things that are similar appear to be grouped together.

PERCEPTUAL ORGANIZATION A theory of perception that suggests that the whole that is perceived is different from the sum of its parts.

GESTALT PSYCHOLOGY Theory of psychology that suggests that an observer sees a whole image as different from the sum of its parts.

For example, dancers often dress alike to form a perceptual group. People also see a pattern in its simplest way possible. For example, a pretzel appears as a figure eight, not as segments of four, five, six, seven, or eight connected line segments.

Gestalt psychologists proposed the concept of **good continuation**, the idea that when points are connected in such a way that they form straight or smoothly curving lines, they appear to follow the smoothest path. They also proposed **connectedness**, or the idea that things that appear physically connected appear to be a unit. **Common fate** refers to the rule that things moving in the same direction appear to be grouped together.

In short, gestalt psychologists argued that people tend to perceive grouped things in the simplest, most unified way, rather than as discrete individual components. In some ways, these ideas are obvious. They are meaningful in the field of perception because they reflect how people impose regular patterns on their view of their environment. Environmental regularity, in turn, is one of the building blocks of knowledge. Perception of the world, when it coalesces into regular patterns, can become stored in human memory. In this way, regular observation leads to an ongoing body of knowledge of the world.

Knowledge and thought both affect perception as well. The ways in which the nervous system responds to stimuli and patterns of stimuli is governed, in part, by the expectations and knowledge that already exist. One is more likely to find a familiar object than an unfamiliar object. Sometimes, even when the object is not even there, one can perceive something familiar. Other times, people ignore what is right in front of their faces because they are not looking for it, do not find it familiar, do not expect to see it, and are not cued to notice it.

GOOD CONTINUATION
Psychological theory suggesting that when points are connected in a way that forms a straight or smoothly curving line, they appear to follow the smoothest path.

CONNECTEDNESS
Psychological theory that things that appear physically connected appear to form a unit.

COMMON FATE Psychological theory that things that are moving in the same direction appear to form a unit.

PSYCHOLOGY & CAREERS: GRAPHIC DESIGN

Gestalt theories of perception have been applied liberally in the graphic design industry. For more than a century, designers of advertising, packaging, logos, and other graphics have been applying the theory that a whole image is different from the sum of its parts. Design rules take advantage of the way the brain relates groups of images to one another.

For example, designers group similar objects near each other, leading them to be perceived as a whole. To create a contrast, one object may appear within a group of similar objects in order to stand out. Graphic designers may create lines or curves that move through an image so that the eye follows that line or curve. Other designs use incomplete images that allow the mind to fill in the blanks. Designers often use repeating patterns or strive to keep logos as simple as possible, as in the golden arches of McDonald's or the Apple logo. Each of these strategies applies the gestalt theory that the mind takes in an image holistically, not as a collection of discrete parts.

HEARING

Hearing is the perceptual signal that takes in and processes sounds. Like vision, hearing gives people signals about what is happening in their environment—warning of danger and informing people of opportunities. For example, a baby's cries alert the parents that the baby needs attention.

Hearing helps people communicate (via speech) and determine where things are located. For example, one can use hearing to identify the location of someone who is speaking or the whereabouts of a train coming down a track with no other perceptual cues. The fact that people have two ears enables them to locate sounds with more precision—and to determine loudness and identify the nature of sounds with more accuracy. The location of a sound is perceived as a result of the difference in times and intensity at which sound arrives in each ear. People can best localize sounds that come from in front of them; sound from behind is the hardest to localize.

Infants use hearing to learn about physical properties of the world, such as how much milk is left in a bottle. Carpenters tap surfaces to gather information about them. Physicians listen to heartbeats to assess health. In addition to helping identify people, perception of voices can suggest different emotional states—whether a person is sad, happy, or bored. Human ears are so sensitive that they can detect movement less than the size of a diameter of a hydrogen atom. Through the perception of rhythm and tone modulation, the ears can detect the stimuli and the brain and emotions can respond to the music.

The psychophysics of hearing begins with the nature of sound waves. These are currents in air created by changes in air pressure. You can visualize a sound wave by thinking of a loudspeaker. The diaphragm of the speaker vibrates quickly, which causes a change in the air molecules around that diaphragm. As the diaphragm pushes out and in, the air molecules increase and decrease their density accordingly. This produces a recurring pattern of air pressure changes— a sound wave.

Sound waves are not electromagnetic radiation, and they move much more slowly than light. Like all waves, they have amplitude and frequency, which correspond to loudness and **pitch**. Frequency is measured in hertz (Hz), which are cycles per second: 1,000 Hz is 1,000 cycles per second. People are most sensitive to a particular range of sound frequency: 20 to 20,000 Hz. **Loudness** is measured in decibels (dB), which is based on perceptual capacity. Humans hear sounds in a range from 0 to 130 dB. The threshold for 1,000 Hz is 0 dB, a whisper is about 30 dB, and conversation at about a five-foot distance is about 55 dB. A truck passing at a distance of about 20 feet is about 80 dB. Noise levels of 85 dB can create permanent hearing loss after eight hours. Noise levels of 100 dB can create permanent damage after 15 minutes of exposure per day. Beyond 130 dB, sound becomes too painful to hear. A jet engine or a gun blast can register at 140 dB. Even short-term exposure to sounds at this level can create permanent hearing loss.

PITCH The frequency of a sound, which causes it to be perceived as "high" or "low."

LOUDNESS The amplitude of a sound, measured in decibels (dB). Humans have the capacity to hear sounds from 0 to 130 dB.

The level of sound in many toys and music players can cause havoc with hearing as well. Some toys can emit noises at levels of 120 dB or higher—levels high enough to create permanent hearing damage, particularly in children. Hearing loss can adversely affect children's language development, and lead to learning difficulties and social isolation.

The number of people with hearing loss is increasing, both because of increasing noise levels in the general environment and because the U.S. population is aging. Yuri Agrawal, Elizabeth Platz, and John Niparko found in a 2008 study that more than 8.5 percent of young adults 20 to 29 years old—and 16 percent of all adults—in the United States have hearing loss that affects speech perception, and the number of people with such hearing loss is increasing. People with hearing loss are less able to use their ears to detect dangers, such as oncoming vehicles. They are also more prone to depression and are generally more socially isolated.

The structures used in hearing sound are primarily located in the ear. In the outer ear, sound first passes through the pinna and auditory canal. These parts of the ear protect the inner part and reinforce incoming sound waves of the same frequency.

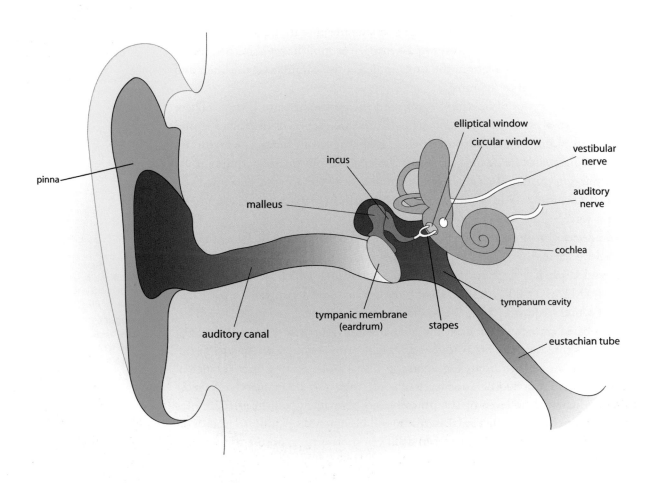

The pinna is the fleshy part of the ear that sticks out from the head. The auditory canal is the canal that leads from the outer ear toward the interior of the head. At the end of the auditory canal is the tympanic membrane, or eardrum, which helps maintain a steady temperature inside the ear. The middle ear contains small bones that work together to press on the membrane covering the oval window; they concentrate the air pressure so that vibrations can be passed effectively to the fluid-filled part of the inner ear.

The inner ear includes the **cochlea**, which is the part of the ear that vibrates in response to the stapes (the vibrations created by the middle ear). Inside the cochlea is the **organ of corti**, inside of which are hair cells that bend in response to changes in pressure. These cells change sound stimuli into electrical signals, which then travel through the nervous system.

COCHLEA Part of the inner ear that vibrates in response to sound.

ORGAN OF CORTI Part of the inner ear that contains sensory hair cells that change stimuli into electrical signals.

The environment in which you hear sound affects the way you hear it. For example, if you are listening to a guitar in an enclosed space, most of what you hear has been bounced off of walls, so it is indirect. Different objects absorb sound at different rates; the same sound may vary widely depending on the room. Most often, hearing is used as a complement to other sensory information, such as visual information.

THE CHEMICAL SENSES—TASTE AND SMELL

Ecological psychologist J. J. Gibson once proposed that chemicals detected through the mouth and nose are useful primarily in signaling potential events. Odors alert a person to what he or she is about to eat or drink. They also tell people when fire or flowers are present or when there are dangerous substances that might lead to illness (including animal waste, mold, and spoiled food). The mouth and skin have receptors for chemical molecules, but the nose is unique because it detects molecules that are about to be assimilated.

THALAMUS The part of the brain that relays sensation and spatial sense to the cortex.

LIMBIC SYSTEM Those parts of the brain that control emotions, consisting of the amygdala, hypothalamus, hippocampus, and pituitary gland.

The nose performs a gatekeeping function by detecting what is bad and needs to be kept out, and what is good and can be brought in to the body. Is the milk fresh? Is the food any good? Is the wine savory? Is the flower plastic or real? The nose can sense these factors before an external object touches the body. Odors also inform people when they are in the presence of potential mates or angry animals. In general, odor is used for pleasure and as support for the other senses but not as a primary day-to-day sense for selecting food, mating, or taking care of babies. An important function of odors is to trigger emotions and emotional memories. These emotions can cause biases for and against certain experiences.

The sense of smell differs from the other senses in the way that sensory information reaches the brain. Instead of traveling to the **thalamus**, where other sensory information travels, sensory information about smell travels to the **limbic system** of the brain, which is where emotion and memories are processed.

HIPPOCAMPUS Area of the brain that deals with memory.

Most people have had an experience in which an odor brought to mind a memory of a long-gone person or past event. For example, the smell of a perfume might bring back childhood memories of a grandmother. French novelist Marcel Proust famously based a critical episode in *Remembrance of Things Past* on the "involuntary memory," as he called it, of the taste and smell of a cookie dipped in tea. In a 2009 study, Yaara Yeshurun and her colleagues examined the basis for long-term memories associated with odors. The researchers found that odors first associated with objects were represented in the **hippocampus** more prominently than were the same odors associated with subsequent objects. They found the likely neural basis for the strong, long-term memories that smell creates.

Emotions are elicited by smell more readily and directly than by other senses. In a 2010 study conducted by Janina Seubert and colleagues, when odors were presented to people, faces that looked disgusted were more easily recognized as disgusted than when no odor was presented; however, odors did not enable people to more easily recognize emotions other than disgust.

Dysfunction in the perception of odors is present in people with psychotic disorders, such as schizophrenia. In a 2008 study, Bettina Pause and colleagues found that negative odors are processed more quickly in schizophrenic people than in people without schizophrenia, while odors that are not negative are processed similarly in people who do and people who do not have schizophrenia.

Odors can indirectly bias people to accurately detect emotion. They can also directly indicate emotions. Pheromones, which are naturally occurring odors, are believed to affect sexual behavior, mood, and even menstrual cycles. In 2000, Denise Chen and Jeannette Haviland-Jones collected samples of body odor from men and women who were watching a funny movie (and were happy) and odor from people who were watching a sad movie (and were sad). They found that men and women who were presented with swabs of these emotions (versus controls) could reliably detect the emotions of fear and happiness in the swabs, suggesting that odor communicates emotion to other people.

A study conducted by Martha McClintock in the early 1970s found that women who live or work together often end up having similar menstrual cycles. McClintock speculated that pheromones released through their skin resulted in the synchronization of their menstrual cycles. Since then, many scientists have argued for or against this notion of synchronization or that the existence of pheromones can affect the length and timing of menstrual cycles.

The rate at which animals sniff and breathe can directly affect the amount of chemical detected. Conversely, the detection of odor can directly affect a person's or an animal's respiratory rate, regulating how much of particular chemicals may be admitted to the body. In a 2008 study, Anna Maria Kleeman and colleagues presented four odors to people—banana, rose, coffee, and lemon. Respiratory rates increased in response to those odors and in response to imagining those odors, and respiratory rates and activity levels decreased in response to noxious odors. (Imagine walking into a room that contains rotting food. Your first impulse would be to cover your nose and mouth—or leave.)

In the modern world, smell is important because in addition to helping people judge natural substances, scent helps them judge the value of commercial products. Retailers and other businesses, such as casinos, attempt to create appealing atmospheres in their places of business. In many cases, these atmospheres include having a distinctive smell that communicates attributes of their brand. Eric Spangenberg, Bianca Grohmann, and David Sprott found in a 2005 study that shoppers rated a store highly when it paired together Christmas-themed music and fragrances. When Christmas fragrances were paired in the same store with other types of music, the store received a lower rating. Scents can work in combination with other factors to attract customers to certain brands and stores.

People who lose their sense of smell often lose their sense of taste as well. Other species use smell more than humans do, to orient themselves, find mates, and hunt for food. People who lose their sense of smell also lose these abilities. For example, they lose the ability to orient themselves to danger (for example, the smell of smoke, signaling that a fire is nearby) or opportunity (the smell of a nutritious meal). In a 2005 study, Thomas Hummel and Steven Nordin found that when subjects could not smell their meals, they often failed to eat enough of the food or were drawn to sweet desserts in order to compensate for the meals' lack of smell. This problem is acute among the elderly population, which includes many people who have lost their sense of smell.

In fact, a significant proportion of people who have lost their sense of smell rate their mood and ability to enjoy food and social interaction as fair to poor; their quality of life is significantly compromised. Some studies indicate that roughly a third of the elderly report dissatisfaction with their chemical senses. Elderly people can lose their sense of smell as a result of changed receptor cells or proteins, or due to changes in the environment in the nose or mouth, such the presence of dentures.

The mouth and nose work closely together to detect chemicals. Between them, they contain a range of receptors that provide the intake for the senses of taste and smell. Humans are capable of perceiving differences in the smells of more than 10,000 different chemicals. Receptors for these chemicals are fragile because they are not guarded by skin and organs as the other senses are. They must renew themselves every six weeks. Humans are less sensitive than other animals because humans have fewer receptors. However, the receptors humans do have are very sensitive, with the ability to sense even a single molecule.

In the nose, the receptors are found in the olfactory mucosa. On the mucosa are cilia, which contain receptor proteins. There are 1,000 types of receptors and odor molecules. This provides a sharp contrast with the visual system, which contains just three types of cones. People do not have many words for odors, yet they can express whether an odor is pleasant; in fact, the essential function of odor may be to determine which chemicals to seek out and which to avoid. The ability to detect intensity differences in odor is about as fine as the human ability to discriminate light in vision. The ability to express these differences is related to emotional valence instead of object recognition. People can learn to identify many odors through concentration and practice; emotional response to odors is nuanced and automatic.

The tongue can detect only chemicals that are salty, bitter, sweet, sour, and umami. (*Umami,* which means *delicious taste* in Japanese, is a word used to refer to the savory, brothy taste of glutamic acid; it is found in breast milk, fish, cured meats, mushrooms, and some fermented products, such as cheeses.) These five qualities of chemicals form the basis for taste. Substances in the mouth create vapors that travel to the olfactory receptors through a cavity in the nose, and these vapors also affect taste. The sense of taste is affected by smell; in fact, what most people consider to be

their sense of taste is actually their sense of smell. (Hence the importance of smell in Proust's cookie episode, even though he primarily describes the taste.)

Information about taste travels from the mouth to the brainstem via three different cranial nerves—the facial nerve, the glossopharyngeal nerve, and the vagus nerve. From nuclei in the **brainstem**, information about taste travels to the thalamus, and then to the cortex.

The chemicals and smells involved in taste represent only a part of what we experience as taste. Other factors also affect taste, such as food's texture, temperature, shape, softness, and solubility. Even visual and auditory factors affect taste, as does socialization. In fact, studies show that people often select food type and quantity based on sensory information other than taste.

BRAINSTEM Portion of the brain that connects it to the spinal cord.

Children and adults treat food in different ways. Children initially may prefer sweet, bland food (an adaptation that may be helpful to survival) before they begin to try new things. They may also experiment with eating nonfood substances, such as dirt. Children may also eat combinations of food that seem bizarre to adults, such as chocolate with ketchup. They place few restrictions on when a food may be eaten, willingly eating "dinner" foods for breakfast or vice versa.

Adults, on the other hand, have definite ideas about the foods that should be eaten at particular times of the day. The contrast between children's and adults' eating experiences indicates that the experience of taste is more learned than innate. Even genetic factors can be less influential on food preferences than the taster's status, age, or gender. In short, the sense of taste is in many ways a social phenomenon.

What is innate about taste? Newborns, who cannot see or hear in a sophisticated fashion, often smile when they taste sweet tastes and grimace when encountering bitter tastes. This finding suggests that tastes are connected to emotions that are hardwired into newborn's brains. Taste, unlike the other senses, is a sense that is intrinsically rewarding—a hot fudge sundae, for example, is fundamentally rewarding in a way that a visual or auditory treat is not. Although tastes of foods signal whether the foods are safe and nutritious (sweet foods are usually safe, and bitter foods are often not), adults in modern society generally eat for pleasure.

THE SKIN

The skin, which is the body's largest organ, has a variety of separate receptors. These are nerve endings that are sensitive to outside stimuli such as heat, pressure, vibration, tickling, physical disruption, and itching. The receptors are located in the epidermis (layers of skin cells, the outermost of which are dead) and the dermis (the layer of skin below the epidermis). Nerves connect back from these layers of skin to the brain, carrying the impulses there, where they are translated into sensations.

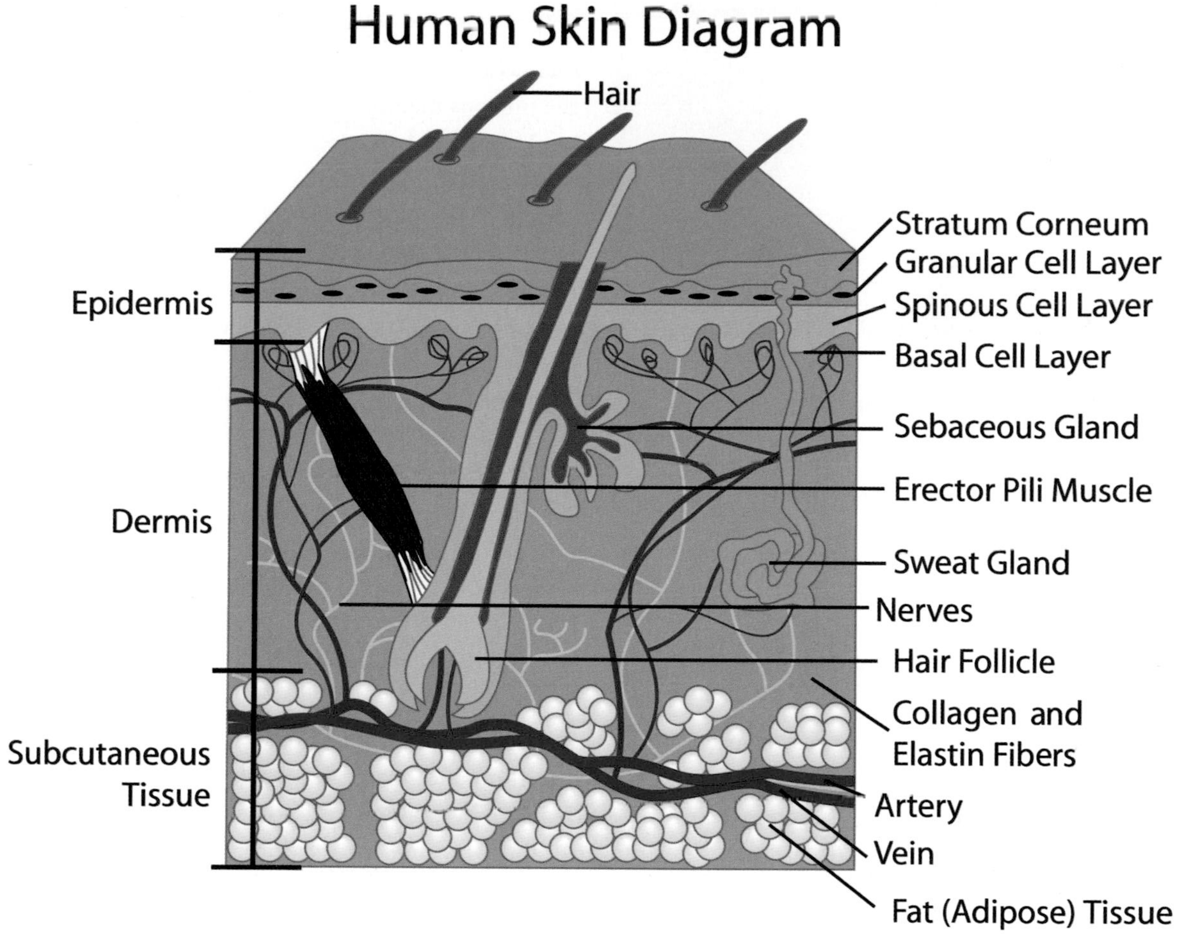

Human Skin Diagram

Hair

Epidermis

Dermis

Subcutaneous Tissue

Stratum Corneum
Granular Cell Layer
Spinous Cell Layer
Basal Cell Layer
Sebaceous Gland
Erector Pili Muscle
Sweat Gland
Nerves
Hair Follicle
Collagen and Elastin Fibers
Artery
Vein
Fat (Adipose) Tissue

The Skin and the Somatosensory System

The process of identifying objects by touch is called **haptic perception**. Sensory, motor, and cognitive functions are used for haptic perception. The system incorporating these functions is called the **somatosensory system**. (The term *somatic* comes from the Greek word *soma*, which means *body*.) The somatosensory system also incorporates proprioception, a sense of the position of the limbs, and kinesthesis, a sense of movement of the limbs. These sensations feel very different, but they are all managed through the same network of nerves and nerve endings. Through these communications, the skin provides the body with pleasure, protection (a certain degree of resistance to objects that threaten to pierce it), reassurance (as in a mother's touch), pain, comfort, and stimulation.

The somatosensory system also has some gaps in capability. For example, haptic receptors easily respond to the onset and offset of pressures, but they do not respond to constant pressure. That explains why you can sit on an uneven surface (such as a patterned chair), unaware of the differences in pressure, and end up with patterns of high and low relief etched into your skin.

Because the somatosensory system is so closely connected with the human skin, it varies according to the type of skin in different parts of the body. Although people often think of themselves as relatively hairless, most of the skin on a human body (male or female) is hairy. The only truly **glabrous skin**, or skin without hair, is on the palms of the hands and the toes and soles of the feet. Another type of skin is the

HAPTIC PERCEPTION The process of identifying objects by touch.

SOMATOSENSORY SYSTEM The system incorporating sensory, motor, and cognitive functions.

GLABROUS SKIN Skin without hair.

mucous membranes, which is the skin found inside body cavities, like the mouth. Finally, **mucocutaneous skin** is present at the transitional edges between the mucous membranes and other skin.

As one might expect from the variety of sensations that skin transmits, the skin is home to a variety of receptors. These different types of receptors respond to pressure of different frequencies, depths, and widths. Different receptors exist in each of these types of skin, each picking up different sensations. They are all oriented toward the mechanical and physical aspects of the environment or the body's position within that environment, and they are located, in varying concentrations, on the different types of skin. All areas of the skin contain more than one type of receptor. The types of receptors include the following:

- **Thermoreceptors**, which respond to temperature
- **Mechanoreceptors**, which respond to tactile pressure and other tactile sensations
- **Nocioreceptors**, which respond to damage to the body, usually in the form of pain

Other receptors exist in other areas of the body. These receptors include **proprioceptors**, which respond to body position and related feedback (such as loss of balance or the presence of something close by); **chemoreceptors** (for smell and taste, located in the nose and mouth); and **photoreceptors** (located in the eye; these respond to light waves).

The receptors in the skin feed into the two major somatosensory pathways that carry information about touch and pain. These are the **dorsal column–medial lemniscal system**, which carries information about touch and **proprioception**, and the **anterolateral system**, which carries information about pain and temperature.

Thermoreceptors, Temperature, and the Hypothalamus

Thermoreceptors respond to temperature. They are located in the skin all over the body, most highly concentrated on the face. Some thermoreceptors are responsive to warmth, others (more numerous in every part of the body) to cold, and still others only to changes in temperature.

The thermoreceptors that respond only to changes in temperature are particularly valuable because they help people regulate their body temperatures. The human body must maintain a consistent body temperature in order to metabolize energy. When there is an increase in warmth or cold in the environment, these thermoreceptors communicate the appropriate response to the **hypothalamus**—a complex structure within the brain, located just above the brain stem, that performs many regulatory and coordinating functions.

In its role as regulator, the hypothalamus is closely linked with the somatosensory system, as well as with many other parts of the brain and body. It transmits signals to other parts of the brain and sends hormones that affect other organs. When a rise in temperature is detected, the hypothalamus stimulates the sweat glands, which cools down the body. When the hypothalamus receives a signal from the thermoreceptors that temperature has decreased, it causes the body to shiver, by sending information to

MUCOCUTANEOUS SKIN Skin that contains mucous membranes.

THERMORECEPTORS Sensory receptors in the body that respond to changes in temperature.

MECHANORECEPTORS Sensory receptors in the body that respond to tactile pressure and other tactile sensations.

NOCIORECEPTORS Sensory receptors in the body that respond to damage to the body, usually in the form of pain.

PROPRIOCEPTORS Sensory receptors in the body that respond to body position and related feedback.

CHEMORECEPTORS Sensory receptors in the nose and mouth that respond to smells and tastes.

PHOTORECEPTORS Sensory receptors in the eyes that respond to light waves.

DORSAL COLUMN–MEDIAL LEMNISCAL SYSTEM Sensory system in the body that carries information about touch and proprioception.

PROPRIOCEPTION The sensation of the positions of different parts of the body.

ANTEROLATERAL SYSTEM Sensory system in the body that carries information about pain and temperature.

HYPOTHALAMUS Complex structure within the brain that performs many regulatory and coordinating functions.

the cortex to activate motor neurons. It can also increase the heart rate to help warm the body when it is too cold. (The hypothalamus also regulates many other body processes, including appetite, sleepiness, gastric reflexes, hair growth, and overall growth. It is affected by changing hormonal levels as women age, and is thus likely responsible for hot flashes.)

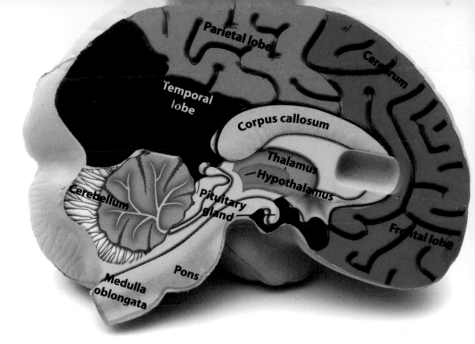

Thermoreceptors also provide other signals to maintain the optimal body temperature for the human body within the range of about 50 to 100 degrees Fahrenheit. When external temperatures exceed that range, receptors sensitive to pain, called nocioreceptors, respond. These receptors trigger more intensive response by the hypothalamus, including coma-like shutdown of bodily function in the case of extreme cold.

Mechanoreceptors and Tactile Pressure

The skin also has receptors that respond to tactile pressure. People can feel fine points more easily on some points of the body than others because of the distribution of these receptors, called mechanoreceptors. Ask someone to lightly trace the outline of a small letter of the alphabet on your back and on your hand. You will probably be able to identify the letter on your hand, because you have a large group of mechanoreceptors there. There are not enough mechanoreceptors on the back to be able to identify a letter traced there. There are more mechanoreceptors on the areas of the body with greatest sensitivity—for example, the face, nipples, and groin.

There are four types of mechanoreceptors:

- Pacinian corpuscles
- Merkel's disks
- Ruffini endings
- Meissner's corpuscles

These four kinds of receptors are found in all parts of the skin. No area of the skin has only one type of receptor.

Pacinian corpuscles, which are onionlike in structure, respond to displacement of the skin. Pacinian corpuscles can also be found in the intestines and joints. They respond best to rapid vibrations between 10 and 500 Hz. They also respond to the onset and offset of pressures. But once the pressure is detected, they rapidly adapt and the sensation diminishes. This is why socks, for example, may initially feel tight but then not be noticed at all.

Merkel's disks and **Ruffini endings** adapt slowly to skin indentation and stretch. Ruffini endings are fibers located inside a cylindrical capsule at the end of nerves (they are also called Ruffini cylinders). **Meissner's corpuscles** are flattened cells in the dermis; they respond to fluttering vibration, which is experienced at frequencies of 3 to 40 Hz. They also respond to other slowly moving stimuli, such as taps on the skin.

PACINIAN CORPUSCLES Sensory receptors in the body that respond to vibration and pressure.

MERKEL'S DISKS Sensory receptors that respond to pressure and texture.

RUFFINI ENDINGS Sensory receptors that respond to pressure and skin stretch.

MEISSNER'S CORPUSCLES Sensory receptors that respond to vibrations and slowly moving stimuli, such as taps on the skin.

Because skin has both fast and slow receptors—Ruffini endings and Meissner's corpuscles, respectively—many forms of pressure will trigger both. A brush rubbed across the skin may evoke the firing of both kinds of receptors, and then the firing of only one. This corresponds to two different types of feelings. The feelings are then projected to a particular segment of the spinal cord. The skin is divided into several discrete areas, called dermatomes, each of which is supplied by a single segment of the spinal cord.

Receptors with Greater Sensitivity: Merkel's Disks and Meissner's Corpuscles

The areas of the skin with the greatest sensitivity have small receptive fields. Receptive fields are areas (on the skin, for example) which, when stimulated, will affect the receptor. Merkel's disks and Meissner's corpuscles are more concentrated on the fingertips than on the rest of the hands, making the fingertips more sensitive.

The cortex takes in signals from these receptors, and its response is directly related to the absolute and relative stimulation of the receptors. This part of the cortex is known as the somatosensory cortex; the more sensitive areas (those with the greatest number of receptors) have a greater area of this part of the brain devoted to them. Researchers evaluate the sensitivity of skin to mechanical pressure using a test called the two-point threshold. The two-point threshold is assessed by determining how far apart two points have to be before they are sensed as two points instead of one. The areas of the skin that have more acuity (a lower two-point threshold) thus have a greater area of cortex devoted to them.

The somatosensory cortex is also plastic. For example, if a finger is amputated, then less of the brain's cortex will be devoted to that finger's representation; adjacent areas of the body will take over that part of the cortex. Increasing stimulation and attention to an area of the body can lead to greater representation in the cortex.

The Perception of Pain

A person's sensation of pain is the result of nocioreceptors and the nervous system working together. The receptor transmits a sudden signal to the central nervous system, where neurons fire. The circuit can be as simple as one synapse: a receptor can synapse on a motor neuron, which will withdraw the appropriate part of the body away from the source of pain. Pain helps people withdraw from harmful stimuli, such as a sharp thorn or a burning log. It tells the body when it has been exercised too hard when the muscles start to hurt or when bruises appear. Those cues signal that it is time to stop the exercise and rest the body. Pain is also affected by culture, mental state, and gender.

Comparisons of the reports of pain from women and men suggest that women experience pain more intensely than their male counterparts do, even when the injuries are similar. Socialization to express pain may contribute to this result, as may biological differences. People from different cultures communicate differently about pain and have divergent understandings of pain.

No one has discovered why, if pain serves to warn people of danger, the experience of pain is so heavily dependent on mental state, culture, and gender. Why, for example, might two soldiers, both of whom have been shot on a battlefield, experience pain differently as a function of their culture? Many religions and cultures have ceremonies in which seemingly painful experiences (such as having their skin pierced by nails) are inflicted on people, and these people do not feel the pain. Pain seems to serve functions other than simply warning about harm.

Pain can also exist when no harm has been done. For example, many people experience chronic pain that does not respond to chemicals that affect receptors. Pain is called the most private of the perceptual experiences, because it can be hard to relate to the pain of others. People often describe the same stimulus in different ways, and pain may mean different things to different people.

There are several theories about the neural mechanisms that underlie the perception of pain. One of the earliest theories is the **gate control theory**. According to this theory, two types of cells in the spinal cord—**substantia gelatinosa (SG) cells** and **transmission (T) cells**—mediate pain.

In the gate control system, there are two types of SG cells. One type of SG cells, known as the SG+ type, opens the pain gate and excites the T cells. The other cells, known as the SG– type, close the gate and inhibit the T cells. Small-diameter fibers stimulate the SG+ cells and large-diameter fibers excite SG– cells. If there is more stimulation of large fibers than small fibers, there should be little pain. If there is more stimulation of the small fibers, there will be more pain. Information travels from the spinal cord to different areas of the brain. Electrical stimulation to those parts of the brain can relieve pain. This theory explains some findings about pain, but it does not account for cultural, religious, or gender differences.

A more recent model of pain is the **biopsychosocial model of pain**. This model considers how psychological, social, cognitive, physiological, and behavioral factors contribute to the experience of pain. It starts with the idea that there is a subjective perception of any physiological insult, which influences the response along with other physical, psychological, and sociocultural factors. In 2007, Johan Vlaeyen and colleagues reviewed the factors that could contribute to pain, such as hereditary resistance (or susceptibility), living conditions (e.g., the physical and emotional climate of a person's home), initiating factors, and maintaining factors (e.g., insomnia). All of these factors contribute to the experience of pain.

Other factors that contribute to pain perception may be psychological or cognitive, related to the mental state of the perceiver. Recent studies have considered the effect of external psychological factors on the pain experienced by burn patients and other badly injured patients. Additional factors, such as anxiety and a feeling of loss of control, increased their perception of pain. Distinguishing pain from anxiety about pain is difficult for those who are treating pain. Pain treatment can be more effective when traditional medicine is accompanied by cognitive and behavioral therapy. For example, cognitive therapy can help direct unnecessary and possibly harmful attention away from the source of pain. Through behavioral conditioning, people may be able to engage in activities that they were previously unable to perform because of anxiety about potential pain.

GATE CONTROL THEORY
Theory that pain is mediated by a series of cells in the spinal cord.

SUBSTANTIA GELATINOSA (SG) CELLS Spinal cord cells that can either release or inhibit pain.

TRANSMISSION (T) CELLS Spinal cord cells that transmit pain.

BIOPSYCHOSOCIAL MODEL OF PAIN A model of pain that considers how psychological, social, cognitive, physiological, and behavioral factors contribute to pain.

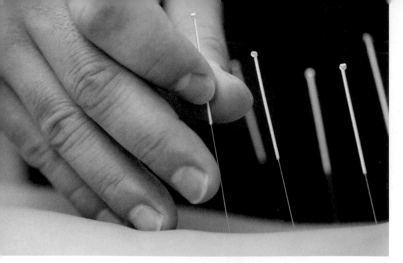

Because pain is a multifaceted phenomenon, treatments that address the factors that contribute to pain better enable patients to manage it. Patients who are treated with an interdisciplinary pain management program improve more on measures of health (psychological and physical) and social functioning than do patients who receive standard therapy for pain.

Another source of evidence for the contribution of social factors to pain is that infants benefit from the presence—visual, auditory, and tactile—of their mothers, and they recover more quickly than infants who do not have mothers present interacting with them. In fact, in a recent study, Celeste Johnson and colleagues found that infants who were held by a parent experienced less pain than infants who were medicated with a powerful drug (oxycodone).

Nonetheless, many traditional treatments can alleviate pain. Drugs can help with many types of pain. Alternative treatments in other traditions include acupuncture and hypnosis. In a hypnotic state, people are focused and relaxed. Hypnosis may activate pathways from the brain to the spinal cord that inhibit pain, or it may shift people's attention away from pain. Acupuncture is the treatment of conditions via needles inserted into the body. It is possible that acupuncture works because large fibers are stimulated that inhibit pain. It is also possible that acupuncture works by a **placebo effect**, in which a treatment with no physiological effect nonetheless reliably changes a symptom. Placebo effects may work by releasing endorphins. **Endorphins**, a naturally produced morphine-like substance in the body, act on opiate receptors in the brain and serve to reduce pain.

PLACEBO EFFECT Phenomenon in which a treatment that has no physiological effect reliably changes a symptom.

ENDORPHIN A morphine-like substance produced by the body to reduce pain and create feeling of well-being.

THE VESTIBULAR SENSORY SYSTEM

Located within the inner ear, the **vestibular sensory system** provides a constant stream of information that allows you to detect, and thus control, the positioning of your body in space. You might not be aware of all the information the vestibular sensory system provides unless it malfunctions. Though not traditionally studied as one of the five senses, the vestibular sensory system is one of the oldest and most important sensory systems in vertebrates. For example, humans have evolved to bipedalism, or the ability to walk upright on two feet, partially thanks to this sophisticated sensory system, which allows the limbs and head to stay in balance while performing complex movements.

The vestibular sensory system is composed of several structures that work closely with the eyes, spine, and muscles to maintain balance. Within the inner ear are three **semicircular canals**, or fluid-filled bone tubes. These semicircular canals are positioned in three different planes in space so that the movement of fluid within them, called **endolymphatic fluid**, gives the body an index to its position and rotation in relation to its surroundings.

The three semicircular canals are positioned at right angles to one another, and they are located symmetrically to the semicircular canals on the other side of the head. If the semicircular canals are working properly, the fluid in the canals on both sides of the head moves symmetrically. This provides a benefit known as sensory redundancy: if an injury harms one of the semicircular canals on one side of the head, the corresponding canal on the other side will be able to receive the same sensory information.

VESTIBULAR SENSORY SYSTEM A system of bony and membranous structures in the inner ear responsible for maintaining the body's sense of balance and orientation in space.

SEMICIRCULAR CANALS Bone tubes in the inner ear, arranged perpendicularly, that are responsive to rotation of the head.

ENDOLYMPHATIC FLUID Fluid that moves inside the semicircular canals to signal rotation of the head to vestibular receptors.

Attached to the membranous portions of the bony semicircular canals are small sensory organs: the **utricle** and **saccule**, which together are called the **otolith organs**. The otolith organs contain tiny calcium carbonate crystals, called **otoconia**, that play a key role in sensing acceleration. The otoconia are encased in a mass of thick fluid that shifts with the motion of the head, and tiny hairs inside the otolith organs respond to the motion of the otoconia. These hairs then send signals to the brain about the head's acceleration through its environment.

The otolith organs and the otoconia they contain are involved in one of the most commonly experienced causes of dizziness, **benign paroxysmal positional vertigo (BPPV)**. Often BPPV goes undiagnosed, but it is the cause of about 20 percent of cases of dizziness, and, in older people, up to 50 percent. BPPV occurs when the otoconia travel into the ear canal from the utricle, either because of injury, infection, or age-related deterioration of the vestibular structures. Usually, the dizziness is brought on by an unusual positioning of the head, so many patients begin to notice it after rolling over in bed, doing Pilates or yoga, or simply craning the neck to look for something on a top shelf. Fortunately, most cases of BPPV can be cured by simple head exercises that gradually shift the otoconia out of the affected portion of the ear canal.

Working in close connection with the eyes, spine, and muscles, a healthy vestibular sensory system participates in several reflexes that give the body a sense of its orientation and balance in space. The **vestibulo-ocular reflex** keeps the vision steady while the head is in motion, while the **vestibulospinal reflex** works with the spine to stabilize the body as it moves. The **vestibulocollic reflex** works with the muscles of the neck in order to keep the head upright.

The vestibular system's powerful sensory role is evidenced by the symptoms that occur when one or more of its functions are compromised. A person with reduced vestibular function may not only experience dizziness, but also **vertigo** (a sense of rotation or spinning while standing still), difficulty walking on an uneven surface, or even an inability to balance while standing upright. Patients with severe loss of vestibular function have been unable to detect the motion of a spinning table when sitting upon it while blindfolded. In such experiments, the other senses, such as the skin, may compensate for a compromised vestibular sensory system by detecting motion and gravity. However, if the patient is submerged in water to control for somatosensory ability to detect gravity, he or she may not be able to distinguish up from down.

Motion sickness when traveling by boat, plane, or car is a classic example of how vestibular reflexes maintain our everyday spatial perceptions. Researchers believe this common ailment is caused by confusion between vestibular sensation and visual perception. For example, if you attempt to read or do other detailed work in a moving car, you may become dizzy and experience nausea or vomiting because your visual system signals that you are in stable surroundings, but your vestibular sensory system is detecting motion. This is known as the **sensory conflict hypothesis** of motion sickness.

Astronauts experience a similar disturbance of the vestibular sensory system known as **space motion sickness**. This ailment, experienced by 60 to 80 percent of space shuttle astronauts during the initial stages of their voyages, can also be explained by the sensory conflict hypothesis. Researchers believe space motion sickness is caused by a conflict between the otolith organs' usual perceptions of acceleration, and the new conditions experienced in space due to altered gravity. Under normal circumstances, the otolith organs take into account the usual force of gravity in their detection of acceleration, but in space, there is a mismatch between expectation and reality, causing motion sickness symptoms similar to those felt in a moving car.

OTOLITH ORGANS Sensory structures (the **utricle** and **saccule**) in the inner ear, responsive to acceleration and gravity.

OTOCONIA Calcium carbonate crystals encased in the otolith organs whose movement signals to the brain the body's acceleration.

BENIGN PAROXYSMAL POSITIONAL VERTIGO (BPPV) Disorder characterized by dizziness and loss of balance, which is caused by movement of the otoconia into sensitive portions of the ear canal.

VESTIBULO-OCULAR REFLEX Vestibular reflex that keeps the vision steady while the head is in motion.

VESTIBULOSPINAL REFLEX Vestibular reflex that works with the spine to stabilize the body as it moves.

VESTIBULOCOLLIC REFLEX Vestibular reflex that works with the muscles of the neck to keep the head upright.

VERTIGO Sense of spinning or rotation while standing still.

SENSORY CONFLICT HYPOTHESIS A theory that proposes conflict between the separate inputs from two sensory systems as the cause of motion sickness.

SPACE MOTION SICKNESS Ailment experienced by space shuttle astronauts in the initial stages of space travel, characterized by dizziness, nausea, and vomiting.

MAL DE DÉBARQUEMENT
Disorder wherein a patient may feel dizziness and a feeling of rocking back and forth for a prolonged period following travel by boat or automobile.

In the past decade, researchers have come to a more complete understanding of another vestibular ailment that is related to motion sickness: **mal de débarquement** (debarkation sickness), also known as landsickness. This occurs after a long boat trip, when a patient may feel pitching and rolling similar to the sensation of ocean waves for several days, or even up to months or years, after returning to land. Mal de débarquement may also occur after riding in an automobile. A study by Dr. Timothy C. Hain, a neurologist at Northwestern University, found that mal de débarquement develops when the vestibular sensory system is able to adapt relatively easily to the conditions of rocking motion on a boat or other vehicle, but resists readjustment upon the patient's return to solid ground. The condition can often be treated with medication and physical therapy to help the vestibular system readapt.

EXTRASENSORY PERCEPTION

EXTRASENSORY PERCEPTION The perception of external events without direct information from the senses.

Extrasensory perception (ESP) is the perception of external events without direct information from the senses. ESP is associated with perceiving things that could not be perceived otherwise: for example, events that are about to take place in the future, or events that the subject could not understand about the present. The ability to predict the future or locate a lost child exemplifies extrasensory perception. ESP experiments have often involved the investigation of imagined sights, sounds, or sensations. Through self-induced or hypnotic meditation, people might imagine hearing voices, seeing where treasure is buried, or feeling pain being relieved. Sometimes these states are induced through guided meditation (hearing someone else lead people through a sequence of imagery while being in a hypnotic state) or through the ingestion of hallucinogens.

In the 1930s, researcher J. B. Rhine developed experiments to test ESP by asking participants to guess the symbols on the back of a series of cards. Rhine claimed that the participants guessed the symbols correctly more often than would be suggested by random chance. Further experiments were conducted in the 1950s and 1960s, each of which had varying levels of confidence in the validity of these results. People who conduct these experiments and who propose that ESP exists are generally not scientists, particularly not perceptual scientists. Moreover, because the experience of these imagined perceptions is all subjective, there is no known way of replicating them.

It is difficult or impossible to confirm in any scientifically credible way that ESP exists. There are no known theories or neural mechanisms that explain how to perceive things without a stimulus. Just as the validity of ESP is difficult or impossible to prove, the nonexistence of ESP cannot be proven either; this perpetuates belief in ESP. Another reason belief in ESP continues is that people do have experiences of perceiving things that do not seem to have come to them through their ordinary senses. An ongoing study of these experiences, known as **mysticism**, goes back as far as recorded human history. But mysticism remains unaligned with any currently recognized form of scientific research.

MYSTICISM The study of experiences that do not seem to have been perceived through known senses.

SUMMARY

Sensation is the experience of information from the physical world that enters sensory receptors and organs. Perception is how that energy in the brain and body is organized and processed. Behavior is in response to the combination of the information from the outside world and neural processing of that information.

The smallest amount of stimulus necessary for a person to notice a stimulus is called the absolute threshold. Senses become less responsive to certain stimuli over time. This is called sensory adaptation. The sense of smell adapts very quickly. At first an odor may smell strong, but over time the olfactory system adapts and experiences the odor with less intensity.

Vision is different for humans than for other types of animals. Fish, for example, live in low light and respond very little to color. The rods and cones are receptors in the retina that regulate these differences.

The sense of motion depends on context. The illusion of motion can exist when a large object is moving by a person who is sitting still. This mistaken perception is due to the relative amount of motion in the center and periphery of the eye. Monocular vision allows one to see two-dimensional depth; binocular vision allows for depth perception and judging distances.

Hearing is produced through sound waves that vibrate in the air with amplitude and frequency, which corresponds to loudness and pitch. The middle ear concentrates air pressure so that vibrations can move to the inner ear where signals travel through the nervous system.

The mouth and skin have receptors for chemical molecules. The nose detects what is "bad" and needs to be avoided before the body makes physical contact with the object. The sense of smell takes a different pathway to the brain than other senses. The information goes to the limbic system in the brain where emotions and memories are processed.

Taste involves substances in the mouth that travel to the olfactory receptors through the nose cavity. Taste is affected by the sense of smell. Taste travels from the mouth to the brainstem via several nerves. The nerve endings in the skin are sensitive to heat, pressure, vibration, and itch. Nerves connect the layers of skin to the brain. Extrasensory perception has not been proven to exist through scientific research, but many people claim to have experienced it.

REFERENCES

Agrawal, Y., Platz, E. A., & Niparko, J. K. (2008). Prevalence of hearing loss and differences by demographic characteristics among US adults: Data from the national health and nutrition examination survey, 1999–2004. *Archives of Internal Medicine, 168*(14), 1522–1530.

Angier, N. (2008, October 27). The unappreciated, holding our lives in balance. *The New York Times.* Retrieved from http://www.nytimes.com/

Angst, F., Verra, M. L., Lehmann, S., Brioschi, R., & Aeschlimann, A. (2009). Clinical effectiveness of an interdisciplinary pain management program compared with standard inpatient rehabilitation in chronic pain: A naturalistic, prospective controlled cohort study. *Journal of Rehabilitation Medicine, 41*(7), 569–575.

Askay, S. W., Patterson, D. R., Sharar, R., Mason, S., & Faber, B. (2009). Pain management in patients with burn injuries. *International Review of Psychiatry, 21*(6), 522–530.

Axelin, A., Salanterä, S., Kirjavainen, J., & Lehtonen, L. (2009). Oral glucose and parental holding preferable to opioid in pain management in preterm infants. *Clinical Journal of Pain, 25*(2), 138–145.

Beer, A. L., Hecke, A. H., & Greenlee, M. W. (2008). A motion illusion reveals mechanisms of perceptual stabilization. PLoS ONE, *3* (7), e2741. doi:10.1371/journal.pone.0002741

Benson, A.J. (1982). The vestibular sensory system. In H.B. Barlow & J.D. Mollon (Eds.), *The senses* (pp. 333-368). New York, NY: Cambridge University Press.

Bruce, C., Desimone, R., & Gross, C. G. (1981). Visual properties of neurons in a polysensory area in superior temporal sulcus of the macaque. *Journal of Neurophysiology, 46*(2), 369–384.

Buonomano, D. V., & Merzenich, M. M. (1998). Cortical plasticity: From synapses to maps. *Annual Review of Neuroscience, 21,* 149–186.

Chen, D., & Jones, J. H. (2000). Human olfactory communication of emotion. *Perceptual Motor Skills, 91,* 771–781.

Coakley, S., & Shelemay, K. (2002). Pain and its transformations: The interface of biology and culture. Cambridge, MA: Harvard University Press.

Davidhizar, R., & Giger, J. N. (2004). A review of the literature on care of clients in pain who are culturally diverse. *International Nursing Review, 51*(1), 47–55.

Elliott, D. B., Vale, A., Whitaker, D., & Buckley, J. G. (2009). Doesmy step look big in this? A visual illusion leads to safer stepping behavior. PLoS ONE, *4*(2), e4577. doi:10.1371/journal.pone.0004577

Feeney, E., O'Brien, S., Schannel, A., & Gibney, E. R. (2010). Genetic variation in taste perception: Does it have a role in healthy eating? *Proceedings of the Nutrition Society, 70*(1), 135–143. doi:10.1017/S0029665110003976

Fillingim, R. B., King, C. D., Ribeiro-Dasilva, M. C., Rahim-Williams, B., & Riley, J. L. III. (2009). Sex, gender, and pain: A review of recent clinical and experimental findings. *Journal of Pain, 10*(5), 447–485.

Gibson, E. J., Gibson, J. J., Smith, O. W., & Flock, H. (1959). Motion parallax as a determinant of perceived depth. *Journal of Experimental Psychology, 58*(1), 40–51.

Gibson, E., & Walk, R. D. (1960). The visual cliff. *Scientific American, 202,* 80–92.

Gläscher, J., Rudrauf, D., Colom, R., Paul, L. K., Tranel, D., Damasio, H., & Adolphs, R. (2010). Distributed neural system for general intelligence revealed by lesion mapping. *Proceedings of the National Academy of Science, 107*(10), 4705–4709.

Hain, T.C. (2011, May 12). Benign paroxysmal positional vertigo. Retrieved from http://www.dizziness-and-balance.com/disorders/bppv/bppv.html

Hain, T.C., & Helminski, J.O. (2007). Anatomy and physiology of the normal vestibular system. In S. Herdman (Ed.), *Vestibular rehabilitation* (3rd ed., pp. 2-18). San Francisco: Davis.

Heer, M., & Paloski W.H. (2006, October 30). Space motion sickness: incidence, etiology, and countermeasures. *Autonomic Neuroscience: Basic & Clinical, 129*(1-2), 77-79.

Highstein, S.M. (2004). Anatomy and physiology of the central and peripheral vestibular system: overview. In S.M. Highstein, R.R. Fay, & A.N. Popper (Eds.), *The Vestibular System* (pp. 1-10). New York, NY: Springer-Verlag.

Hummel, T., & Nordin, S. (2005). Olfactory disorders and their consequences for quality of life: A review. *Acta Oto-Laryngologica, 125,* 116–121.

Johnston, C. C., Rennick, J. E., Fillon, F., Campell-Yeo, M., Goulet, C., Bell, L., … Ranger, M. (2011). Maternal touch and talk for invasive procedures in infants and toddlers in the pediatric intensive care unit. *Journal of Pediatric Nursing.* Advance online publication. doi:10.1016/j.pedn.2010.12.016

Julesz, B. (1969). Foundations of cyclopean perception. *Journal of the Optical Society of America, 59,* 1544.

Kleeman, A. M., Kopietz, R., Albrecht, J., Schopf, V., Pollatos, O., Schreder, T., & Wiesmann, M. (2008). Investigation of breathing parameters during odor perception and olfactory imagery. *Chemical Senses, 34*(1), 1–9.

Kleiner, A. (2008). The age of heretics: A history of the radical thinkers who reinvented corporate management. New York, NY: Jossey-Bass.

Koffman, J., Morgan, M., Edmonds, P., Speck, P., & Higginson, I. J. (2008). Cultural meanings of pain: A qualitative study of black Caribbean and white British patients with advanced cancer. *Palliative Medicine, 22*(4), 350–359.

Kriegeskorte, N., Mur, M., Ruff, D. A., Kiani, R., Bodurka, J., Esteky, H., … Bandettini, P. A. (2008). Matching categorical object representations in inferior temporal cortex of man and monkey. *Neuron, 60*(6), 1126–41.

Lee, D. N., & Reddish, P. E. (1981). Plummeting gannets: A paradigm of ecological optics. *Nature, 293,* 293–294.

Nir, Y., & Tononi, G. (2010). Dreaming and the brain: From phenomonology to neurophysiology. *Trends in Cognitive Science, 14*(2), 88–100.

Pause, B. M., Hellmann, G., Goder, R., Aldenhoff, J. B., & Fersti, R. (2008). Increased processing speed for emotionally negative odors in schizophrenia. *International Journal of Psychophysiology, 70*(1), 16–22.

Rawson, N. E. (2003). Age-related changes in perception of flavor and aroma. *Generations, 27*(1), 20–26.

Schiff, W., & Oldak, R. (1990). Accuracy of judging time to arrival: Effects of modality, trajectory, and gender. *Journal of Experimental Psychology: Human Perception and Performance, 16*(2), 303–316.

Seubert, J., Kellermann, T., Loughead, J., Boers, F., Brensinger, C., Schneider, F., & Habel, Y. (2010). Processing of disgusted faces is facilitated by odor primes: A functional MRI study. *Neuroimage, 53*(2), 746–756.

Shepherd, G. M. (2007). The major senses: Sight, hearing, taste, smell, and touch. In F. E. Bloom and M. F. Beal (Eds.), *The Dana guide to brain health*. New York, NY: The Dana Foundation.

Sørensen, L. B., Moller, P., Flint, A., Martens, M., & Raben, A. (2003). Effect of sensory perception of food intake: A review of studies on humans. *International Journal of Obesity, 27*(10), 1152–1166.

Spangenber, E. R., Gerhmann, B., & Sprott, D. E. (2004). It's beginning to smell (and sound) a lot like Christmas: The interactive effects of ambient scent and music in a retail setting. *Journal of Business Research, 58*(11), 1583–1589.

Svoboda, E. (2007, June 12). When seasickness persists after a return to solid ground. *The New York Times*. Retrieved from http://www.nytimes.com/

Toomey, M. (2008). Update for nurse anesthetists part 4: Gender differences in pain: Does X = Y? *American Association of Nurse Anesthetists Journal, 76*(5), 355–359.

Vlaeyen, J. W. S., Crombez, G., & Goubert, L. (2007). The psychology of chronic pain and its management. *Physical Therapy Reviews, 12,* 179–188.

Winn, P. (Ed.). (2001). *Dictionary of biological psychology*. London: Routledge.

Yang, M., Clarke, A. M., & Crawley, J. (2009). Postnatal evidence against a primary role for the corpus callosum in mouse sociability. *European Journal of Neuroscience, 28*(8), 1663–1677

Yeshurun, Y., Lapid, H., Dudai, U., & Sobil, N. (2009). The privileged brain representation of first olfactory associations. *Current Biology, 19*(21), 1869–1874.

Yeshrun, Y., & Soble, N. (2010). An odor is not worth a thousand words: From multidimensional odors to unidimensional odor objects. *Annual Review of Psychology, 61,* 219–241.

States of Consciousness

"It is on the whole probable that we continually dream, but that consciousness makes such a noise that we do not hear it."

—Carl Jung

CONSCIOUSNESS

What makes people conscious? Several theories attempt to answer this question. Some suggest that consciousness is a physical function—the reason why the human body can perform each of its vital functions without having to be initiated. Other theories suggest that consciousness is social—that it is controlled by each society's perception of what is important and what is not. Still others argue that consciousness is spiritual.

In short, the study of consciousness is relatively new, and scientists are still learning about what it is and what it means. From William James, an early scholar of psychology who taught the subject at Harvard University in the late 1800s, to Sigmund Freud, considered the founder of psychoanalysis because of his work in the late nineteenth and early twentieth century, to Charles Tart, a well-known contemporary psychologist, consciousness has inspired great minds to actively think about how people think.

Awareness

CONSCIOUSNESS An individual's awareness of his or her own feelings, memories, thoughts, sensations, and environment.

AWARENESS The act of focusing on feelings, memories, thoughts, sensations, and environment.

Many people think consciousness means being awake, but it is so much more than that. The state of **consciousness**, in a psychological sense, refers to each individual's **awareness** of his or her own unique feelings, memories, thoughts, sensations, and environment. Consciousness is different for each individual—each person focuses his or her awareness on different things—and it even varies within the same person. Consciousness is always changing.

One's attention and awareness is constantly shifting. The brain has to prioritize a host of internal and external **stimuli**, focusing on what it considers most important at the time. The human brain is even programmed to attend to that which is most important to survival. For example, in an era when human survival depended on awareness of surroundings—a person's ability to hear a saber-tooth tiger approaching even if a baby was crying, for example—awareness was critical. These shifts in consciousness can happen very quickly and without actually "thinking" about them.

STIMULUS A thing or event that causes a reaction, feeling, thought, or change in behavior; stimuli can be either internal or external.

The brain is so good at shifting attention, or multitasking, that one can cook dinner and have a conversation at the same time, jog through the mountains and think about last night's party, or read this chapter while walking on a treadmill. However, in general, a person can be conscious of only one thing at a time. So, if Tara is making dinner and talking on the phone, she will likely barely remember making dinner. And, according to researcher Wolf Singer, for most people, conscious attention will be focused on the task they have the least amount of experience with. This means that if Tara is making dinner and talking on the phone and has never cooked that meal before, she will focus more on cooking than on the conversation.

KEY CONCEPTS

1. The state of consciousness refers to an individual's awareness of his or her own unique feelings, memories, thoughts, sensations, and environment. See page 81.

2. Sleep and dreams are important to the study of consciousness. Although researchers are not exactly sure why humans sleep, they are certain that sleep is a necessary and critical function for health and survival. See page 83.

3. Consciousness can be altered in several ways, including by legal drugs for psychiatric reasons, legal drugs for recreational use, illegal drugs, hypnosis, and meditation. See page 88.

The amazing thing about consciousness is that it is a sort of awareness without awareness. In essence, we are aware, but we are not aware that we are aware. Consciousness shifts dramatically and constantly in the blink of an eye. A person can be conscious of one thing one second and of something completely different the next. However, even though his or her consciousness is busy processing new information, the person is completely unaware of this constant shift from one stimulus to another.

Consciousness

Medically speaking, consciousness and unconsciousness are opposite states. Psychologically speaking, consciousness is a bit more complicated. It is possible to exist in varying states of consciousness. In fact, it is probable. In reality, you are likely living in varying states of consciousness every minute of every day. Remember, a person can focus on many different things at the same time even though the brain will prioritize which thought, task, or sensation will receive the most attention at any given moment.

Unconsciousness, in the psychological sense, means being unaware of something. Though people do not realize they have unconscious thoughts, memories, and more, their brains register just about everything. So, even though you do not think you remember something, it is probably buried somewhere deep in your brain. The brain registers nearly every stimulus it encounters, and then processes each one individually. If a person does not actively remember or notice something, it is likely because he or she does not need to or does not want to.

UNCONSCIOUSNESS An individual's lack of awareness of thoughts, memories, feelings, sensations, or environment.

Freud was one of the first to study and theorize about consciousness. His theories were considered controversial, even shocking, to many, and his work is still the subject of debate among some of today's psychology experts. Psychoanalysis, which Freud founded, focuses on the theory that consciousness and unconsciousness are a hierarchy of memory and thought storage, sort of like the layers of an onion. The conscious mind is at the top of the hierarchy (the onion peel), housing everything people are aware of. Freud believed that memories that can be easily recalled—one's childhood home address or phone number, or what happened at the prom—are stored in the preconscious mind (the outer layers of the onion), not exactly conscious, but not unconscious either.

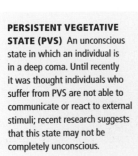

Freud believed that the unconscious mind (the heart of the onion) houses everything people do not want to remember. He theorized that memories and urges that are painful, unpleasant, unacceptable, or that cause people to feel anxiety or conflict, are relegated to the unconscious mind, where they must be "dug out" if a person truly wants to recognize them. According to Freud, the unconscious mind influences behavior even if the individual is not aware of that influence. This influence can result in what he called psychological conflict.

PERSISTENT VEGETATIVE STATE (PVS) An unconscious state in which an individual is in a deep coma. Until recently it was thought individuals who suffer from PVS are not able to communicate or react to external stimuli; recent research suggests that this state may not be completely unconscious.

The study of consciousness is relatively new, holding interest for many researchers only since the mid-1950s. Varying states of consciousness, such as dreams, hypnosis, and the effect of drugs, are major areas currently under study. One area of study that has recently received attention is the study of brains of individuals in a **persistent vegetative state** (PVS). British and Belgian scientists have used magnetic resonance imaging (MRI) technology to explore brains of patients who suffer from PVS; MRI imaging has indicated that some patients may not only be able to

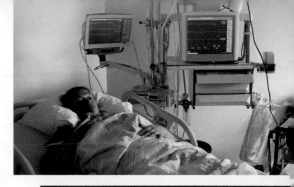

respond to external stimuli, including spoken words, but they may also be able to communicate with those around them.

Another area of interest is synaesthesia, a condition whereby stimulation in one sensory mechanism causes an experience in another sensory mechanism. For example, affected individuals experience a blending of sensations that are normally experienced separately by others. Some may hear a musical note when viewing a particular color or feel a particular shape while tasting foods.

Synaesthesia is automatic, and whether it is a conscious perceptual experience, a perception hidden from the consciousness, or merely a memory association is a hotly debated topic. Richard Cyotowic, a neurologist, has argued that affected individuals experience a shutdown of the left hemispheric cortex, and that the perceptions are normally hidden from the conscious mind. His book *The Man Who Tasted Shapes* profiles synaesthetes.

SLEEP AND DREAMS

Sometimes a person has complete control over his or her consciousness, and sometimes the body takes over. One example of the body controlling consciousness is when people are asleep. Sleeping and dreaming are natural, but also critical, events. Although scientists are not sure why people need to sleep or why people dream, *not* sleeping and dreaming can lead to serious physical and mental problems.

Circadian Rhythms

The suprachiasmatic nucleus is a tiny region in the anterior hypothalamus that is believed to be responsible for controlling circadian rhythms. A **circadian rhythm** is the body's natural internal clock. The term *circadian* comes from a Latin term meaning *around the day.* A circadian rhythm is a 24-hour sleep–wake cycle during which the body uses external and internal cues to determine what activity occurs when. Light is the factor that most affects the body's circadian rhythms. The presence or absence of light stimulates circadian rhythms and turns the body's clock on and off. People become accustomed to these rhythms and tend to sleep and wake at certain times because of them. If you have ever been frustrated because you wake up at roughly the same time on the weekend as during the week even when you want to sleep in, it is because your body's circadian rhythms are programmed to wake you up.

Scientists study circadian rhythms because they appear to be closely related to physical and mental health. But most research does not involve human subjects. Instead, subjects such as mice or algae are subjected to controlled light experiments and then studied to determine if any changes, even those that occur at a genetic level, are evident. These studies are important because they can lead to an increased understanding of biological systems and further may lead to innovative new treatments for sleep disorders.

CIRCADIAN RHYTHM The body's natural 24-hour internal clock, or sleep–wake cycle, that uses external and internal cues such as lightness and darkness to determine when the body should sleep and wake.

Circadian rhythms control important functions such as sleep–wake cycles, hormone release, and body temperature. Research indicates that they may also have a genetic component. A hormone called **melatonin** is released according to light levels, which are sent to the brain by receptors located near the optic nerves. This is why one tends to be sleepy at night, when light levels are low and more melatonin is released, and why one has more energy during the day, when light is bright and less melatonin is present. It is believed that heightened secretions of melatonin during the winter cause some people to slow down and feel sluggish and depressed. Some people experience seasonal affective disorder (SAD), a depressive disorder that occurs seasonally—particularly during months of the year that have less sunlight, such as fall and winter.

When the body's circadian rhythm is interrupted, problems ranging from jet lag to bipolar disorder may result. In cases of jet lag, circadian rhythms stay the same even though one may enter a different time zone. The body wants to continue the sleep–wake routines it has established. People may even experience changes in their eating habits.

Say you have traveled from California to Connecticut. The time difference is three hours. When you wake up the next day in Connecticut at 6 a.m., your body thinks it is 3 a.m. It only takes a few days for your body's internal clock to reset to the new time zone, but, in the meantime, you may feel sluggish and disoriented even if you have gotten a full eight hours of sleep. Disrupted sleep–wake cycles have been linked to insomnia and other sleep disorders, depression, seasonal affective disorder, and bipolar disorder.

Stages of Sleep

When people fall asleep, they are not merely resting. Their brains are leading them in and out of two different types of sleep: **non–rapid eye movement (NREM) sleep**, sometimes called quiet sleep, and **rapid eye movement (REM) sleep**, also called active sleep or paradoxical sleep. There are four stages of NREM sleep. Researchers use the analysis of brain waves to determine which stage of sleep a person is experiencing.

NREM sleep is divided into four stages, known simply as Stage 1, Stage 2, Stage 3, and Stage 4. Before reaching Stage 1, one is still mostly awake and somewhat alert. During this time, the brain is producing **beta waves**—small, fast brain waves. As the brain begins to move toward sleep, it relaxes and begins to produce **alpha waves**, which are more relaxed and slower than beta waves. During this phase, people sometimes experience some interesting sensations, such as hearing their name called or feeling like they are falling. People sometimes also experience an event known as a **myoclonic jerk**. For no apparent reason at all, the body jerks as it does when a person is startled. This type of sleep event is very common and is no cause for alarm.

During the first stage of sleep, one is sleeping lightly and the body is transitioning between being awake and being asleep. The brain produces alpha waves and also begins to produce **theta waves** (see Figure 5.1)—very slow, higher-amplitude brain waves. This period of sleep generally lasts only five or ten minutes. Most people who are awakened during this phase do not realize they were actually asleep.

MELATONIN A hormone released according to low light levels that causes increased sleepiness.

NON–RAPID EYE MOVEMENT (NREM) SLEEP A type of sleep, sometimes called quiet sleep, that has four stages and occurs before REM sleep.

RAPID-EYE MOVEMENT (REM) SLEEP A type of sleep that usually occurs about 90 minutes after falling asleep and is associated with fast eye movement, active brain waves, and relaxed muscles.

BETA WAVES Small, fast brain waves often associated with being awake or just beginning a sleep cycle.

ALPHA WAVES Brain waves that are slower than beta waves and occur as the body relaxes at the beginning of the non-REM sleep cycle.

MYOCLONIC JERK The common sensation of the body jerking near the beginning of the non-REM sleep cycle.

THETA WAVES Brain waves that are slower than alpha and beta waves and occur during Stage I of non-REM sleep during the transition between being awake and asleep.

Stage 1 sleep

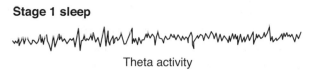

Theta activity

FIGURE 5.1 Stage I Sleep

The second stage of sleep lasts about 20 minutes. During this phase, the brain produces theta waves and also what are known as **sleep spindles**—bursts of rapid, rhythmic brain waves—and **K-complexes**, which are less frequent, high peaks of brain waves (see Figure 5.2). During Stage 2 sleep, one begins to feel drowsy, as the heart rate decreases and the body temperature begins to lower.

Stage 2 sleep

Sleep
spindle   K-complex

FIGURE 5.2 Stage II Sleep

SLEEP SPINDLES Bursts of rapid, rhythmic brain waves that occur during Stage II sleep in which the heart rate decreases and the body temperature begins to lower.

K-COMPLEXES Brain waves that are less frequent than sleep spindles but have higher peaks.

Stage 3 sleep serves as a transition between light sleep and deep sleep. During this stage, the brain begins to produce some **delta waves**—slow, deep brain waves.

Stage 3 sleep

Delta activity

FIGURE 5.3 Stage III Sleep

DELTA WAVES Slow, deep brain waves that mark the transition between light sleep and deep sleep during Stage III of non-REM sleep.

During the fourth stage of sleep, the brain produces only delta waves. Because of this, the fourth stage is often called **delta sleep**. Stage 4 sleep is deep, lasts for about 30 minutes, and is the stage during which events like bed-wetting and sleep-walking happen.

DELTA SLEEP Deep sleep that occurs during the fourth stage of non-REM sleep and lasts about 30 minutes.

Stage 4 sleep

Delta activity

FIGURE 5.4 Stage IV Sleep

Some people consider REM sleep the fifth stage of sleep, but REM sleep is really a different type of sleep altogether. Most people enter REM sleep about 90 minutes after they start to fall asleep. Sleep cycles are continuous, with REM sleep lasting longer each time. After a period of REM sleep, a person returns to Stage 2 sleep, then Stage 3, Stage 4, then back to Stage 3 and Stage 2. After the person completes a phase of REM sleep, he or she usually returns to Stage 2 and repeats the cycle. Sleep does not occur in exactly the same pattern throughout the night. As sleep progresses and the pattern repeats as many as four or five times, it is possible to spend as much as one full hour in REM sleep.

REM sleep is also known as **paradoxical sleep** because this type of sleep is a study in contradictions. During REM sleep, the eyes move quickly, the respiration rate increases, and brain activity increases, but the voluntary muscles are relaxed to the point of paralysis. Most dream activity happens during REM sleep.

REM sleep

Theta activity   Beta activity

FIGURE 5.5 REM Sleep

Functions of Sleep

If you have ever been awake for an extended period of time or lost sleep for one reason or another, you probably know how important it is to sleep. There is much debate about why people sleep. Scientists are unsure exactly why people sleep; they know it is important, however, because all mammals do it and consequences are often severe when sleep needs are not met.

Although simple rest appears to be one important function of sleep, other functions seem to include "resetting" the brain and processing memories. While people are awake, their brains use as much as 80 percent of their energy to engage in synaptic activity. This massive amount of energy use means that the brain needs some downtime to refresh, regroup, and be ready for more activity the next day.

Many scientists believe that sleep may also be a time the brain uses to process memories. Researcher Jie Zhang found that among her subjects, everything that happened during their day is either stored or deleted from memory. Researchers believe that the incredible amount of brain activity during sleep indicates that the brain is processing information even while the body is resting. The brain uses sleep to "clear out" information and prepare for a new day of processing.

Dreams

Scientists have yet to agree on why people dream; some theories include memory consolidation, emotional regulation, and that dreams hold information about unconscious thoughts and emotions or predictions about the future (premonitions).

Function of Dreams

Freud believed that dreams are an interpretation of what people experience during sleep. He thought that if a sleeper has a full bladder, for example, he or she might dream of going to the bathroom; if hungry, the same sleeper might dream of digging into a huge all-you-can-eat buffet of favorite foods. Jung, in contrast, theorized that dreams are reflections of a person's waking personalities. If people are outgoing in their waking lives, they are outgoing in their dreams. If people are shy in their waking lives, their dreams will reflect the same.

Other researchers believe that dreams may serve as a sort of method of solving problems—unresolved problems in a person's waking life that are tackled by the person's brain during sleep. Many people believe that dream analysis may be the key to solving problems that trouble people in their waking lives.

Interpreting Dreams

"Dream" can refer to three things:

- An experience during sleep
- What is remembered upon awakening
- What is reported to others

Although dream reports are theoretically an actual depiction of what the dreamer remembers, what is remembered may not actually be correct; parts may be missing or misinterpreted as the dream fades. In addition, people's age, gender, ethnicity, and cultural experiences can influence how they interpret their own dreams. Because there is no way to determine exactly what a person's dream was, and because personality so influences how a person presents his or her dream to others, dream interpretation is difficult. Some researchers believe that dream analysis is best done "blind," meaning that the person completing the analysis has no information about the dreamer other than that individual's gender and age. Others believe that the person analyzing a dream needs as much information about the life of the dreamer as possible.

Sleep Disorders

About 60 million Americans each year suffer from long-term and short-term sleep disorders, according to the National Institute of Neurological Disorders and Stroke. Doctors have described more than 70 sleep disorders, which may be the result of disruptions in the body's natural circadian rhythms or have their roots in physical or mental disorders. The following are a few of the most common disorders.

INSOMNIA A sleep disorder that causes difficulty falling asleep or staying asleep.

SLEEP APNEA A sleep disorder that is characterized by interrupted breathing during sleep.

Insomnia

Almost everyone at some point experiences **insomnia,** which is characterized by having trouble falling asleep and/or staying asleep. Primary insomnia is a state of insomnia that appears to have no cause. Comorbid insomnia means that another disorder or health problem is preventing sleep. Treatment for insomnia may include behavioral therapy, relaxation, or medication.

Sleep Apnea

Sleep apnea is a disorder that causes interrupted breathing during sleep. Obstructive sleep apnea is caused by an obstruction of the airway during sleep and may be treated with weight loss, mechanical devices, or oral appliances. In central sleep apnea, the brain fails to signal the lungs to breathe.

Hypersomnia

People with **hypersomnia** experience frequent episodes of daytime sleepiness or prolonged sleep at night. These people get enough sleep at night but still feel very sleepy during the day. In some cases, hypersomnia is caused by another sleep disorder (like sleep apnea). It may also be caused by medications, head injury, or medical conditions. Treatment for hypersomnia focuses on the symptoms of the disorder.

HYPERSOMNIA A condition in which a person experiences frequent episodes of daytime sleepiness, or excessive or prolonged deep sleep at night.

PSYCHOLOGY & CAREERS: A HEALTH CARE CAREER IN A SLEEP LAB

People who work in sleep labs are called *polysomnographic technicians*. These specialists help doctors diagnose and treat sleep disorders such as sleep apnea, snoring, and disruptions in sleep patterns. Polysomnographic technicians may also help researchers study the way people sleep in order to help develop drugs and theories about sleep.

Sleep lab technicians use diagnostic equipment to monitor patients while they sleep. They perform and evaluate the body during sleep, monitoring such functions as brain wave activity, heart activity, temperature, heartbeat, blood pressure, and more.

ALTERED STATES OF CONSCIOUSNESS

Consciousness can be altered intentionally or unintentionally. Consciousness can be altered via drug use (legal and illegal), hypnosis, and meditation. Just how beneficial or harmful each of these altered states is over the long term is still to be determined. However, a great deal of research has been done about altering consciousness.

Drug Use

Drugs are perhaps the most widely used method of altering consciousness. Many people use common drugs, such as alcohol, marijuana, tobacco, and prescription medications, to change the way they feel, think, and perceive the world around them.

Many drugs that modern societies have deemed illegal have been used for centuries as treatments for a host of diseases and disorders. Some of the drugs that are illegal in the United States are now being used as medical treatments. Drugs originally tagged as having no medical benefits, such as marijuana, psilocybin mushrooms, and methylenedioxymethamphetamine (otherwise known as MDMA or ecstasy), are now prescribed by some doctors for a range of conditions. Marijuana can be used to treat anxiety and glaucoma and to ease side effects of chemotherapy. Psilocybin mushrooms, a hallucinogenic, can be used to treat cluster headaches,

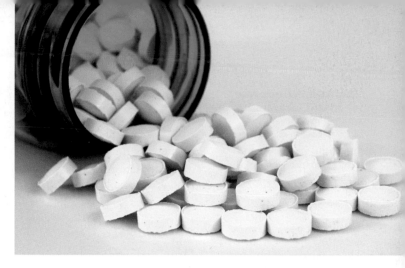

obsessive-compulsive disorder, anxiety, depression, and even drug dependence. They are also sometimes suggested as a treatment for anxiety in patients near the end of life. MDMA is being used for post-traumatic stress disorder–related anxiety.

Psychologist Timothy Leary was well known in the 1960s and 1970s for his experiments with LSD (lysergic acid diethylamide). He believed that LSD had numerous therapeutic, emotional, and spiritual benefits. He was responsible for the **Harvard psilocybin project**, a series of psychological experiments involving psychedelic drugs. One part of the project was the Concord prison experiment, during which Leary and colleagues gave psilocybin mushrooms to prisoners in an effort to reduce their rate of repeat crimes. As another part of the project, the Marsh chapel experiment, one of Leary's graduate students gave psilocybin to divinity students in an effort to induce profound religious states. At the time of the Harvard project, psilocybin was not illegal, and Leary encouraged its use to explore emotional and spiritual feelings. He was terminated by Harvard in May 1963, but he continued his research on his own. In the early 1970s, Leary developed his **8-circuit model of consciousness**, an attempt to quantify altered states of consciousness into one theory that stated that the brain was actually composed of eight mini brains and that each of these brains, or mini circuits, was responsible for a particular aspect of human consciousness.

Stanislav Grof, another well-known psychiatrist, has spent much of his research on the therapeutic and transformative powers of non-ordinary states of consciousness, which is rooted in his experimentation with LSD. He has argued that personal spiritual experiences can be gained during altered states of consciousness. Much of his work revolves around conducting therapy with mind-altering substances like LSD and working with clients who are going through spiritual crises. He is also involved with holotropic therapy, which involves using breathing techniques, suggestive music, and other techniques to alter clients' consciousness.

Whether legally prescribed or illegally used, many drugs are known to alter consciousness. Many legally prescribed drugs, especially those used in psychiatry, are prescribed in an effort to intentionally alter consciousness for the better. Drugs prescribed for physical illnesses may unintentionally affect consciousness, especially in older people, and may need to be discontinued or adjusted as a result. However, drugs obtained and used illegally are generally used to intentionally alter consciousness for recreation or in an effort to avoid unpleasant feelings or experiences.

HARVARD PSILOCYBIN PROJECT A series of experiments led by psychologist Timothy Leary exploring the effects of psilocybin mushrooms.

8-CIRCUIT MODEL OF CONSCIOUSNESS A theory developed by Timothy Leary that suggests the brain is composed of eight mini circuits that are each responsible for specific aspects of consciousness.

Substance Abuse

Psychoactive drugs are drugs that affect people psychologically. Psychoactive drugs such as alprazolam (Xanax), thioridazine (Mellaril), and haloperidol (Haldol) are commonly prescribed for anxiety, depression, insomnia, psychosis, and mania. Psychoactive street drugs like heroin, LSD, and ecstasy are used recreationally or to self-medicate. Substance abuse is a way that people intentionally alter consciousness and may also include the use of legal drugs such as alcohol and tobacco. Substance abuse can lead to addiction and dependence.

PSYCHOACTIVE DRUGS A category of drugs that affect people psychologically. Examples include legal prescription drugs, such as alprazolam (Xanax), thioridazine (Mellaril), and haloperidol (Haldol), as well as illegal drugs, such as heroin, LSD, and ecstasy.

Addiction

SEDATIVE-HYPNOTICS Drugs such as alcohol, barbiturates, and minor tranquilizers that are addictive and often abused.

ADDICTION A physiological and/or physical dependence on a substance.

Alcohol, barbiturates, and minor tranquilizers are considered **sedative-hypnotics**. They are also widely abused. These drugs are addictive, meaning they may result in a physical and/or psychological dependence. **Addiction** may lead to serious physical damage to the nervous system or liver, and even death due to overdose. In some cases, addiction is situational, meaning it is more related to when, where, and how the drug is used than any real physical dependence.

Dependence

DRUG DEPENDENCE A physical tolerance that is a result of a physiological process involving the liver and metabolism. This type of tolerance often results in increased use of drugs and sometimes overdose or death.

Drug dependence happens as the body develops a tolerance to the substance. It takes more and more of the drug to get the same feeling a smaller amount once produced. This can lead to exponential increase of use of the drug, which may result in death by overdose. Dependence is a physiological process that involves the liver and metabolism. Dependence may develop quickly, especially with narcotics such as morphine and heroin.

Hypnosis

HYPNOSIS A method of accessing the unconscious mind by inducing a trance state resembling sleep.

Have you ever had the experience of pulling your car into the driveway, parking in front of the garage, and being so deep in thought that you did not remember driving home? Sometimes when people mull over their workday, run errands, or fixate on a problem, they run on autopilot. At times, people do not need to be more than minimally conscious of what they are physically doing and are able to concentrate instead on larger issues.

Other examples of being lost in thought include looking out the window of a bus and realizing that you have already reached your destination but not remembering the bus making any stops, or watching TV and, as one program ends and another begins, realizing that you are so deep in thought that you are not paying attention to what you are watching.

These "lost in thought" events are known as trances, and they are a form of **hypnosis**. Other forms of hypnosis occur with the aid of professionals who guide patients into a state of consciousness that is similar to sleep, but is not sleep. Hypnosis is in fact an altered state of consciousness because awareness is shifted toward sleep without sleep actually occurring. Hypnosis encourages relaxation, awareness, and a separation between the self and one's surroundings. The person being hypnotized is neither alert nor asleep, but somewhere in between.

Hypnosis is a voluntary process. Not everyone can be hypnotized, and it is not something that can be done against a person's will. There are many theories about how hypnosis works—the general consensus is that hypnosis accesses the unconscious mind—but no one knows for sure. Many people believe that hypnosis works with the unconscious mind and bypasses the barriers the conscious mind has constructed. It can be used to help people quit smoking, manage their weight, build confidence, or even to eradicate pain during surgical or dental procedures.

Meditation

Meditation is an individual-driven form of consciousness. The way meditation is perceived and practiced varies from culture to culture, making it difficult, in some respects, to study. The process of meditation refers to engaging the brain in deep thought in a way that means the person is someplace between excitement and dullness; in meditation, stability and clarity are perfectly balanced.

Many people believe that meditation is not simply a form of relaxation because relaxation implies dullness. For this reason, meditation practices are not generally undertaken lying down, as this could result in too much relaxation and, possibly, sleep, which is not the goal. Meditation, therefore, is a state that requires relaxation but also requires awareness. Meditation is a form of altered consciousness because the "normal" state of alertness that the body generally requires to function is bypassed so that the person engaging in the meditation process can access a deeper consciousness and thought.

Research studies have shown that practicing meditation changes the brain. These studies have shown that the changes take place in the gray-matter density in the hippocampus, an area in the brain that plays a role in learning and memory. Ritchie Davidson, a psychiatrist at the University of Wisconsin-Madison, has spent much of his scientific research on meditation, which is a field now known as contemplative neuroscience. His work focuses on how meditation changes processes in the brain and how it affects attention and emotion.

MEDITATION A form of altered consciousness that engages the brain in deep thought.

KEY THINKERS IN PSYCHOLOGY: CHARLES TART

Charles Tart, who is on the faculty of the Institute of Transpersonal Psychology in Palo Alto, California, is known for his study of the nature of consciousness, specifically altered states of consciousness. His work focuses on bridging the gap between science and spiritualism. He is the author of more than a dozen books about varying states of consciousness, among them *Altered States of Consciousness* (1969) and *Transpersonal Psychologies* (1975). His most recent title, *The End of Materialism: How Evidence of the Paranormal Is Bringing Science and Spirit Together* (2009), is critical in the field of transpersonal psychology, the study of the spiritual and transcendent aspects of the human experience.

Tart studied engineering at MIT before becoming interested in psychology. He completed his undergraduate, master's, and doctoral studies at the University of North Carolina at Chapel Hill. He went on to receive postdoctoral training in hypnosis research at Stanford University.

Tart is partly retired after half a century of work in psychology, but he is a part-time faculty member at the Institute, as well as a consultant and speaker.

SUMMARY

From the human body's natural regulation of consciousness to individual attempts to alter consciousness, scientists have learned that consciousness is a complicated and intricate function of the human mind. Consciousness consists of several components, including awareness, which is consciousness itself, and the unconscious mind, studied by Freud and many other prominent researchers. New research into how consciousness works has uncovered brain activity in patients in persistent vegetative states, meaning that people who have suffered a traumatic brain injury may be conscious even though the doctors and loved ones who attend to them do not think they are.

Sleep and dreams are important to the study and state of consciousness. There are two types of sleep, non-REM and REM. With non-REM sleep are four stages. Each of these types and stages of sleep appear to be important in their duration and sequence. Although researchers are not exactly sure why humans sleep, they are certain that sleep is a necessary and critical function for health and survival. Common sleep disorders include insomnia, sleep apnea, and hypersomnia.

Although consciousness is a constant, it is not unalterable. People alter consciousness both intentionally and unintentionally. One of the most recognizable ways to alter consciousness is via drug use. Legal drugs, prescribed for psychiatric reasons, alter consciousness intentionally by affecting brain receptors. Drugs prescribed for nonpsychological medical reasons may also unintentionally alter consciousness. These types of drugs may need to be discontinued if consciousness is altered to the detriment of the patient.

Drug abuse, whether through illegal drugs or legal drugs used in illegal ways, is also a way that people alter consciousness. This type of consciousness alteration is intentional and is usually a way for the drug user to escape a difficult situation, feelings, or emotions. Substance abuse may result in addiction and/or dependence.

Hypnosis and meditation are two ways that people seek to alter consciousness to access their inner minds. Hypnosis, a form of relaxation, is a way for people to work through difficult experiences and feelings and is thought to open the unconscious mind. Meditation is a way that individuals hover between a state of alertness and relaxation, helping them to focus and concentrate on issues, emotions, and feelings.

REFERENCES

Cleveland Clinic. (n.d.). *Sleep disorders in older child and teen.* Retrieved from http://my.clevelandclinic.org/documents/sleep_disorders_center/factsheets_collection.pdf

Domhoff, G. W. (2004). *Finding meaning in dreams: A quantitative approach.* Retrieved from http://psych.ucsc.edu/dreams/Library/fmid1.html

Domhoff, G. W. (n.d.). The "purpose" of dreams. Retrieved from http://psych.ucsc.edu/dreams/Library/purpose.html

Griffiths, R., Richards, W., Johnson, M., McCann, U., & Jesse, R. (2008). Mystical-type experiences occasioned by psilocybin mediate the attribution of personal meaning and spiritual significance 14 months later. *Journal of Psychopharmacology, 22*(6), 621–632.

Hall, R. (n.d.). Stages of sleep. Retrieved Psychology World website: http://web.mst.edu/~psyworld/sleep_stages.htm

Levy, N. (2006). *Consciousness and the persistent vegetative state.* Melbourne, AUS: University of Melbourne.

Lutz, A., Dunne, J. D., & Davidson, R. J. (2005). Meditation and the neuroscience of consciousness. In P. Zelazo, M. Moscovitz, & E. Thompson (Eds.), *Cambridge handbook of consciousness* (pp. 499–554). Retrieved from http://brainimaging.waisman.wisc.edu/~lutz/Meditation_Neuroscience_2005_AL_JDD_RJD_2.pdf

Marano, H. E. (2005, March 1). Why we dream. *Psychology Today*. Retrieved from http://www.psychologytoday.com/articles/200504/why-we-dream

Monti, M. M., Vanhaudenhuyse, A., Coleman, M. R., Boly, M., Pickard, J., Tshibanda, L., … Laureys, S. (2010). Willful modulation of brain activity in disorders of consciousness. *New England Journal of Medicine, 362*, 579–589.

National Institute of General Medical Sciences. (2008, July). Circadian rhythms fact sheet. Retrieved from http://www.nigms.nih.gov/publications/factsheet_circadianrhythms.htm

National Institute of Neurological Disorders and Stroke. (2007, May 21). Brain basics: Understanding sleep: Sleep disorders. Retrieved from http://www.ninds.nih.gov/disorders/brain_basics/understanding_sleep.htm#back

Nicholson, C. (2006). Memory and consciousness: Consciousness to unconsciousness and back again. *Observer, 19*(8). Retrieved from http://www.psychologicalscience.org/observer/getArticle.cfm?id=2028

Owen, A., Coleman, M., Boly, M., Davis, M., Laureys, S., & Pickard, J. (2006). Detecting awareness in the vegetative state. *Science, 313*(5792), 1402.

Psychoanalysis—psychoanalytic theory of mind. (n.d.). Retrieved from http://science.jrank.org/pages/10900/Psychoanalysis-Psychoanalytic-Theory-Mind.html

Public Library of Science. (2008, August 27). Exploring the function of sleep. *ScienceDaily*. Retrieved from http://www.sciencedaily.com/releases/2008/08/080825203918.htm

Ryder, J. (2009, May 29). Is hypnosis really an altered state of consciousness? [Web log post]. *Psychology Today*. Retrieved from http://www.psychologytoday.com/blog/hypnosis-the-power-trance/200905/is-hypnosis-really-altered-state-consciousness

Singer, W. (2000). Phenomenal awareness and consciousness from a neurobiological perspective. In T. Metzinger (Ed.), *Neural correlates of consciousness: Empirical and conceptual questions* (pp. 121–138). Boston, MA: MIT Press.

Timothy Leary. (2004). In *Encyclopedia of world biography*. Retrieved from http://www.encyclopedia.com/doc/1G2-3404703777.html

Timothy Leary. (n.d.). Retrieved from http://www.timothyleary.us/

Weil, A. T. (n.d.). *Altered states of consciousness* (Drug Abuse Survey Project, Staff Paper No. 6). Retrieved from http://www.druglibrary.org/schaffer/library/studies/dwda/staff6.htm

Zhang, J. (2004). Memory process and the function of sleep. *Journal of Theoretics, 6*(6). Retrieved from http://www.journaloftheoretics.com/Articles/6-6/Zhang.pdf

Developmental Psychology

"The best years of your life are the ones in which you decide your problems are your own. You do not blame them on your mother, the ecology, or the president. You realize that you control your own destiny."

—Albert Ellis

WHAT IS HUMAN DEVELOPMENT?

Human development encompasses all the changes that occur during the span of human life, from prenatal development through death. Developmental psychologists study these changes in humans and develop theories to explain how and why these changes occur. Some of these theories are described in this chapter.

NATURE VERSUS NURTURE

What makes a person—the environment he or she is raised in or the DNA encoded in his or her cells? This question—nature versus nurture—is one of the most prominent debates among psychology researchers. Some theorists believe that nature, or biological factors, control and affect human behavior. These biological factors occur inside the human body and include brain chemistry and DNA.

Other theorists believe that nurture, which essentially means environmental factors, are responsible for molding human behavior. Environmental factors can include everything from how much and what types of food one eats to the educational opportunities one receives in kindergarten. The importance of nurture is often associated with family relationships, particularly parent–child relationships. Many psychologists now believe that human development is a combination of both nature and nurture.

HUMAN DEVELOPMENT The complete set of physical, cognitive, social, and emotional changes experienced by a person during the course of a lifetime.

GENES The basic biological unit of heredity.

Genetic Influences

Proponents on the nature, or biological, side of the nature versus nurture debate argue that if genes determine one's hair color, height, eye color, and other physical characteristics, they must play a similar role in one's personality and behavior. **Genes** are the basic biological unit of heredity, and each person has thousands of them.

But what else do genes control? Is your personality genetically determined? What about intellectual potential or sexual orientation? Do genes control how you will respond to stress or grief? These are controversial questions, and today, genetic researchers are searching for the answers. Many behavioral geneticists believe that further analysis of the human genetic code will reveal a powerful connection between genetics and behavior.

These researchers believe a link exists between genetics and behavior because they have repeatedly observed connections in natural settings. Animals repeat behaviors that serve them well, such as the mating rituals of various species of chickens or the herding behaviors exhibited by German shepherds or collie dog breeds—even among dogs who are family pets and not "working dogs." Certain human behaviors are inherited traits. For example, many types of mental illness, such as schizophrenia or bipolar disorder, run in families.

KEY CONCEPTS

1. The nature versus nurture debate addresses how genetic makeup and the environment affect a person's potential. See page 95.

2. The biological basis of behavior is a theory about development that considers the biological components of human behavior. See page 95.

3. Stage theories suggest that development takes place in discrete phases, or stages. See page 97.

4. Cognitive development is the series of events by which a person's capacity for thought, reflection, and awareness occur. See page 100.

5. Social-emotional development examines a person's interactions with his or her surroundings. See page 103.

6. Moral development occurs when growing awareness of the effect of words and deeds on others leads to the willingness to consider others' needs in advance. See page 108.

KEY THINKERS IN PSYCHOLOGY: ERIK ERIKSON

German-born psychologist Erik Erikson, born in 1902, created one of the most prominent theories of human development. His theory focuses on the social–emotional development of people from birth through death.

At the age of 25, Erikson moved to Vienna to work in a small school. He was trained in psychotherapy techniques by Sigmund Freud's daughter, Anna, but Erikson's work departed from Anna's version of her father's five-stage psychosexual development model by 1930. The Freuds believed that human emotional development halted once a child reached adulthood. Erikson disagreed and created a model that accounted for social and emotional development across the lifespan.

In the early 1930s, Erikson and his family left Vienna to escape the threat of the Nazis. They sought safety first in Copenhagen, Denmark, and eventually settled in the United States, where Erikson worked for the rest of his career in universities and private practices on both coasts. During his career, he widened his influences beyond psychology to include anthropology and social justice. He studied child development in the Native American communities of the Sioux and Yurok.

Erikson was appointed as a professor of human development at Harvard University in 1960. He taught there until his retirement in 1970, at which point he continued to research. Harvard named an academic center after Erikson.

The family returned to Cambridge, Massachusetts, in 1987, and Erikson planned to continue a more limited schedule of work and research. Sadly, however, Erikson began to exhibit signs of mental decline soon after the move, likely due to the onset of Alzheimer's disease. He died in 1994.

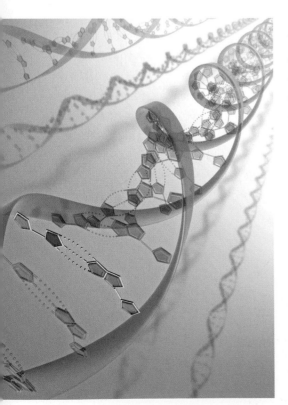

This powerful influence of genetics on human behavior is just beginning to be revealed. Between 1990 and 2003, genetic researchers conducted the Human Genome Project, which involved mapping the entire human genetic code. Although this mapping goal was reached, continued analysis of the human genome will occur for many years to come.

Psychologists remain interested in how genetics affects human behavior. In contemporary Western society, for example, some people argue that sexuality is controlled by genetics, while others believe it is influenced by environmental factors. The depth of genetic influence on behavior and development is difficult to pinpoint.

Further complicating matters is the fact that sometimes study findings are misconstrued or misrepresented. If, for example, scientists announce the discovery of a particular gene that is believed to influence intelligence, the discovery may become distorted in its reporting. The public may assume that a single gene is responsible for intelligence in humans, but in reality the genetic and environmental realities shaping intelligence are far more complex.

Despite the success of the Human Genome Project, the connection between genes and trait development remains unknown. Even if researchers are able to isolate a gene as indicating the existence of a specific trait, understanding how that gene becomes activated and deactivated over the course of a person's life may remain in question. Environmental factors may prove to be the scale that balances how and when genes are expressed during a person's life.

Environmental Influences

Proponents of the nurture side of the debate maintain that the interactions among people and their environments affect human development. People who are properly nourished grow to be taller and stronger than those who are undernourished. Though malnourished people may possess genetic directions to be taller than average, they may not reach their full height potential without the assistance of ideal environmental conditions, such as getting enough to eat and having a balanced diet. It is easy to see how environmental factors can affect human physical development.

It is more difficult to determine how environmental factors influence human cognitive, social, emotional, and moral development. You may be aware of how your own life experiences and environments influenced your development. For example, a child who is exposed to excessive violence at the hands of abusive parents is at a higher risk for emotional disturbances throughout life than a child who was raised in a healthy, nonviolent home. However, the child from the nonviolent home could be exposed to other detrimental factors, such as poor eating habits, which are likely to be influential into adulthood as well.

Environmental influences are not limited to a person's family or small community. Humans exist within a historical period, and in the current era of globalization and instant communication, the environment in which people live has expanded considerably. The citizens of today's world are influenced by international events in a way that previous generations were not. This influence is just beginning to be recognized and explored by psychologists. The effects of technology and "screen time"—whether those screens are computer, television, or video game— on developing minds is a growing concern for many parents and teachers. These influences, and others, open the doors to new areas of study for developmental psychologists.

As human beings develop throughout their lives, different types of development interact with one another. Isolating social development from emotional, cognitive, and moral development, for example, presents a challenging research dilemma. Psychologists design experiments to single out the one factor they are attempting to investigate. This is how they study the environmental effects of the elements of human nature. Even when experiments successfully isolate the factor under investigation, researchers cannot force their subjects to suppress emotional reactions to the experiments.

LIFE STAGES

Human development can be divided into several periods during which people share similar physical, cognitive, social, and emotional experiences. Dividing development into identifiable stages is helpful for understanding the events occurring during each stage. However, many developmental psychologists argue that human development is a continuous process.

This chapter explores the prenatal period, newborn period, childhood, adolescence, adulthood, and late adulthood. Developmental psychologists typically study physical development, cognitive development, emotional development, social development, and moral development. These areas of study tend to overlap, as many factors can affect human development.

Prenatal Development

PRENATAL DEVELOPMENT
Human development from conception through birth.

Prenatal development includes human development from conception through birth. The gestational period for humans is approximately 40 weeks in length, and during this time the fetus undergoes dramatic changes.

Development

ZYGOTE The new cell containing all the genetic material to create a new human being.

EMBRYO The third week after fertilization, when an embryo's heart is formed and beating.

FETUS After the eighth week, the embryo is called a fetus, which is capable of spontaneous movement.

The remarkable changes that occur during a pregnancy begin as soon as a man's sperm unites with a woman's egg. This new cell, now called a **zygote**, contains all the genetic material needed to create a new human being. The zygote divides rapidly, and by the third week the **embryo**'s heart is formed and beating. The heartbeat is considered the embryo's first behavior.

After the eighth week, the embryo gets a new name—it is now called a **fetus**. The fetus is capable of spontaneous movement and begins to take advantage of the space in the woman's uterus, completing flips and turns and moving what will soon become arms and legs. At approximately the sixteenth week, the fetus is large and strong enough to be felt by its mother. Some women feel their babies' movements this early, but others will not notice until several weeks later. As the pregnancy progresses, the fetus's movements become stronger and more noticeable.

By the end of the first 13 weeks (the end of the first trimester), the fetus's organs are fully formed and will continue to develop for the remainder of the pregnancy. One of the most striking prenatal developments occurs within the brain. Much of the brain matter is made up of neurons that allow the structures of the brain to communicate with the rest of the body. A fetus generates new neurons at a rate of 250,000 per minute, and by the time birth occurs, 100 billion neurons have been created in the newborn's brain.

Environmental Influences

Although a fetus is protected from the outside world by its mother's body, it is still subject to the environment within the womb. Once connected to its mother

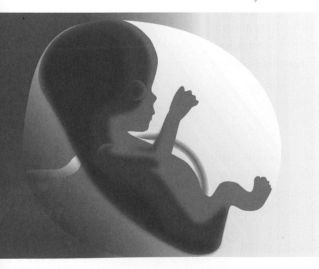

through the umbilical cord, the fetus receives nourishment directly from its mother. Whatever the mother does or does not consume is also consumed by the growing fetus.

For example, if a mother contracts certain illnesses, such as rubella or German measles, they can cause physical and mental defects in her fetus. Babies of malnourished women are at a higher risk for miscarriage and developmental defects. Women who smoke cigarettes or drink alcohol place their babies' healthy development at risk: Alcohol can cause developmental disabilities, preterm labor, and increase the risk for miscarriage. Cigarette smoking can cause preterm labor and low birth weight of babies.

Some prescription and illegal drugs can negatively impact fetal development. Cocaine is a vasoconstrictor, which means that it causes blood vessels to constrict. Because the fetus receives the same substances ingested by the mother, cocaine will cause the blood vessels in the placenta to constrict. Cocaine can also cause placental abruption, which occurs when the placenta pulls away from the uterine wall and bleeding occurs. These consequences result in less oxygenated blood reaching the fetus, which can cause mental handicaps or fetal death.

Many women choose to improve their lifestyles and diets upon discovering that they are pregnant. These measures may include taking prenatal vitamins to make sure they ingest the right amount of folic acid and iron, eating more vegetables and lean meats, and avoiding potentially harmful chemicals and other substances. Some women and their partners play music and talk to the fetus as a way to bond with it. Even though human development seems to be controlled only by genetics during the prenatal period, the effects a mother can have on the environment of her growing fetus are profound. The tension between the effects of nature and nurture truly begins at the moment of conception.

Newborns

Doctors and researchers once believed that newborns were helpless beings incapable of promoting their own survival. More recent research paints a very different picture of newborns' capabilities. During the first hour or two after birth, a baby is amazingly alert. This is typically the period in which parents begin the bonding process with their child by feeding, holding, and talking to their newborn child. Newborns have excellent hearing and respond most noticeably to their mothers' voices, which they heard in utero for many months.

Newborns, however, do not have fully developed eyesight; they can only see in black and white. Their optimum viewing distance is approximately eight inches. Interestingly, when a newborn is held in a cradling position, the newborn's face is about eight inches away from the face of the person holding him or her. This allows the newborn and parent to study one another's features and bond even more effectively.

Reflexes

Infants have several reflexes that are meant to promote their survival. Perhaps the most noticeable reflex is crying. Crying is the newborn's way of communicating with caregivers in order to express hunger, tiredness, boredom, pain, or feeling overwhelmed. Parents who carefully observe their infants are able to discern the differences between these cries and respond accordingly to meet their children's needs.

The **suckling reflex** occurs when the baby's lips are stimulated. In this event, a baby will instinctively make a sucking motion. This reflex ensures that newborns can take in nourishment by suckling either at their mothers' breasts or on bottle nipples. Infants suck both for nourishment and for comfort.

SUCKLING REFLEX When a baby's lips are stimulated, the baby will instinctively make a sucking motion.

The **rooting reflex** occurs when an infant's cheek is brushed. The baby will turn toward the touch, looking for something to suck. The **Moro reflex**, which is also known as the startle reflex, occurs when an infant is startled by something or his or her head drops back. The Moro reflex causes a newborn to throw open his or her arms, with the hands open and thumbs extended. Following this, the infant pulls his or her arms close to the body, with elbows in, before relaxing. Doctors use this reflex to test newborns for any neurological damage that could have occurred in the womb or during birth.

Most reflexes present at birth disappear within the first year of a child's life. Persistence of the presence of a reflex may indicate a neurological problem. For example, a Moro reflex present on only one side of a newborn's body may indicate a broken shoulder or nerve damage. Pediatricians check these reflexes to make sure they are present and may continue to check them to be sure they fade appropriately over time.

Childhood

Childhood includes the period from infancy through the onset of puberty in early adolescence. Tremendous physical, cognitive, social, and emotional changes occur during childhood.

Physical Development

During childhood, physical development is dramatic—especially during the first year. Thriving infants typically double their weight in the first six months of life and triple it by their first birthdays. They spend their first year coordinating gross motor movements, learning to roll over, sit, crawl, and eventually stand and walk. Some children reach these physical milestones earlier than others, but "normal" development includes a wide range of time. For example, one child may learn to crawl at six months and another may not crawl until eight months, but both children are developing within the normal range. Children develop gross motor control first, followed by fine motor control. As they grow and develop, they continue to refine their motor skills. These skills are evident in their expressions of physical play.

During childhood, boys and girls develop in similar ways. Their bodies grow into proportion with their heads, which are 60 percent of their adult size at birth. They grow taller and gain muscle strength and control, but their reproductive organs do not change until they enter puberty.

Cognitive Development

Cognitive development refers to the mental processes people use to make observations, solve problems, and communicate their ideas. Human cognitive development begins at birth, but many of the products of cognitive development are difficult to recognize until the child learns to communicate with caregivers more clearly. Although cognitive development is discussed in

the childhood section of this chapter, it actually occurs across the human lifespan. It is crucial for people to maintain healthy cognitive function throughout life.

Piaget

The most prominent theorist in the field of cognitive development was Jean Piaget, a Swiss psychologist and biologist who was born in 1896. After earning his doctorate at the University of Geneva, Piaget worked for Alfred Binet, the influential creator of the first intelligence tests. Working in Paris, Piaget administered tests to school-aged children. He found that he was intrigued most by the wrong answers the children gave and set out to understand the reasoning behind those answers using diagnostic interviews. These interviews were what propelled him into his investigation of children's cognitive development.

Piaget's theory of cognitive development rests on an understanding of three concepts: assimilation, accommodation, and equilibration. **Assimilation** is the process by which a person incorporates external stimuli or observations into a previously developed framework for understanding the world. For example, when a child is introduced to a new toy that has wheel-like features, but he does not know what it is, he may play with it in the same way he plays with a toy car or a train. The boy fits the new toy into his existing understanding of toys that have wheels. He is assimilating, or incorporating, this new object into his understanding of toys.

Accommodation complements assimilation. **Accommodation** is the process by which a person modifies understanding of a concept to include newly acquired information or experiences. For example, a young brother and sister with a dog for a pet may believe that all pets are dogs. When the siblings encounter an iguana as a pet in another family's home, they will adjust their cognitive framework for pets to include iguanas and perhaps other animals. This adjustment is an example of accommodation. Generally, assimilation and accommodation work together to allow people to regulate their understandings of reality over time.

Equilibration is the concept that brings assimilation and accommodation together. Equilibration posits that people want to bring their understandings of their environments into balance. Assimilation and accommodation are the tools used to find and maintain that cognitive equilibrium.

Piaget's theory of cognitive development is a stage theory. He postulated that children must accomplish the cognitive tasks of one stage before moving on to the next. His theory includes four stages:

- Sensorimotor
- Preoperational
- Concrete operational
- Formal operational

The **sensorimotor** stage, which lasts from birth to age two, is marked by using the senses to understand the environment. Infants and toddlers develop their cognitive schemes, or mental frameworks, based on what they experience and observe. According to Piaget, the most integral task of this stage is acquiring object permanence. **Object permanence** is described as the principle of understanding that an object continues to exist even when it cannot be seen.

ASSIMILATION The process by which a person incorporates external stimuli or observations into a previously developed framework for understanding the world.

ACCOMMODATION The process by which a person modifies understanding of a concept to include newly acquired information or experiences.

EQUILIBRATION The concept that people want to bring their understandings of their environments into balance.

SENSORIMOTOR The stage of development from birth to age two that is marked by using the senses to understand the environment.

OBJECT PERMANENCE The understanding that an object remains in existence despite being out of sight.

Piaget tested this by removing interesting objects from the view of babies and watching their reactions. Although infants can follow objects with their eyes before three months of age, at that age they do not bother to look for missing objects when they are removed from view. At around three months, babies continue looking at the place where the object disappeared. Sometime between 8 and 12 months, babies begin to look for the object that disappeared.

Piaget observed that these changes in behavior indicated a change in the child's understanding that includes a mental representation of the object in addition to a visual confirmation of its existence. In essence, the child remembers the object and believes in its existence even though he or she cannot see it. Piaget believed that this was the beginning of symbolic thinking in children.

The **preoperational stage** begins at age two and continues until approximately age seven. This stage is marked by egocentrism and improved use of symbolic thought. Egocentrism occurs because children can only reason from their own perspective, not from the perspective of others. A casual observer might consider a child of this age to be self-centered or even selfish, but according to Piaget, the child simply has not developed the cognitive skills necessary to see the world from another viewpoint. Though many toddlers begin using language earlier, this stage is also marked by rapidly developing language skills. Language is perhaps the most functional manifestation of symbolic thought. Children increasingly use words to represent people, objects, desires, and feelings as they age.

A child's imagination develops swiftly in the preoperational stage. For example, children begin to use toys as symbolic representations of characters in their imaginary games and stories. Children in the preoperational stage also have difficulty distinguishing between what is real and what is imaginary. They may believe that cartoon characters or stuffed animals are alive because they are animated or have believable facial features.

Finally, preoperational children experience **centration**, which is characterized by the inability to focus on more than one idea at a time. Children may be able to process many details about a situation in quick succession, but they are unable to process those details simultaneously. This is why a preoperational child cannot understand that the same amount of liquid poured into two differently sized glasses is the same amount of liquid, even if one glass is filled to the brim and the other is only partially full.

The **concrete operational stage** lasts from approximately age 7 through age 12. During this stage, a child develops the ability to perform mental operations without visual cues. For example, children in this stage are able to perform mental mathematical operations, including adding and subtracting quantities in their minds. Prior to developing this ability, children use their fingers or other manipulatives to add and subtract.

At this time, children also come to understand the concept of conservation, which is misunderstood in earlier stages. Conservation is the understanding that the characteristics of a substance remain the same even if its outward appearance

PREOPERATIONAL STAGE The stage of development from age two and until approximately age seven that is marked by egocentrism and improved use of symbolic thought.

CENTRATION The cognitive inability to focus on more than one idea at a time.

CONCRETE OPERATIONAL STAGE A development stage from approximately age 7 through age 12 in which a child develops the ability to perform mental operations without visual cues.

changes. The classic Piagetan example of this skill is the lemonade demonstration: identical amounts of lemonade are poured into two identical glasses. Children in the preoperational and concrete operational stages agree that both glasses contain the same amount of liquid. Then the lemonade is poured from one glass into a tall, thin glass. The lemonade from the second glass remains in the original glass. Children in the preoperational stage report that the tall, thin glass contains more lemonade than the original glass of lemonade. Children in the concrete operational stage report that both glasses contain the same amount of lemonade, even though the amounts appear to be different. Understanding that the amount of liquid has not changed is a manifestation of conservation.

Children in this stage also develop the ability to consider two or more details of a situation simultaneously. This is why a concrete operational child can ascertain that the identical liquid in two different-sized containers is the same. The child considers the height and width of the new container simultaneously, thereby allowing the child to judge that the amount of liquid has not changed.

The **formal operational stage** begins around age 12 and continues throughout adulthood. In fact, Piaget believed that some never progress through this stage; they simply remain in the concrete operational stage throughout their adulthood. Most children, however, do reach the formal operational stage.

During this stage, people begin using abstract thought. This type of thinking allows people to perform logical cognitive operations. For example, once a child has reached the formal operation stage, she is mentally prepared to understand the abstract logic needed to solve algebraic equations. Abstract thinkers can also understand and engage complex concepts like justice and human consciousness. When people think abstractly, they can develop higher-order thinking skills like analysis, interpretation, and evaluation. Abstract thinking is used to imagine the realities of others and respond with empathy, successfully linking cognition with emotion.

FORMAL OPERATIONAL STAGE A development stage beginning around age 12 that continues throughout adulthood; during this stage people begin to use abstract thought.

Social and Emotional Development

Social and emotional development may be more challenging to isolate because of the unique role that cultural values play in human interaction. Different cultural groups place varying amounts of value on life stages. Some cultures revere their elderly population as a source of wisdom and experience. Other cultures place special value on the transition from childhood to adulthood, marking such development with special ceremonies or rituals. Noting the powerful influence of culture is essential to understanding human social and emotional development.

Erik Erikson

Erik Erikson, one of the most prominent theorists in human emotional development, was trained in psychoanalysis by Anna Freud, Sigmund Freud's daughter. He believed that people develop in the context of their environments, with the forces of culture exerting strong influences on the social world of people in all phases of development. Through his work with children in Vienna, Austria, Erikson began to develop his **psychosocial stages of development**.

The first stage in Erikson's theory is **trust versus mistrust**, and it lasts from birth through 18 months of age. During this stage, a child must successfully develop an attachment to a caregiver in order to establish trust and a feeling of

PSYCHOSOCIAL STAGES OF DEVELOPMENT Erik Erikson's eight stages of psychological development; in Erikson's model, each stage includes a crisis that requires a resolution.

TRUST VERSUS MISTRUST A stage of psychosocial development lasting from birth through 18 months; during this period, a child develops an attachment to a caregiver.

safety. This is accomplished when the child's needs for food, physical closeness, and affection are met by his or her caregiver. If the child's needs are not met, then the child is likely to develop feelings of anxiety and insecurity.

The second stage, **autonomy versus self-doubt**, begins at approximately 18 months of age and lasts until the child is three years old. During this stage, children are avid explorers of their surroundings. They also manifest a need to control objects within their environments. Too many restrictions or demands on a child during this stage can result in strong feelings of self-doubt because the child cannot experience successes and failures as a person. Likewise, if children are pushed into advanced activities too early, such as toilet training, or treated harshly while learning such skills, they may develop doubts about the ability to exert control of self or of the environment.

Erikson's third stage is **initiative versus guilt**, and it begins around age three and lasts until age six. During this phase, children experiment with initiating mental and physical activities. If parents respond to a child's initiations with enthusiasm, interest, and trust, a positive sense of self-worth is developed in the child. If parents or other caregivers respond with discouragement or disdain, the child will develop guilty feelings associated with initiating activities. Successful resolution of this stage results in feelings of freedom and self-confidence that are used during the next stage.

AUTONOMY VERSUS SELF-DOUBT A stage of psychosocial development lasting from 18 months to three years of age; during this period, children explore their surroundings and their control over objects in their environment.

INITIATIVE VERSUS GUILT A stage of psychosocial development lasting from age three to age six; during this period, children begin to develop mental and physical activities that develop self-confidence.

COMPETENCE VERSUS INFERIORITY A stage of psychosocial development lasting from age six to until puberty; during this period, children develop social and intellectual skills and become confident in their talents and competencies.

IDENTITY VERSUS ROLE CONFUSION A stage of psychosocial development that begins in adolescence; during this period, people understand themselves in many dimensions and take on many roles in life.

Competence versus inferiority, which is also known as industry versus inferiority, defines Erikson's fourth stage. Beginning at age six and lasting through puberty, the main task of this stage is developing successful social and intellectual skills. This is the first stage in which children look beyond their primary caregivers for feedback. They typically begin school during this stage and receive social and intellectual feedback from teachers and peers. They also become involved in extracurricular activities, which teach and test a variety of their motor, social, and mental skills. If children experience success in some of these areas, they build an internal belief that they have individual talents and competencies that are worth developing. If they experience excessive failure or social detachment during this stage, children are likely to develop feelings of inferiority regarding their skill sets, sustaining damage to their sense of self-confidence.

Successful resolution of the previous stages prepares the adolescent for the main task of the next stage, identity development. Erikson named this stage **identity versus role confusion**. From this stage forward, Erikson did not connect the stages with particular ages because he understood that movement through the next four stages is based more on life events than on chronological ages. Adolescents begin to understand themselves in many dimensions and are able to self-identify as sons or daughters, friends, students, athletes, musicians, risk-takers, or cautious types, among other roles. During adolescence, people must become comfortable with themselves, accepting the various facets of their identities and integrating these facets into a coherent whole. As people age, they engage in different roles in different situations. If adolescents cannot successfully navigate this stage, their identities never fully form, and they are left without a clear sense of self.

Adolescents who are secure and have a clear sense of identity can begin Erikson's next stage, **intimacy versus isolation**. During this stage, people develop the ability to maintain intimate relationships with another person. This is typically when many young adults develop romantic relationships, but the traditional commitment of marriage may or may not occur for some time, or ever. Culture is a strong influence during this stage. Young adults in some cultures may feel pressure to demonstrate a commitment through marriage, while those in other cultures may feel no such pressure. Regardless of cultural mores, however, Erikson believed that people need intimate relationships with others to fend off feelings of loneliness and to successfully move to the next stage.

The seventh stage in Erikson's theory is **generativity versus stagnation**. During this period, adults widen their focus to include the welfare of others, typically their families and communities. The activities of these years are marked by the guidance of children and involvement in work and social commitments. At this stage, people begin to feel a desire to create and give something lasting, whether that means starting a family, making a significant donation to charity, or some other enduring gift to humanity. If earlier stages are not resolved, this stage may also remain unresolved. This stage requires an external focus rather than an internal one, and as such people who are unable to resolve this stage may be considered selfish and may question the life experiences of their past.

Ego integrity versus despair is Erikson's final stage of development. This stage occurs in older adulthood and is marked by a person's integration of life experiences into a coherent whole. Older adults who are at peace with their life choices and experiences typically experience a sense of inner integrity, while those saddled with many regrets may experience a sense of disappointment with their lives. When people resolve the crises at each stage of development, they look back over their lives with a sense of pride. Those who move through life with unresolved crises are more likely to experience despair at the end of life.

Attachment

Perhaps the most crucial task of infants is to develop a sense of attachment to a caregiver, usually a parent. At first, attachment serves to ensure the child's survival, as infants cannot feed or care for themselves. Later, the establishment of a close emotional bond between baby and parent creates a sense of security in the child that serves as a jumping-off point for future exploration of the world.

Developmental psychologist Mary Ainsworth investigated attachment between infants and their mothers in both naturalistic and laboratory settings. Her most famous study, which is known as the Strange Situation experiment, involved observing the attachment responses of toddlers to their mothers. In the experiment, a mother and child would enter an unfamiliar room filled with toys. The child was encouraged to play with the toys. Soon after, a strange woman entered the room, spoke to the mother, and played with the baby. Then the mother exited the room briefly and returned.

INTIMACY VERSUS ISOLATION A stage of psychosocial development during which people learn to maintain intimate relationships.

GENERATIVITY VERSUS STAGNATION A stage of psychosocial development during which adults widen their focus to include the welfare of others—typically their families and communities.

EGO INTEGRITY VERSUS DESPAIR A stage of psychosocial development in older adulthood that is marked by a person's integration of life experiences into a coherent whole.

Ainsworth found the reunion behaviors of the children most compelling. She found that about 70 percent of children responded to their mothers' return with a desire for closeness and comfort. This response indicates a secure attachment to their mothers. The other 30 percent of children Ainsworth considered to be insecurely attached, with two different response types. Insecurely attached–avoidant children responded to their mothers' return by ignoring her. Insecurely attached–ambivalent/resistant children responded to their mothers' return with a desire for closeness, but they resisted her attempts at comforting and sometimes exhibited aggressive behaviors toward her.

Longitudinal studies reveal that these attachment types remain relevant throughout children's lives. Those who have formed secure attachments to their parents exhibit healthier behaviors during their school years, making friends more easily and experiencing less social anxiety than peers with insecure attachments to their parents. Research indicates that attachment styles are related to the quality and characteristics of individuals' future relationships with intimate and romantic partners, friendships, and emotional well-being and functioning.

Parenting Styles

Parenting styles are influenced by several factors, including parents' and children's personalities and temperaments, social norms, and cultural values. As anyone with children knows, parenting styles tend to evolve over time for most parents. A parent may begin guiding a child in one way and later develop other, and hopefully more effective, methods over time.

Four main parenting styles have been identified by psychologists. These styles are based on two dimensions: demandingness and responsiveness. Demandingness refers to parents' desire to socialize their children somewhat forcibly and is a measure of how the parent expresses demands on the child's behavior. Responsiveness refers to parents' acknowledgment of their children's autonomy and is a measure of how parents respond to their child's personality and individual needs in the context of the family.

The four main parenting styles are indulgent, uninvolved, authoritarian, and authoritative:

■ **Indulgent** parents make few demands on children while being accepting of children's individuality. Children of indulgent parents may fail to understand social rules and may attempt to get away with a variety of unsavory behaviors. At the same time, they feel loved and accepted by their parents, so although they may perform at lower levels in school, they typically have high self-esteem and adequate friendships.

■ **Uninvolved** parents make few, if any demands on children's behaviors and also reject their child's individuality. Uninvolved parents are generally neglectful, placing their own needs before those of children. Such a style takes its toll on children, and children subject to this parenting style often exhibit low self-esteem, poor scores in school, and perhaps dysfunctional relationships.

INDULGENT Parents who make few demands on their children, who therefore may not understand social rules but typically have high self-esteem and adequate friendships.

UNINVOLVED Parents who make few demands on children's behaviors and also reject their child's individuality, are generally neglectful, and place their own needs before those of children.

■ **Authoritarian** parents exhibit high demands on children's behaviors combined with a strong need for power and control in the parent–child relationship. Children of authoritarian parents are allowed to make very few decisions and may respond by rebelling as they enter adolescence and young adulthood. Authoritarian parents aim to control both their children's behavior and their psychological processes.

■ **Authoritative** parents have high behavioral demands for their children, but they simultaneously respect their children's individuality and need to make at least some of their own decisions. Children of authoritative parents perform better in academic, social, and emotional situations than children of parents who follow the other three parenting styles.

Sex Role Development

The understanding of sex roles can begin when a child is just a few months old. Children observe how men and women behave and note the similarities and differences in those behaviors. Over time, children develop a comprehensive understanding of how men and women are expected to behave within the context of their families and cultures. These behavioral patterns and expectations are known as **gender roles**. A child also begins to develop a **gender identity** at an early age. Gender identity includes an understanding of self as a male or female as well as an acceptance of that understanding. Although gender identity is not dependent on a person's physical sex characteristics, gender identity and biological sex typically match.

Psychologist John Money devoted much of his research to gender role identity. In fact, Money coined the term "gender role" to include nonsexual functioning, activities, behaviors, and expectations that are defined by societal norms to apply either to males or females. In other words, gender is not necessarily biological and innate; rather, it is a function of learned behavior. In studying hermaphrodites, who are people born with both male and female reproductive organs, Money and his colleagues argued that the sex of assignment and rearing is a more powerful predictor of a hermaphrodite's gender role than the sex gene. He argued for the plasticity of gender identity due to environmental factors, but that the assignment had to be made between 18-24 months of age.

Although parents and social norms are strong influences on gender for their children, children are also governed by their biology. Eleanor Maccoby, a developmental psychologist at Stanford University, has researched this connection. She conducted an experiment among nonhuman primates in which doses of testosterone were given to female fetuses late in the gestational period. These female primates who received the testosterone exhibited more masculine behavior after their birth. This led her to conclude that testosterone levels in utero play a major role in guiding future behavior.

Researchers have discovered that physical differences in the structures of the brain occur as a result of biological differences in men and women, and not just as a product of their social upbringing. The study of sex role development is particularly rich with nature–nurture interactions. It is unlikely that there will ever be undeniable proof that biology or environment is solely responsible for sex role development.

AUTHORITARIAN Parents who place high demands on their children and have a need for power and control in their relationships with their children.

AUTHORITATIVE Parents who have high demands for their children and also respect the children's individuality.

GENDER ROLES Behavioral patterns and expectations shared by a culture based on "maleness" and "femaleness."

GENDER IDENTITY Understanding and accepting oneself as male or female; typically, gender identity matches biological sex.

MORAL DEVELOPMENT

As Erik Erikson noted, an adolescent's main task is to develop a coherent identity with which to enter adulthood. People do this by integrating the many roles they play in their daily lives and by identifying possible avenues for their futures as adults that contribute to society. As adolescents' brains develop, so do their decision-making abilities.

As Piaget describes in his theory of cognitive development, adolescents typically achieve the formal operations stage during their teenage years. Formal operational-stage adolescents are capable of abstract thinking and understanding another person's point of view. These skills also allow them to make increasingly complex value judgments when faced with moral dilemmas. The following sections examine the views of two prominent researchers in moral development: Kohlberg and Gilligan.

Lawrence Kohlberg

Lawrence Kohlberg, an American psychologist from Bronxville, New York, developed a foundational theory of human moral development that was modeled on Piaget's stages of cognitive development. In fact, the progression a person experiences through Kohlberg's stages mirrors the progression of Piaget's stages of cognitive development. Kohlberg crafted his theory after interviewing boys from middle- and lower-class families in Chicago about moral reasoning.

The result of Kohlberg's investigation was a three-level, seven-stage theory of moral reasoning. Kohlberg believed that people functioning at the lower levels of his theory were motivated by self-interest, while those operating at higher levels focused on serving the common good, regardless of personal outcomes. He also believed that people could operate in only one stage at a time, that people in all cultures progress through the stages in the same prescribed order, and that each stage is more complex than those it precedes.

Kohlberg named the first level preconventional morality. This level includes two stages, the pleasure–pain orientation and the cost–benefit orientation. Children at this level are typically in their preschool or early school-age years. When operating from the pleasure–pain orientation, children make decisions based on seeking pleasure and avoiding pain. In the mind of the preconventional child, avoiding pain is synonymous with avoiding getting caught. Kohlberg identified stage two as the cost–benefit orientation because children in this stage are motivated to act morally in order to receive a reward. Preconventional morality has an external locus of control, because in that stage, people are externally motivated to make moral decisions.

Level two, conventional morality, is usually seen in the later elementary school and middle-school years. Very young adolescents exhibit level-two morality, and most reach stage four by late adolescence. Stage three is the good-child orientation and stage four is the law-and-order orientation. In the good-child orientation, children behave morally in order to be accepted by their caregivers or peers and to avoid criticism. In the law-and-order orientation, children are motivated by rules and regulations. People with law-and-order orientation do not want to be caught by authority figures. Many people remain in stage four throughout adolescence and young adulthood, which means that they continue to be externally motivated to act in a moral fashion.

Level three, principled morality, is rarely seen before young adulthood. This level includes three stages (stages five, six, and seven), but the third stage proved difficult for Kohlberg to research reliably. In level three, the motivations behind moral behavior have become internalized. People in level three make moral decisions based on what they believe to be right, rather than what the possible outcome of their choice may be.

Stage five is the social-contract orientation. In this stage, people desire to promote the common good and make moral decisions that reflect that value. Stage six is the ethical-principle orientation, the goal of which is to adhere to a few specific values that guide a person's moral choices. These values can include a desire to promote justice, equality, or human dignity. People in this stage would violate the law or other social contracts without hesitation in the name of their principles, if necessary (for example, stealing antibiotic drugs from a hospital in order to give them to the poor).

Stage seven, a somewhat hypothetical stage, is called cosmic orientation or transcendental morality. Kohlberg believed that very few people could reach this stage, and he had a difficult time empirically proving its validity. This stage links moral decision making to religion and suggests that people in this stage wish above all else to follow the tenets of their beliefs, even if doing so defies all existing social norms.

Carol Gilligan

The American psychologist Carol Gilligan is best known for her rebuttal of Kohlberg's moral development stage theory. Kohlberg conducted a long-term study recording the responses of boys age seven through adolescence to dilemmas requiring a moral choice. In the study, Kohlberg concluded that children and adults move through six stages in the development of moral reasoning.

In her own studies, Gilligan noticed that women and girls scored lower than men and boys on Kohlberg's measures of moral decision making. She did not believe that this finding meant that females had weak moral skills—on the contrary, she believed that Kohlberg's theory was only applicable to men and boys because he only interviewed boys in his research and used those interviews in the development of his theory.

Gilligan set out to uncover how girls and women made moral decisions. In 1982, Gilligan published *In a Different Voice*, a book that detailed her own moral reasoning theory. In it, she argued that girls and women made moral judgments that were based upon caring for others. Kohlberg's theory, on the other hand, focused on a morality based on justice.

Gilligan's theory, which she called the stages of the ethic of care, included three stages: preconventional, conventional, and postconventional. Gilligan noted that females progress from one stage to the next as the result of changes in identity rather than cognitive developments.

- In **Gilligan's preconventional stage of morality**, the goal is individual survival. The main task for a girl moving forward from this stage is to move from a place where she can make decisions only based on selfishness to one where she can take responsibility for others.
- **Gilligan's conventional stage of morality** is marked by the belief that self-sacrifice is equivalent to goodness.
- Girls and women progress to **Gilligan's postconventional stage of morality** by letting go of a desire to be good through self-sacrifice. At this stage, a woman

GILLIGAN'S PRECONVENTIONAL STAGE OF MORALITY A stage of the ethic of care in which an infant or young girl believes her primary goal is for individual survival at any cost.

GILLIGAN'S CONVENTIONAL STAGE OF MORALITY A stage of the ethic of care that is marked by a girl's belief that self-sacrifice is equivalent with goodness.

GILLIGAN'S POSTCONVENTIONAL STAGE OF MORALITY A stage of the ethic of care that is marked by a woman's ability to let go of a desire to be good through self-sacrifice to realizing that she, too, is a person of importance. This stage is reached when a woman adopts a belief in nonviolence toward others as well as toward herself.

realizes that she, too, is a person of importance. In this final stage, morality is reached when a woman adopts a belief in nonviolence toward others as well as toward herself.

Adolescence

Adolescence is the period of human development that bridges the psychological gap between childhood and adulthood. Adolescence is most readily defined by obvious physical changes. Adolescents do, however, experience profound cognitive changes during this period, which in turn promote social, emotional, and moral development.

Physical Development

The comprehensive physical changes experienced by adolescent boys and girls are impossible to ignore. At the end of the childhood period, both boys and girls experience a prepubescent growth spurt. This growth spurt is typically the cause of the gangly appearance of many prepubescent children. Because children's extremities grow before their torsos do, both boys and girls can tend to appear clumsy. During this growth spurt, people may grow a dramatic three to six inches over the course of a year. Many children experience rapid weight gain during this period as well. This growth spurt is a signal that the period of sexual maturation, **puberty**, is approaching.

Beginning with puberty, an adolescent embarks on a physical journey set forth prior to birth, when their biological sex was determined in the womb. For girls, puberty results in **menarche**, which is a girl's first menstruation cycle. The normal age range for menarche is 11 to 15 years old, but some girls may begin their cycles as young as 9 years old. Before menarche, adolescent girls experience growth of pubic hair, underarm hair, and breast buds, which will develop into mature breasts throughout adolescence. They also experience a change in physical proportions; young women develop wider hips for later use carrying and giving birth to children.

In boys, sexual maturation culminates in the production of live sperm, typically between the ages of 12 and 14. Puberty begins with the development of pubic hair, body and facial hair, and the growth of the testes, scrotum, and penis. Boys' voices deepen during this period as well. Boys usually experience their first ejaculation about a year into puberty.

For both sexes, these dramatic physical changes cause an increase in sexual feelings. This is a natural part of the development process, as this increase is genetically programmed to result in reproduction—arguably the chief goal of any species. Adolescents, do not, however, acquire the decision-making ability of adults as soon as they reach physical sexual maturation. The brain also undergoes dramatic structural changes as adolescents' bodies develop.

Adolescents' frontal lobes, the part of the brain behind the forehead, experience the most change during adolescence. Teenagers experience rapid growth of gray matter—brain tissue—in the frontal lobes of the brain during early adolescence. The frontal lobes are responsible for executive functioning, which includes planning,

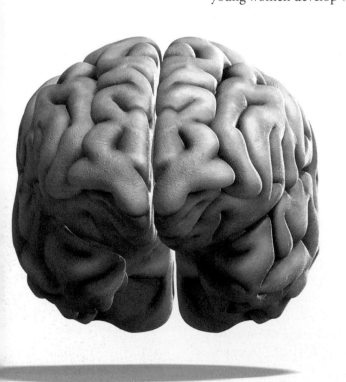

emotional regulation, and decision making. Adolescents do not develop adult decision-making skills overnight. The increase in gray matter within the frontal lobes is important, but equally significant is the increase and improvement in how teenagers use their newfound brain power. This takes time to develop and mature.

Brain researchers with the National Institutes of Mental Health have measured the maturation of gray matter by measuring the amount of white matter found in various brain structures. White matter is the name given to mature neural connections between and within brain structures. Scientists use "white" to describe these nerves because of the white myelin sheaths that cover the nerves and make them more efficient communicators of information. Neural connections that are more mature have nerves with more myelin protection than those with immature neural connections. When researchers compare magnetic-resonance imaging (MRI) scans of adolescent and adult brains, they find more white matter in the adult brains. This indicates that adults use their brains more efficiently than adolescents.

The more you use your muscles, the stronger they become. The same is true for mental strength. As adolescents use the neural connections in their brains, the myelin grows and the connections become stronger and more efficient. If adolescent brains are not challenged with planning and decision-making situations, they are likely to lose some of their adult mental potential. Regardless of how much or how well adolescents use their developing brains, a pruning process occurs in which unused neural connections are severed, presumably in order for efficient neural connections to develop and strengthen.

Adulthood

Adulthood is the developmental stage at which a human is functionally capable of sexual and emotional maturity, within which periods of growth and development continue to occur. Adulthood was a developmental period once ignored by developmental psychologists, simply because they believed that very little, if any, development occurred during the adult years. Modern psychology, however, acknowledges the many changes and developments experienced by adults through the course of their lives.

ADULTHOOD The developmental stage at which a human is functionally capable of sexual and emotional maturity, within which periods of growth and development continue to occur.

Physical Development

Once adolescents reach young adulthood, most of the physical changes associated with maturation have completed. Many people enjoy good health and physical strength throughout most of their adulthood. Most choose to raise families during their young-adult and middle-adult years, and they tend to have the physical strength and energy needed to keep up with their growing children during this time.

Adults may begin to notice declines in their physical abilities as early as their thirties. Depending on individual lifestyles, for example, some adults may notice skin damaged by excessive sun exposure during childhood and adolescence. Overall, adults can affect their physical appearances and abilities in positive ways during adulthood by maintaining healthy diets and lifestyles. Physical changes during this period are quite minimal compared to those of childhood and adolescence.

Midlife

Focusing psychiatric research on the midlife period is a relatively new trend. Researcher Daniel Levinson identified several transitional periods within the various eras of adulthood. Levinson found that a transition takes place during the ages of 40 to 45, during which adults move out of the energy and passion of younger adulthood into middle adulthood, which lasts from ages 45 to 60. During this period, adults begin to mentor adolescent and young adult children who will soon become full-fledged adults. The lives of most adults during this period are likely to revolve around their families or significant others and around their occupations.

Depending on how satisfied adults are with their life choices, some may experience difficulties at midlife. According to Levinson, adults periodically progress through transition phases in which they reevaluate their previous choices and possibly make changes to their current life goals and situations. Such transitional periods may be dramatic, reflecting a stereotypical "midlife crisis" often portrayed in popular culture. Transitions are, however, more likely to be incorporated into the normal fabric of life, prompting people to make adjustments to their beliefs, activities, and relationships to create coherence with their ever-developing personalities.

The study of adult development is relatively new in comparison to other developmental areas, but Levinson and others believe that adults do experience significant change from their early adult years through late adulthood and death. Levinson has argued for a collaborative approach that examines these developments through the eyes of the biological sciences, psychology, social science, and the humanities.

The World of Work

Work and career are two of the most important parts of an adult's life. Most adults spend more time working than performing any other task (other than sleeping). Many adults want to experience challenges and successes in their work lives, as these experiences can bring about feelings of efficacy and pride. Work–life balance can be a challenge for adults, as work demands can interfere with family commitments.

Late Adulthood

The phase of late adulthood begins around age 65, when many people retire from work. At this age, most adults have seen their children grow up and become fully functioning adults themselves. Adults in this phase of life can easily remain active and engaged in their communities.

Physical and Mental Changes

Older adults are likely to experience more physical difficulties than younger people. However, researchers have confirmed that the old adage "Use it or lose it" is absolutely true in terms of physical strength. It seems that declines in physical abilities come from a lack of use rather than a breaking down of physical abilities. A few areas are inevitably affected by age: hearing, vision, and sexual function.

Many older adults experience hearing loss. As people age, their abilities to hear higher-pitched noises and voices decrease. Vision is affected by age as well. As the lens of the eye ages, it becomes less flexible and yellows. The results of these changes include a diminished ability to distinguish between blue and green hues. Older adults sometimes experience diminished night vision as a result of their lenses' decreased flexibility.

Sexual function changes in late adulthood. Though older adults still enjoy sex, they become less likely to procreate as they age. Around age 50, women experience **menopause**, a period of physical transition which is marked by the end of the menstrual cycle. Although their period of transition is somewhat less dramatic, men also experience a decrease in sperm development and seminal fluid. Despite these physical changes, men and women continue to enjoy sexual activity throughout late adulthood. Sex has the potential to strengthen couples' emotional bonds and can serve as a form of aerobic exercise, both of which improve health in late adulthood.

MENOPAUSE The period of transition during which a woman's menstrual cycle stops.

Mental changes in older adults demonstrate an interesting mix of outcomes. Many older adults experience some memory loss in addition to a slowing of mental processing speeds. On the other hand, older adults' intelligence is not diminished by age. When older adults participate often in engaging intellectual and social activities, they are more likely to maintain or improve their mental acuity over time.

The Social World in Late Adulthood

Social connections and relationships can be extremely rewarding at this stage of human development. By the time many people have reached later adulthood, they have discarded relationships that mean little to them and have maintained only the relationships that bring them satisfaction and happiness. Researcher Laura Carstensen developed the socioemotional selectivity theory, which argues that people become more discriminating about their social relationships as they age. Older adults may have fewer friends, but the friends they do have help them meet their emotional and social needs.

Bernice Neugarten

Bernice Neugarten, who was one of psychology's preeminent authorities on adult development until her death in 2001, studied at the University of Chicago and taught the nation's first course on adult development and aging at the school for more than 30 years. She was a vigorous opponent of ageism, the practice of discriminating against older people, and insisted that social services offered to seniors be based on economic resources rather than on age alone. Her advocacy for older adulthood helped shape legislative changes to the U.S. Social Security system and brought consideration for older adults and their varying needs into the national conversation.

Her pioneering work into the personality and social development of adults changed the way psychologists view the adult years. Neugarten challenged social myths about older adults, including proving that the commonly held beliefs that empty nesters were miserable without their children and that menopausal women were devastated by the "change of life" were not true for millions of older people. Her concept of social clocks challenged the conventional concept of biological clocks for influencing behavior, postulating that older adults judge whether they were socially "on time" or "off time" based on cultural cues about age-appropriate behaviors. Neugarten recognized and defended the diversity present in adult life, honoring the process of aging and promoting continued human development across the lifespan.

PSYCHOLOGY & CAREERS: THE EDUCATOR'S ROLE IN STUDENTS' PSYCHOLOGICAL DEVELOPMENT

Educators, whether they are teachers, counselors, or administrators, have the potential to affect students' psychological development. Educators at different levels of academia can affect their student populations in different ways. The way a preschool teacher influences a student's development, for example, will probably be different from the way a college counselor influences a high school student's development.

The role of a teacher is to assist students as they develop a body of knowledge within a particular field of study. Educators are often subject-matter experts, but they can also serve as mentors for students at different points in their lives. Teachers can use their content area as a vehicle to expose students to life skills they may not experience outside the classroom. Through various projects, discussions, and activities, teachers can expose students to new perspectives on a variety of topics, thereby widening their academic and social horizons.

Teachers can also encourage students to engage in moral reasoning activities by presenting them with dilemmas faced by past leaders. Student groups can participate in discussions and debates about how different cultures might approach the same challenges, whether those challenges arise in the discipline of social studies, science, or literature.

Other educators serve students as counselors. School counselors guide and support students through their educational experiences in elementary, middle, and high school. They assist students with issues they may be having in the classroom or on school property, perhaps difficulties with a teacher or another student. They also assist students in selecting a course of study that is appropriate for students' academic levels and academic goals.

At the same time, school counselors are often trained to help school personnel deal with the challenges of students with various special needs. Counselors may also be called upon to help the members of a school community address the larger issues that may influence day-to-day life in a school. Counselors must understand issues of identity development in their students, including race and gender issues. They must also be aware of the potential power of social hierarchies within their schools, whether such influence arises from gangs or cliques or sports teams. Over time, counselors become experts on their schools' cultures and work with individual students as well as the larger school community to make their school environments safe, healthy, and appropriately challenging for each member.

Although many administrators do not play a direct role in day-to-day interactions with students, they use their educational expertise to shape student experiences throughout the school year. They are the designers of policy and practice within schools, often choosing or even developing elements of the curriculum with the assistance of teachers. Administrators must also enforce school policy, and at times such enforcement brings them face to face with an opportunity to shape the psychological development of a student or group of students. When an administrator must set consequences for a violation of school policy, for example, he or she is demonstrating the importance of agreeing to the social contract at work in the school—a social contract of which students are typically well aware.

Because students spend a great deal of their childhood and adolescence working and playing within a school community, the influence of an educator's role cannot be overlooked. It is an educator's job to help provide a safe, challenging, and socially engaged school community, one in which students can develop their gifts and personalities freely.

Death and Dying

In the 1960s, psychiatrist Elisabeth Kübler-Ross began to investigate how people cope with the knowledge of their own death. Working with terminally ill patients, she developed a stage theory to explain this coping process. Her theory's stages included denial, anger, bargaining, depression, and acceptance. Because studying the intellectual and emotional process of dying is difficult, and because her research was based on her clinical impressions rather than on empirical methods, some consider Kübler-Ross's theory to be little more than a theory. Some bias is inherent because her theories are primarily narrative-based, but Kübler-Ross's studies are complemented by other studies.

Researcher Charles Corr responded to the Kübler-Ross theory by recognizing the highly individualized experience of dying. He notes that people develop, reject, and redevelop coping strategies throughout the end-of-life process and that caregivers must be alert and open to these changes in their patients. Corr also stresses that the dying must be empowered to make as many decisions as possible, and that even the dying are still living people coping with great stress.

During a series of interviews with dying people, psychologist Debbie Messer Zlatin found a pattern of what she called "illness-understandings" among their stories. These understandings seem to arise out of specific life themes, or the ways that the people explained their experiences of dying. Zlatin realized that these themes could be used to improve and further personalize the care that dying patients receive from caregivers. She also noted that using life themes as a touch point for communicating with dying persons had the potential to improve interactions between doctors and patients and improve patients' overall satisfaction with medical care.

SUMMARY

The nature versus nurture debate remains a powerful theme in developmental psychology. Psychologists continue to debate this issue and the motivations for human behavior. Are the motivations based in human biology, or are they based in how humans experience their environments?

As genetic researchers discover more about the human genome, the links between genetic influences and human behavior are becoming clearer. What remains unclear is the extent to which genes *cause* human behaviors. Researchers are aware of the limitations of their investigation into the biological basis of behavior.

Physical development can influence other ways that humans develop, particularly during the adolescent years. The rapid physical changes of adolescence trigger a variety of emotional responses, ranging from excitement about growing into adulthood to feeling like a stranger in one's own skin. Similar comparisons can be drawn during older adulthood, when the body may begin to slow down yet the mind remains active and sharp. Such challenges demonstrate how biological and emotional experiences can interact.

The theories of Erikson and Piaget are considered foundational theories of psychology. Their influence on later psychologists remains profound within the world of psychological research. Piaget's theory of cognitive development attempts to explain how the human mind develops from infancy through young adulthood. Erikson's social-emotional stages of development examine a set of eight crises experienced during different phases of life. Each crisis must be successfully resolved in order for a person to continue to successfully move through the remaining stages. Erikson was one of the first psychologists to place value on the social-emotional development of adults.

Kohlberg's stages of moral development explore how people make moral choices throughout their lives. He noted that most people begin with an external motivation for moral behavior and progress to internally motivated reasoning for moral behavior as they gain life experience with increased age.

REFERENCES

American Pregnancy Association. (2008, October). Using illegal street drugs during pregnancy. Retrieved from http://www.americanpregnancy.org/pregnancyhealth/illegaldrugs.html

Bretherton, I. (1992). The origins of attachment theory: John Bowlby and Mary Ainsworth. *Developmental Psychology, 28,* 759-775. Retrieved from http://www.psychology.sunysb.edu/attachment/online/inge_origins.pdf

Gerrig, R. J., & Zimbardo, P. G. (2009). *Psychology and life*. Boston, MA: Pearson.

Gilligan's *In a Different Voice*. (n.d.). Retrieved from http://www.stolaf.edu/people/huff/classes/handbook/Gilligan.html

Green, M., & Piel, J. A. (2002). *Theories of human development: A comparative approach*. Boston, MA: Allyn & Bacon.

Human Genome Project. (2008, September 16). Behavioral genetics. Retrieved from http://www.ornl.gov/sci/techresources/Human_Genome/elsi/behavior.shtml

Human Genome Project. (2010, December 31). Human genome project information. Retrieved from http://www.ornl.gov/sci/techresources/Human_Genome/home.shtml

Levinson, D. (1986). A conception of adult development. *The American Psychologist 41*(3), 3–13. Retrieved from http://www.imamu.edu.sa/topics/IT/IT%206/A%20Conception%20of%20Adult%20Development.pdf

Messer Zlatin, D. (1995). Life themes: A method to understand terminal illness. *OMEGA-Journal of Death and Dying, 3*(3), 189–206.
Retrieved from http://baywood.metapress.com/app/home/contribution.
asp?referrer=parent&backto=issue,2,5;journal,123,245;linkingpublicationresults, 1:300329,1

National Institutes of Mental Health. (2010, September 10). Teenage brain: A work in progress (Fact sheet). Retrieved from http://www.nimh.nih.gov/health/publications/teenage-brain-a-work-in-progress-fact-sheet/index.shtml

Palo Alto Medical Foundation. (2011). Puberty—Changes for females. Retrieved from http://www.pamf.org/teen/health/puberty/girlschanges.html

Palo Alto Medical Foundation. (2011). Puberty—Changes for males. Retrieved from http://www.pamf.org/teen/health/puberty/girlschanges.html

Perring, C. (n.d.). Kübler-Ross and other approaches. Retrieved from http://www.uky.edu/~cperring/kr.htm

Stevens, R. (2008). *Erik Erikson: Shaper of identity.* New York: Palgrave Macmillan.

Cognition, Memory, and Language

"Every man's memory is his private literature."

—Aldous Huxley

INTELLIGENCE

What is intelligence? Is there one single aspect of intelligence, or do people have multiple intelligences? The answers to these questions might rely on cultural norms and need. If you ask a New Yorker, intelligence might include the ability to successfully navigate the subway system—which is not something that is of paramount importance to a villager in rural China. A major league pitcher who can instantly select and deliver the best pitch to strike out a batter—seemingly a test of intelligence—might have trouble completing a standardized test. Does his prowess on the field really show intelligence, and can that ability be measured in a standardized test? To what extent is his ability the result of the environment in which he developed his skills, and to what extent is it pure biological ability?

INTELLIGENCE A person's capacity to understand, reason, and adapt to the world based on cultural norms.

These questions give rise to various theories and tests on intelligence. In psychology, **intelligence** is a person's capacity to understand, reason, and adapt to the world based on cultural norms.

Given the cultural elements of intelligence, it can be challenging to make uniform assessments of it. Over the years, numerous intelligence tests have been developed to identify who has normal intelligence and who has higher and lower intelligence—and what "normal" means in this context. Scores on intelligence tests have been used to determine cognitive or learning impairment, to place students in college, and to help select vocational and educational goals.

French psychologist Alfred Binet (1857–1911) developed one of the first intelligence tests based on age and projected ability for each age group. Binet assigned mental ages as numerical scores based on how many questions a person got right on the test. Using a mental age worked when comparing children of similar ages, but it did not provide an accurate assessment when comparing the intelligence across different ages. In children, intelligence scoring ranges dramatically from year to year—an unsurprising finding, considering the rapid developments and new experiences that children undergo as they age. A 21-year-old adult scoring at the level of a 19-year-old is therefore not comparable to a 5-year-old child scoring as a 2-year-old. A 5-year-old with a mental age of 2 would have far more limited intelligence than a 21-year-old with a mental age of 19.

The solution to the limitations of the mental age test was to combine mental age and chronological age in a formula that creates an intelligence quotient, or IQ score. The original formula divided the mental age (MA) by the chronological age (CA) and multiplied that total by 100—the IQ score assigned to a person whose chronological and mental ages are equal. The formula looks like this:

$$\text{IQ score} = \text{MA} \div \text{CA} \times 100$$

If mental age exceeds chronological age, the IQ is over 100. If mental age is less than chronological age, the IQ is less than 100.

KEY CONCEPTS

1. Intelligence is a person's capacity to understand, reason, and adapt to the world based upon cultural norms. See page 119.

2. Various theories of intelligence examine different types of intelligence, such as creative, analytical, emotional, or logical intelligence. See page 121.

3. New studies of the brain, genetics, and societal interactions clarify how memories are formed and how learning occurs. See page 126.

4. Genetic predisposition, cultural environment, or some combination of both affect language acquisition and development. See page 138.

5. Theorists Cattell, Gardner, and Sternberg examined the complex nature of intelligence. See page 121.

While an average IQ score is still 100, the method of determining IQ has changed. Statistics play a larger part, and deviation IQ scores are now the standard. A score of 100 is assigned based on the average test score for all people of the same age who take the test. For example, if the average test score is 85, that test score is assigned an IQ of 100. Students who score higher or lower are scored based on the differences, or deviations, between their score and the average score.

The collection of resulting IQ scores normally forms a bell-shaped curve on a graph, with a peak somewhere between 85 and 115 that drops and tapers off as scores fall further from the average. The average IQ scores cluster around the 100 mark on either side. This is called a **bell curve**, which is a graph that represents the normal distribution of data.

BELL CURVE A graph that represents the normal distribution of data.

Binet's original test has been revised many times to meet changing needs and is now called the Stanford–Binet Intelligence Scale, Fifth Edition (SB5). Test components are now more age-specific. The test is administered orally and has progressive levels of difficulty with each subsequent question. Once the test-taker is no longer able to answer questions correctly, the test is over. The mental age has been established and strengths and weaknesses have been identified.

David Wechsler devised a different approach to intelligence tests in his Wechsler Adult Intelligence Scale—III (WAIS-III) and Wechsler Intelligence Scale for Children—IV (WISC-IV). The Wechsler scales have two parts: a verbal scale and a performance scale.

MENTAL RETARDATION A condition whose diagnosis is based on a combination of low test scores and a person's inability to adapt to and understand his or her living environment.

The Binet and Wechsler scales are the most commonly administered individual tests available today. Other intelligence tests can be administered to groups of test-takers at the same time by a single test administrator. These tests are designed as standard written tests, much like the standardized state tests children take in school.

Mental Retardation

The lower end of the bell curve includes people whose performance on the intelligence assessment was below average. People with intelligence scores below 70 will be diagnosed as having **mental retardation** (MR) if they also exhibit a limited ability to adapt to and understand their environment. The degree of MR depends upon the approximate intelligence score. MR is diagnosed in about 1 percent of the population, with a

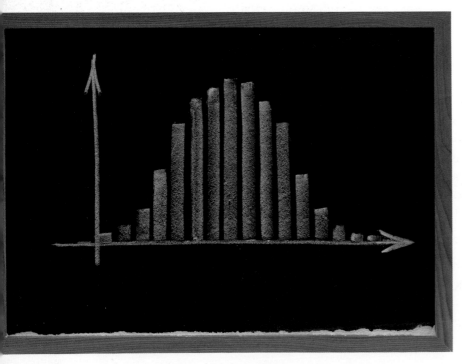

50 percent higher prevalence among males. Two identifiable physical causes of MR are Down syndrome and fetal alcohol syndrome.

Down syndrome is a genetic condition. People with Down, which is also known as trisomy 21, have an extra chromosome—47 instead of the usual 46. The extra chromosome, a copy of chromosome 21, causes complications in development.

Fetal alcohol syndrome (FAS) can occur in children whose mothers drink alcohol during their pregnancy. It is unclear how much alcohol triggers FAS; some believe that even a single binge drinking episode could have severe consequences. FAS has become the leading cause of mental retardation in the United States today, according to a 2000 report by researcher Chrysanthy Ikonomidou and colleagues.

The families and support system of a patient with MR must adjust their lifestyles to accommodate the needs and level of ability of the patient. Some people with MR live in supportive group-home environments and some live with their families. Many people with MR work or volunteer as well.

DOWN SYNDROME An inherited condition caused when an extra chromosome 21 is transmitted during conception.

FETAL ALCOHOL SYNDROME (FAS) An induced form of mental retardation that may occur when pregnant women drink during pregnancy.

Giftedness

On the other side of the bell curve is giftedness. People who score higher than 115 on an IQ test are on the gifted side of the curve. As scores increase, people are labeled as *gifted* or *gifted and talented*. These people show a strong aptitude for the material tested in IQ assessments. The federal government defines **gifted and talented** children as being capable of high performance in general intellectual ability, specific academic aptitude, creative or productive thinking, leadership ability, or visual and performing arts.

GIFTED AND TALENTED Children who are capable of high performance in general intellectual ability, specific academic aptitude, creative or productive thinking, leadership ability, or visual and performing arts.

Some people are quick to assume that gifted and talented children, with their accelerated learning capacity, may be maladjusted. In an effort to determine the extent of maladjustment in giftedness, in California in 1921 psychologist Lewis Terman began studying 1,500 school children with IQ scores higher than 135. These children were revisited at regular intervals over the next 70 years. The researchers found that most of the children went on to achieve graduate degrees and enter professions that require a high level of responsibility, including medicine, law, academia, and science.

Theories of Intelligence

Three major researchers who contributed theories of intelligence are Howard Gardner, Robert Sternberg, and Raymond Cattell. Their theories are outlined in Figure 7.1 and discussed in-depth in the following paragraphs.

THEORY	THEORIST	EXPLANATION OF THE THEORY
Multiple intelligences	Howard Gardner	Includes nine types of intelligence: linguistic, logical–mathematical, spatial, musical, bodily–kinesthetic, interpersonal, intrapersonal, naturalistic, and existential.
Triarchic theory of intelligence	Robert Sternberg	Categorizes intelligence into analytical, creative, and practical.
Trait theory	Raymond Cattell	Describes 171 personality traits that can be categorized into 16 traits that are the source of all human personality.
Wechsler theory of intelligence	David Wechsler	Intelligence is defined as performance based—that is, the ability to adapt and solve problems relative to the environment. Wechsler developed IQ tests for adults and children.
Stanford-Binet IQ test	Alfred Binet and Lewis Terman (from Stanford)	Binet defined intelligence as the ability to judge, reason, and comprehend. Later Lewis Terman revised Binet's IQ test, which is now known as the Stanford–Binet Intelligence Scale.

FIGURE 7.1 Theories of Intelligence

Howard Gardner's Theory of Multiple Intelligences

Howard Gardner theorized that intelligence consisted of nine types. **Gardner's multiple intelligences** are the following:

- Linguistic: the ability to speak and write language(s), including telling stories, memorizing, and recalling and recounting events
- Logical–mathematical: the ability to think logically and abstractly, reason, and perform mathematical equations
- Spatial: the ability to visualize and imagine, read maps, mentally manipulate objects, and recognize concepts like distance
- Musical: the ability to understand and appreciate tone, rhythm, and timbre
- Bodily–kinesthetic: the ability to control oneself physically and exhibit fine motor skills
- Interpersonal: the ability to interact well with and relate to others
- Intrapersonal: the ability to reflect on oneself
- Naturalistic: the ability to identify patterns and relationships in nature
- Existential: the ability to understand and try to answer deep questions

Gardner's theory gives a large range of intelligences, and it is difficult to create a standardized set of assessment criteria for some of them. For example, how can intrapersonal intelligence or existential intelligence be measured?

Robert Sternberg

Robert Sternberg also presented a theory of multiple intelligences, but described three intelligences—analytical, creative, and practical—rather than nine in his **triarchic theory of intelligence**:

- Analytical intelligence: normally assessed in intelligence and standardized tests, with questions that have specific predetermined answers
- Creative intelligence: addresses how well a person reacts and adapts to novel situations and ideas
- Practical intelligence: refers to an ability to think through and complete everyday tasks; often applied to problems that are ill-defined, with more than one possible solution

GARDNER'S MULTIPLE INTELLIGENCES A theory that there are nine types of intelligences, including linguistic, logical–mathematical, spatial, musical, bodily–kinesthetic, interpersonal, intrapersonal, naturalistic, and existential.

TRIARCHIC THEORY OF INTELLIGENCE A theory that people have three types of intelligence—analytical, creative, and practical.

WHAT IS YOUR INTELLIGENCE TYPE?

A variety of intelligence surveys can give you a sense of your intelligence strengths. Different intelligence strengths often line up with a certain learning style. For example, if you are strong in linguistic intelligence, you are more likely to feel most compatible with a visual learning style. If, on the other hand, you rate higher in bodily–kinesthetic intelligence, you are probably a tactile/kinesthetic learner. There are no absolutes in matching learning style to intelligence type, because everyone learns differently. Someone who rates high in spatial intelligence, for example, may learn best by hearing a lesson (auditory learning).

Emotional Intelligence and Practical Intelligence

Sternberg's practical intelligence theory may explain why many upper-level managers (and even a few U.S. presidents) with only average intelligence scores go on to become highly successful in leadership positions. Practical intelligence focuses not on general knowledge but on a person's ability to assess and work out solutions to both simple and complex problems. Practical intelligence tests are often designed to identify top management prospects, testing (among other things) an ability to motivate others, solve problems, and document events. These tests place emphasis on navigating daily activities and unexpected issues that come up in life.

Emotional intelligence pertains to skills in assessing, expressing, and regulating emotions. It is the ability to recognize and categorize the feelings and emotions of others based on behaviors and other outward symptoms. Emotional intelligence gives rise to empathy, which is the ability to recognize and vicariously experience others' feelings. Emotional intelligence is not easily measured, and where and how it should be taught is also the subject of debate. Concern for and awareness of others, for example, is often modeled in the home, rather than in schools. A primary factor in emotional intelligence is cultural sensitivity.

EMOTIONAL INTELLIGENCE
The ability to recognize and categorize the feelings and emotions of others based on behaviors and other outward symptoms.

Cattell's Theory

Psychologist Raymond Cattell rated a large sample of people for 171 personality traits. Then, using factor analysis, he identified related traits and narrowed his list to 16 key personality traits. Cattell believed that the following 16 traits are the source of all human personality:

- Abstractedness
- Apprehension
- Dominance
- Emotional stability
- Liveliness
- Openness to change
- Perfectionism
- Privateness

- Reasoning
- Rule-consciousness
- Self-reliance
- Sensitivity
- Social boldness
- Tension
- Vigilance
- Warmth

Some of these traits are common, while others are rare. The traits can be divided into three domains: temperament (how a person behaves), motivation, and ability. Cattell also identified second-order traits, which include extraversion/introversion and anxiety. Dynamic traits include attitudes about a particular action or in response to a situation. Other dynamic traits are innate drives, such as sex, hunger, and companionship. Are these personality traits inherited? Cattell's research indicated that the ability to adapt to new material is very likely inherited, as is intelligence.

CREATIVITY The ability to create new and innovative ideas without help.

VERTICAL THINKING The thought process used in school for processing facts and thinking within the bounds of set criteria.

LATERAL THINKING Thinking in a way that does not follow conventional patterns and normal methods.

CREATIVITY AND IMAGINATION

Creativity, the ability to create new and innovative ideas without help, seems at first glance to be intertwined with intelligence. What makes a person creative? Do creative people think differently? Some of history's greatest innovators, such as Albert Einstein, Stephen Hawking, and Andy Warhol, were creative people.

Some researchers propose that creativity is based in a difference in thinking. **Vertical thinking** is the thought process used in school for processing facts and thinking within the bounds of set criteria. **Lateral thinking,** on the other hand, is thinking in a manner that does not follow conventional patterns and normal methods. Lateral thinking may be more conducive to creativity.

The Torrance Test of Creative Thinking (TTCT) and similar tests are widely used in schools as part of the kindergarten testing process, and they continue throughout childhood and adulthood. For example, a test may ask a preschooler to draw family members. If the people a child draws are more detailed than simple stick figures, that child may be assessed as having more advanced creative thought processes.

Sternberg proposed six interrelated resources that produce creativity: intellectual abilities, knowledge, styles of thinking, personality, motivation, and environment. Everyone has some degree of each of the six resources. Intellectual abilities include the ability to recognize relevance and value, the ability to convince others of this relevance and value, and the ability to see problems outside the bounds of conventional thinking. Knowledge in creativity is the ability to use prior knowledge to help adjust to new and innovative thoughts without becoming entrenched in routine.

Styles of thinking refer to the way a person processes information and the way intelligence and cognition are used to respond to that information. For example, legislative-style thinkers like to think and decide in new ways and are likely to exhibit creativity in thought. In contrast, hierarchical thinkers recognize which questions are important and which are not.

Personality and creativity combine through people's willingness to overcome obstacles or take risks and the belief that they can do what they set out to do. In addition to confidence in their success, people must have motivation to drive the creative push for success. An environment that supports and rewards creative ideas is better for creative thinkers than an uncreative environment is. Many creative thinkers face circumstances that block creativity and must decide whether to persevere through unfavorable forces or to allow the environment they are in to limit their work. Thus, reasoning and decision-making are part of the creative process.

Deductive and Inductive Reasoning: Divergent Thinking

Reasoning processes are used to evaluate information and to reach a conclusion. **Deductive reasoning** looks for a specific conclusion based on general information. When people reason using a deductive approach, they take general information and narrow it down to the specific.

DEDUCTIVE REASONING
The use of general information and observations as a basis for drawing a more specific conclusion.

This reasoning process can get you into trouble if you make a conclusion based on biased or faulty information. For example, if you begin with a premise that only women can bear children and then proceed to determine that since women bear children, all women are mothers, you reach an inaccurate conclusion. However, if you begin with the same premise—that only women can bear children—and conclude that men cannot bear children, you have an accurate conclusion.

Likewise, if you have a bag of colored candies and pull out six green candies in a row, you might conclude that the bag contains only green candies. If there are only six candies in the bag, that is an accurate conclusion, but if there are more and the bag is supposed to include a mix of colors, your deductive reasoning may not be valid.

Deductive reasoning helps create shortcuts in thought processes based on information you are receiving and what you

already know. If you are traveling in a city far from home and see a billboard for a fast-food restaurant you have never visited before, you might reason that since most fast-food restaurants you go to have hamburgers on their menus, this one will too. You are making that assumption based on what you know about restaurants and what you have personally experienced. However, if you concluded that since your favorite fast-food restaurant serves its hamburgers with sweet potato fries, this one must have sweet potato fries, too, you might be mistaken. Thus, deductive reasoning can be valid or invalid depending on the information used and the conclusions reached.

INDUCTIVE REASONING
The use of specific information and observations to infer a more general principle.

With **inductive reasoning**, you take a specific piece of information and work outward to a more general conclusion. Think about the fast-food restaurant again using inductive reasoning. While you are standing in line at the restaurant, you watch the clerks as they wait on the customers. Clerk A has a frown on her face, Clerk B looks bored, and Clerk C is throwing the food into bags as quickly as possible. You might deduce from your observations that the hamburger restaurant is not a nice place to work.

In this example, you used specific pieces of information (your observations) to infer a general principle (the fast-food restaurant is not a nice place to work). As with deductive reasoning, this might or might not be correct.

EXPLORE A CREATIVITY TEST

Indiana University's website (www.indiana.edu) features a collection of various types of creativity tests, including divergent thinking tests (the Torrance Test of Creative Thinking, Guilford's Alternative Uses Task), convergent thinking tests, artistic assessments, and self-assessments, among other selections. Enter "Indiana University" "creativity test" into a search engine and give one of the tests a try.

PSYCHOLOGY & CAREERS: VISUAL TALENT IN A FASHION DESIGN CAREER

What are you wearing today? Does each piece of your ensemble match? Is your ensemble bold or sensible? Can *you* mix plaids and stripes and still come up with a look that is pleasing to the eye?

Anna Sui took center stage in the fashion world in 1991 when she introduced a bold and feminine style at her first runway show. She studied at New York's Parsons The New School for Design and then worked as an assistant to other designers while developing her own line. Sui combines various textures, prints, and colors to create designs that work together, and her business has managed to stay afloat even in difficult economic times. Sui has noted that while her visual design has long created excitement about her line, her practical intelligence plays a part in her business success as well—even an avant-garde designer must work within the boundaries of what her suppliers can provide, when they can provide it, and whether her selections are within her budget.

MEMORY

Imagine that you walk to work on the same route each day. One sunny Thursday on your way to the office, you find yourself in the middle of a robbery at a corner store. A man dressed in black runs out of the shop with something in his hand, and you can hear people inside the store screaming about a gun. The man in black runs right past you.

The police are on the scene in moments. After a few minutes, a police officer interviews you. When the officer asks you to recount what you saw, you suddenly draw a blank and are unable to think of anything. You sit on the curb for a few minutes and think carefully about what you saw, and after doing so, you are able to give the police more information: the suspect was a man, dressed in black, who was carrying a gun. He jumped into a red car parked across the street. He was tall and smelled of cigarette smoke.

Then the officer asks you a few specific questions: Was the suspect wearing a jacket? Did he have any facial hair? You are unable to remember either detail. Next, you are asked whether there were any other passersby on the street. You are unable to remember anyone else—until suddenly you remember seeing a woman in purple pants at the bus stop on the corner.

Why do you remember some details of the event more clearly than others? How accurate do you think these descriptions really are of what actually happened?

The Biology of Memory

Advanced brain scanning techniques revealed that certain areas and structures in the brain specialize in certain memory functions. The **limbic system,** which includes the **hippocampus** and the amygdala, is the main area of the brain involved in memory. The hippocampus acts as the neurological message system, passing along information for long-term storage in the cerebral cortex. Different areas of the hippocampus are thought to be involved in different activities, such as consolidation of spatial memories.

The **amygdala** is a part of the brain associated with memories involving emotion. It provides a means of retrieval by pairing emotion in an event with the memory of the event. For example, if you receive a special award on your graduation day, you are likely to remember your graduation as a happy event. Future mention of graduations will probably bring to mind feelings of happiness. Although this example is a happy one, the amygdala is also implicated in fear responses and natural fight-or-flight reflexes. Unhappy, scary, or dangerous events will present with stronger memories and reactions.

While the hippocampus and amygdala play active roles in the memory process, the brain is an interactive organ. Some areas might specialize more highly in a given function, but no memory function takes place in a single area of the brain.

LIMBIC SYSTEM The parts of the brain that control emotions; the system includes the amygdala, hypothalamus, hippocampus, and pituitary gland.

HIPPOCAMPUS Part of the limbic system that helps transfer short-term memory to long-term memory.

AMYGDALA Part of the brain that pairs emotion and memory; it is part of the limbic system.

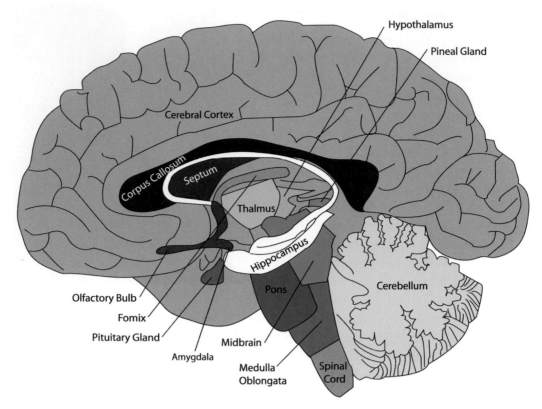

FIGURE 7.2 Human Brain

Memory function is distributed throughout the brain and relayed through neural networks.

Memory Systems

Memory is a complex process that entails more than simply looking at something and later remembering what you saw. Memory comprises different systems that are in charge of different types of memories. Some memories are automatically recalled, while others need a little more help. Memories are more easily recalled when the environmental context is the same during encoding and retrieval. This means that if you study in a classroom setting, you are more likely to recall the information in a classroomlike setting. This might be due to cues in the environment or to the similarity of circumstances during encoding and retrieval.

Explicit versus Implicit Memories

Explicit and implicit memories are part of the long-term memory system. **Explicit memories** are purposely pulled from long-term storage and are specific in nature. Explicit memory is what you use to remember details such as a relative's birthday or state capitals. You might not know when or where you first learned the information, but it is stored away and must be consciously recalled in order to bring it to mind.

  Implicit memories are brought to mind automatically without intentional, conscious recall. Implicit memory is more automatic than explicit memory—the classic example of explicit memory is never forgetting how to ride a bike. Once you have learned something with implicit memory, your responses come without thinking. There is no conscious recall. Figure 7.3 gives some examples of explicit and implicit memory.

TASKS REQUIRING EXPLICIT MEMORY	TASKS REQUIRING IMPLICIT MEMORY
Recalling a birth date	Riding a bicycle
Solving a mathematical equation	Reciting the alphabet
Identifying the current president	Tying shoes
Writing a term paper	Singing part of a familiar song

FIGURE 7.3 Explicit and Implicit Memory

Retrospective versus Prospective Memory

Retrospective memory is based on information that has already been presented. The memory processes discussed to this point have all been forms of retrospective memory, which means that they are based on knowledge from the past. But how many times have you attempted to remember to do something in the future? **Prospective memory** is used when you create the intention of doing something in the future, such as remembering to buy milk at the store. People have time-based and event-based prospective memories. With time-based memories, you must remember to do something within a certain period of time, or at a certain time, such as going to an upcoming doctor's appointment. With retrospective memory, recall is triggered by a request or need for the information.

Prospective memory, on the other hand, is self-initiated. If you forget to buy milk and you do not have a back-up plan to help you remember what you needed (retrospective memory), you will likely forget that you need to get it. The prospective memory process actually has a retrospective element, as you must cue yourself— remembering to remember the upcoming issue.

RETROSPECTIVE MEMORY Memories based on information that has already been presented.

PROSPECTIVE MEMORY The system of memory with which one creates the intention of doing something in the future.

Memory Processes

Memory processing occurs based on what you experience and how you perceive these experiences. People process new information into their memory systems through the way they understand what they process. Experiences and biological systems contribute to memory as people encode, store, and retrieve.

Encoding

Encoding is the initial process of recording and identifying information. The encoding process determines how information is remembered as it is acquired. Perception and understanding play a role in encoding. People encode information and get it ready for storage based on what they believe the information to mean. Thus, encoding is based on what you *think* exists rather than what might actually exist. In the story at the beginning of this section, in which you witnessed a robbery, you did not actually see a gun in the offender's hand—you saw *something* in the man in black's hand, but a gun seemed to make sense, so you *believed* you saw a gun.

Additionally, processing time has a bearing on how well people store information. When one spends a great deal of time trying to process information, the likelihood increases that information will be lost. More time spent processing means more time for other information to crowd in, waiting to be processed—thus causing attention to switch from one message to the other.

ENCODING The initial process of recording and identifying information.

Storage

Once information is encoded, it is placed in storage based on how it is encoded. Memories can be stored in more than one place. Think of storage as a road map. There are a number of ways to get to a destination, and each way is a different method of storage. One method of remembering something is to pair it with something else that is easy to remember and associate with the first object. If you use this pairing memory technique by connecting something you need to remember with an event that was happening when you first learned the information, for example, you will create a memory trace between the information and the event. Storage is not an active process; rather, it is the state of the information once it has been successfully committed to memory.

Retrieval

RETRIEVAL The process of bringing up stored memories to a conscious level.

Retrieval is the process of bringing stored memories to a conscious level. The retrieval process relies greatly on the encoding process and the cues or techniques used to get the material through the encoding process. When material is encoded properly, it is often easily accessible. If no cues are given, however, it might be available but not accessible.

For example, say you remember the word *red* paired with the cue *flag*. When you then try to remember the word *red* without pairing it with the cue *flag*, you might not be able to remember it. The word *red* is available, but it might not be accessible without the cue *flag*. Available material must also be accessible in order to properly retrieve it. Thus, it is not simply a matter of attending to what you are trying to remember. It must be properly encoded to be retrievable.

This is where mnemonic devices and other memory techniques you may have learned in grammar school begin to pay off—if you paid attention. Do you recall the mnemonic device Roy G. Biv, which is a reminder of the seven conventional colors of the rainbow (red, orange, yellow, green, blue, indigo, and violet)?

Some people try to make stories up to remember certain information, while others connect one word to another to create cues and memory trails. Acronyms, for example, can help people remember a list of items. If you need to remember

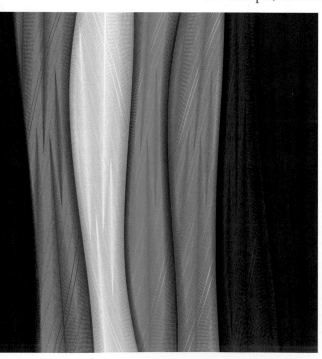

the psychological terms *memory, intelligence, kinesthetic,* and *encoding,* you can create an acronym using the first letter of each word and arranging them so they form a word that makes sense to you: MIKE. The use of a mnemonic technique provides you with cues and prompts when encoding that can be used during the retrieval process. The mnemonic (MIKE) also reminds you how many items (four) need to be remembered.

Some information may cause you to incorrectly remember what you initially encoded. Think about the example in which you witnessed the robbery. You initially had some trouble piecing together the events as they occurred when you were being interviewed by the police. You did not actually pay attention to the event until you became a part of it. Instead, you were probably thinking about what you needed to do when you got to work.

When people experience a traumatic event, they experience stress and other emotions. These factors can affect what and how they remember. They can also affect what

KEY THINKERS IN PSYCHOLOGY: ELIZABETH LOFTUS'S FALSE MEMORY AND EYEWITNESS TESTIMONY

How accurate are you when you remember and report an incident? In the past, some psychiatrists have used forms of therapy, including hypnotherapy, to help bring out repressed memories and buried "truths" from their patients. In a few cases, patients have reported circumstances so severe that criminal charges were levied. In one case, a church counselor helped a woman remember that her father, a clergyman, had repeatedly raped her during her childhood. The woman began to recall detailed memories of the rapes, including two pregnancies that resulted from them. Her father resigned his position, and the community learned of the daughter's accusation. Subsequently, the daughter underwent a medical examination that revealed the memories could not possibly be true—she was still a virgin and had never been pregnant.

Elizabeth Loftus, a psychologist who is an expert on memory, studied how influential exposure to misinformation can be in creating false memories. She believed that when people are suggestively interrogated or provided with new (and false) information about an event they have experienced, the old information may get incorrectly mixed with the new information. To prove this point, Loftus performed a study that provided participants with a list of three events from their childhood along with one event that did not happen, but was not distinguished from the others on the list. The participants were asked to write what they remembered about each event, or if they did not remember it, to simply write they did not remember the event. In the end, 25 percent of the participants wrote that they remembered the fictitious event.

people focus on during the event. For example, you were unsure that you had seen a gun in the offender's hand, but you heard people in the store shouting about a gun. That led you to assume that the object in the offender's hand was a gun. Memory is open to suggestion—for example, when a person is asked leading questions.

Stage Model of Memory

The **stage model of memory** describes the basic structure and function of memory. Richard Atkinson and Richard Shiffrin developed this model in 1968. Their model contains three separate memory systems: sensory memory, short-term memory, and long-term memory.

STAGE MODEL OF MEMORY
A structural and functional model for memory describing three separate memory systems—sensory, short-term, and long-term memory—that operate in stages.

Sensory Memory

Sensory memory, the initial storage system for memory, is the processing of brief sensations noted through one of the five senses. Each sense produces its own form of sensory memory. For example, a brief flash of lightning followed by a clap of thunder is processed through visual and auditory senses. Sensory memory that is not passed to short-term memory lasts a very brief time and is typically forgotten within a second. Sensory memory that is passed on to short-term memory is transferred based on some awareness of sensory stimuli that have some meaning.

While sensory memory is fleeting when a stimulus is removed quickly, sensory input creates strong cues for memory recall. Have you ever walked into a room and noticed a scent, one that instantly transported you back to a certain time and place? How about when you hear a song from your high school days? This sudden, involuntary access is thought to be the result of emotional memories associated with sensory input. The stronger the emotions associated with the memory, the stronger the memory.

Short-Term Memory

Short-term memory, which lies between the transient sensory memory and the extensive long-term memory, is also referred to as *working memory*. An active, working process that manages new material from sensory memory and older material from long-term memory, short-term memories are temporary. Short-term memory briefly holds information that resides in current consciousness. The information stored in short-term memory lasts about 15 to 25 seconds if it does not get transferred to long-term memory.

Duration is not the only limitation of short-term memory. Capacity is also a concern, as one's memory span—the string of information a person can recall immediately—is limited. According to researcher Klaus Oberauer, most people remember items in groups of seven. The definition of items, however, has been expanded to include the notion of chunking. Chunking allows a person to remember more digits or parts as they are broken up into chunks. The magic number of chunks one can remember still seems to be seven, but each chunk can have multiple parts. An example is ABC DEF GHI JKL MNO PQR STU—seven chunks of three letters each. Thus, the memory includes twenty-one letters, again in seven items (chunks).

Transfer of information to long-term memory occurs mainly through **rehearsal**—the repetition of the short-term information. People rehearse in two different ways. If rehearsal is merely repetition of the information, as in a phone number or combination repeated over and over until it is used, the information will likely disappear once it is used. If the information is attended to and organized in some way, it is more likely to be transferred to long-term memory. This method is called **elaborative rehearsal**.

Long-Term Memory

Many of the systems already discussed pertain to long-term memory, including the explicit, implicit, retrospective, and prospective systems. There are two types of long-term memory: episodic and semantic. **Episodic memory** pertains to memory of events that have been experienced personally. It includes facts about the experience, including who, what, when, and where. Your memory of your last birthday party is episodic—you experienced it, and your memory is based on those experiences.

Episodic memories have a high likelihood of being forgotten unless the event is connected to something else that aids recall of specific details. Do you remember everything that happened on your birthday three years ago? Probably not. You might remember some parts of the day, but if something special happened, you might remember more of it.

The information stored in episodic memory is not always useful. For example, you might remember an occasion when you walked to the library when you were nine years old. While it might be a pleasant memory, this information will probably not help you with your shopping list. Episodic memory includes sensory components and often includes an emotional element. The walk to the library might be brought to mind quickly, although the actual date on which it happened might be lost. Instead, you will be more likely to remember the weather or other sensory input gained on the walk and whether or not it was a good experience.

Semantic memory is based on knowledge or information that you know but have not personally experienced. They are not personal memories that place you in the event. For example, you may remember that Christopher Columbus sailed the ocean blue in 1492, but you were not there. Semantic memories are less likely to be forgotten than episodic memories, and are often useful memories needed to pass tests in school or navigate daily life. Semantic memories do not normally have sensory or emotional components to them because they were not personally experienced.

SEMANTIC MEMORY
Memory based on knowledge or information that you know but have not experienced.

Long-term memory does not have the time constraints of sensory and short-term memory, yet there are factors that affect people's ability to retrieve a long-term memory. Attention is a key factor in passing information from short-term to long-term memory systems. If you do not attend to what you are trying to remember, you likely will not remember it well, if at all.

Imagine sitting in class and staring out the window. Your teacher is speaking about psychoanalytic theory. You may be physically hearing her speak, but if you are thinking more about what you are going to do when you get out of class than about Freud, you will probably have trouble remembering anything the teacher said.

Attending allows you to take in the material you need to take in, but it does not commit it to long-term memory. The material must be repeated or used frequently in order to gain a stronger hold in memory. Does that mean that if you repeat your psychology terms over and over again an hour before the test, they will all sink in? Probably not. Some of them might, but it is unlikely that they will all come back to you during the test. Likewise, most of the terms will be forgotten before the end of the day, which means you did not really learn the material. Because the goal is to learn information you

will need for a final exam, for another class, and ultimately for real-world application, last-minute repetition and cramming might not be in your best interest. When people use such repetition, they often try to put too much information into their memories at one time; as a result, they rarely store all of it.

If you space out repetitions, you have a better chance of learning the material such that you will not as easily forget it by the end of the day. Spacing provides multiple encodings, which means the information is retrieved and stored multiple times. Learning is even better if the material is also rehearsed, or thought about, as it is repeated. Once the information is encoded and stored in long-term memory, it awaits retrieval, unless something happens that causes you to forget or replace the information.

Forgetting

Forgetting is a function most often associated with the process of failing to retrieve stored memories. That makes for a rather simplistic description of memory failure. Forgetting can occur in both short-term and long-term memory systems for different reasons and through different processes. Short-term memory failure differs from long-term memory issues because material is lost from short-term memory fairly quickly. In short-term memory, two main mechanisms are thought to be responsible for information loss: interference and decay.

Interference Theory

INTERFERENCE THEORY
Theory that proposes that information remains until other information comes along to crowd it out.

RETROACTIVE INTERFERENCE
When new information interferes with the ability to keep older information.

PROACTIVE INTERFERENCE
When old information gets in the way of new information.

Interference theory proposes that information remains until other information comes along to crowd it out. Imagine that you are repeating a phone number over and over again in an effort to remember it, and suddenly someone comes along and asks you what time it is. You stop repeating the phone number long enough to tell the other person what time it is, and when you return to your task, you will probably not remember the phone number.

As new information comes in and is processed, it can crowd out older information. **Retroactive interference** occurs when new information interferes with our ability to keep older information, as the phone number example shows. **Proactive interference** works in the opposite way, preventing new information from entering.

When you take your final exams, you are usually trying to remember information from more than one course. Imagine that you take an algebra exam first, and then a psychology one. When you get into your psychology exam, algebra equations keep popping into your head, preventing you from remembering the psychological theories you need to remember for the exam. The older information—the algebra—is interfering with your ability to bring up the psychology information.

Decay

The passage of time is also a factor in the process of forgetting some information.

Decay occurs as information that has been encoded is lost or because information is improperly encoded initially. Do you remember all of the formulas from every algebra class you have ever taken? If you do not use the formulas, you will likely forget them. As more time passes and new information asks for attention, it is likely you will forget how to use the formulas. The process of decay is unclear and is inconsistent from person to person; for example, many older adults can remember facts or figures from 60 years earlier. Memory loss might be caused by decay that causes the loss over time, or it may be caused by interference, as new information comes in that is more useful in your daily activities.

Amnesia

Amnesia has fed television storylines for years. Someone suffers a blow to the head and wakes up in the hospital unable to remember the events of his or her life to that point. **Amnesia** is the inability to remember previously stored information due to some form of damage to the brain. It is unclear whether the information is still stored and inaccessible or simply gone.

In most cases, the type and severity of the amnesia is determined by where and how serious the damage is in the brain. Memory loss in cases where there is damage to the brain other than Alzheimer's disease is relatively rare. One form of amnesia, however, does not seem to have anything to do with injury—infantile amnesia.

Infantile Amnesia

Infantile amnesia, which is also called childhood amnesia, is the inability to remember early events in your life. Think back to your earliest memories. Do you remember your mother changing your diapers? Do you remember looking at a mobile over your crib? It is doubtful that you can come up with memories of things that happened when you were younger than age two or three. Some people might remember some snippets, or think they remember something from when they were younger than this, but few can recall memories from before the age of three.

Why? Brain development in the first few years of life occurs at a rapid pace, and areas associated with memory may not yet be available for the encoding, storage, and retrieval process. Memory development seems to coincide with language development, perhaps indicating a connection between the two. Or perhaps memory is formed only after children can understand what they are encoding.

Anterograde Amnesia

Another form of injury-related amnesia is **anterograde amnesia**, in which people are unable to process information properly from short-term to long-term memory from the time of injury onward. They remember information already stored in long-term storage but cannot add new information to it.

Retrograde Amnesia

Retrograde amnesia is the loss of information stored in long-term memory before the event that caused the amnesia. A person with retrograde amnesia does not normally lose all memories stored, and the loss is not always permanent. Memories are often regained as time goes on and brain injuries heal. In some cases, cues from daily life help people retrieve some of the memories that were lost or inaccessible.

People can suffer from either anterograde or retrograde amnesia, or they can suffer from both. One famous case involves K.C., a man who suffered a serious closed-head injury in a motorcycle accident at age 30. As a result of the accident, K.C. developed both anterograde and retrograde amnesia. K.C.'s cognitive abilities and intelligence remained intact, along with his knowledge of many important dates and places in his life, including his birth date and the address of his parents' summer cottage.

However, K.C.'s episodic memory stopped functioning correctly. He became unable to remember personal experiences, no matter how often they had occurred. At the same time, his retrograde semantic memory remained intact. He could remember general knowledge of the world and material he learned in school before the accident. But he could not retain large amounts of semantic knowledge presented after the accident for more than a very short time.

Korsakoff Syndrome

KORSAKOFF SYNDROME The inability to form new memories, loss of memories already stored in long-term memory, inventing and repeating untrue stories, and having hallucinations.

A person who engages in heavy alcohol use over an extended period of time risks the effects of Korsakoff syndrome. **Korsakoff syndrome** is characterized by an inability to form new memories, loss of memories already stored in long-term memory, inventing and repeating untrue stories, and having hallucinations. Not all symptoms appear in all cases, and severity depends on damage done and whether or not the person stops drinking. Damage in Korsakoff syndrome is irreversible, although it is unclear whether the information is lost or inaccessible even with cues.

Memory issues might someday be eliminated; current research seeks to manipulate genes in an effort to improve learning and memory systems. One study looked for ways to increase the plasticity of the synapses used for the acquisition and retention of information. Some researchers have found that enhancements to specific receptor genes have produced positive learning and memory function. While this information signals positive steps toward limiting and ultimately eliminating some cognitive issues, such as Alzheimer's disease, it is still unclear how these manipulations affect other functions in the brain.

Alzheimer's disease is a form of dementia, which is a cognitive disorder that involves memory loss. Alzheimer's disease was first identified in 1901 by Alois Alzheimer, a German physician. It typically starts with mild memory losses, attention problems, and difficulties with communication and language. As the symptoms worsen, an individual diagnosed with Alzheimer's disease can have difficulty performing simple tasks, remembering basic activities, and even recognizing loved ones.

Alzheimer's disease is the cause of approximately 60 percent to 80 percent of all dementia cases. In 2010, the National Institutes of Health estimated that more than five million Americans had the disease. Age is a predictor, as the late-onset form of Alzheimer's disease is typically diagnosed in those 60 years of age and older.

COGNITION AND METACOGNITION

Cognition refers to a variety of mental processes, including memory, judgment, perceptions, information processing, learning, evaluating, and problem solving. Metacognitions are the sets of information that people are aware of regarding their own cognition and internal states, as well as the coping strategies that affect cognition and internal states. Metacognition has been linked to depression, anxiety, post-traumatic stress disorder, and obsessive-compulsive disorders.

The theory of metacognition was developed by Adrian Wells, who believed that the underlying basis for most psychological disturbances rests on individuals' assumptions. For example, anxiety stems from beliefs about worrying. A person's beliefs about worrying may include both positive and negative dimensions. On the positive side, people might think that worrying will help them think things through in their minds. They will then examine every angle of a situation and the threats of the situation—and end up worrying constantly. On the negative side, they might think that it is bad for them to worry about the issue. Because society has socialized people to think worrying is bad, they will then believe that worrying is harmful and cannot be controlled.

LANGUAGE AND COGNITION

Language is the cornerstone of how people think and communicate. Language consists of using spoken, written, and signed words in some combination to convey meaning and thought. Language is a way of passing down traditions, culture, and history.

Language consists of three basic structural units: phonemes, morphemes, and grammar. **Phonemes** are the basic sounds used in language. The English language has about 40 phonemes, including both vowel and consonant phonemes. When you say *but*, you utter the phoneme sounds *b*, *u*, and *t*. When you say *brush*, you utter the phoneme sounds *br*, *u*, and *sh*. In general, consonant phonemes carry more information. Consider the following sentence:

> *Tha cunsenents ure tha sime in thes suntance, but meny of tha vuwals ure wrung.*

You are probably able to read the sentence, even though many of the vowels were incorrect.

The second structural unit is the morpheme. A **morpheme** is the smallest unit of language that conveys meaning. In the English language, morphemes are also phonemes. The letter/word *I* is both a unit of sound and a basic unit of meaning. Some morphemes are words, like *dog*. Other morphemes are only parts of words, including suffixes and prefixes. The word *hunted*, for example, has *hunt* and *ed*, which shows tense.

The third structural unit is grammar. **Grammar** is the dual set of rules used in a language to promote consistency in application and meaning. The two rule sets are semantics and syntax. **Semantics** are the rules used to produce specific meaning from morphemes, words, and sentences. Semantics differ with each language. In the English language, the use of certain morphemes would signify quantity and tense. Other morphemes or words could be used in other languages.

Syntax determines word order in a sentence. Each language has its own order for parts of a sentence that set it apart from others. Syntax often causes problems for English-speaking adults who are trying to learn Spanish, for example, as the

PHONEMES The basic sounds used in language.

MORPHEME The smallest unit of language that conveys meaning.

GRAMMAR The dual set of rules used in a given language to promote consistency in application and meaning.

SEMANTICS The rules used to produce specific meaning from morphemes, words, and sentences.

SYNTAX Determines word order in a sentence.

order of adjectives and nouns is different in each language. In English, adjectives precede nouns, but in Spanish nouns precede adjectives. Once a person learns a certain syntax and uses it for a long period of time, it is difficult to switch to another form. For this and other reasons, childhood is the best time to learn new languages.

Language and Culture

There are three primary theories of language acquisition. The **nativist approach** suggests that language is an innate skill. Linguist Noam Chomsky proposed that all languages share a universal grammar, or common underlying structure. Chomsky described a language-acquisition device that is part of the neural system in the brain and allows humans to learn language. This is confirmed by some research and brain imaging studies that suggest that certain genes may be specific to certain aspects of language.

The **learning theory approach** bases language development on nurture and the repetition of observed behaviors. Children learn from their home environments and speak the language modeled in their family. When a child repeats sounds and words correctly, he or she is often rewarded with a hug or smile. These actions reinforce acquisition of language as parents understand and continue to shape how the child thinks and speaks.

The **interactionist approach** views language development as a combination of biological and environmental circumstances. People have the capacity for language and understanding based on genetic factors. People learn language usage and meaning based on what they experience in their environments.

There is debate about whether language shapes culture or culture shapes language. Original information about language led to the proposal that language shapes how people view the world and is ultimately responsible for how people think. This is known as the **linguistic-relativity hypothesis**. The opposite of that is the hypothesis that thought produces language. In other words, we create our language based on how we think. Recent research seems to indicate a combination of the two. For example, people of different cultures will pick the same true red when asked to identify the basic shade but will exhibit cultural distinctions in concepts of number and content.

Language Development

Language begins to develop around four months of age when babies normally begin to utter natural, spontaneous sounds. This first stage of language development is the babbling stage. The sounds uttered at this stage do not seem to reflect the language of the infant's household. This seems to indicate that the influence of nature begins before nurture in language development. By about the age of ten months, the sounds are more identifiable and consistent with the language sounds within the house, indicating the influence of environment.

Babies begin to speak single, intelligible words around the time of their first birthday, and they generally continue speaking single words for the next year. Their speech at this point conforms to the culture of the house. Infants learn, on average, one new word per week at this stage.

NATIVIST APPROACH Theory suggesting that language is an innate skill, a skill people are born with.

LEARNING THEORY APPROACH Theory suggesting that language development is based on nurture and repetition of observed behaviors.

INTERACTIONIST APPROACH Theory suggesting that language development is a combination of both biological and environmental circumstances.

LINGUISTIC-RELATIVITY HYPOTHESIS Language shapes how people view the world and ultimately is responsible for how people think.

Around age two, toddlers begin to put together two-word strings of words with meaning, such as "want juice." The words normally follow syntax rules and are presented in the order dictated by the language of the family. Word acquisition increases from one word per week to one word per day. After age two, toddlers begin a more rapid increase in language use and length of word strings. There does not seem to be a three-word string period, however; when toddlers get beyond two-word strings, they begin to speak in longer phrases.

Nonverbal Communication

Communication is not limited to language and verbal expression. People also communicate with each other through body language and behavior. Nonverbal communication can provide clues when communicating with people whose languages you do not understand. Cultural norms provide us with clues on how to interact with people in different countries, including the meaning behind facial expressions, seating, and physical proximity.

Physical Space

Physical space is the region of comfort surrounding each person that dictates how close others should come. Different relationships denote different measures of distance: intimate, personal, social, or public distance.

Intimate distance is the shortest; in the United States, it normally measures 0 to 1.5 feet. Intimate distance is most often associated with loving relationships. Personal distance is next, at 1.5 feet to 4 feet between parties. This space is usually maintained by those who are close, such as friends or family members. Social distance runs from 4 to 12 feet and is reserved for interactions with people who do not know each other well. Public distance is measured at 12 feet and beyond and is used in formal settings where distance is dictated.

The size of physical space needed varies based on culture, as each culture sees space in a different way. Some cultures, such as those of China and Japan, are more comfortable being physically closer, while other cultures, such as that of the United States, value greater distance.

PHYSICAL SPACE The region of comfort surrounding each person that dictates how close others should come.

Movement and Body Position

Body movement and position can transmit signals about emotion and comfort. If a person's space is infringed upon, it is likely that the person will react by moving away or turning away. A child who is bored will often fidget and look around. When a person is comfortable in a situation, his or her posture is normally relaxed. The hands might be loosely clasped or resting gently in his or her lap or on a table. When we sit facing people with whom we are speaking, we tend to lean toward them slightly to signify that we are paying attention to what they are saying.

When we are uncomfortable or angry, we often close our posture and show signs of tension. We might shift our position and swing our legs. If we feel our physical space has been invaded, we might cross our arms and legs and turn away from the offending person. Our position can be defensive or open, depending on what situation we are in. Think about how you sit when you are in a work meeting compared to how you sit when you are at a dinner table with friends.

Gaze

A person's gaze has long been thought to provide a window to the truth. Many believe that people who cannot look others in the eye when they speak are likely to be lying. This is not necessarily the case; in fact, many studies have found that people who are lying can look someone in the eye while doing so. Some people are more comfortable with direct eye contact, while others might be more shy and unable to withstand direct gaze. Facial expressions can show emotion. Smiles normally signify happiness, while a glare or frown might signify anger.

Ethnic and National Differences in Nonverbal Behaviors

Each culture has its own method of maintaining nonverbal communication. In some cultures people prefer to sit closer together with an indirect gaze, while in others the opposite is true. Thus, at an international conference, someone from one country might be most comfortable sitting next to the person they are speaking with, while a person from another country might wish to sit across the table and speak and look directly at someone else.

MISCOMMUNICATION

This age of communication via e-mail, Internet social networking sites, and instant messaging leads to an increased risk of misunderstanding. Nonverbal communication is usually absent because we often cannot see or hear the person with whom we are communicating online. Miscommunication is normally thought of as a negative event that goes hand-in-hand with conflict. However, misunderstanding can also lead to clarifying and refining meaning for other people as we attempt anew to

communicate purpose or desire. The message itself can lead to conflict or mutual discussion depending on whether the message threatens integrity, satisfaction, or meaningful relationships. If any one of these factors is threatened, conflict is more likely than communication.

Have you ever had to explain yourself after sending an instant message or e-mail? Because the recipient of your message cannot see your facial expressions, he or she must rely on the written message alone to determine meaning. What if the recipient reads a message you intended to be nonprovocative and reacts with hurt and anger? A simple miscommunication can easily become a conflict.

Message Accuracy and Inaccuracy

Message accuracy is based on how the message is presented and how it is received. One issue that interferes with accuracy is ambiguity. Ambiguity occurs when the subject is unclear or can be interpreted in multiple ways, and ambiguity can be intentional or unintentional. For example, the statement "I am sorry for what happened" could mean that the speaker is sorry that she did something. It could also mean that she is sorry that something happened to someone else. Some people employ this type of statement because it allows them to express regret without actually apologizing.

Unintentional inaccuracy can occur as cultural elements come into play. Different languages have different rules of grammar. These rules can create situations where the message is meant one way and interpreted another. As discussed earlier, in the Spanish language, the adjective follows the noun. In the English language, it precedes it. Thus, someone who speaks Spanish as a first language could ask for directions to the *house white,* meaning the White House. This could be interpreted to mean a house that is white rather than the home of the president of the United States. While the message is the same, it might not be interpreted the same way. This example shows a relatively benign situation. There are, however, other times where message accuracy is crucial.

Unintentional inaccuracy can stem from styles of communication. People from a high-context culture communicate more often with indirect modes of communication, vague descriptions, less talk, and less eye contact. They rely on assumed recollection of shared experiences. However, people from low-context cultures use direct patterns of communication and clear descriptions and terms and assume that meanings are described explicitly.

Message accuracy in hospitals and other health care settings is critical to diagnosing medical issues and providing proper treatment. Miscommunication between patients and health care workers occurs often and can lead to health care errors. Studies have found that patients are unlikely to speak up and clarify information if they do not feel that information will be heeded or if they feel that it will be derided. Communication accuracy relies on our ability to communicate effectively and with confidence. When people are unsure of their audience or the reception their message might produce, they communicate with less accuracy.

Understanding occurs when the listener grasps the speaker's objective, ideas, and intent. Thus, the other component of communication involves actively trying to understand what is being communicated as it is stated. The listener must see the message from the perspective of the person relaying it.

Actively understanding what another person is communicating becomes important in work environments. Consider basic communication guidelines. For example, a human resources professional conducting an interview with a potential new employee should ask open-ended questions to elicit more responses from the job candidate. Open-ended questions require more than a "yes" or "no" answer, such as, "Tell me more about…" It is also important to check in with the speaker to make sure you understand his or her message. You might say, "Let me see if I understood you correctly" and then restate what the person said to you. Doing so facilitates active listening.

Deception

Miscommunication is not always accidental. Deception is a form of miscommunication intentionally designed to mislead. There has been much research on how to tell when one person is deceiving another. Deception can occur when someone lies,

hides, or fails to provide all information or manipulates information so that it leads in a different direction.

This might seem like something that happens only occasionally, but deception is actually a large part of social interaction. In one study, people admitted to using deception in 14 percent of e-mails, 27 percent of in-person interactions, and 37 percent of phone conversations. According to researchers Stephen Porter and Leanne ten Brinke, most people lie approximately twice per day.

Everyday lies seem to go undetected more often than not. Why? Because most people are not looking for signs of deception over small things. These lies are often less complex and require less thought, and the potential outcome is not usually as severe as when someone lies about committing a crime. The higher emotional content of a crime and the fear of getting caught can interfere with the consistency of story, facial features, and confidence needed to pull off the deception.

It is not always possible to detect deception by simply using common sense—especially in higher-stakes lies. Judges and other legal decision-makers have reported relying on cues that are commonly thought to be effective but in reality do little to detect deception. Paul Ekman, a prominent psychologist known for his work in emotions and facial expressions, has argued that facial expressions are universal, rather than culturally specific. He developed the Facial Action Coding System, which is a classification of human facial expressions. Ekman's research also focused on facial expression and microexpressions.

Using these unreliable clues can often lead to false positive identification of deception. False positives can also occur in polygraphy (commonly called lie detector tests). Polygraphy relies on physiological changes that indicate nervousness, following the misconception that nervousness indicates guilt. In fact, some deceivers maintain a calm, unruffled demeanor, while some who are innocent become stressed out and seem guilty simply because they must take the test. One test of truth that may have some reliability is sentence length. Unprepared liars tend to take longer to voice responses than truth-tellers do, while prepared liars tend to provide shorter responses than those telling the truth.

SUMMARY

Intelligence is influenced by various factors, and quantifying intelligence is not an easy task. Recent research has expanded our thinking about the different types of intelligence and their measurement. While by definition most people fall into the normal range, some people are mentally retarded or gifted. There are different methods for determining intelligence. Types of intelligence can include emotional, practical, and creative, for example. Measuring such types of intelligence can make it easier to determine where people's strengths lie and how they think. Ideally, this can make people aware of the different types of intelligences and talents and help them to adjust to different ways of thinking.

Memory is a complicated process. There are different types of memories, and there are many ways to make, store, and retrieve them. Memory can be shaped; for instance, you can devise tricks to help you remember something, or your mind can falsely remember something that has been suggested to you. Many different factors are responsible for memory loss. Current studies seek to learn how to manipulate genes so that memories can be more easily accessed when retrieval failure occurs.

Like memory, the process of communication is complex. There are several theories about how people acquire language. Language development generally follows the same steps at the same time. People communicate through many different modes, including nonverbal communication and distance communication along with traditional spoken communication. However you communicate, think about the cultural norms of the person with whom you are communicating, as this can help to avoid unintentional miscommunication. Also keep in mind that intentional deception is commonplace when communicating.

REFERENCES

Arnold, R., & Colburn, N. (2011, January 1). It's never too early. *School Library Journal, 57*, 20–28. Retrieved from http://www.schoollibraryjournal.com/slj/printissuecurrentissue/888330-427/its_never_too_early_parents.html.csp

Axmacher, N., Haupt, E., Cohen, M. X., Elger, C. E., & Fell, J. (2009). Interference of working memory load with long-term memory formation. *Cognitive Neuroscience, 29*, 1501– 1513. doi: 10.1111/j.1460-9568.2009.06676.x

Best, J. (2009). Need to override your heuristic system? Better bring your deductive competence. *North American Journal of Psychology, 11*(3), 543–582.

Bhatti, A. A. (2009). Performance analysis and comparison of a minimum interconnections direct storage model with traditional neural bidirectional memories. *IET Nanobiotechnology*, 3(4), 81–102. doi: 10.1049/iet-nbt. 2009.0002

Chamorro-Premuzic, T., & Furnham, A. (2004). A possible model for understanding the personality-intelligence interface. *British Journal of Psychology, 95*(Pt 2), 249–264.

Chandra, P. (2007). Review of language, mind, and brain: Some psychological and neurological constraints on theories of grammar. *Cognitive Systems Research, 8(1),* 53–56.

Chomsky, N. (1968). *Language and mind*. New York, NY: Harcourt Brace Jovanovich.

Daviglus, M. L., Bell, C. C., Berrettini, W., Bowen, P. E., Connolly, Jr., E. S., Cox, N. J., … Trevisan, M. (2010). National Institutes of Health state-of-the-science conference statement: Preventing Alzheimer's disease and cognitive decline. *Annals of Internal Medicine*, 153(3), 176–W.65.

Enchanted Mind. (2002). Creativity test. Retrieved from http://www.enchantedmind.com/html/creativity/iq_tests/creativity_test.html

Furnham, A. (2009). The validity of a new, self-report measure of multiple intelligence. *Current Psychology, 28*(4), 225–239. doi:10.100//s12144-009-9064-z

Garand, D. (2009). Misunderstanding: A typology of performance. *Common Knowledge, 15*(3), 472–500. doi: 10.1215/0961754X-2009-024

Ikonomidou, C., Bittagau, P., Ishimaru, M. J., Wozniak, D. F., Koch, C., Genz, K., … Olney, J. W. (2000). Ethanol-induced apoptotic neurodegeneration and fetal alcohol syndrome. *Science 2000, 287*, 1056–1060.

Kearney, J. (2009). Rogerian principles and the writing classroom: A history of intention and (mis)interpretation. *Rhetoric Review, 28*(2), 167–184. doi: 10.1080/07350190902740034

Kennedy, D. P., Gläscher, J., Tyszka, J. M., & Adolphs, R. (2009). Personal space regulation by the human amygdala. *Nature Neuroscience, 12*, 1226–1227. doi: 10.1038/nn.2381

Koppel, J., & Goldberg, T. (2009). The genetics of episodic memory. *Cognitive Neuropsychiatry, 14*(4–5), 356–376. doi: 10.1080/13546800902990438

Kryukov, V. I. (2008). The role of the hippocampus in long-term memory: Is it memory storage or comparator? *Journal of Integrative Neuroscience, 7*(1), 117–184. doi: 10.1142/S021963520800171X

Kvavilashvili, L., & Fisher, L. (2007). Is time-based prospective remembering mediated by self-initiated rehearsals? Role of incidental cues, ongoing activity age, and motivation. *Journal of Experimental Psychology: General, 136*(1), 112–132.

Kvavilashvili, L., Kornbrot, D. E., Mash, V., Cockburn, J., & Milne, A. (2009). Differential effects of age on prospective and retrospective memory tasks in young, young-old, and old-old adults. *Memory, 17*(2), 180–196.

Lee, Y., & Silva, A. J. (2009). The molecular and cellular biology of enhanced cognition. *Nature Reviews: Neuroscience, 10*, 126–140. doi: 10.1080/09658210802194366

Loftus, E. F. (1997). Creating false memories. *Scientific American, 277*(3), 70–75. Retrieved from http://faculty.washington.edu/eloftus/Articles/sciam.htm

Oberauer, K. (2007). In search of the magic number. *Experimental Psychology*, 54, 245–246.

Ornat, S. L., & Gallo, P. (2004) Acquisition, learning, or development of language? Skinner's "verbal behavior" revisited. *Spanish Journal of Psychology, 7*(2),161–170.

Parker, A., Dagnall, N., & Coyle, A. M. (2007). Environmental context effects in conceptual explicit and implicit memory. *Memory, 15*(4), 423–434. doi: 10.1080/09658210701309834

Porter, S., & ten Brinke, L. (2010). The truth about lies: What works in detecting high-stakes deception? *Legal and Criminological Psychology, 15*(1), 57–75. doi: 10.1348/135532509X433151

Raica, D. A. (2009). Effect of action-oriented communication training on nurses' communication self efficacy. *Medsburg Nursing, 18*(6), 343–346, 360.

Simonton, D. K., & Song, A. V. (2009). Eminence, IQ, physical and mental health, and achievement domain: Cox's 282 geniuses revisited. *Psychological Science, 20*, 429–434. doi: 10.1111/j.1467-9280.2009.02313.x

Spada, M. M., Georgiou, G. A., & Wells, A. (2010). The relationship among metacognitions, attentional control, and state anxiety. *Cognitive Behaviour Therapy, 39*(1), 64–71.

Sporer, S. L., & Schwandt, B. (2006). Paraverbal indicators of deception: A meta-analytic synthesis. *Applied Cognitive Psychology, 20*(4), 421–446.

Sternberg, R. J. (2006). The nature of creativity. *Creativity Research Journal, 18*(1), 87–98.

Torrance, P. E. (2008). *Torrance Test of Creative Thinking*. Scholastic Testing Service. Retrieved from http://ststesting.com/ttctbro.pdf

Trebay, G. (2009, November 2). Testing her strong suit. *The New York Times*. Retrieved from http://www.nytimes.com

Tulving, E. (2002). Episodic memory: From mind to brain. *Annual Review of Psychology, 53*, 1–25.

Unsworth, N., Redick, T. S., Heitz, R. P., Broadway, J. M., & Engle, R. W. (2009). Complex working memory span tasks and higher-order cognition: A latent-variable analysis of the relationship between processing and storage. *Memory, 17(6)*, 635–654. doi: 10.1080/09658210902998047.

Zhang, Q., He, X., & Zhang, J. (2007). A comparative study on the classification of basic color terms by undergraduates from Yi nationality, Bai nationality and Naxi nationality. Acta *Psychologica Sinica, 39(1)*, 18–26.

Learning

"Taking charge of your own learning is part of taking charge of your life, which is the sine qua non in becoming an integrated person."

—Warren G. Bennis

CLASSICAL CONDITIONING

Classical conditioning is a type of learning that uses a stimulus to train a learner to perform a particular behavior at a particular time. Learners experiencing classical conditioning learn a new response to a stimulus.

CLASSICAL CONDITIONING
A type of learning that uses a stimulus to train a learner to perform a particular behavior at a particular time.

One experiences this type of learning when one associates a stimulus with a particular outcome—whether the two are related or not. You may associate a visit to a particular doctor's office with pain because you once had a painful experience there. Or you may associate a visit to a local barber shop with embarrassment because you received a bad haircut there three months ago. Some of these associations are conscious, and others are not.

The Basics of Classical Conditioning

Classical conditioning gets its name from the experiment that was designed to examine the phenomenon of learning by association. When a particular stimulus, or condition, is present, a reaction, or conditioned response, is the result. When that particular stimulus is not present, the response given is considered unconditioned. The example of Ivan Pavlov and his salivating dogs clarifies this point.

Pavlov's Dogs

Ivan Pavlov was the first scientist to develop an experiment to test these associations. Pavlov, a Russian physiologist, set out to design an experiment to understand the processes of digestion in the early 1900s. He had no immediate interest in learning what stimuli caused various behaviors. His original goal was to measure how much dogs salivated when a meat powder was placed in their mouths.

Something remarkable began to happen, however. Pavlov and his team noticed that the dogs would begin salivating before the meat powder was placed in their mouths. In fact, the moment the dogs saw the assistant who usually gave them the meat powder, the dogs began salivating. Pavlov realized that the dogs' behavior had changed because they began to associate eating food not only with food itself, but also with the sight of the assistant who fed them.

Pavlov modified his inquiry to investigate this association. He now wanted to understand the relationship between a stimulus and a learned response. Pavlov and his team always placed the dogs in harnesses during their experiments. Once the dog was harnessed, a tone—like one from a tuning fork—was struck. After the tone played, the dog was given a small piece of food. At first, the dog only turned to look for the origin of the tone.

UNCONDITIONED RESPONSE
A response that is reflexive, not learned.

UNCONDITIONED STIMULUS A stimulus that occurs naturally, eliciting a reflexive, or unconditioned, response in an organism.

Of course, the dogs salivated when they received their food. Salivation of this kind is an example of an **unconditioned response**, one that occurs naturally, like a reflex. An unconditioned response is caused by an **unconditioned stimulus**, which is a stimulus that

---

1. Classical conditioning is a type of learning that involves a stimulus and a response and can help encourage positive behavior or get rid of unwanted behavior. See page 147.

2. When a person or animal makes a connection between a stimulus and a response, this is operant conditioning. See page 153.

3. Previous behaviors can be reinforced to ensure that they will be repeated. See page 155.

4. Punishment may be positive or negative, such as a "time out" or restricting access to something the subject wants. See page 155.

5. Cognitive learning involves thinking and perceiving in order to learn. See page 158.

6. Observational learning occurs when a behavior is witnessed and then a person learns from that experience. See page 159.

occurs naturally within the organism's life. Any stimulus that elicits a reflexive response is an example of an unconditioned stimulus. With Pavlov's repetitive pairings of the sound and the food, however, the dogs developed a **conditioned response**, salivating when the tone was sounded, regardless of whether or not food was given after the tone. The salivation was caused by the sound of the tone, a **conditioned stimulus**, rather than by the unconditioned stimulus of the food.

Acquisition is the process of learning that leads to the development of the conditioned response in an organism. Acquisition of a conditioned response occurs after repeated pairings of the unconditioned stimulus and the conditioned stimulus. As an animal learns to associate the unconditioned stimulus with the conditioned response, the conditioned stimulus can be removed. Once the unconditioned stimulus is shown to reliably cause the conditioned response, successful classical conditioning has taken place.

Pavlov was consistently able to elicit the dogs' salivation when he sounded the tone. This breakthrough was striking—his research now opened the door to understanding one process of learning. In 1904, he and his team won the Nobel Prize for their experiment.

Applying Conditioning Principles to Human Behavior

Conditioning affects human behavior both consciously and unconsciously. Richard Gerrig and Philip Zimbardo use the example of the type of music used in a horror film. When a certain type of suspense-inducing music begins to play during a scene, the viewer "just knows" that something terrible is about to happen. The music itself is not terrifying, yet the viewer feels scared upon hearing it. The horrifying or repulsive scene that ultimately follows the music is the unconditioned stimulus, which elicits revulsion—the unconditioned response. The music is the conditioned stimulus, which the viewer comes to associate with horrifying and repulsive scenes in horror movies. When you hear that type of music, your brain and body begin to react in anticipation, expecting to see the horrifying scenes that always seem to come after that music is played. When it comes to human behavior, classical conditioning is not just about entertainment. Conditioning is used in a variety of settings to deter or eliminate bad habits and to develop good habits. In what ways can conditioning be used to modify human behavior?

Advertisers use conditioning methods to entice consumers to purchase their products. When a car manufacturer advertises its shiny, fast sedan with a shot of the car parked in front of a mansion, the viewer is left to associate the car with wealth. Over time, viewers may believe that if they own such a car, others will assume that they live in a large house and have a lot of money.

The same is true for advertisements that employ sexy models to sell a company's clothing. The message is that when you wear that company's clothes, you are transformed into a sexy, attractive person. Many adults have the presence of mind to at least note the underlying meaning of such commercials, but younger viewers may not notice that the advertisements use strong emotional desires to sell their products.

Classical conditioning can be used to extinguish unwanted behaviors, such as phobias or smoking. For example, if you are afraid of dogs, you might use a process called systematic desensitization to change the feelings of fear associated with

dogs. Every time you encounter a dog, you could take three long, deep breaths and visualize your favorite, most relaxing place. Over time, you will form a new association with encountering a dog. The association will be between the dog and your favorite place, thereby eliminating the fear that you felt when you saw a dog.

To use classical conditioning to quit smoking, you might associate an unpleasant stimulus with the act of smoking or even the desire to smoke. What if every time you reached for a cigarette, for example, you got a shock on your lips? It is likely that you would soon associate the pain from the shock with the desire to smoke—thus making smoking much less appealing, which, in turn, should help you to quit.

NEW DEVELOPMENTS IN LEARNING THEORY

Recent research has led to significant new developments in learning theory. For example, consider the changes that have taken place in college classrooms in the last decade. Once, it was standard for teachers to lecture at a blackboard. Now, it is common to find classrooms with a computer for every student, or entirely virtual classrooms where students interact online. Some schools have virtual whiteboards or handheld remote controls so students can solve problems and engage with class materials as they are presented. Certainly, these changes are evidence of dramatic changes in technology and culture. But they also reveal changes in the psychological learning theories that schools use to plan their curriculums, which have come to place new emphasis on the active role of the learner.

Constructivism

New learning theories, known under the broad category of constructivism, maintain that learning is a highly subjective, interactive process on the part of the learner. This is in contrast to classical conditioning, which usually emphasizes instructor-focused training, the goal being the same objective outcome for each learner. The most well-known constructivist was the French thinker Jean Piaget, whose ideas have influenced many other twentieth-century psychologists. Central to Piaget's theory was that each individual builds knowledge based on his or her own internal understanding of the world.

As an example of Piaget's constructivism, imagine a four-year-old girl playing with a set of watercolor paints. She dips her brush in blue paint and then applies it to paper. She notices this makes a blue brushstroke. Then, she dips the same brush into yellow paint. She notices to her surprise that the stroke on the paper comes out green, not yellow. She tries a new brush, dipping it in the blue paint, then the yellow—and sees that this also makes green. Then she tries the reverse: yellow paint first, then blue—also green! This child has taught herself, or constructed, the principle that yellow and blue together, in either order, make green.

For Piaget and other constructivists, there are several important principles involved in this type of learning. Even in the presence of an expert or authority figure, humans construct knowledge primarily experimentally, rather than receiving

CONSTRUCTIVISM One of the main schools of learning theory; maintains that learning is a subjective, relative, and active process on the part of the learner.

it passively. Knowledge is also constructed from the learner's existing mental frameworks. For example, this child knows something about paints and paintbrushes already, and she probably has played with mixing her paints before. So development is an important factor in Piaget's theory. Learners need to be at an age, or developmental stage, where they have the capacity to respond to new experiences, or **assimilate** them into previously existing knowledge.

As children develop, they also become more able to engage in the process of **accommodation:** modifying existing knowledge or mental frameworks when these don't fit with reality. For example, the child expected yellow paint, not green paint, but she was able to accommodate the contradiction into her existing knowledge. **Equilibration** is Piaget's term for this process of self-regulating one's own knowledge and reorganizing what is observed.

Vygotsky's Social Development Theory

An important aspect of constructivism is the idea that knowledge is subjective and unique to the individual. This becomes central to the work of one of Piaget's contemporaries, the Russian psychologist Lev Vygotsky (1896-1934). Like Piaget, Vygotsky believed the child was active in constructing knowledge, but Vygotsky emphasized the sociocultural nature of that construction. For Piaget, the context in which children are raised shapes not only what they learn, but the very mental tools they use for learning. For example, in social contexts children are shown different strategies for learning, such as note taking, memorization techniques, or maybe playing with watercolor paints, depending on where they are raised. So learning processes are not universal but socially mediated.

Vygotsky's social development theory further stresses the importance of social relationships, specifically the need for an authority figure, to help the child learn. Vygotsky theorized the **zone of proximal development** as the difference between what a child can learn on his or her own and with an expert companion present. For Vygotsky, a relationship with an expert companion makes an activity easier to learn because the companion will provide **scaffolding**—that is, less complex, step-by-step variations on the activity. The companion also will give verbal instructions, which the child learns to repeat to him or herself in **private speech**, or speaking instructively to oneself. Vygotsky's social development theory has become quite influential. However, some critics have noted that the highly social model of learning may apply to the skills needed in cultures where work is more collaborative, but not as much to cultures where such skills are less valued.

Kolb's Experiential Learning Theory

A recent constructivist theory that has gained wide application is David A. **Kolb's experiential learning theory**. In the early 1970s, influenced by Piaget's ideas of assimilation and accommodation, Kolb identified two ways of "grasping" experience—concrete experience and abstract conceptualization—and two ways of transforming (processing or understanding) experience—reflective observation and active experimentation. According to Kolb, everyone uses these four skills in a cycle. When you have a new experience, you reflect upon it. Then you form an abstract concept based on your reflections, which you test through experimentation.

Importantly, Kolb also argued that people are unable to use all of these skills at the same time, so they choose. For example, imagine it's your first day at a new job and you're given a confusing new task that has to be finished in two hours. You

---

ASSIMILATION Piaget's term for the learner's process of incorporating new experiences into existing knowledge.

ACCOMMODATION Piaget's term for the learner's process of adjusting mental frameworks to fit with observed reality.

EQUILIBRATION Piaget's term for self-regulating one's own knowledge and mentally reorganizing what is observed.

VYGOTSKY'S SOCIAL DEVELOPMENT THEORY Learning theory that stresses the role of sociocultural context, particularly the presence of an expert companion, in a child's construction of knowledge.

ZONE OF PROXIMAL DEVELOPMENT Vygotsky's term for the difference between what a child can learn on his or her own and with an expert companion present.

SCAFFOLDING Simpler, step-by-step variations on a complex activity provided to a learner by an adult or expert.

PRIVATE SPEECH Vygotsky's term for instructions or guidance spoken to oneself while learning.

KOLB'S EXPERIENTIAL LEARNING THEORY Theory of a four-step learning cycle consisting of (1) concrete experience, (2) abstract conceptualization, (3) reflective observation, and (4) active experimentation.

could use the available books and manuals to learn the rules as well as you can (abstract conceptualization), or just dive right in and hope for the best (active experimentation)—but you don't have the time to take both options. So you make a choice. The patterns of choosing you develop in such situations over time come to characterize your individual **learning style**.

In 1971, Kolb developed the **learning style inventory (LSI)** to assess which combination of categories were most common, finding that the majority of test subjects fell into one of four learning styles:

- *Diverging*—Using primarily concrete experience and reflective observation, these learners excel at brainstorming concrete solutions to a problem and examining it from many angles.
- *Assimilating*—Using primarily abstract conceptualization and reflective observation, these learners excel at bringing together large amounts of information and organizing it concisely.
- *Converging*—Using primarily abstract conceptualization and active experimentation, these learners excel at finding practical uses for theories.
- *Accommodating*—Using primarily concrete experience and active experimentation, these learners learn by "jumping right in" to new experiences, following impulses, and improvising.

Kolb's LSI has been applied to many different fields. Schools use it as a way to design curriculums for different student needs. The LSI is also used in the workplace, as learning style has been found to be linked to management styles and decision-making styles.

Extinction

Extinction refers to the elimination of a conditioned response in an organism. Before extinction can occur, the organism must acquire the conditioned response. As you learned earlier in the chapter, **acquisition** is the process of learning that leads to the development of the conditioned response in an organism. Acquisition of a conditioned response occurs after repeated pairings of the unconditioned stimulus and the conditioned stimulus. Once the unconditioned stimulus is shown to reliably cause the conditioned response, successful classical conditioning has taken place.

Extinction follows a similar but somewhat opposite pattern. When the conditioned stimulus is removed, the conditioned response begins to weaken and eventually disappear. In the case of Pavlov's dogs, when the tone was no longer sounded to predict giving food powder, the dogs stopped salivating over time. So in this case, the tone may continue to be sounded, but the dogs would not receive the food powder. Soon, the dogs learn that the sound of the tone does not indicate that they will be fed. This break in the association between the tone and the food causes them to stop salivating when they hear the tone.

Pavlov continued his experiment long enough to notice an interesting phenomenon. After a brief rest period during which the dogs were not exposed to the unconditioned stimulus (the food), the conditioned response suddenly returned. Pavlov named this phenomenon **spontaneous recovery**. If the conditioned response reappears after this rest period, it is weaker than before extinction took place.

Although behaviors learned through classical conditioning are not necessarily permanent, the associations between the conditioned stimulus and the conditioned response can be renewed quite easily. Pavlov also noted that when he restarted the experiment by pairing the conditioned stimulus (tone) with the unconditioned stimulus (food) again, the time it took the dogs to associate the conditioned stimulus

LEARNING STYLE Kolb's term for the learning skills that individuals tend to choose and develop over time.

LEARNING STYLE INVENTORY (LSI) Kolb's test that determines which combination of learning skills an individual tends to use.

EXTINCTION The elimination of a conditioned response.

ACQUISITION The process of developing a conditioned response.

SPONTANEOUS RECOVERY The sudden reemergence of the conditioned response after a rest period.

with the conditioned response (salivation) was greatly diminished. He reasoned that this quick reacquisition of the desired behavior is evidence that the dogs did not completely forget the association they had learned previously.

Generalization and Discrimination

GENERALIZATION The idea that several related stimuli can potentially cause an organism to give a conditioned response.

If a child is scratched on the cheek by a neighbor's orange cat, he might come to associate his fear of being scratched by that cat with cats of every color. **Generalization** refers to the concept that a variety of similar stimuli has the potential to elicit a conditioned response. The child who is scratched might also generalize his fear to other household pets, like dogs or hamsters. If the fear intensifies, he may even begin to see all four-legged animals as potential threats.

Such a fear is obviously irrational and must be extinguished. Humans and other animals use generalization as a protection from potential threats or predators. An animal's ability to generalize information about a potentially harmful stimulus allows it to steer clear of trouble. If a zebra hears the growl of a hunting lioness rather than seeing her face, the zebra can still make the connection that the lioness is an immediate threat and it should flee. The zebra benefits from its ability to generalize about the conditioned stimulus with its survival.

DISCRIMINATION The process that guides an organism to respond only to certain stimuli in certain situations.

Discrimination is the opposite of generalization. An animal uses discrimination when it responds to one stimulus among several similar stimuli. If Pavlov's dogs heard tones of several frequencies prior to being fed, but were only fed after hearing a tone with a frequency of 1200 Hz, over time they would learn to salivate only after hearing the tone of 1200 Hz. The dogs will begin to discriminate between the various tones, only salivating when they hear the one at 1200 Hz.

Watson, Rayner, and "Little Albert"

John Watson was a behavioral psychologist interested in understanding fear responses. He and colleague Rosalie Rayner designed an experiment to further this understanding. This experiment's design boldly violates today's ethical principles. Watson and Rayner trained an infant to fear certain objects. By today's standards, such an experimental design would make most researchers squirm with discomfort. This experiment would not be allowed in research settings today.

Little Albert was the name given to the infant that Watson and Rayner used in their study of fear responses. The study involved changing Little Albert's emotional associations with a white rat. Little Albert was initially fond of the rat—that is, until Watson and Rayner began their experiment. The white rat became the conditioned stimulus.

Each time they presented the rat to Little Albert, they also banged a large steel bar with a hammer. This loud noise, the unconditioned stimulus, terrified the baby. His distressed response was initially unconditioned because it was the result of being upset by the loud bang, but soon enough, just the sight of the white rat sent Little Albert into a fearful and distressed state. In fact, it only took seven trials to elicit the conditioned response from the baby. His response then became generalized to other furry animals and objects, including dogs, rabbits, and a Santa Claus mask.

Little Albert's mother, presumably horrified and upset by what was happening to her son, removed him from the experiment and was never heard from again. This is troubling, especially because conditioned fear responses are quite strong and require intensive desensitization and extinction to be removed. Watson and Rayner never had the opportunity to recondition the infant's learned fear response because the experiment ended so abruptly.

OPERANT CONDITIONING

Edward Thorndike, an American scientist, observed cats as they attempted to escape from puzzle boxes. His observations led him to believe that the cats learned how to escape from the boxes by making a connection—or association—between a stimulus and a response. In terms of Thorndike's cats, the stimulus was the puzzle box.

The cats' responses may have originally occurred spontaneously, but eventually the cats began to understand that swiping or clawing at a loop or button gave them a temporary respite from the box. Once they learned the association between the stimulus (the puzzle box) and the response (swiping at the loop), the cats performed that behavior over and over to release themselves from their confinement. Thorndike referred to this connection as the **law of effect**.

LAW OF EFFECT The connection between a behavior and the behavior's outcome.

The Basics of Operant Conditioning

Operant conditioning relies on the use of reinforcement to shape behavior. This is different from classical conditioning because in operant conditioning, the outcome of the behavior affects an animal's future behaviors. **Operant conditioning** is a type of learning in which future behaviors are affected by the consequences of current behaviors. An **operant** is defined as any behavior that affects the animal's environment.

OPERANT CONDITIONING Learning in which future behaviors are affected by the consequences of current behaviors.
OPERANT Any behavior that affects an organism's environment.

In classical conditioning, the conditioned response is elicited by a specific stimulus. In operant conditioning, the likelihood that certain responses will be repeated are contingent upon the kind of reinforcement an animal receives. In Thorndike's study, the operant was the cat's behavior—swiping at the loop. Behavioral psychologists test an organism's behaviors by changing the consequences of that organism's behavior.

The details of operant conditioning can be complex, but the basic understanding of behaviorism lies at its center. True behaviorists believe in studying observable behavior only. All other potential influencers on behavioral choices, such as thoughts or emotions, are considered irrelevant unless such intangibles are shown as behaviors. Behaviorists also believe that humans and all other animals are born with a *tabula rasa*—a blank slate. This blank slate is the unformed mind.

DISCRIMINATIVE STIMULUS A factor that determines the conditions under which a behavior is reinforced or not reinforced.

Of course, the mind does not remain blank for long; many perceptions and experiences begin to shape an infant's development almost immediately following birth. Operant conditioning also assumes that individuals freely give responses, rather than having responses elicited from them, and that it is the reinforcement felt after those responses that causes learning.

The basic foundations of operant conditioning include a reliance on observable behaviors and the use of reinforcers to mold future behaviors. Though behaviorists tend to focus most on observable behaviors, they also weigh the influence of certain mitigating factors on those behaviors. Perhaps the most important one of these mitigating factors is the **discriminative stimulus**. A discriminative stimulus helps an organism determine if performing the desired behavior will result in reinforcement or not.

KEY THINKERS IN PSYCHOLOGY: SKINNER

B. F. Skinner, the "father of behaviorism," is among history's best-known psychologists. Skinner was born in 1904 in Susquehanna, Pennsylvania. He attended Hamilton College and graduated with a degree in English literature. A somewhat disillusioned writer, Skinner decided to change his career focus to psychology after learning about the research of John Watson. He earned a PhD from Harvard University in 1931 and stayed on as a researcher through 1936. After working at other universities, in 1948 he returned to Harvard, where he remained for the rest of his career.

Early in his career, at the University of Minnesota, Skinner trained pigeons to guide bombs for use during World War II. Although his research was applicable and important, it was discontinued because the military chose to fund other research projects, including the development of radar systems.

Skinner and his wife had two daughters, Julie and Deborah. Skinner designed a crib for one of his daughters that he named the "Baby Tender," and he intended the crib to be a model of cleanliness and safety. *Ladies' Home Journal* profiled the design and distorted the realities of his invention by titling the article "Baby in a Box." Unfortunately, some confused this with his "Skinner box" and assumed he was executing operant conditioning experiments on his own children—which he clearly was not.

Throughout his career, Skinner was fascinated with efficiency in teaching and learning. For example, he developed a teaching machine that broke complex concepts and skills into manageable steps. Students who used the machines were able to perform skills that they could not accomplish prior to using the machine. Skinner may have been ahead of his time, as educational methods are trending toward using more online learning, which is self-directed and contains frequent opportunities for reinforcement. Skinner's machine proved too cumbersome to maintain, and most companies did not want to invest in producing materials for a machine unlikely to endure in the marketplace.

Ultimately, Skinner is best known for his focus on observable behaviors and the development of operant conditioning. He believed observable behaviors were the most important feature of human or animal life.

Consider an alarm clock going off, or the ringing of a school bell that signals the end of the school day. In the latter case, the bell is the discriminative stimulus because it sets the scene for ending the school day. Students know that when the bell rings, they will be dismissed. The bell signals favorable conditions for the behavior of leaving school. The consequences for the students are feelings of freedom associated with no longer being in class. If a student tries to leave the classroom at a different time of day, however, the behavior is likely to be punished. Students learn quickly that the proper context for leaving depends on the bell being rung.

B. F. Skinner

B. F. Skinner is often referred to as the father of behaviorism. He identified four factors that served as the foundation for his model of operant conditioning: behavior, past learning, present conditions, and genetic endowment. Skinner developed the tenets of operant conditioning through his research. Using an operant chamber, Skin-

ner tested rats' ability to learn a behavior by controlling the consequences of that behavior. By reinforcing the rats' behavior choices, Skinner observed their learning.

The operant chamber, also known as a Skinner box, reinforced certain observed behaviors with food. For example, when a rat pressed the middle button in a series of three buttons, it got a food pellet. The positive reinforcement of the food pellet shaped the rat's future behavior. Once the animal learned that pressing the middle button resulted in a food pellet, it was much more likely to consistently press the middle button rather than one of the other buttons.

POSITIVE REINFORCERS, NEGATIVE REINFORCERS, AND PUNISHMENT

How does reinforcement shape future behavior? Recall that behaviorists focus only on observable behaviors. A **reinforcer** is an outcome that is dependent upon a previous behavior. For example, if Marlon is given a raise every time he makes a new sale, he is likely to continue to make more sales.

Reinforcers can be positive or negative, but all reinforcers increase the likelihood that a behavior will increase in the future. A **positive reinforcer** is almost synonymous with a reward. For the rat who presses the middle button in the Skinner box, the positive reinforcer is the food pellet. For the student who studies for an extra hour for her midterm exam, the better grade on the test is the positive reinforcer.

A **negative reinforcer** is a bit more complex. If the rat receives a small shock until it presses on the middle button in the operant chamber, it will learn to press the middle button in order to avoid receiving the shock. This is also known as escape conditioning because the animal is performing a particular behavior to escape from an unpleasant experience. Negative reinforcement can also take the form of avoidance conditioning, in which an animal performs a behavior in order to avoid a future unpleasant experience.

REINFORCER An outcome dependent upon a previous behavior.

POSITIVE REINFORCER A desirable outcome that is dependent on previous behavior.

NEGATIVE REINFORCER Removal of an undesirable outcome that is dependent on previous behavior.

The Pros and Cons of Punishment: Why Reinforcement Prevails

Punishment is fundamentally different from reinforcement. Punishment is the imposition of an undesirable outcome when an animal exhibits an incorrect behavior. Most people have experienced various forms of punishment in their lives, whether at home, in school, or at work, for a variety of "bad" behaviors or choices. Punishment theoretically decreases the likelihood of a particular behavior over time.

Punishment, like reinforcement, comes in positive and negative varieties. Positive punishment occurs when an uncomfortable or painful consequence is added to a situation. For example, if Ramona is spanked after stealing a dollar from her father's wallet, she is experiencing positive punishment.

The spanking, an uncomfortable and painful consequence, occurred as a result of the child's behavior. Negative punishment occurs when a desirable stimulus is removed. Imagine that a manager plans to take the employees in his department to the theater when they finish a project. Upon discovering that the department did not complete their project on time, the manager decides not to provide the tickets for the department to see the play. The manager has removed the desirable stimulus of the theater tickets from the department's immediate future as a result of being late with the project. This is negative punishment.

Punishment is a tricky way to shape behavior. For example, punishment usually does not completely extinguish a behavior; it simply suppresses it. In order for punishment to be effective, it must adhere to certain requirements. Punishment must be immediate, relevant, and carry the appropriate intensity to match the action it is attempting to prevent in the future. The punishment must also be administered after each wrong behavior for maximum effectiveness. Punishment is a weaker method for changing future behaviors because it does not present the individual with an alternative correct behavior; it merely identifies the incorrect behavior.

Punishment tends to be associated with childrearing, but it can also be found in the workplace. If punishment is used to shape behavior in the workplace, the results are likely to be mixed. Punishment does not cause an employee to exhibit good behavior—it just motivates that person to stop the bad behavior. Employees may also behave properly around the individual responsible for administering punishment, but when that individual is gone, employees may resume undesirable behaviors.

Depending on why a punishment is given, its subject can become angry and resentful of the person administering it. In addition, the constant threat of being punished could cause employees' work performance to suffer. Employees may feel anxious about potential punishment, which could cause a drop in worker effectiveness.

Shaping

SHAPING A process by which a new behavior is learned through reinforcement of behaviors that are progressively more similar to the desired learned behavior.

For an organism to learn a new behavior in the context of a laboratory experiment, **shaping** may need to be used prior to the beginning of the experiment. Shaping is exactly what it sounds like: a method used by a researcher to mold an organism's behavior until it learns the desired behavior that will be used in the experiment. So, when shaping his dog's behavior, Jorge might reward it with a food treat when it lifts its paw off the ground while standing. Then Jorge might reinforce the dog lifting its paw while sitting. Next, he would reinforce the dog when it sits, lifts its paw, and brushes Jorge's hand with it. Finally, Jorge would reinforce the dog when it sits, lifts its paw, and places it in Jorge's hand.

Another way to think about shaping is to think about reinforcing behaviors that approximate the desired behavior. As the animal learns, the trainer becomes more and more selective with reinforcement, only reinforcing behaviors that are successively closer and closer to the desired final behavior. Eventually the animal learns the desired behavior and only receives reinforcement for performing correctly.

The Schedules of Reinforcement

B. F. Skinner uncovered an important facet of reinforcement while working with his rats. In order to efficiently use the food pellets he kept in his lab, he did not give the animals a pellet after each successful performance of the desired behavior. Skinner only gave the rats pellets when they exhibited the desired behavior after a certain length of time.

This is called a partial reinforcement schedule, because reinforcement is not given after each correct behavior. Partial reinforcement schedules create a stronger affinity for performing the desired behavior than do immediate reinforcement schedules. Skinner observed that extinction of the behavior happened more slowly for rats that experienced partial reinforcement than those that experienced immediate reinforcement. This discovery was important for understanding some of the mechanisms behind learning. Psychologists began studying **schedules of reinforcement** in an attempt to determine which type of schedule would yield optimal learning results.

Researchers focused on four different schedules of reinforcement: fixed ratio, variable ratio, fixed interval, and variable interval. Each of these schedules is explained in greater detail in the following section.

Fixed- and Variable-Ratio Schedules

In a **fixed-ratio schedule**, reinforcement is given after an animal exhibits a set number of correct responses. Skinner's original experiment is an example of a fixed-ratio schedule because the rats received a food pellet after a certain number of correct responses. If a dog is given a treat after "shaking hands" five separate times, the schedule is a fixed-ratio-5 schedule, abbreviated as FR-5. Over time, the dog learns to expect a food treat after each fifth shake. Fixed-ratio schedules produce strong, consistent responses because there is a clear connection between the animal's response and the reinforcement it receives. This type of schedule is resistant to extinction, as long as the number of responses does not get too high.

In a **variable-ratio** (VR) **schedule**, reinforcement is given after a varied number of correct responses. For example, when training his dog to shake on command, Jorge would vary the number of shakes the dog would need to perform before reinforcing the behavior with a food treat. A VR-5 schedule could mean that the trainer reinforces the desired behavior after 1 response, 5 responses, or 10 responses. The number used in the naming convention is generally an average, even though the reality is varied. This reinforcement schedule produces the strongest learning behaviors in operant conditioning. Animals trained using this schedule type respond with the desired behavior more consistently than with other schedules, and the behavior associated with variable-ratio schedules is harder to extinguish than behaviors on other schedules.

Fixed and Variable-Interval Schedules

In a **fixed-interval schedule**, reinforcement is given after an animal gives a correct response, but subsequent reinforcers are not given until a set interval of time has

SCHEDULES OF REINFORCEMENT Patterns of how reinforcers are given during operant conditioning.

FIXED-RATIO SCHEDULE A schedule of reinforcement in which the reinforcer is given after a set number of correct behavioral responses.

VARIABLE-RATIO SCHEDULE A schedule of reinforcement in which the reinforcer is given after a changing number of correct behavioral responses.

FIXED-INTERVAL SCHEDULE A schedule of reinforcement in which the reinforcer is given after a set period of time has passed and a correct response has been given.

passed. Recall the dog training example. In a fixed-interval schedule that is set on a three-minute interval, Jorge reinforces the dog's shake with a food treat the first time it occurs. He would not reinforce the dog's subsequent shakes until the three-minute period had completely passed, even if the dog shook fifty times during that three-minute interval. Once the interval has passed, he would then reinforce the next shake with a food treat.

The results of this reinforcement schedule are not as strong as fixed-ratio or variable-ratio schedules. In effect, a fixed-interval schedule teaches the organism that its responses will not be reinforced until the set time period has passed. The organism, therefore, does not perform the desired behavior much during the interval period.

VARIABLE-INTERVAL SCHEDULE A schedule of reinforcement in which the reinforcer is given after varied periods of time have passed and a correct response is given.

In a **variable-interval schedule**, reinforcement is given after a varied amount of time. Typically, the schedule is named based on the average time interval between reinforcements. For example, in a VI-30 schedule, reinforcement is given, on average, every 30 seconds. Using this schedule to train his dog to shake on command, Jorge would vary the amount of time between giving his dog reinforcement for shaking. After the first correct behavior he would reinforce the shake with a food treat. Then he might wait 20 seconds before reinforcing the next correct behavior with a food treat. The third reinforcement might come after a 40-second interval. Variable-interval schedules have a similar naming convention to the rest of the reinforcement schedules. A VI-5 schedule could mean that the trainer reinforces the desired behavior after 1 second, 5 seconds, or 10 seconds. The number used is generally an average interval time.

Robert Rescorla and Allan Wagner proposed a model of classical conditioning that is called opponent process theory. In this model, learning is based upon the discrepancy between what is anticipated or expected to occur and what actually occurs. Essentially, the effect of surprise would determine how much conditioning would occur. There are four main tenets of the theory:

1. There is a maximum associative strength that can happen between the conditional stimulus (CS) and the unconditional stimulus (UCS).
2. This associative strength will go up with each trial; however, the amount is influenced by the amount of previous training. More associative strength will occur earlier, rather than later.
3. The rate of conditioning is a function of the CS and the UCS that are given.
4. The level of conditioning is then a function of the amount of learning before the conditioning of the stimulus and the level of conditioning to the stimulus associated with the UCS.

COGNITIVE APPROACHES TO LEARNING

Learning is a complex process that involves interrelated factors. Different researchers take different perspectives on how learning occurs. The cognitive approach to understanding learning is fundamentally different from the conditioning approaches to learning. Conditioning focuses on observable behaviors only, while cognitive approaches to learning involve the mental processes of thinking and perceiving. This chapter highlights latent learning and observational learning.

Edward Tolman and Albert Bandura are two psychologists who focused their research efforts on cognitive approaches to learning. Bandura focused on observational learning, which will be explained in greater detail later in the chapter. Tolman, whose research predates Bandura's, wanted to show that animals use more than simple stimulus-response or operant-reinforcer associations to learn about their environments.

Tolman and his colleagues designed experiments that demonstrated the cognitive nature of learning. They created a maze with three possible paths leading to a food box. Locating the food box served as the reinforcer for the rats that ran through the maze. To test the rats' understanding of the maze, Tolman placed two barriers in the maze to block two of the three routes to the food box. When the barriers were both in the "up" position, the rats chose the shortest route to the food box. When one barrier was down, blocking the shortest route, the rats chose the next best route to the food box, even though this route was not previously reinforced. Tolman and his colleagues realized that the rats had created a mental schematic, or **cognitive map**, to make their way through the maze despite the barriers.

COGNITIVE MAP A mental representation of an actual location or space.

Evidence of cognitive maps is abundant in the natural world. Salmon, sea turtles, and many other animals return to specific breeding grounds year after year to bear their young. Humans create cognitive maps when they recall a driving route from memory. Squirrels and birds, among other animals, create cognitive maps to recall where they have stored food to retrieve in colder months. In a sense, Tolman simply identified and named an important mental process that animals use for survival.

Latent Learning

Sometimes a parent does not realize that a child has learned a new word or skill until the child uses it with great proficiency. Learning that occurs without being immediately expressed is known as **latent learning**. Because learning is demonstrated through observable behaviors, those observing will not know if a new skill has been learned until the organism expresses that learning through its behavior.

LATENT LEARNING Learning that occurs without being immediately expressed.

Tolman's investigation of cognitive maps is one example of latent learning. When the rats chose another path to the food box, they expressed an understanding of the maze that went previously undetected because they chose the most efficient route to the food when that route was available. The rats did not express what they had learned until the need to express it arose. Latent learning also tends to occur without the use of reinforcement. How organisms learn without reinforcement is one question at the center of Albert Bandura's investigation into learning.

Observational Learning

Observational learning occurs after an organism observes the behavior of another organism. When a person learns through observation, her or she is integrating different pieces of information and relating them to her current observation of a particular situation.

OBSERVATIONAL LEARNING Learning that occurs after an organism observes the behavior of another organism.

For example, Selena is observing her significant other, Brian, eating a particularly spicy meal. She watches as Brian's face turns red and his eyes begin to water. The redness climbs down Brian's neck and spreads across his collarbone. His nose even begins to run. After wiping his face on his napkin, he drinks an entire glass of ice water. As Selena observes his behavior, she recalls a memory of an unpleasantly spicy meal she had two years ago at the same restaurant. When Brian offers her a bite of his food, she declines. Using her own observations and her memory, she learns that the food is too spicy for her tastes. She did not experience the heat of the food herself this time, but she learned that it was likely to be too spicy for her tastes, so she refuses a bite.

Bandura and the Bobo Doll

Observational learning was further promoted by Albert Bandura, who investigated the link between observing an aggressive behavior and acting aggressively. Bandura began teaching at Stanford University, where he continues to work today. His research marked the beginning of a new focus in the field of psychology called social learning theory. **Social learning theory** postulates that humans learn appropriate and inappropriate behaviors by participating in and observing social interactions with others.

Bandura focused much of his research attention on aggression and social learning, as evidenced by his now-famous Bobo doll experiment. Bandura and a graduate student, Richard Walters, focused their attention on observational learning by investigating the connections between the actions of parents and their children. They were especially interested in aggressive behaviors. They believed that children learned to act aggressively from their parents, both through observation and reinforcement. Bandura and Walters found that extremely aggressive teenagers generally also had aggressive parents. Following this line of reasoning, Bandura and Walters designed an experiment to test the way a child might learn aggressive behaviors simply by being exposed to them.

SOCIAL LEARNING THEORY
The theory that humans learn appropriate and inappropriate behaviors by participating in and observing social interactions with others.

PSYCHOLOGY & CAREERS: VIDEO GAMES AND VIOLENCE FROM THE PERSPECTIVE OF A GAME DESIGNER

Eric Zimmerman, a New York–based digital game designer, prefers to create interactive digital games that are challenging. His work includes teaching others about the art, sport, and psychology of video games, and he owns the company Gamelab.

Games include large amounts of information and automatic, complex processes and can give the player immediate feedback on an action. Video games can engender a cross-cultural and cooperative spirit, particularly as individuals network and play with other players, some of whom live on the other side of the world. Some video games also include political and social content, thus engaging players in a dialogue with current events.

What makes Zimmerman's game designs different than more violent video games? His company offers adventure games, simulations, and team sports—many types of games that are not driven by violence. Zimmerman believes that although violent games tend to be popular, video games can portray types of conflict that are fun but non-violent. After all, violent games only have power if consumers buy them and use them. Less violent video games involve play that is meaningful and necessitates making good choices.

The experiment began with children observing an adult hitting, kicking, and punching a Bobo doll, a large inflatable clown doll that rocked back and forth when hit. After the children observed the adult's behavior, they were individually exposed to the Bobo doll. The children were observed by the researchers, but they believed that they were alone. The children in the experimental group demonstrated similar behaviors to the ones they observed from the aggressive adult.

A separate control group of children did not observe the adult acting aggressively toward the doll. Those in the control group exhibited significantly fewer aggressive behaviors than the experimental group.

The ramifications for Bandura's research have been extensive. Social psychologists continue to investigate the effects of watching violent television programs on children's levels of aggression. The results of Bandura's research also affect parenting behaviors. Parents who regularly use corporal punishment to discipline their children may notice an increase in aggression in their children's behavior. At the same time, certain qualities must be present for a model's behavior to produce lasting effects for the observer. The model must be respected by the observer, the observer must feel a connection to the model, the model's behavior is reinforced in some way, and the observer is reinforced for giving the model attention. If the model or the behavior is not compelling in some way to the observer, behavior is more likely to be discounted rather than noticed and remembered.

SUMMARY

Classical conditioning is the most basic learning theory. In classical conditioning, an organism learns an association between a stimulus and a response. In Pavlov's experiment, the sound of the tone predicted that the dogs would receive food. The dogs were conditioned to associate the sound of the tone with food; they salivated when they heard the tone because they anticipated eating. Associations made by animals between events can support their survival. On a more complex level, advertisers use classical conditioning to associate various products with positive feelings, thereby enticing consumers to purchase the products. Classical conditioning creates powerful associations that individuals may not realize influence their behaviors.

Operant conditioning is based on consequences—events that follow a behavior rather than precede it. Operant conditioning is a powerful shaper of future behaviors. Behaviors are controlled by reinforcers and punishers. Positive reinforcers are desirable consequences of a behavior. Negative reinforcement occurs when an organism can avoid an undesirable consequence following a correct behavior. Punishment is a negative consequence following an incorrect behavior. Research has shown that positive and negative reinforcement are more effective at modifying future behaviors than punishment. Reinforcement can be given on various schedules to obtain maximal behavioral results.

Cognitive approaches to learning are based on the understanding that it is not necessary for an organism to experience a behavior or consequence in order to learn a new behavior. Most research reveals the way humans learn by observing others' behaviors and modifying their own behaviors accordingly.

REFERENCES

Cole, M., & Wertsch, J.V. Beyond the individual-social antimony in discussions of Piaget and Vygotsky. Retrieved from http://www.massey.ac.nz/~alock/virtual/colevyg.htm

Gallagher, J.M., & Reid, D.K. (1981). *The learning theory of Piaget and Inhelder.* Lincoln, NE: Authors Choice.

Gerrig, R. J., & Zimbardo, P. G. (2009). *Psychology and life* (19th ed.). Boston, MA: Allyn & Bacon.

Green, M., & Piel, J. A. (2002). *Theories of human development.* Boston, MA: Allyn & Bacon.

Kolb, D.A., Boyatzis, R.E., & Mainemelis, C. (2000). Experiential learning theory: Previous research and new directions. In R. J. Sternberg & L. F. Zhang (Eds.), *Perspectives on thinking, learning, and cognitive styles.* Mahwah, NJ: Lawrence Erlbaum.

Leonard, D.C. (2002). *Learning theories, A to Z.* Westport, CT: Greenwood Press.

Milbourn, G., Jr. (1996, November 17). Punishment in the workplace creates undesirable side effects. *Wichita Business Journal.* Retrieved from http://www.bizjournals.com/wichita/stories/1996/11/18/focus3.html

Pajares, F. (2004). Albert Bandura: Biographical sketch. Retrieved from http://www.des.emory.edu/mfp/bandurabio.html

Pritchard, A. (2009). *Ways of learning: learning theories and learning styles in the classroom.* New York, NY: Routledge.

Pritchard, A., & Woollard, J. (2010). *Psychology for the classroom: Constructivism and social learning.* New York, NY: Routledge.

Salen, K., & Zimmerman, E. (2003). *Rules of play: Game design fundamentals.* Cambridge, MA: MIT Press.

Sasso, N. (Producer & editor). (2009, December 8). A conversation with Eric Zimmerman [Audio podcast]. Interview by C. J. Pratt. *Another Castle.* Retrieved from http://gamedesignadvance.com/?page_id=1616

Shaffer, D.R. (2009). *Social and personality development* (6th ed.). Belmont, CA: Wadsworth, Cengage Learning.

Smith, L., & Tomlinson, P. (1997). *Piaget, Vygotsky and beyond: Future issues for developmental psychology and education.* New York, NY: Routledge.

Vargas, J. (2005). A brief biography of B. F. Skinner. Retrieved from http://www.bfskinner.org/BFSkinner/AboutSkinner.html

Emotion and Moods

"Any emotion, if it is sincere, is involuntary."

—Mark Twain

WHAT IS EMOTION?

Humans are emotional beings. The emotions exert a powerful influence on human thought, behavior, communication, and perception. Emotional expression starts in infancy and contributes significantly to a person's experience of life. Emotions are more than just feelings. They are physical experiences as well. Emotions are automatic responses to thoughts, events, and experiences. They are an adaptive response that helps you focus and respond to challenges. The term **affect** is used to describe emotions and motivations. Affect is one of three components of psychology, in addition to behavior and cognition. **Cognition** includes thinking, attention, and processing and using information. **Behavior** is a person's actions and how they respond to other people and events.

AFFECT Emotions and motivations.

COGNITION Thinking, attention, and processing and using information.

BEHAVIOR A person's actions and how they respond to other people and events.

EMOTION

Emotions involve arousal, a physiological response by the autonomic nervous system; cognitive experiences, such as thoughts and memories; and expressive behaviors, such as smiling or shaking a fist. For instance, a person experiencing fear may have an increased heart rate, nausea, trembling, and worried thoughts. Animals experience and express emotions as well, which supports the theory that emotions have a biological basis.

EMOTION Aroused physiological response of the autonomic nervous system to which cognitive experiences and expressive behaviors contribute.

The relationship between emotion, cognition, and behavior is a subject of great debate among psychologists. Psychologist Richard Lazarus believed that people must think about an experience in order to feel emotion. According to Lazarus, emotions occur through the process of conscious or unconscious cognitive appraisal, physiological arousal, and then emotional response and action. For instance, if you see a man carrying what seems to be a gun, you might think, "He has a gun!" Your heart might start to pound as you become afraid and decide to flee. When you think you are safe again, you may feel euphoric relief.

Robert Zajonc, a social psychologist, disagreed with Lazarus. Zajonc believed

KEY CONCEPTS

1. Emotional awareness and growth have innate and cultural sources in the individual. See page 167.

2. There is current interest in facial expressions as a clue to emotional states, especially as seen in different societies. See page 171

3. Researchers disagree about whether emotions are directly tied to cognitive awareness or occur independently of cognition. See page 165.

4. Studies of emotion and linguistics have an interesting relationship to each other: verbal skills may help individuals to express and understand their emotions better. See page 173.

that emotional reaction and cognition are separate processes. Zajonc observed that emotional reactions may occur faster than conscious thoughts and criticized Lazarus's notion of unconscious cognition. The direct path from the retina of the eye to the hypothalamus enables a faster-than-thought emotional reaction to sensory input. For example, if you are walking in the forest and hear a rustling in the leaves, you might jump in fear before you determine whether a snake, or just the wind, made the noise.

TRY IT!

The following is a checklist for qualities associated with emotional intelligence. Place a check mark by each of the following characteristics that describe your emotional intelligence in the categories of self-awareness, self-regulation, and self-motivation.

Self-Awareness

❑ Do you know which emotions you are feeling and why?

❑ Can you accurately assess your strengths and limitations?

❑ Do you voice your point of view even if it is unpopular?

Self-Regulation

❑ Can you handle impulsive feelings and difficult emotions well?

❑ Do you stay focused and think clearly under pressure?

❑ Are you flexible enough to handle changes and adapt?

Self-Motivation

❑ Do you pursue challenges and take calculated risks?

❑ Are you able to commit to the goals of a group?

❑ Do you proceed with optimism and hope in pursuing goals, despite obstacles?

Determining the Range of Emotions

The basic range of human emotions includes fear, anger, sadness, joy or happiness, surprise, excitement or interest, guilt, shame, disgust, and contempt. Emotions vary in intensity and duration. Research psychologist Paul Ekman describes emotions as having a set of characteristics including a feeling or experienced sensation, brief time span, personal meaning, cognitive appraisal, and a signal that tells other people how an emotional person is feeling.

MOOD A broad outlook on life that is less intense than an emotion and less likely to be triggered by a specific event; it may last for an extended period of time.

Moods are similar to emotions, but they last longer. While most people can identify the cause of a particular emotion, moods may not be so easy to explain. Emotions have a short duration and last for seconds or minutes, while moods may last for hours or days. Emotions may change quickly or exist in conflicting states. A mood is a long-lasting emotional state that tends to be positive (good) or negative (bad). Moods involve both physical arousal and the conscious elements of energy or tiredness, and calm or tension. People generally feel best when they are in a state of energy and calm and worse when they are in a state of tiredness and tension.

Moods can be controlled or changed by emotions, physiology, and conscious thought. Psychologist Robert Thayer surveyed a range of adults to find out the methods they used to identify and change bad moods, enhance energy, and reduce tension. The most common methods reported for changing a bad mood were cognitive self-control, such as recognizing a bad mood and giving yourself a pep talk; social strategies such as visiting or talking with friends; and analysis reflection, or figuring out the reason for the mood.

The Roots of Emotions

At the beginning of the 20th century William James, a medical doctor and psychologist at Harvard University, founded the field of functional psychology. Functional psychology explains mental states as adaptations to the environment. Carl Lange, a Danish physician and psychologist working at the University of Copenhagen during the same time period, also contributed to the field. Both James and Lange independently proposed the theory that emotional experiences follow physiological arousal in response to environmental stimuli.

Emotions are controlled by the **limbic system**. The limbic system includes the amygdala, hypothalamus, hippocampus, and pituitary gland. The **amygdala** is associated with the emotions of fear and anger. It consists of a pair of almond-shaped clusters of neurons located next to the hippocampus, just behind the pituitary gland. The **hypothalamus**, which is the pleasure center of the brain, regulates the **pituitary gland**, which is called the master endocrine gland because it secretes hormones that regulate growth, metabolism, thirst, temperature, and sexual behavior. The **hippocampus** is involved with memory and navigation.

LIMBIC SYSTEM Those parts of the brain that control emotions, consisting of the amygdala, hypothalamus, hippocampus, and pituitary gland.

AMYGDALA Part of the brain that pairs emotion and memory; it is part of the limbic system.

HYPOTHALAMUS The pleasure center of the brain; it regulates the pituitary gland.

PITUITARY GLAND The master endocrine gland that secretes hormones regulating growth, metabolism, thirst, temperature, and sexual behavior.

HIPPOCAMPUS Part of the brain implicated in memory; it is part of the limbic system.

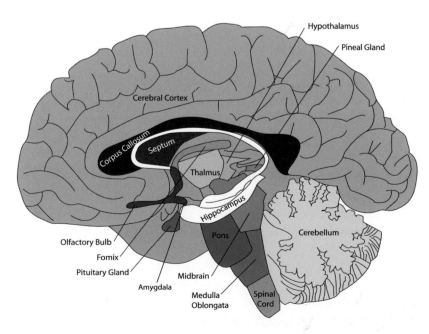

FIGURE 9.1 The Brain

The **autonomic nervous system** controls physiological arousal. This self-regulating system controls the glands and internal organs. The autonomic nervous system is not under conscious control. It regulates processes such as digestion, temperature, fluid regulation, heartbeat, and the muscles of the eyes. This system is made up of two parts, the sympathetic and parasympathetic nervous systems. The **sympathetic nervous system** is responsible for arousing and energizing the body in response to stress—much like the gas pedal of a car. When you are angry or frightened, your sympathetic nervous system stimulates your **adrenal glands** to release the hormones **epinephrine** (adrenaline) and **norepinephrine**, which are responsible for the fight-or-flight reaction to threats or stress. These substances accelerate your heartbeat, slow digestion to raise the blood sugar, dilate the pupils and arteries, and cause perspiration.

The hypothalamus also produces fear reactions because when a person is faced with a stressor the hypothalamus signals to the pituitary gland to secrete adreno-corticotropic hormone (ACTH), the body's major stress hormone. ACTH then stimulates the adrenal cortex, the outer layer of the adrenal glands, to secrete yet another stress hormone, cortisol. Next, it travels throughout the body, generating fear and arousal. When it reaches the hippocampus, it will then turn off the body's arousal.

The **parasympathetic nervous system** is responsible for calming the body and controls the processes of "resting and digesting." If the sympathetic nervous system is like a gas pedal, the parasympathetic system acts like the brake. When you calm down, the parasympathetic nervous system has the opposite effect of the sympathetic nervous system. It conserves energy by stimulating digestion, lowering the blood sugar and heart rate. The parasympathetic nervous system regulates salivation, digestion, defecation, urination, and crying. The parasympathetic nervous system is regulated by the neurotransmitter acetylcholine. Acetylcholine also plays a role in learning and memory.

Many psychologists have theorized about the nature and cause of emotions. The historic debate about the nature of emotions has focused on the importance of and relationship between the physiological, cognitive, and behavioral elements of emotional expression. Psychologists have proposed three classic theories to explain emotions: the James-Lange, Cannon-Bard, and two-factor theories.

The James-Lange Theory of Emotion

The **James-Lange theory of emotion** states that emotions result from an awareness of physiological responses. Emotions are experienced only after perception of an event and physical reaction to the perception. Imagine you are walking down a dark street late at night and notice a stranger walking toward you. You might experience fear as he gets closer, which turns to relief as he greets you in passing and goes on his way. According to the James-Lange theory, you feel fear because your heart is pounding and your palms are sweating.

William James believed that people could control their emotions by changing their behavioral responses. For instance, whistling a tune can help you feel less

AUTONOMIC NERVOUS SYSTEM A two-part, self-regulating system that controls the glands and internal organs.

SYMPATHETIC NERVOUS SYSTEM The part of the human nervous system responsible for activating the body, which triggers its fight-or-flight responses among others.

ADRENAL GLANDS Glands located above the kidneys that release hormones in response to stress.

EPINEPHRINE A hormone released by the adrenal gland to create the fight-or-flight reaction by accelerating the heartbeat, raising blood sugar, dilating pupils, and causing perspiration; also known as adrenaline.

NOREPINEPHRINE A hormone similar to epinephrine that is released by the adrenal gland to create the fight-or-flight reaction by accelerating the heartbeat, raising blood sugar, dilating pupils, and causing perspiration.

PARASYMPATHETIC NERVOUS SYSTEM The part of the human nervous system responsible for calming the body; it controls the processes of "resting and digesting."

JAMES-LANGE THEORY OF EMOTION A theory stating that emotions result from an awareness of physiological responses and are experienced only after the perception of an event, and the physical reaction to the perception, have occurred.

afraid, and standing up straight, relaxing your face, and smiling can help relieve sadness and anxiety. On the other hand, giving in to strong emotions such as panic, grief, or anger intensifies those emotions.

Carl Lange studied the physiological reactions expressed with different emotions. Sorrow is associated with fatigue, weakness, dry mouth, tears, and reduced blood flow, which could lead to pale skin and poor health if the sad emotional state lasts for a long time. Joy is associated with the opposite of the response to sorrow. Blood vessels dilate and the function of muscles and nerves is enhanced. The facial muscles contract, which causes smiling and creasing in the eye muscles. Joy increases blood flow, which brings more oxygen to all the parts of the body and improves overall health, energy, and cognitive function.

Lange considered sorrow and fear to be the opposite of joy and anger. Fear is similar to sorrow, but it also involves the contraction of blood vessels and major muscle groups, resulting in shivering or paralysis. Anger is associated with increased blood flow but may involve noticeable swelling of the veins. Joy may cause a person to be more active and lively, but anger causes agitation and sometimes aggressive displays such as shouting, staring, or fist shaking.

Cannon-Bard Theory of Emotion

Walter Cannon served as chairman of the department of physiology at Harvard Medical School around the turn of the 20th century. His studies of human digestion led him to make observations about the changes made in the body during various emotions. Cannon believed different emotions were associated with similar physiological changes—that physiological arousal and emotional response occur simultaneously.

Philip Bard, who was one of Cannon's graduate students, later became director of the department of physiology at Johns Hopkins Medical School. Bard's research involved mapping various emotions to parts of the brain, and he discovered that the hypothalamus controls sexual behavior.

Cannon and Bard believed that emotions and physiological responses occur simultaneously. They performed experiments to observe changes in animals following surgical removal of various parts of the brain. According to the **Cannon-Bard theory of emotions**, a frightening experience causes both the emotion of fear and the physiological response of a faster heartbeat, but an increased heartbeat alone does not cause fear. Cannon and Bard did not think that physiological responses by themselves are enough to generate emotions such as fear, anger, or love.

CANNON-BARD THEORY OF EMOTIONS The belief that emotions and physiological responses occur simultaneously.

Two-Factor Theory of Emotion

Stanley Schachter and Jerome Singer developed the **two-factor theory of emotion**, which proposed that emotions develop from a physiological response and also a cognitive label or thought that describes or defines the physical arousal. Schachter and Singer performed experiments in which they injected college-aged men with either a mild stimulant, like epinephrine, or an inert saline solution, as a control. The test subjects were given different information about the side effects from the injection—the truth, no information at all, or misinformation. They were then left in a waiting room with a participant actor who acted either angry or euphoric. The actor's mood was more likely to affect participants when they were unaware of the side effects of the injection. The uninformed group was most likely to be affected by and react similarly to the mood of the actor, either angry or euphoric.

SCHACHTER-SINGER TWO-FACTOR THEORY OF EMOTION Proposal that emotions develop from both a physiological response and a cognitive label or thought that describes or defines the physical arousal.

James-Lange theory	The belief that emotions result from an awareness of physiological responses and are experienced only after the perception of an event, and the physical reaction to the perception, have occurred.
Cannon-Bard theory	The belief that emotions and physiological responses occur simultaneously.
Schachter-Singer two-factor theory	The belief that emotions develop from both a physiological response and a cognitive label or thought that describes or defines the physical arousal.

FIGURE 9.2 Theories of Emotion

Emotions and Culture

Emotional expression is influenced by culture. Paul Ekman, a research psychologist, studied emotions and human facial expressions. Facial expressions indicate how a person is feeling, and studies indicate that facial expressions are universal across cultures. Ekman performed an experiment in which he showed a series of photographs of different facial expressions to individuals from the United States, Chile, Argentina, Brazil, and Japan. He asked participants to identify the emotion being expressed. Regardless of culture, most subjects agreed on the emotion that each facial expression represented.

Variations in the social expression of emotions are regulated by what Ekman terms display rules. **Display rules** are learned rules about appropriate displays of emotions. In one study, American and Japanese people displayed the same expressions after watching disturbing films of accidents and surgeries. However, those who participated in the study responded differently when a scientist observed them as they watched the films—the Japanese subjects were more likely than the Americans to mask their negative expressions. On the other hand, the study found that Japanese are more likely to express respect or sympathy than Westerners.

Your facial expressions affect your emotions. If you smile, you will likely feel happier, and if you frown, you are more likely to feel angry. Charles Darwin noticed similarities between the facial expressions of humans and nonhuman primates. He proposed that facial expressions are a universal means of nonverbal communication. Darwin believed that facial expressions and emotional gestures are adaptive mechanisms of communication. Like other animals, humans stare or turn away as indicators of aggression or submission. Surprise and fear widen the eyes, letting them take in more information.

Regardless of a person's culture, a smile indicates happiness or pleasure; wide eyes and a tense expression indicate fear; and a scowl indicates anger. People who are blind also display predictable facial expressions in response to various emotions even if they have never seen another person. The predictable patterns of facial expressions support Darwin's idea that facial expressions evolved to communicate information and influence behaviors.

Genetics also influence facial expressions. In one study by Ekman and his colleagues, 28 sets of twins separated at birth were shown films

DISPLAY RULES Learned rules about appropriate displays of emotions.

chosen to cause certain emotional responses. One film was pleasant, showing gorillas in a zoo, ocean waves, and a puppy. The second film was a safety film that showed men being careless and getting hurt at work, and the third, a medical training film, showed the treatment of burns and surgery. A hidden camera videotaped the test subjects as they watched the films.

The subjects' responses were then analyzed according to the **facial action coding system** (FACS) that was developed by Ekman, Wallace Friesen, and Joseph Hager. The system measures changes in facial activity according to 44 different action units (AU) that produce the variety of movements of facial muscles—such as those around the eyes, brows, nose, mouth, chin, dimples—and also head and eye positions and tilting. The emotions expressed were classified as happiness, surprise, sadness, fear, anger, and disgust. Significant correlations for positive emotional expression were observed in the twins, but correlations were not found for negative emotions or disgust. In addition to facial expression, gestures, and other displays, emotions may be communicated vocally and through music and art.

Different emotions cause different physiological responses. Negative emotions, moods (including depression), and personality types show more activity in the right side of the prefrontal cortex, while positive emotions, moods, and personalities show more activity in the left lobe. Fear excites the amygdala more than anger. Fear, anger, and joy all accelerate the heart rate but involve different facial muscles. Lifting of the inner eyebrows indicates worry, while raising and pulling the eyebrows together shows fear. A natural smile uses the muscles around the eyes, while false smiles do not extend to the eyes and start and stop more abruptly than a natural smile. Emotions can be difficult to conceal due to their autonomic physiological responses.

FACIAL ACTION CODING SYSTEM (FACS) A system that measures changes in facial activity according to 44 different action units (AU) that produce the variety of movements of facial muscles—such as those around the eyes, brows, nose, mouth, chin, dimples—and also head and eye positions and tilting.

FACIAL FEEDBACK HYPOTHESIS

The **facial feedback hypothesis** states that feedback from the facial muscles influences a person's experience of emotion. Facial expressions may influence how people describe their emotions and how they recall events. They are also associated with physiological changes, including heart rate, skin temperature and conductance, and blood volume.

Researchers have tested the facial feedback hypothesis by asking subjects to contract different facial muscles and then measuring the subjects' reported moods. The experiments were designed so that test subjects manipulated their facial expressions without emotional stimulus or cognitive interpretation of the expression. One experiment involved asking subjects to rate their amusement while looking at cartoons while holding a pen in three different positions—in their nondominant hand, in their lips, or between their teeth. Holding the pen between the lips causes an expression similar to frowning, while holding a pen in the teeth causes an expression similar to smiling. The people who held the pens in their teeth rated the cartoons as funnier. People holding the pen between their lips were prevented from smiling, and they rated the cartoon as less amusing. These studies indicate that controlling facial expressions does have an influence on emotions.

FACIAL FEEDBACK HYPOTHESIS The theory that feedback from the facial muscles influences a person's experience of emotion.

Facial Affect Programs

Paul Ekman researched the ability to recognize facial clues indicating emotion. He formulated a system called a **facial recognition program**, which is a more or less universal tendency to equate certain facial expressions with particular emotions: when you feel happy, the muscles of your face contract in a certain way, and people around you recognize from your facial expression that you are happy. The same pattern of facial expressions exists for a range of emotions. These patterns of facial expressions are known as **facial affect programs**.

Facial affect programs consist of several distinct processes; some are thought to be universal, while others are believed to be culturally specific. The most basic or primal emotions involve the neurochemical responses sent by the brain to move or contract certain facial muscles. There are seven basic emotional facial expressions that are recognized in every culture: sadness, anger, surprise, contempt, fear, happiness, and disgust. These emotions trigger specific reactions in the muscles of the face. The expressions associated with surprise and fear, for example, are universal, but the conditioning that governs the responses can be culturally generated.

Facial affect programs can vary in different cultural settings. In Japan, smiling while casting the eyes downward indicates embarrassment or disappointment; in Western societies, the same expression is usually interpreted as shyness or reluctance.

People who are unfamiliar with the cultural contexts of facial expressions risk making mistakes in communication. People from Western and Asian cultures interpret the intensity of emotions differently, for example. People from Western cultures may have a tendency to interpret facial emotional expressions as an external or "surface" indicator, whereas people from Asian cultures may interpret subtle nuances in facial expression as indicators of extreme emotional responses.

Happiness and Sadness

Happiness is a complex group of associated feelings, including lightness, openness, and peace. The experience of happiness involves pleasure and gratification. Pleasures, such as comfort or exuberance, induce positive emotions. Gratifications are enjoyable activities, such as playing games, dancing, making music, or spending time with friends. Seeking feelings of pleasure (such as comfort or exuberance) and activities that provide gratification (such as playing games or spending time with friends) can increase happiness. Other ways to be happier include managing your time, getting enough rest, finding your purpose, and nurturing your relationships.

While most people do not think of happiness or sadness as conscious choices, acting happy actively increases health and happiness. This is the idea behind the **positive psychology** movement, which was founded by psychologist Martin Seligman. This movement focuses on mental health and positivity rather than mental illness.

According to the tenets of positive psychology, people can enhance their lives by developing positive subjective well-being, positive character, and positive groups and communities. Positive subjective well-being is a measure of a person's sense of happiness, satisfaction, and quality of life. Virtues such as wisdom, courage, love, justice, and spirituality are components of positive character. Positive groups, communities, and cultures promote education, health, families, and civic responsibility.

According to Seligman, a person's general level of happiness is defined by three factors: a person's biological disposition; his or her life circumstances, such as wealth or marital status; and voluntary factors, which are under a person's control from day to day, such as anxiety, moods, and optimism. **Positive self-talk** has proven effective in dealing with many voluntary factors, leading to increased happiness.

Dysphoria refers to the negative emotions of anxiety, sadness and depression, and anger. Anxiety and worry can persist even when people have plenty of money, health, and friends. The tendency to worry and consider worst-case scenarios may have been an evolutionary advantage to early humans. Anxiety warns of danger and can inspire people to take action, but it can be a problem if it is irrational, paralyzing, or overpowering.

Depression and sadness are a response to a sense of helplessness and failure. Depression is characterized by factors such as pessimistic or negative thinking, a sad or anxious mood, indecisiveness, or (in extreme cases) suicide. It can also include physical symptoms such as pain, changes in sleep patterns or appetite, and fatigue. Cultivating a habit of optimistic thinking can help relieve depression.

Anger

Anger is a response to perceived threats or harm. People get angry because of the actions of other people or at annoyances such as noise, traffic, temperature, or odors. Anger involves three elements:

- Thought
- Bodily reaction
- Attack

Chronic anger is related to high blood pressure and heart disease. While the expression of anger is often considered healthy, expression of angry or sad feelings actually tends to increase the emotion. For instance, if another driver cuts you off in traffic, you may feel your muscles tense and heart pound as you shake your fist at the offensive driver. That anger may carry forward into the rest of your day as well.

The best way to reduce anger is to wait, calm down, and control your thoughts. Sympathetic nervous system arousal subsides with time. Ruminating on, or thinking about, all the things that annoy you increases anger. Exercise, talking, relaxation, religious practice, and music can be effective tools for changing a bad mood. Communicating grievances without resorting to attacks against another person is also an effective way to deal with anger.

PSYCHOLOGY & CAREERS: WORKING IN HUMAN RESOURCES AND DEALING WITH ANGER

Human resources representatives are frequently called upon to resolve conflicts between employees in the workplace. Many businesses have established firm policies regarding sexual harassment or other forms of illegal discrimination. Anger management in the workplace, however, is more subjective than a specific set of policies can address. Beyond addressing the possibility of exposing your business to legal risks or even violence, it is important for anger issues to be addressed and resolved. Allowing unresolved anger issues to fester in the workplace can be extremely detrimental to employee productivity and morale. Anger issues have a variety of causes, only some of which are work-related: it is perfectly normal to get angry occasionally, as personal circumstances and career issues sometimes cause extreme if temporary stress. These incidents are a part of normal human interaction; they are usually resolved quickly and things return to normal, many times with a greater understanding of the needs of coworkers or task requirements.

Stress

STRESS A physical response to threatening or emotional events.

Stress is a physical response to threatening or emotional events. Stressful events include catastrophes, such as natural disasters or wars; life-changing events, such as marriage or divorce, the birth of a child, the death of a friend or relative, getting fired or retiring from work, injuries, or illness; and even annoyances. Even relatively minor issues—like waiting in lines or traffic, losing your keys, having a busy schedule, social stressors such as racism or bullying, and dealing with the challenges of being a parent, spouse, or roommate—can add up quickly and lead to stress.

What Is Stress?

FIGHT-OR-FLIGHT RESPONSE The first, or "alarm," stage of the sympathetic nervous system's GAS response to physical or psychological threats.

GENERAL ADAPTATION SYNDROME (GAS) The sympathetic nervous system's three-stage response to threats (alarm, resistance, exhaustion) caused by increased levels of epinephrine and norepinephrine.

The sympathetic nervous system's **fight-or-flight response** is the body's natural reaction to stressful situations. The fight-or-flight response helps you be energetic, alert, and focused in times of danger or challenge. The sympathetic nervous system responds the same way to physical or psychological threats, so a traffic accident or fight with a loved one causes the same sensations and production of epinephrine and norepinephrine.

Hans Selye described the stress response as a three-stage **general adaptation syndrome (GAS)** consisting of:

- Alarm
- Resistance
- Exhaustion

The alarm response is the fight-or-flight response. Resistance results when stress continues and becomes chronic and may be seen in bodily changes such as increased temperature, blood pressure, and respiration. If the state of stressed arousal continues, exhaustion may set in, resulting in illness or death. Illnesses associated with stress include hypertension, headaches, and heart disease. Prolonged stress may weaken your immune system because stress hormones suppress lymphocytes, which fight disease.

Coping with Stress

Factors that influence your ability to tolerate stress include your attitude, sense of control, support network, and ability to manage your emotions. A pessimistic attitude generates a depressed mood. Feelings of not being able to control one's environment contribute to stress and illness.

Learned helplessness, a tendency to passively accept that bad things happen outside of one's control, is similar to pessimism. People who give themselves positive messages are more likely to take action to change negative situations. Having a sense of hope improves mood and overall health.

Seligman's work focused on changing attitudes of pessimism, depression, and helplessness. Experiments he performed using electroshock treatment of dogs indicated that the dogs became listless after learning they could not escape the shock. Three groups of dogs were exposed to different conditions:

- The first group received an escapable shock; they could turn off the shock by pushing a panel.
- The second group received the same shock as the first dogs but had no way of turning off the inescapable shock.
- The third group received no shock at all.

The dogs were then placed in a large box with two compartments separated by a low divider. They could move from one side of the box to the other by jumping over the wall. The first and third groups learned they could escape the shocks by jumping over the barrier. The second group, which had received the inescapable shocks, became passive, lay down, and did not try to escape.

Seligman concluded that the second group had learned helplessness, or had become passive, because they learned that their actions had no effect on their environment. The dogs that had learned to be helpless could be trained to go over the barrier, and then would move to escape the shock. Similar results were observed in experiments with people using loud sounds.

Social Support

Social support is a helping network made up of friendships, close relationships, and the larger communities in which people live. Being part of a social network helps people handle stress. Having a social support network of people to talk to about things that bother a person improves health and longevity. Married people or those with close friendships or support groups tend to recover faster from illness and survive longer than people who live alone.

LEARNED HELPLESSNESS The passive acceptance that bad things happen outside of the individual's control.

SOCIAL SUPPORT A helping network made up of friendships, close relationships, and the larger communities in which people live.

HOW STRESSED ARE YOU? A TEST

Stress is an unavoidable part of life, but psychologists agree that one's reaction to stress is what determines whether the stress is perceived to be severe or not. Here is a test to measure your relative stress level. *Note: This is an exercise only; it does not indicate a true stress level or your associated health risks.*

Select a relative value based upon how relevant the following statements are to your experiences:

4 = Always
3 = More often than not
2 = Occasionally
1 = Never

1. Are you aware of the current time of day?
2. Do you wish you had more authority over your coworkers?
3. Do you have trouble with unstructured time?
4. Do you focus on winning games?
5. Are you concerned with the amount of work you complete in a day?
6. Do you feel the need to finish projects as soon as possible?
7. Do you look for something else to do when your tasks are complete?
8. Do you become impatient with lengthy explanations or sets of instructions?
9. Do you consider yourself to be driven to succeed?
10. Are you reluctant to take time for yourself?
11. Do you enjoy leisure activities?

If your total score is 11–16, you are in need of more motivational stimulation. If your score is 17–25, you are comfortable with your lifestyle and handle stress well. If your total score is 26–37, you may need to find more time to enjoy yourself. If you score 38 or higher, you may need to take on less responsibility and focus more on down time.

Rational Emotive Behavior Therapy

Psychologist Albert Ellis was the founder of **rational emotive behavior therapy (REBT)**, a cognitive behavioral therapeutic approach to coping with stress. He developed the ABC model—which stands for activating event, belief, and consequence. Ellis theorized that adversity is an event or thought that causes distress due to irrational beliefs or judgments about the adversity. Disputing negative thoughts is a way of changing thoughts and avoiding pessimistic pitfalls. Eliminating pessimism involves focusing on specific, changeable, and nonpersonal causes of adversity.

REBT has become one of the fundamental methods cognitive therapists use to help their patients change inflexible and unhealthy psychological behaviors, but it is confrontational and often emotionally charged. Many of Ellis's peers criticized him for his use of curse words and his often brutal challenges to his patients' spiritual or cultural beliefs. However, because of its ability to be tailored to the specific needs of the patient, REBT has been incorporated into many types of counseling, such as addiction and recovery, grief and loss, and family or relationship therapy.

KEY THINKERS IN PSYCHOLOGY: ALBERT ELLIS

Albert Ellis theorized that the unreasonable beliefs people held were the cause of their unhappiness and conflict with others. As a therapeutic exercise, he separated his patients' unreasonable beliefs into three categories, or the "three basic musts":

1. The approval of others is the key to positive self-esteem.
2. Others who treat you poorly deserve to be condemned as "bad people" and punished.
3. If you want something, it is acceptable to be impatient and demanding.

Ellis believed that these three sets of beliefs caused people to make unreasonable demands on themselves and others around them. As he continued his therapeutic exercises, he challenged his patients to justify their belief that they must seek the approval of others, that others must be punished for treating them poorly, and that it was appropriate to be demanding and inflexible when they want something.

As his patients began to justify their beliefs, Ellis encouraged them to examine their reasoning and try to understand that the inflexible nature of their reactions was the underlying cause of their psychological distress. He then challenged his patients to identify the inflexible beliefs as dysfunctional and to work to change those beliefs to more flexible and less absolute expectations.

Ellis did not believe that a warm or caring relationship was necessary in order for therapist–patient encounters to be successful; rather, the therapist must only communicate an attitude of unconditional acceptance of the patient. Ellis theorized that people needed the tools to identify and correct their dysfunctional beliefs in order to continue the positive effects of REBT. If a person could not continue his or her own self-improvement, then the person had not been helped.

SUMMARY

Emotions are physiological responses of the autonomic nervous system, including changed heart rate, facial expressions, and the release of chemicals in the body. Many theories have been proposed about the nature of emotions. The James-Lange theory suggests that people experience emotion when they become aware of their own physiological responses to stimuli, whereas the Cannon-Bard theory posits that the physiological and emotional experiences occur simultaneously. The two-factor theory states that our emotions arise from both physiological responses and cognitive thought.

Whatever the mechanism that produces emotion, people around the world tend to express emotions in the same way—a smile for happiness, widened eyes for fear, or a scowl to show anger. However, a person's culture can influence whether he or she displays certain emotions or masks them.

Emotions can influence thoughts, health, and behaviors. They can be the foundation of a happy and healthy life or the cause of stress and illness. Evidence continues to support the theory that there is a connection between thoughts, emotions, and health. Improved physical and emotional health can be gained by changing and directing your thoughts to be positive and optimistic. Positive thoughts lead to positive moods and emotions, which in turn create opportunities for positive experiences and increased health and happiness. Discovering and pursuing that which gives you meaning is a way to create and live a positive emotional life.

REFERENCES

Brodal, P. (2004). *The central nervous system: Structure and function* (3rd ed.). New York, NY: Oxford University Press.

Cannon, W. B. (1920). *Bodily changes in pain, hunger, fear and rage.* New York, NY: D. Appleton and Company.

Duenwald, M. (2005, January). The physiology of… facial expressions. *Discover Magazine.*

Ekman, P. (1972). Universals and cultural difference in facial expressions of emotion. In J. Cole (Ed.), *Nebraska symposium on motivation, 1971* (Vol. 19, pp. 207–280). Lincoln, NE: University of Nebraska Press. Retrieved from http://www.paulekman.com/wp-content/uploads/2009/02/Universals-And-Cultural-Differences-In-Facial-Expressions-Of.pdf

Ekman, P. (1992). Are there basic emotions? *Psychological Review, 99*(3), 550–553.

Ekman, P. (2003). *Emotions revealed: Recognizing faces and feelings.* New York, NY: Henry Holt and Company.

Ekman, P. (2004). Emotional and conversational nonverbal signals. In J. M. Larrazabal & L. A. Perez (Eds.), *Language, knowledge, and representation* (pp. 39–50). The Netherlands: Klewer. Retrieved from http://www.paulekman.com/wp-content/uploads/2009/02/Emotional-And-Conversational-Nonverbal-Signals.pdf

Ekman, P., Friesen, W., & Hager, J. (2002). *Facial action coding system: The manual.* Salt Lake City, UT: A Human Face. Retrieved from http://face-and-emotion.com/dataface/facs/manual/TitlePage.html

Ellis, A. (2001). *Feeling better, getting better, staying better.* Atascadero, CA: Impact Publishers.

Ellis, A. (2001). *Overcoming destructive beliefs, feelings and behaviors: New directions for rational emotive behavior therapy.* Amherst, NY: Prometheus Books.

Emotional Intelligence Consortium. (n.d.). Emotional competence framework. Retrieved from http://www.eiconsortium.org/reports/emotional_competence_framework.html

Harrison, T. (1997). *Archibald Philip Bard: A biographical memoir.* Washington, DC: National Academies Press. Retrieved from http://www.nap.edu/readingroom.php?book=biomems&page=pbard.html

Hillstrom, K., & Hillstrom, L. C. (Eds.). (2011). Workplace anger. *Encyclopedia of Small Business.* Retrieved from http://www.enotes.com/small-business-encyclopedia/workplace-anger

Kendler, K. S., Halberstadt, L. J., Butera, F., Myers, J., Bouchard, T., & Ekman, P. (2008). The similarity of facial expressions in response to emotion-inducing films in reared-apart twins. *Psychological Medicine, 38,* 1475–1483.

Lange, C., & James, W. (1922). *The emotions.* Baltimore, MD: Williams and Wilkins Company.

Lewis, M., Haviland-Jones, J., & Barret, L. (2008). *Handbook of emotions.* New York, NY: Guilford Press.

Matsumoto, D. R. (2001). *The handbook of culture and psychology.* New York, NY: Oxford University Press.

Myers, D. (2005). *Exploring psychology.* New York, NY: Worth Publishing.

Plutchik, R. (2001). *The emotions.* New York, NY: University Press of America.

Schachter, S. (1964). The interaction of cognitive and physiological determinants of emotional state. In L. Berkowitz (Ed.), *Advances in experimental social psychology* (pp. 49–79). London, England: Academic Press.

Seligman, M. E. (1990). *Learned optimism.* New York, NY: Alfred A Knopf.

Seligman, M. E. (1995). *What you can change and what you can't.* New York, NY: Alfred A Knopf.

Seligman, M. E. (2002). *Authentic happiness.* New York, NY: Simon and Schuster.

Shimoff, M. (2008). *Happy for no reason.* New York, NY: Simon and Schuster.

Sibbald, B. (2003). Adrenaline junkies. *CMAJ, 169*(9), 942–943. Retrieved from http://www.canadianmedicaljournal.ca/cgi/reprint/169/9/942

Stone, F. (2003). Managing today's angry workforce. In *Business: The ultimate resource.* Cambridge, MA: Perseus Publishing.

Strack, F., Martin, L., & Stepper, S. (1988). Inhibiting and facilitating conditions of the human smile: A nonobtrusive test of the facial feedback hypothesis. *Journal of Personality and Social Psychology, 54*(5), 768–777.

Zajonc, R. B. (1984). On the primacy of affect. *American Psychologist, 39*(2), 117–123.

Motivation

"To find your own way is to follow your bliss. This involves analysis, watching yourself and seeing where real deep bliss is—not the quick little excitement, but the real deep, life-filling bliss."

—Joseph Campbell

THEORIES OF MOTIVATION

People are motivated to act by different needs. These needs may be biological, such as hunger and thirst; social, such as the need to belong to a group; spiritual, such as a search for meaning; or behavioral, such as seeking reward or avoiding punishment. Psychologists have proposed theories to explain motivation of human behavior. These include instinct and evolutionary theory, drive-reduction theory, humanistic theory, and the hierarchy of needs.

Instinct and Evolutionary Theory

A **motivation** is an urge or desire that causes some type of behavior. The **instinct and evolutionary theory** of motivation was influenced by the work of Charles Darwin. It attributes behaviors to instinctive urges. **Instincts** are species-specific, unlearned behaviors. According to the instinct theory, capacities for social behavior and reasoning, as well as physical characteristics, must have undergone natural selection and evolved as adaptations to environmental conditions.

MOTIVATION A drive that causes behavior.

INSTINCT AND EVOLUTIONARY THEORY A theory of motivation suggesting that human behaviors are a result of evolutionary adaptation.

INSTINCT Species-specific, unlearned patterns of behavior.

Instinctive behavior is a fixed pattern of actions, such as infant rooting or sucking, and migratory or nest-building behavior of birds and animals. Instincts have survival value and can be for any basic need such as hunger, thirst, sexuality, or belonging to a group. These fixed actions contain an underlying drive and an urge to engage in that instinctive pattern.

German biologist Ernst Haeckel, who was also influenced by Darwin's work, contributed to the evolutionary perspective with his **recapitulation theory**, which suggested that the development of an individual organism repeats in an abbreviated way the evolutionary history of its species. Human embryos pass through phases in which they look like fish, amphibians, and so on. The recapitulation theory was not biologically sound, but it influenced the evolutionary thinkers of the late 1800s, who theorized that instincts are expressed during child development as remnants of various stages of human evolution.

RECAPITULATION THEORY A theory of motivation suggesting that the development of an individual organism repeats in an abbreviated way the evolutionary history of its species.

Drive-Reductionism and Homeostasis

The instinct theory was replaced by the drive-reduction theory. According to **drive-reduction theory**, needs create drives, which in turn produce drive-reducing behavior. Basic drives include hunger, thirst, sex, and escape from pain.

A physiological need results in an aroused state, which motivates behavior to reduce the need and maintain a stable state called homeostasis. **Homeostasis** is the body's automatic regulation of a consistent internal state, such as temperature or blood sugar. As Abraham Maslow put it, "If the body lacks some

DRIVE-REDUCTION THEORY A theory of motivation suggesting that physiological needs create an aroused state or drive that motivates behavior to reduce the need.

HOMEOSTASIS Regulation and maintenance of a balanced internal state.

1. Motivation may be biological or psychological. See page 181.

2. Motivation energizes and directs behavior in order to meet some need or desire. See page 181.

3. Abraham Maslow described the importance of various motivations in his hierarchy of needs. See page 182.

4. Physiological factors such as hormones, neurotransmitters, and genetics play a role in motivation. See page 184.

5. Culture and environment are also important influences on motivation. See page 182.

6. Achievement theories explain why some individuals are more motivated to learn, set goals, and work toward success than others. See page 191.

7. Motivation researchers look for ways to inspire goal setting, encourage work and positive thinking, and increase productivity in students and workers. See page 191.

chemical, the individual will tend to develop a specific appetite or partial hunger for that food element."

People are also motivated by positive or negative **incentives**. An incentive is any factor that influences behavior. For instance, a worker does labor both for the positive incentive of money and the negative incentive of being fired for not doing the job. Hunger is a drive that is caused by the need for food, and the scent of cooking food is the incentive that motivates the drive-reducing behavior of eating. Physical needs and the attempt to fulfill them may direct and meet other needs as well. For example, an adult who has a craving for ice cream may be satisfying a need to eat something cool, or may be seeking comfort in addition to fulfilling the need to eat.

Humanistic Theory

Humanistic psychology began as a movement in the 1950s designed to take a holistic approach to understanding the nature of what it is to be human. Humanistic psychology addresses human values such as love, compassion, creativity, and individuality. Humanistic psychology is considered the third force of psychology; behaviorism and psychoanalysis are the first and second forces.

The humanistic movement grew out of a conference held in 1964 in Old Saybrook, Connecticut. Abraham Maslow, Rollo May, Carl Rogers, Clark Moustakas, and many other psychologists attended the conference. Maslow was particularly interested in motivation. Along with Rogers, he supported the idea of self-actualization—realizing one's full potential—as a path to psychological well-being. May integrated creativity, mythology, and the arts with psychology. Moustakas studied love and loneliness with a focus on the integration of philosophy, research, and psychology.

According to the Association for Humanistic Psychology (AHP), humanistic psychology is "a value orientation that holds a hopeful, constructive view of human beings and of their substantial capacity to be self-determining. It is guided by a conviction that intentionality and ethical values are strong psychological forces, among the basic determinants of human behavior." Humanistic psychologists seek to better understand the experience of being human and take special interest in culture and consciousness, love and social issues, self-awareness and sensitivity, personal responsibility, psychotherapy, and the search for meaning.

Maslow's Hierarchy of Needs

Maslow developed a hierarchy of human needs to describe the order of importance of various motivations. According to Maslow, physiological needs take priority over all other needs. People must fulfill their basic need for food and water before they can take care of the need for safety. Safety needs include

INCENTIVE A positive or negative stimulus that motivates behavior.

HUMANISTIC PSYCHOLOGY A holistic approach to understanding human psychology that is focused on meaning, values, spirituality, and self-actualization.

security and shelter; stability and protection; freedom from fear, anxiety, and chaos; and structure, order, law, and limits.

Maslow believed that when a society's members feel safe and protected "from wild animals, extremes of temperature, criminal assault, murder, chaos, tyranny, and so on," then the next level of needs would emerge. He considered religion and philosophy to be safety-seeking mechanisms created by people to organize and understand the universe and society. The common human tendency to prefer familiar things over exotic choices is another example of an attempt to seek safety and stability in the world.

Only when individuals have met the most basic needs for food and safety are they able to pursue higher needs such as love, self-esteem, and self-actualization. The need for love and belonging involves giving and receiving affection. Maslow was careful to make a distinction between sex as a purely physiological need and the reciprocal expression of love and affection. He also focused on nurturing and unconditional love as essential parts of development of a healthy sense of self.

Once the need for love and belonging is met, a desire for self-esteem arises. Maslow identified two sets of needs: self-esteem and prestige. **Self-esteem** is a person's opinion and assessment of his or her own worth. It includes the desires for achievement and adequacy, competence and confidence, and independence. **Prestige** is the desire for recognition from others, including appreciation, attention, fame, and status. This need is exemplified today by the popularity of television shows in which individuals gain fame from using their innate desires, interests, and skills to win competitions.

Satisfying the need for self-esteem leads to feelings of self-confidence and adequacy, but failure to meet this need causes feelings of inadequacy and helplessness. He believed that healthy self-esteem derives from competence and deserved respect rather than fame or celebrity.

Maslow believed that such needs as freedom of speech, information, and expression; self-defense; and social order are preconditions for the satisfaction of basic needs (see Figure 10.1). These preconditions, according to Maslow, "are defended because without them the basic satisfactions are quite impossible, or at least severely endangered."

SELF-ESTEEM A person's opinion and assessment of his or her own worth.

PRESTIGE The desire for recognition from others, including appreciation, attention, recognition, fame, and status.

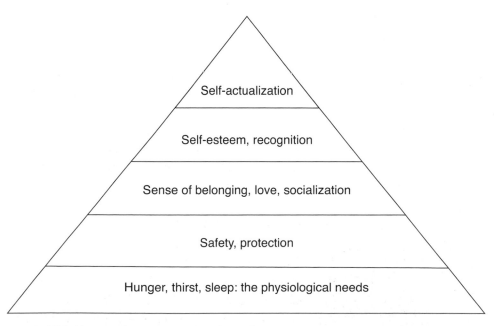

FIGURE 10.1 Maslow's Hierarchy of Needs

Self-Actualization

SELF-ACTUALIZATION The desire of a person to achieve his or her full potential.

Self-actualization is the desire of a person to achieve his or her full potential or, in Maslow's words, "to become everything that one is capable of becoming." Maslow believed that a healthy society would be one in which people's basic needs were met, allowing them to focus on developing their highest creative purpose. Maslow believed that even when individuals' basic needs have been met, they cannot be content unless they are involved in activities dedicated to fulfilling their potential.

HUMAN NEEDS

Human life is centered on meeting basic needs. Quality of life depends on how well these needs are met. The ability to meet basic needs depends on environmental factors. Individual survival depends on the need for food and safety, and survival of the species depends on sex and reproduction. When people fulfill basic needs, they seek social fulfillment and achievement. The next section looks at hunger and the need to eat.

Hunger and Eating

HUNGER The sensation of needing food.

HYPOTHALAMUS A part of the brain that links the nervous system to the endocrine system and regulates body temperature, hunger, thirst, and sleep.

Hunger is the sensation of needing food. It is associated with stomach pangs—the contractions of an empty stomach—and with changes in hormones and blood chemistry. Hunger is regulated by the **hypothalamus**, which responds to various hormones circulating in the bloodstream. Ghrelin is a hormone secreted by the empty stomach that signals hunger, and orexin, another hunger-signaling hormone, is secreted by the hypothalamus in response to low blood sugar levels.

Blood sugar is a measure of blood glucose levels. Glucose, the simple sugar molecule that the body breaks down to create energy, is either metabolized into energy or converted to fat by the pancreatic hormone insulin. Leptin and Peptide YY are hormones secreted by the digestive tract that signal fullness (also called satiety or lack of hunger) to the brain.

Insulin plays an important role in metabolism and hunger. Insulin breaks down glucose in the bloodstream. Excess glucose is converted into fat for energy storage. Many diets, in fact, focus on reducing or eliminating foods that are high in carbohydrates, because they cause the body to generate excess insulin—which in turn causes the accumulation of fat.

Regulation of Hunger

Experiments on laboratory mice and rats have elucidated the hypothalamus's role in regulating hunger. Electrical stimulation of different areas of the hypothalamus causes changes in hunger and appetite. Stimulating the sides of the lateral hypothalamus causes well-fed animals to eat, while destruction of that area causes animals to have no interest in food. The lower-middle ventromedial hypothalamus reduces hunger. Stimulating that area causes animals to stop eating, while destroying the area causes animals to overeat and become fat.

In addition to hormonal factors, hunger and satiety are controlled by a combination of gastric distension caused by food in the stomach and nutrient content absorbed by the intestines. Animals that are fed a low-calorie diet eat more than animals who are fed a high-calorie diet. The number of calories consumed by a resting body's basic metabolic functions is called the **basal metabolic rate**. In general, body weight is maintained by the homeostatic regulation of food intake and energy expenditure. The basal metabolic rate decreases when caloric intake is

BASAL METABOLIC RATE The amount of energy expended by the body in a resting state.

reduced but can be increased through exercise and increased muscle mass.

Hunger is not just a physiological response, as evidenced by the tendency of people and animals to overeat given unlimited access to food. Hunger is also affected by psychological influences. Culture influences **appetite** in the way that people learn to enjoy or reject various salty, spicy, and bitter foods, or different types of meat. People eat for comfort and pleasure and learn to avoid foods they associate with illness or unpleasant experiences.

One theory, the homeostatic-hedonistic model of hunger, suggests that two very different motivations for hunger exist. Homeostatic hunger has been attributed to an energy deficiency, but most people do not go without food long enough to experience real physiological hunger. Instead, the theory suggests, there must be another motivation to eat.

Researchers Michael Lowe and Allen Levine have focused their research on dieting that limits food intake and on reasons people eat when they are not hungry. Lowe and Levine argued that the modern trend of dieting among normal-weight people in an effort to become even thinner contributes to both eating disorders and obesity. Reducing caloric intake lowers the basal metabolic rate and makes it harder to lose weight.

Research on animals and human volunteers has indicated that the body weight of most individuals has a homeostatic **set point** that is regulated by the hypothalamus. People feel less hungry when their weight is above the set point and more hungry when their weight is below the set point. The set point is maintained by the basal metabolic rate (BMR), although the BMR may change as caloric intake or energy expenditure changes. However, people and animals may overeat when access to food is unlimited, and obesity may result.

APPETITE Psychological hunger that is motivated by emotional needs and the presence of appealing food.

SET POINT A person's normal homeostatic body weight.

Social and Environmental Factors

In many countries, nearly unlimited amounts of food are available, and most people get far less exercise than their ancestors because of modern transportation and sedentary work and leisure pursuits. High-calorie convenience food is readily available—and more important, it is often less expensive than more nutrient-rich and lower-calorie foods. Throughout the developed world, an increasing number of people have become overweight or obese as a result of excessive food intake and decreased activity.

Television has influenced the trend toward obesity. Watching TV leads to reduced activity and increased eating—through the influence of advertising. In addition to contributing to the epidemic of obesity, television and other forms of media also portray an unrealistic (and unhealthy) ideal of slimness for both men and women. This ideal of thinness contributes to the popularity of dieting and unhealthy eating behaviors.

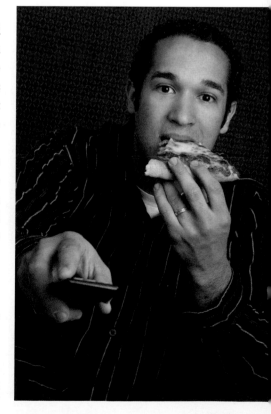

Obesity and Eating Disorders

Obesity and overweight are the conditions that result when an individual's weight is higher than what is healthy in proportion to his or her height. The ratio of body weight to height is called the body mass index (BMI).

BMI = weight (kg or pounds multiplied by .45) / squared height in meters (or inches divided by 4)

A person whose BMI is greater than 25 is considered overweight, and a person whose BMI is greater than 30 is considered obese. Obesity is a serious public health problem in America and can lead to early death and increased risk of diabetes, heart disease, stroke, and cancer.

Obesity can be caused by behavior, genetics, or environmental factors. Behavioral factors include overeating, eating foods that are high in fat and sugar, and not getting enough exercise. Genes influence appetite, weight set point, and metabolic rate. Studies of twins raised apart have indicated that two-thirds of body mass is related to genetic factors, but a person's environment influences his or her food choices and can limit physical activity. For example, a person who lives in an area with abundant opportunities for exercise is less likely to be obese than someone who has fewer exercise opportunities.

Fundamentally, obesity results from the accumulation of fat, a type of energy storage cell that is made when calories ingested exceed the calories consumed by metabolism. Once fat cells are made, they shrink or expand, but they do not decrease in number. Fat cells do not need as much energy as other types of cells do. Becoming overweight or obese also changes an individual's basal metabolic rate. Once a person is overweight, he or she requires less food to maintain the fat than was needed to accumulate it. For this reason, dieting is often ineffective.

In addition to adverse physical health effects, obesity also can cause psychological and social problems. Fat people are more likely to be depressed and experience discrimination. Obese individuals are less likely to be married, are likely to earn less money, and are less likely to be hired or promoted than those who are not obese.

Obesity is influenced by genetic, social, and environmental factors, but sometimes it has roots in disease. Prader-Willi syndrome is a genetic disease with symptoms that begin during the first year of life. Children with Prader-Willi syndrome experience uncontrollable feelings of hunger, leading to excessive eating and obesity that can be life threatening. This syndrome is a result of a chromosomal abnormality. People with Prader-Willi also have behavioral problems, poor muscle tone, cognitive delays, and sex organs that do not mature completely.

Eating disorders such as anorexia occur around the world but are more prevalent in Western cultures that idealize thinness. **Anorexia nervosa** is an eating disorder in which a normal-weight person dramatically decreases food intake and becomes more than 15 percent underweight. The effects of **bulimia nervosa**, in which a person follows a pattern of binge eating and purging through vomiting, fasting, excessive exercising, or using laxatives, may be harder to detect.

Women are especially susceptible to negative self-images about weight and appearance when media images of beauty portray an unnaturally thin ideal. Women are 10 times more likely than men to develop eating disorders. Those who are dissatisfied with their body's appearance may feel depressed and ashamed and develop eating disorders or resort to constant dieting to achieve thinness.

In societies and cultures where food is scarce, as in parts of Africa, a larger body type is favored, and there are fewer incidences of eating disorders. Home and family life play an important role in body image development. Studies have shown that girls whose mothers are preoccupied

ANOREXIA NERVOSA Eating disorder associated with intentional starvation and extreme weight loss to a body weight of more than 15 percent below normal.

BULIMIA NERVOSA Eating disorder associated with cycles of binge eating and purging through the use of laxatives, vomiting, or excessive exercise.

with weight and body image are more likely to develop eating disorders. Bulimia is more common in people whose family members suffer from alcoholism, obesity, or depression. Families and friends may influence eating disorder behavior by complimenting and expressing envy about a thin appearance.

Much research is focused on obesity prevention. Incidences of obesity and eating disorders have increased in recent decades. Researchers Jess Haines and Dianne Neumark-Sztainer examined the prevention of obesity and eating disorders with a consideration of shared risk factors. They considered obesity and eating disorders to be related conditions that may share a source, noting that many studies have shown that dieting does not stop weight gain—on the contrary, many of these studies, as well as other studies, show a link between dieting and weight gain. Haines and Neumark-Sztainer advocate for a practical, single-intervention approach to address obesity and prevent eating disorders: People who want to lose weight should increase their level of activity to boost their metabolism and should eat nutritious food throughout the day.

PSYCHOLOGY & CAREERS: INTERIOR DESIGN TO SERVE HUMAN NEEDS

In the early 1990s, psychologist Roger Ulrich theorized that the design and layout of health care facilities have a significant influence on patients' ability to heal and recover. He also theorized that the staff members employed in health care facilities are profoundly influenced by their surroundings and the quality of care they provide has a relationship to the interior design of the facility. The theory that Ulrich promoted is known as supportive design. Today, psychologists use supportive design to help architects and healthcare facility designers create a supportive environment for patients and staff.

Ulrich believed that medical facilities, such as nursing homes and hospitals, should not be cold or unwelcoming. Ulrich found evidence that patient wellness is decreased by facilities with poor designs. Hence the need for supportive design, which helps to promote patient recovery and complements treatment plans.

(Continued on next page)

(Continued from previous page)

According to Ulrich, there are two major sources for patient stress in a hospital setting:

■ the illness itself, which can reduce physical capacities, increase uncertainty, and necessitate painful medical procedures

■ the physical environment of the hospital or health care facility

Has anyone you know had a hard time getting needed rest in the hospital due to frequent interruptions by nurses and staff performing scheduled duties?

When staff members at a health care facility are under stress, an unfriendly, institutional environment can result—which can reduce the quality of healthcare and affect patient wellness. To promote wellness, health care facilities should be designed to provide an environment that reduces stress among patients and staff alike. There are three key components that affect stress and wellness:

■ a sense of control of one's physical and social surroundings

■ access to social support

■ the presence of positive distractions in the surroundings

These components have been shown to lower stress in a varied range of health care situations and groups of people. Ideas that support this end include allowing patients to wear gowns that provide more privacy, providing televisions that patients can control, and providing pleasant outdoor areas for patients to walk through or sit in. A nursing home setting might include open, easily accessible areas that allow residents to pursue personal interests or hobbies. Patient interaction can also be increased by arranging comfortable furniture into gathering places.

Staff workspaces should be designed to avoid unwanted interruptions by visitors yet encourage interactive care with patients. Because common areas filled with patients and their visiting families are often quite chaotic, staff should have quiet, limited-access areas where they can eat, exercise, take a shower, or simply relax during break times or slow periods in their schedules.

The need for the second component, social support, has been firmly established by studies in behavioral medicine and clinical psychology. Supportive design focuses on how the design of a treatment facility can foster social support, such as in the following ways:

■ It can allow families who live far from the facility to stay overnight.

■ It can provide comfortable visiting areas for family and friends, allowing them to support patients and one another.

■ It can provide outdoor areas such as gardens, providing opportunities for patients and visitors to spend time together in a pleasant setting.

Studies have also shown that having pets in nursing homes improves the quality of patients' lives. A supportive design could include space and facilities for companion animals.

Research in environmental psychology has suggested that physical surroundings can provide a sense of well-being. Some of the elements include interacting with other people, having windows that face natural settings, and having access to animals, trees, plants, and water.

SEXUAL MOTIVATION

Sexual motivation differs from other needs, such as hunger, because people do not need to have sex in order to survive. However, the species depends on sexual motivation for survival. Sexual motivation in humans represents a mix of biological, psychological, and sociocultural factors.

The Sex Drive

The **sex drive**, or the libido, is the urge to procreate. Biologically, sexual intercourse is an exchange of genetic material for the purpose of creating new life. However, sexual motivation in humans is different from the motivation of animals, because in humans, sex is more than an instinctive urge to engage in reproductive behavior.

Humans engage in sexual activity for the purposes of reproduction, recreation, and emotional bonding. Sexual expression can also affirm the need to belong. Humans are sexually motivated by a number of factors including hormones, sexual orientation, internal and external stimuli, and culture. The variety of human sexual expression points to the complex nature of human sexuality; for example, different cultures express different values regarding sexual expression and education.

Sex hormones control sexual development and drive behavior. In females, the sex hormones are **estrogen** and progesterone. Estrogen fluctuates throughout the menstrual cycle and peaks during ovulation; progesterone also cycles during the menstrual cycle and plays a role in maintaining pregnancy. **Testosterone**, the male sex hormone, regulates male sexual development and influences personality, aggression, competitiveness, and sexual motivation. In animals, estrogen makes females sexually receptive, but testosterone levels also influence a human woman's sex drive. Diminished sex drive in both males and females can be restored via testosterone replacement therapies.

Hormones play a role in human sexuality, but human sexuality is also motivated by various stimuli. Internal stimuli include memories and fantasies of sexual experiences. External stimuli include the sight of sexually attractive people or erotic material, such as sexually explicit books, movies, magazines, or websites. Both men and women become aroused by sexually explicit materials, but different people may have different responses to the arousal and perceive it as either pleasant or disturbing.

In some studies, people have been shown to be habituated (accustomed and less responsive) to repeated exposure to stimuli. Cultural expressions of erotic stimuli also change over time. For instance, the sight of a woman's leg or a kiss in a movie was considered erotic in the United States in the 1920s but barely evokes any response today; conversely, most films made in India today still feature modestly dressed people, and kissing in films is still largely taboo. Some studies have shown that exposure to erotic material can have adverse effects, such as reduced satisfaction with one's partner, unrealistic expectations, or the false idea that women enjoy being coerced into sexual activity.

Kinsey

Alfred Kinsey, a biologist at Indiana University in the 1940s, conducted a series of interviews to gather data about human sexuality and later founded the Institute for Sex Research, which is now called the Kinsey Institute. Kinsey and his colleagues published the findings of their studies in two books, *Sexual Behavior in the Human Male* and *Sexual Behavior in the Human Female* (commonly called the Kinsey Reports). At the time, Kinsey's research was highly controversial. It openly discussed sexual activity and behavior of many types, including nudity, masturbation, fantasy, petting, sexual practices and orientation, and marital and extramarital sex. Kinsey's work was also often criticized for being misleading and unscientific due to nonrandom sampling and the use of leading questions.

SEX DRIVE Sexual desire or motivation.

ESTROGEN Female sex hormone that regulates ovulation and sexual receptivity.

TESTOSTERONE Male sex hormone that regulates the growth of male sex organs and influences sex drive in males and human females.

The Sexual Response

In the 1960s, gynecologists William Masters and Virginia Johnson studied the physiological responses of sexually aroused volunteers. They observed 312 men and 382 females engaging in sexual activity and recorded their findings. They observed over 10,000 sexual acts and described a **sexual response cycle** with four stages:

■ Excitement
■ Plateau
■ Orgasm
■ Resolution

During the excitement phase of the sexual response cycle, the genitals fill with blood, which causes the penis to become erect in men and the clitoris and labia in women to swell. In the female, vaginal lubrication increases and the nipples swell. The physiological elements of sexual response are vasocongestion (increased blood flow to tissue) and muscle tension.

SEXUAL RESPONSE CYCLE Four stages of sexual response include excitement, plateau, orgasm, and resolution.

During the plateau phase, breath rate, blood pressure, and pulse increase. The clitoris retracts, and the penis becomes fully engorged and may emit preejaculatory fluid from the tip.

During the orgasm phase, strong muscle contractions occur in the penis and vagina and throughout the body. The vaginal contractions aid the reproductive cycle as well—they encourage conception by drawing in and retaining sperm near the uterus.

During the resolution, the final stage of the sexual response cycle, the body returns to normal. Men may experience a refractory phase (lasting anywhere from minutes to days) during which they are unable to achieve another orgasm. Women generally have a shorter refractory period; they may be capable of experiencing repeated orgasms with continued stimulation.

Like Alfred Kinsey, William Masters and Virginia Johnson were pioneers in the field of sexual research (sexology). They wrote numerous books, including their classic text *Human Sexual Response,* and founded the Masters and Johnson Institute to treat sexual disorders, such as premature ejaculation and erectile disorder in men and orgasmic disorder in women. Masters and Johnson were among the first to openly document and discuss human sexuality.

Sexual Orientation and Gender Role Identity

Sexual orientation refers to a person's attraction to members of his or her own (homosexual) or the opposite (heterosexual) gender. Sexual orientation generally manifests during puberty; it is innate, and not chosen. Homosexuality occurs among all cultures, regardless of social attitudes or acceptance. According to studies conducted by Kinsey and his colleagues, a significant percentage of the population will have had at least some homosexual experiences in the course of their lifetime.

The factors that determine sexual orientation are unknown. Recent studies indicate there is a biological element to homosexuality. Researcher Simon LeVay discovered differences in the hypothalamus of homosexual humans. Exposure to atypical

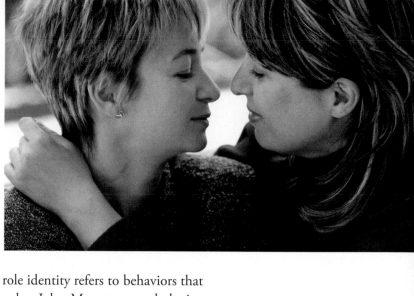

hormone levels during prenatal development has also been associated with homosexuality. Birth order may be influential; statistical evidence has indicated that men who have older brothers may be more likely to be homosexual. In studies, differences in fingerprint patterns, occupational preferences, age of puberty in males, and auditory and spatial perception have been noted between homosexual and heterosexual people.

Gender identity is a term that refers to a person's realization and sense of affiliation with either the male or female gender. Gender role identity refers to behaviors that are associated to either the male or female gender. John Money, a psychologist, coined these terms, and he is best known for his mid-twentieth century research on intersexed people (people with ambiguous genital formations).

Money and his colleagues were the first to study children with intersex conditions, undertaking a study of 105 children in the 1950s. In the study, Money argued that since hermaphrodites are "neither exclusively male or female, [they] are likely to grow up with contradictions existing between the sex of assignment and rearing, on the one hand, and various physical sexual variables, singly or in combination, on the other" (p. 333). Money found that the assignment of the sex and socialization are better predictors of an individual's gender role identity than chromosomal or hormonal sex.

ACHIEVEMENT MOTIVATION

Achievement motivation is a person's desire for accomplishment and competence. In 1938, Henry Murray defined achievement motivation as a basic need to strive for the accomplishment of goals. This may be expressed through the desire to learn and master skills, abilities, or ideas; be in control; or achieve goals.

ACHIEVEMENT MOTIVATION The desire for learning, mastery, and achieving a high standard of performance.

Achievement motivation relates to self-worth and esteem. Factors that affect achievement motivation include intrinsic and extrinsic motivation, interest, self-assessment of competence, and value of achievement. People with low levels of achievement motivation may choose easy tasks, while people with high achievement motivation work to achieve goals that require more effort. Factors that contribute to high achievement motivation include praise and encouragement to be independent during childhood.

Emotions such as pride, anger, hopelessness, or gratitude related to a person's expectations about a given task influence goal achievement motivation. For adults, setting specific, challenging, and attainable goals leads to higher achievement. People are encouraged by success just as they may be reluctant to try again after failing.

However, the causes for success or failure also affect motivation. A person's perception of his or her chances for success depends on the stability or instability of the reason for failure. For instance, if a person fails a class because they lack aptitude for the subject matter (a stable cause) rather than failing because they experience a temporary illness (an unstable cause) they may be less willing to take the class again.

Need for Achievement

What motivates you to achieve at school or work? Many researchers study achievement motivation in order to understand ways to encourage individuals, such as students or workers, to set and work toward higher performance goals. Motivation theorists are interested in subjects such as people's perceptions of control and competence in different situations; children's goals, interests, and motivation for learning; and how children value different achievements.

A **mastery goal** is a personal attempt to improve one's own performance for the purpose of learning and self-improvement. A **performance goal** is assessed competitively in terms of how one performs relative to others. **Performance-approach goals** involve trying to outperform others, such as by getting good grades or running to win a race. **Performance-avoidance goals** center on avoiding performing more poorly than other people—for example, desiring not to fail a class. Performance-avoidance goals have a negative effect on performance. A multiple-goal perspective that involves setting a combination of mastery and performance-approach goals motivates better performance. Patterns of multiple-goal pursuit in an educational setting include

- additive goal patterns, in which a single outcome provides positive effects for mastery and performance goals
- interactive goal patterns, in which performance goals depend on mastery
- specialized goal patterns, in which mastery and performance goals affect different outcomes, such as interest in subject (mastery) and grades (performance)
- selective goal patterns, where individuals focus on different goals at different times

An example of multiple-goal pursuit is a student reading a text both to master the material and to prepare for a test.

Key Thinkers

This section examines the work of two key motivation theorists: David McClelland and Frederick Herzberg. McClelland's theory proposes that human motivation is influenced by the need for achievement, affiliation, and power. Herzberg's theory addresses employee motivation and attitudes.

David McClelland

David McClelland is best known for his **three needs theory**, which argues that human motivation is dominated by three needs: achievement, affiliation, and power.

- Achievement is the need to succeed, achieve, and excel.
- Affiliation is the need for human interaction and positive relationships with others.
- Power is the need to make an impact and lead others.

McClelland, whose career spanned from 1941 through 1998, studied achievement and motivation in different societies by analyzing children's stories. One component of his work involved a widely used psychological test, the Thematic Apperception Test (TAT), which was developed by Henry A. Murray and Christiana D. Morgan in the 1930s. McClelland established new scoring systems for the TAT to measure intrinsic

MASTERY GOAL A personal attempt to improve one's own performance for the purpose of learning and self-improvement.

PERFORMANCE GOAL A goal that is assessed competitively in terms of how one performs relative to others.

PERFORMANCE-APPROACH GOALS Trying to outperform others—for example, by getting good grades or running to win a race.

PERFORMANCE-AVOIDANCE GOALS Avoiding performing more poorly than other individuals—for example, desiring not to fail a class.

THREE NEEDS THEORY A theory that human motivation is dominated by three needs: achievement, affiliation, and power.

motivation. People were asked to tell stories about pictures, describing what the depicted characters were thinking and doing. Based on their narratives, researchers determined each individual's levels of achievement motivation. The need for power can be exhibited in one of two ways: either as a need for personal power that can be expressed as a need to have power over others, or as a need for institutional power, which a person can use to direct team or organizational efforts.

The three needs theory states that these needs vary from person to person and are affected by a person's cultural background. A mix of these needs can be used to influence and motivate a person's behaviors.

Frederick Herzberg

In his 1959 book *The Motivation to Work*, Frederick Herzberg conducted studies to gain a greater understanding of employee motivation and attitudes. He found that the factors linked to job satisfaction were different from the ones that cause job dissatisfaction. He explained the results in his **motivation-hygiene theory**, which is also called the two-factor theory. Motivators such as achievement, recognition, the nature of the work, responsibility, advancement, and growth generate job satisfaction. Hygiene factors include company policies, supervision and relationship with management, work conditions, salary, and relationship with peers. According to Herzberg, motivators are the primary causes of job satisfaction, while hygiene factors are the cause of unhappiness.

Managers must provide their employees with these hygiene factors in order to avoid employee dissatisfaction, and managers also need to offer intrinsically motivating factors to increase job satisfaction. Herzberg recommended job enrichment to motivate employees—that a job itself should include challenges that fully engage workers' abilities. Employees who show increased levels of productivity and new abilities should be assigned increasing levels of responsibility. If a person is unable to reach his or her full potential in a job, motivation will suffer.

MOTIVATION-HYGIENE THEORY A theory that posits that factors linked to job satisfaction are different from factors linked to job dissatisfaction.

CASE STUDY: BRAIN DAMAGE AND MOTIVATION

Brain injuries may occur as a result of disease, lack of oxygen, or trauma from accidents, falls, or blows. There are three types of head injuries: penetrating, crushing, and closed. Penetrating injuries may be caused by gunshot wounds, machine accidents, or car accidents. Crushing injuries are a result of the head being caught between objects, such as the wheel of a car and the road. Closed injuries are the most common—there is not a penetrating wound, but the brain moves inside the skull. Closed injuries can result from falls or shaking.

Symptoms of brain injuries can range from mild to severe. Even mild brain injuries can cause changes in thinking, sleep patterns, memory, mood, and motivation. Mild brain injuries

(Continued on next page)

(*Continued from previous page*)

may be associated with dizziness, brief unconsciousness, headaches, fatigue, vision or hearing changes, and cognitive or mood changes. More serious brain injuries may include severe lasting headaches, amnesia or loss of memory, vomiting and nausea, seizures, unconsciousness or coma, loss of coordination, confusion, and personality changes. Acute injuries may heal entirely or can lead to chronic conditions. Internal bleeding or hemorrhaging at the site of head injuries can lead to further injury or death if not treated quickly. Factors associated with recovery from brain injuries include length of period of unconsciousness following the injury; extent of bleeding, lesions, and inflammation; patient's personality before injury; and degree of motivation to recover.

Traumatic brain injuries with hemorrhaging frequently lead to anxiety, depression, and passivity or loss of motivation. The clinical term for loss of motivation after brain injury is **abulia**. Abulia includes decreases in speech, thought, movement, and emotional reactions. Loss of attention and interest in activities can slow recovery and lead to withdrawal from other people, resulting in social isolation. When brain injuries result in memory loss or impaired cognitive function, patients may feel self-consciousness and a loss of identity and consequently become passive, neglectful, and unmotivated to complete tasks. Apathy, depression, and anxiety are common behavior changes following injury to the frontal lobe and limbic system.

Depression and loss of motivation have been associated with injuries to the dopamine pathways. Dopamine is a neurotransmitter associated with pleasure responses, eating, drinking, and sex. Treatment with drugs that activate dopamine receptors can improve mood and motivation in patients with traumatic brain injuries.

Traumatic brain injuries are a serious public health issue, particularly for veterans dealing with combat injuries. Rehabilitation after brain injuries may involve physical therapy, speech therapy, occupational therapy, and cognitive rehabilitation, as well as individual and family psychotherapy to teach patients how to do and enjoy daily activities. Alternative therapies such as art therapy, theater, dance, and writing are effective tools for increasing motivation and gratification in patients with traumatic brain injuries.

ABULIA Loss of motivation after brain injury.

SUMMARY

Motivation may be biological or psychological. It energizes and directs behavior to meet some need or desire. Needs may be biological, such as hunger or sexuality, or psychological, such as the need to belong to a group or gain a sense of personal achievement. Some behaviors result from a combination of needs. Physiological needs lead to aroused psychological states aimed at reducing needs and tensions. Some motives are universal, but individuals may be motivated by different needs. Motivations may be intrinsic (from within a person) or extrinsic (from outside sources). Some needs are more important than others. Maslow described the importance of various motivations in his hierarchy of needs.

Physiological factors such as hormones, neurotransmitters, and genetics play a role in motivation. Culture and environment are also important influences. Motivation researchers attempt to define the needs that cause behaviors.

Achievement theories attempt to explain why some individuals are more motivated to learn, set goals, and work toward success than others. Motivation researchers look for ways to inspire goal setting, encourage work and positive thinking, and increase productivity in students and workers. Goals and habits are intrinsic motivators. Reward, feedback, and recognition are extrinsic motivators. Motivation is influenced by emotions, praise and criticism, interest, and competence. Setting achievable goals and deadlines for mastery, performance, and improvement increases motivation.

REFERENCES

Aanstoos, C., Serlin, I., & Greening, T. (2000). A history of division 32 (humanistic psychology) of the American Psychological Association. In D. Dewsbury (Ed.), *Unification through division: Histories of the divisions of the American Psychological Association* (Vol. V, pp.1–46). Washington, DC: American Psychological Association. Retrieved from http://www.apa.org/divisions/Div32/pdfs/history.pdf

Association for Humanistic Psychology. (2006). Five basic postulates of humanistic psychology. *Journal of Humanistic Psychology, 46*, 239. doi: 10.1177/002216780604600301

Association for Humanistic Psychology. (2010). Humanistic psychology overview. Retrieved from http://www.ahpweb.org/aboutahp/whatis.html

Baker, S. (2007, January 1). The sex hormone secrets. *Psychology Today*, 1–4. Retrieved from http://www.psychologytoday.com/articles/200612/the-sex-hormone-secrets

Baumeister, R. F., Catanese, K. R., & Vohs, K. D. (2001). Is there a gender difference in sex drive? Theoretical views, conceptual distinctions, and a review of relevant evidence. *Personality and Social Psychology Review, 5*(3), 242–273. Retrieved from https://www.csom.umn.edu/Assets/71520.pdf

Bovet, P. (2006). *The fighting instinct.* (J. Y. T. Greig, Trans.). Whitefish, MT: Kessinger Publishing.

Brooks, G. (n.d.). Rehabilitation of mind, motivation, and identity after traumatic brain injury. Retrieved from http://www.northeastcenter.com/rehabilitation-of-mind-motovation-and-identity-after-traumatic-brain-injury.pdf

Carson, R. C., & Butcher, J. N. (1992). *Abnormal psychology and modern life* (9th ed.). New York, NY: Harper Collins.

Cooper, C. L., & Pervin, L. A. (1998). *Personality: Critical concepts in psychology.* New York, NY: Routledge.

Crain, W. (2005). *Theories of development: Concepts and applications* (5th ed.). Upper Saddle River, NJ: Pearson Prentice Hall.

Darwin, C. (2005). *The descent of man and selection in relation to sex.* In W. Crain, *Theories of development: Concepts and applications* (5th ed.). Upper Saddle River, NJ: Pearson Education. (Original work published 1871)

Darwin, C. (2005). *The origin of species.* In W. Crain, *Theories of development: Concepts and applications* (5th ed.). Upper Saddle River, NJ: Pearson Education. (Original work published 1859)

Garner, D. (2009, June 25). Books of the Times: Out of the bedroom, into the clinic. *The New York Times*, C28. Retrieved from http://www.nytimes.com/2009/06/26/books/26book.html

Graham, S., & Weiner, B. (1996). Theories and principles of motivation. In D. Berliner & R. Calfe (Eds.), *Handbook of educational psychology* (pp. 63–84). New York, NY: Macmillan.

Granacher, R. P. (2008). *Traumatic brain injury: Methods for clinical and forensic neuropsychiatric evaluation* (2nd ed.). Boca Raton, FL: CRC Press/Taylor and Francis Group.

Haines, J., & Neumark-Sztainer, D. (2006). Prevention of obesity and eating disorders: A consideration of shared risk factors. *Oxford Journal of Health Education Research, 21*(6), 770–782. Retrieved from: http://her.oxfordjournals.org/content/21/6/770.full

Harackiewicz, J. A., Barron, K. E., Pintrich, P. R., Elliot, A. J., & Thrash, T. M. (2002). Revision of achievement goal theory: Necessary and illuminating. *Journal of Educational Psychology, 94*(3), 638–645. doi: 10.1037//0022-0663.94.3.638

Hastak, S. M., Gorawara, P. S., & Mishra, N. K. (2005, September). Abulia: No will, no way. *Journal of the Association of Physicians of India, 53*, 814–818. Retrieved from http://www.japi.org/september2005/CR-814.pdf

Herzberg, F. (1987). One more time: How do you motivate employees? Cambridge, MA: *Harvard Business Review*. (Reprint, with commentary, of original article published January–February, 1968, pp. 88–96). Retrieved from http://www.facilitif.eu/user_files/file/herzburg_article.pdf

Herzberg, F., & Snyderman, B. B. (1959). *The motivation to work*. New York, NY: John Wiley and Sons.

Huitt, W. G. (2007). Maslow's hierarchy of needs. *Educational Psychology Interactive*. Valdosta, GA: Valdosta State University. Retrieved from http://www.edpsycinteractive.org/topics/regsys/maslow.html

Kinsey, A. C., Pomeroy, W. R., & Martin, C. E. (2003). Voices from the past: Sexual behavior in the human male. *American Journal of Public Health, 93*(6), 894–898. Retrieved from http://ajph.aphapublications.org/cgi/content/full/93/6/894

Lowe, M. R., & Levine, A. S. (2005). Eating motives and the controversy over dieting: Eating less than needed versus less than wanted. *Obesity Research, 13*(5), 797–806. Retrieved from http://lowelabs.com/publications/2005_Obesity_Research.pdf

Marx, K. (1970). *Introduction to a contribution to a critique of Hegel's Philosophy of Right*. (J. O'Malley, Trans.). Oxford, England: Oxford University Press. Retrieved from http://www.marxists.org/archive/marx/works/download/Marx_Critique_of_Hegels_Philosophy_of_Right.pdf (Original work published 1844).

Maslow, A. (1943). *A theory of human motivation* (Classics in the history of psychology). *Psychological Review, 50*, 370–396. Retrieved from: http://psychclassics.yorku.ca/Maslow/motivation.htm

Maslow, A. (1954, 1970). *Motivation and personality* (3rd ed.). New York, NY: Harper and Row.

Masters, W., & Johnson, V. (2010). *Human sexual response*. New York, NY: Ishi Press International.

McClelland, D. C. (2010). *The achieving society*. Eastford, CT: Martino Fine Books.

Money, J., Hampson, J. G., & Hampson, J. L. (1957). Imprinting and the establishment of gender role. *Archives of Neurology and Psychiatry, 77*, 333–336.

Myers, D. G. (2010). *Exploring psychology* (9th ed.). New York, NY: Worth Publishers.

National Institute of Neurological Disorders and Stroke. (2011). Traumatic brain injury information page. Retrieved from http://www.ninds.nih.gov/disorders/tbi/tbi.htm

Ogden, J. A. (2005). *Fractured minds: A case study approach to clinical neuropsychology*. New York, NY: Oxford University Press USA.

Polivy, J., & Herman, C. P. (2002). Causes of eating disorders. *Annual Review of Psychology, 53*(1), 187–213. Retrieved from http://comp.uark.edu/~nlwilli/polivy02.pdf

Powell, J. H., al-Adawi, S., Morgan, J., & Greenwood, R. J. (1996). Motivational deficits after brain injury: Effects of bromocriptine in 11 patients. *Journal of Neurology, Neurosurgery, and Psychiatry, 60*(4), 416–421. Retrieved from http://jnnp.bmj.com/content/60/4/416.full.pdf

Read, N. W. (1992, May). Role of gastrointestinal factors in hunger and satiety in man. *The Proceedings of the Nutrition Society, 51*(1), 7–11.

Reiss, S. (2004). Multifaceted nature of intrinsic motivation: The theory of sixteen basic desires. *Review of General Psychology, 8*(3), 179–193. doi: 10.1037/1089-2680.8.3.179

Seligman, M. E. P. (2002). *Authentic happiness: Using the new positive psychology to realize your potential for lasting fulfillment*. New York, NY: Free Press.

Simons, J. A., Irwin, D. B., & Drinnien, B. A. (1987). Maslow's hierarchy of needs. In W. G. Huitt (Ed.), *Psychology: The search for understanding* . New York, NY: West Publishing.

Ulrich, R. S. (1991). Effects of interior design on wellness: Theory and recent research. *Journal of Health Care Interior Design*, 97–109. Retrieved from http://www.majorhospitalfoundation.org/pdfs/Effects of Interior Design on Wellness.pdf

Weiner, B. (1985). An attributional theory of achievement motivation and emotion. *Psychological Review, 92*(4), 548–573. Retrieved from http://education.ucsb.edu/janeconoley/ed197/documents/weinerAnattributionaltheory.pdf

Wigfield, A., Eccles, J. S., Schiefele, U., Roeser, R. W., & Davis-Kean, P. (2006). Development of achievement motivation. In W. Damon & N. Eisenberg (Eds.), *Handbook of child psychology* (6th ed., Vol. 3, pp. 1–39). Hoboken, NJ: Wiley.

Personality

"The meeting of two personalities is like the contact of two chemical substances: If there is any reaction, both are transformed."

—Carl Jung

PERSPECTIVES IN PERSONALITY

The word *personality* comes from the Latin word *persona*, which means "mask." What you may refer to as personality is really an interpretation of the persona, or mask, that each person wears. Your personality is the "face" you project to those around you. From a psychological perspective, personality is also the experience collectively referred to as the self.

In many ways, you highlight your own personality each time you use the word "I." Any sentence that begins with the word "I" is a summary about you. In "I" sentences, you list your hopes, fears, likes, dislikes, strengths, or weaknesses. The study of personality attempts to explain how and why people differ from one another.

Definition of Personality

Personality is a combination of a person's behavioral, temperamental, emotional, and mental characteristics. But personality is never simple. Humans assess personality all the time, making judgments about their own and others' personalities every day. Whether you realize it or not, you are constantly trying to figure out why other people do what they do, and why you do what you do.

PERSONALITY A combination of behavioral, temperamental, emotional, and mental characteristics; a complex of individual experiences collectively referred to as "I" or "the self."

Personality is unique. Every personality is different. Additionally, personality tends to remain constant once it is developed. That means that most people maintain a relatively consistent personality throughout their lives.

Although personality is a psychological concept, it is largely physiological as well. Much of what determines personality is a mixture of psychology and biology. Many people tend to view personality as the factor that drives behavior. However, personality does not merely influence the way people respond to events; it causes them to act in certain ways.

Personality does more than influence behavior. It influences nearly every aspect of human life. Personality influences the way people think, feel, and manage relationships and social interactions.

The scientific view is that personality is each person's compilation of patterns of thought, behavior, and emotions. Gordon Allport, an American psychologist and forerunner in the field of personality research, strove to understand the individual as someone with specific attitudes and prejudices based on character and experience—i.e., both internal and external factors.

Trait

TRAIT A primary quality or inherited characteristic present in each person in varying degrees, a cluster of which make up the personality.

A **trait** is both a distinguishing quality and an inherited characteristic. Much of personality research is based on the assumption that individual personalities are composed of more than one quality or characteristic. If you think about someone you know

KEY CONCEPTS

1. Personality is a combination of a person's behavioral, temperamental, emotional, and mental characteristics. See page 199.

2. The different theories of personality include the trait, psychoanalytic, humanistic, biological and evolutionary, and sociocultural theories. See page 199.

3. Two frequently used personality tests are the Myers-Briggs Type Indicator (MBTI) and the Minnesota Multiphasic Personality Inventory (MMPI). See page 214.

and attempt to list the characteristics of that person, you will probably find yourself listing more than one quality. You may describe your best friend, for example, as outgoing and impulsive. You may describe your brother as loyal, pragmatic, and steady. Perhaps you describe your mother as caring, knowledgeable, and energetic. Rarely do people attribute only one characteristic to any one person. Trait theories of personality are different from psychoanalytic or humanistic theories, because the trait approach highlights what is unique to each person rather than what is the same.

Trait Theory

TRAIT THEORY A personality theory based on the idea that personality is made up of three basic qualities or characteristic traits: introversion/extroversion, neuroticism, and psychoticism.

Trait theory is based on the idea that personality is made up of more than one quality or characteristic. British psychologist Hans Eysenck believed that an individual's personality was based on three primary traits: where you scored on the scale for each trait determined your personality. According to Eysenck, everyone

possesses each of these traits in varying degrees. In his 1952 book *The Structure of Human Personality*, Eysenck theorized that variations of introversion/extroversion, neuroticism, and psychoticism comprised human personality. His theory that human personality can be defined in these terms led to the development of the Maudsley Personality Inventory (also known as the Eysenck Personality Inventory), a personality test that was, at the time, considered highly reliable in measuring introversion/extroversion and neuroticism.

Introversion/Extroversion

According to Eysenck, everyone is either an **introvert** or an **extrovert**, or some combination of the two. Introverts focus on inner thoughts and experiences, while extroverts focus their thoughts and experiences outward. In general, introverts are quiet and maybe even shy. Extroverts, with their focus on other people and the world around them, tend to be outgoing and more social. A low score on the **introvert/extrovert scale** means you are introverted, and a high score means you are extroverted. The scale also includes a range between introverted and extroverted.

Neuroticism

Emotional stability is sometimes measured on a scale ranging from moodiness to even-temperedness. The emotional stability scale measures a person's tendency to be either emotional and upset (**neuroticism**) or calm and level-headed (**emotional stability**). Like the introvert/extrovert scale, emotional stability encompasses a range of personality. A high score on the neuroticism/emotional stability scale means that the person tends toward nervousness and emotional behavior. According to Eysenck, people who scored high on the neuroticism scale were more likely to suffer from phobias, obsessions, compulsions, and depression than those who scored low on the scale.

Psychoticism

Based on his years spent studying people with mental illnesses, Eysenck concluded that his theory needed to explain personality disorders as well as general personality traits. This is why he added the scale of psychoticism to his trait theory. **Psychoticism** measures a person's tendency toward psychosis and psychotic behavior. This scale attempts to measure how a person deals with reality.

A low score on the psychoticism scale means you are relatively normal. A high score may indicate problems with antisocial behavior, hostility, and lack of empathy. High scorers may also be manipulative. A score in the middle of the scale may indicate eccentricity, meaning that the person may be unconcerned about others' opinions, ignore norms, and take added risks in pursuit of some unusual interest or goal.

INTROVERT A person who focuses on inner thoughts and experiences; is probably quiet or even shy.

EXTROVERT A person who focuses thoughts and experiences outward, on other people and the world around him or her, and who tends to be outgoing and more social.

INTROVERT/EXTROVERT SCALE A measure of internal versus external emotional focus; a low score means the person is introverted and a high score means the person is extroverted.

NEUROTICISM A tendency to be less emotionally stable in general and more likely to suffer from phobias, obsessions, compulsions, and depression.

EMOTIONAL STABILITY The general degree of a person's steadiness in moving through life events; the likelihood that he or she will respond to challenges with equanimity.

PSYCHOTICISM A tendency toward psychosis and psychotic behavior.

WHAT DO YOU THINK? PERSONALITY SCALE

The following questions are representative of questions on scales measuring extroversion/introversion, neuroticism, and psychoticism.

Extroversion

- Do you like to meet new people and talk to others?
- Are you energetic and gregarious?
- Do you like going to parties?

Neuroticism

- Do you have mood swings often?
- Do you ever feel miserable for no reason?
- Are you easily irritable?

Psychoticism

- Are you preoccupied with what others think of you?
- Would you be very worried if you were in debt?
- Do you often break rules, preferring to do your own thing?

Factors of Personality

SIXTEEN PERSONALITY FACTORS THEORY Cattell's theory of personality considering 16 pairs of traits, developed in response to Eysenck's scale.

English psychologist Raymond Cattell, who worked for most of the 20th century, developed the **sixteen personality factors theory**. As its title indicates, Cattell's theory pinpoints 16 specific components of personality. From this theory, Cattell developed the 16PF Personality Questionnaire, which is still in use today. Cattell's scale contains the following personality factors:

- Warmth: People who score low on this scale tend to be reserved, impersonal, distant, cool, detached, formal, and aloof. People who score high tend to be warm, outgoing, kind, easygoing, and attentive.
- Reasoning: People who score low on the reasoning scale may be less intelligent and less able to think in the abstract. People who score high may be more intelligent, with a higher general mental capacity.
- Emotional stability: People who score low on this scale tend to be emotionally reactive, less stable, and easily upset. People who score high on the emotional stability scale may be adaptive, mature, and calm.
- Dominance: People who score low on the dominance scale may be deferential, cooperative, humble, submissive, docile, and accommodating. People who score high may be forceful, assertive, aggressive, competitive, stubborn, and bossy.
- Liveliness: People who score low on the liveliness scale tend to be serious and introspective. People who score high may be animated, spontaneous, enthusiastic, cheerful, and impulsive.
- Rule-consciousness: People who score low on the rule-consciousness scale are generally nonconforming and self-indulgent. People who score high may be rule-conscious, moralistic, and dutiful.
- Social boldness: People who score low on the social boldness scale may be shy, timid, hesitant, and easily intimidated. People who score high are often bold and uninhibited.

- **Sensitivity:** People who score low on the sensitivity scale may be objective, tough, and self-reliant. People who score high are likely sensitive, sentimental, intuitive, and refined.
- **Vigilance:** People who score low on the vigilance scale may be trusting, unsuspecting, and accepting. People who score high may be suspicious, skeptical, and distrustful.
- **Abstractedness:** People who score low on the abstractedness scale may be grounded, practical, and conventional. People who score high may be imaginative, impractical, and absent-minded.
- **Privateness:** People who score low on the privateness scale tend to be genuine, open, naïve, and unpretentious. People who score high tend to be discreet, shrewd, and worldly.
- **Apprehension:** People who score low on the apprehension scale tend to be self-assured, secure, untroubled, and confident. People who score high may be worried, insecure, and prone to guilt.
- **Openness to change:** People who score low on the openness to change scale may be traditional and conservative. People who score high may be liberal, flexible, and freethinking.
- **Self-reliance:** People who score low on the self-reliance scale tend to be group-oriented and dependent. People who score high may be solitary, resourceful, and self-sufficient.
- **Perfectionism:** People who score low on the perfectionism scale may be flexible, undisciplined, impulsive, and uncontrolled. People who score high may be organized, compulsive, and self-disciplined.
- **Tension:** People who score low on the tension scale may be relaxed, tranquil, and patient. People who score high may be energetic, impatient, driven, and easily frustrated.

Cattell's theory was a response to Eysenck's scale, as Cattell believed that Eysenck's theory did not account for nearly enough personality factors. However, critics of Cattell's theory assert that the theory considers far too many components of personality.

The Big Five

The Big Five theory of personality is a merging of Cattell's 16 personality factors and Eysenck's trait theory. Many researchers believed that Cattell focused on too many personality traits and Eysenck's theory focused on too few, and the Big Five is a result of those beliefs.

The Big Five, sometimes called the **five-factor model of personality**, focuses on five specific personality traits: extroversion, agreeableness, conscientiousness, neuroticism, and openness. These personality categories are far broader than Eysenck's theory and more streamlined than Cattell's theory. Researchers have found that these five personality traits tend to occur together in most people.

- **Extroversion:** Like Eysenck's theory, this trait includes individual attributes, such as assertiveness, emotional expressiveness, talkativeness, sociability, and excitability.
- **Agreeableness:** Agreeableness measures such prosocial characteristics as trust, altruism, kindness, and affection. A high score on the agreeableness scale means

FIVE-FACTOR MODEL OF PERSONALITY A merging of Cattell's 16 personality factors and Eysenck's trait theory, that focuses on extroversion, agreeableness, conscientiousness, neuroticism, and openness.

that a person tends to be friendly and accommodating. Note that agreeableness is not the same as being an extrovert. One can be an introvert and score high on the agreeableness scale. Agreeable people tend to be popular because they compromise and conform, which is not objectively a good thing. People who score low on the agreeableness scale tend to stick to what they believe in—even if those beliefs are unpopular.

■ Conscientiousness: People who are conscientious tend to be thoughtful, goal-directed, and have a firm grasp on impulse control. People who score high on this scale tend to be organized and detail-oriented. People who score low may be more laid-back and less worried about appearances, deadlines, and neatness.

■ Neuroticism: The Big Five neuroticism scale is sometimes referred to as the emotional stability scale. People high in neuroticism may be overly emotional, moody, anxious, irritable, and sad.

■ Openness: Openness is sometimes referred to as *culture* or *openness to experience*. This scale measures imagination, insight, and interest. People high on the openness scale tend to be open to new experiences and have a wide range of interests.

Psychoanalytic Theory of Personality

The **psychoanalytic theory of personality**, the brainchild of Sigmund Freud, focuses on levels of awareness or consciousness, components of personality, defense mechanisms, and psychosexual stages.

Conscious, Preconscious, and Unconscious

Freud believed that there were three levels of awareness, or consciousness—the conscious, the preconscious, and the unconscious. Your **conscious mind** is also known as your working memory. In your conscious mind are the things that you are thinking about in the here and now. These contents are easily accessed and remembered.

Your **preconscious mind** houses thoughts, memories, wishes, feelings, and knowledge that you are not currently accessing. These contents are easily retrieved when you need them.

According to Freud, the **unconscious mind** stores all the thoughts and knowledge that you are not aware of. These contents are stored but not accessible. The unconscious mind actively prevents you from being aware of what is stored within.

Id, Ego, and Superego

According to the psychoanalytic theory of personality, human personality is composed of the id, the ego, and the superego.

■ The **id**, which is present from birth, is the primary component of human personality. The id is housed entirely in the unconscious mind and drives all instinctive and primitive behaviors. It seeks immediate gratification without compromise and generates all of the energy of the personality.

■ The **superego** acts as the conscience. Residing in the preconscious, the superego strives to retain a person's morals and ideals. Humans do not develop a superego until they are about four or five years old. Much of what a person's superego believes is based on what his or her society and family taught. According to Freud,

PSYCHOANALYTIC THEORY OF PERSONALITY Freud's personality model, which focuses on levels of awareness or consciousness, components of personality, defense mechanisms, and psychosexual stages.

CONSCIOUS MIND A person's awareness of his or her own feelings, memories, thoughts, sensations, and environment.

PRECONSCIOUS MIND The area of the mind that houses thoughts, memories, wishes, feelings, and knowledge that a person is not currently accessing but can easily retrieve if needed.

UNCONSCIOUS MIND The area of the mind that stores all the thoughts and knowledge that a person is not aware of.

ID Primitive sexual and aggressive energy that corresponds to the deepest part of the unconscious mind.

SUPEREGO Higher ideals and standards of maturity and morality, as embodied by parents and society.

without a superego, people would behave like animals, searching to immediately satisfy their needs and pleasures. (See Figure 11.1 for a graphic representation of the id, ego, and superego.)

■ The **ego** acts as a sort of negotiator between the id and the superego. It resides in all levels of awareness. The ego tries to give both the id and the superego what they want, but it strives to do so in socially appropriate ways.

A person whose id, ego, and superego are in balance is mentally healthy. Conflict between the id and the superego, unmediated by a strong ego, tends to lead to mental imbalance and personality problems.

EGO The area of the mind responsible for balancing the drives of the id with the ideals of the superego.

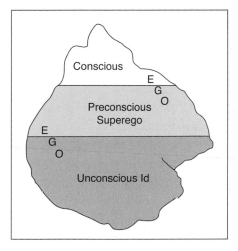

FIGURE 11.1 Freud's Iceberg Analogy of the Human Mind

Defense Mechanisms

The ego struggles daily to strike a balance between the id and the superego. Some days it is easier than others. When the ego cannot maintain an acceptable balance, the person suffers from anxiety. Freud identified three types of anxiety:

■ **Neurotic anxiety** occurs when the unconscious mind is concerned that the person will lose control of the id's urges. The unconscious worries that this loss of control may lead to punishment for inappropriate behavior.

■ **Reality anxiety** occurs when a real event causes worry. Reality anxiety is the fear of something real such as falling off a ladder or being hit by a car while walking on the highway. Most people avoid reality anxiety by avoiding the threat.

■ **Moral anxiety** occurs when the person fears violating his or her own moral principles.

NEUROTIC ANXIETY A feeling that occurs when the unconscious mind is concerned about losing control of the id's urges.

REALITY ANXIETY A feeling that occurs when a real event causes worry.

MORAL ANXIETY A fear of violating one's own moral principles.

Defense mechanisms help people fight off anxiety, both consciously and unconsciously. Used sparingly, defense mechanisms can be adaptive, but overuse of defense mechanisms is psychologically unhealthy. Defense mechanisms include:

■ Denial: Arguing that anxiety-provoking stimuli do not exist. For instance, a person who has a serious illness or disease may refuse to believe that he or she is sick, even when presented with factual information to the contrary.

■ Repression: Hiding in the unconscious.

■ Suppression: Shoving into the unconscious.

■ Displacement: Taking frustrations out on a less threatening target.

■ Sublimation: Acting out unacceptable impulses in a socially acceptable way. For example, angry people often sublimate their feelings of anger in socially

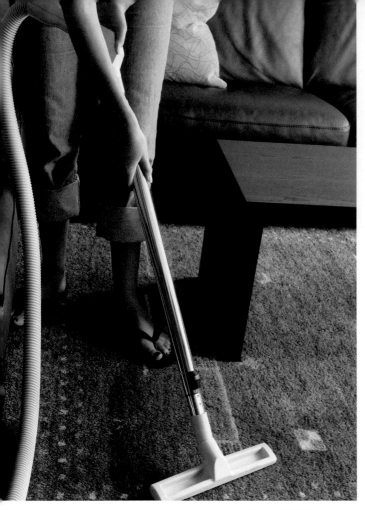

appropriate ways. A woman who is angry may seek to expend her anger by cleaning the house from top to bottom, until it is spotless. She focuses all her energy on cleaning, which is socially acceptable, rather than on anger, which is discouraged.

■ Projection: Transferring your own unacceptable impulses to someone else.

■ Intellectualization: Focusing on the intellect in order to avoid unacceptable feelings.

■ Rationalization: Supplying a reason, but often not the real reason, for an event. For example, someone who cheats on his taxes may rationalize his or her actions by insisting that the government wastes taxpayer money.

■ Regression: Reverting to a previous stage of development.

■ Reaction formation: Believing differently in order to avoid anxiety.

Freud worked with his daughter, Anna Freud, to develop the psychoanalytic theory. Since then, several researchers have added to the list of defense mechanisms. Other defense mechanisms may include:

■ Acting out: Focusing on actions rather than thinking about feelings.

■ Affiliation: Turning to others for confirmation.

■ Aim inhibition: Accepting a lesser goal rather than what one really wants.

■ Altruism: Satisfying one's own internal needs through helping others.

■ Avoidance: Avoiding dealing with events, objects, or situations that seem unpleasant.

■ Compensation: Overachieving in one area to compensate for a lack of success in another area.

■ Humor: Highlighting what is funny or ironic about a situation.

■ Passive-aggression: Expressing anger indirectly, as opposed to directly.

Psychosexual Stages

One of the most controversial components of Freud's psychoanalytic theory was his position on psychosexual development. His **psychosexual stages theory** dictates how early experiences set the stage for later personality development and behavior.

The theory of psychosexual stages focuses on particular phases a child experiences during development. During these stages, the personality is driven by certain pleasure-seeking energies of the id called the **libido**. Particular erogenous areas generate these energies.

Assuming a person passes through each stage successfully, he or she will develop a healthy personality. If the person retains unresolved issues stemming from one or more conflicts during the stage, he or she may become fixated (persistently focused, or stuck) in that stage. Following are descriptions of the psychosexual stages:

■ Oral
■ Anal
■ Phallic
■ Latent
■ Genital

PSYCHOSEXUAL STAGES THEORY Freud's theory that early erogenous experiences influence personality growth and set the stage for later personality development and behavior.

LIBIDO Pleasure-seeking energies of the id, generated by particular erogenous areas.

The oral stage begins at birth. A newborn is very orally motivated, as evidenced by its biological urge to root and suck. It is through oral stimulation that the infant learns trust. The primary conflict during this stage is weaning. Oral fixation during this stage may lead a person to later develop negative habits, such as excessive drinking or eating, smoking, or nail biting.

During the anal stage, the libido focuses on controlling bladder and bowel movements. The primary conflict during this stage is toilet training. A child who toilet trains successfully becomes independent, but a child who does not may become stuck in this stage. Fixation may lead to either an anal-expulsive or anal-retentive personality.

The phallic stage leads the libido to focus on the genitals. Freud believed that boys vie for their mother's attention against the rival father (known as the Oedipus complex) and that girls vie against the mother for the attention of the father (known as the Electra complex). Conflict during this stage could lead to castration anxiety for boys and penis envy for girls. Freud believed that boys were more likely than girls to resolve the conflicts of this stage, and that girls would retain some level of penis envy for the rest of their lives. This belief has been challenged by researchers who note that it is sexist and inaccurate to claim that boys are more likely to resolve this issue than girls.

Around the time children enter school there is a period of calm that Freud called the latent period. Although the libido is still active during this period, it is somewhat suppressed as the ego and the superego develop. During this period, children focus on intellectual pursuits, social interactions, communication skills, and self-confidence.

The genital stage is the last of Freud's five psychosexual stages. During this stage, people turn their focus outward and become more interested in others—especially (among heterosexuals) people of the opposite sex.

NEO-FREUDIAN PSYCHOANALYSIS

Freud had many followers who were interested in his theories. However, as students of his theories sought to change and expand psychoanalytic thought, Freud remained steadfast in his beliefs. This led to the development of neo-Freudian psychoanalysis. Three of psychology's greatest thinkers were involved in changing the face of psychoanalytic theory: Carl Jung, Karen Horney, and Alfred Adler.

Neo-Freudian thought developed Freud's key beliefs. Carl Jung, a favored student of Freud's and the father of analytic psychology, believed that the unconscious mind was far more extensive than Freud had theorized. Jung theorized that time and culture did little to change fears, behaviors, and thoughts. This led to his assertion that humans possessed what he called a *collective unconscious*.

Karen Horney, who studied Freud's work but was never his student, added a feminine insight to psychoanalytic theory. Although she agreed with many of the premises of Freud's assertions, she did not believe that men and women were as inherently different

(Continued on next page)

(*Continued from previous page*)

as Freud did. Horney, the founder of the American Institute for Psychoanalysis, believed that the differences that *did* exist between male and female personalities were due more to society and culture than biology. To that end, she countered many of Freud's concepts with those of her own, such as countering penis envy with womb envy, the male envy of the female's ability to bear children.

In the early 1900s, psychologist Alfred Adler split from Freud over his challenges to Freud's theories and Freud's unwillingness to accept other avenues of thought. Adler believed that personality was not merely the result of biology, but rather the result of a sense of inferiority, birth order, and parenting styles.

KEY THINKERS IN PSYCHOLOGY: CARL JUNG

Nearly a full century ago, Swiss psychiatrist Carl Gustav Jung penned 205 pages of what was simply titled *Liber Novus*, which is Latin for "New Book." The book, bound in red leather and illustrated by Jung himself, was written between 1914 and 1930. It remained hidden in a Jung family vault until his heirs agreed to its publication. The text is popularly known as *The Red Book* due to its distinctive binding.

The Red Book serves as a pictorial diary of Jung's own "confrontation with the unconscious." After his split from Freud, Jung employed what he called "active imagination" to explore his own spiritual unconscious and develop his own psychoanalytic theories on archetypes, collective unconscious, and self-awareness.

Newly published for the masses, *The Red Book* has been referred to as both a book of infinite wisdom and the work of a psychotic. Regardless, Jung considered *The Red Book* his greatest work and the basis for his insight into the development of human personality.

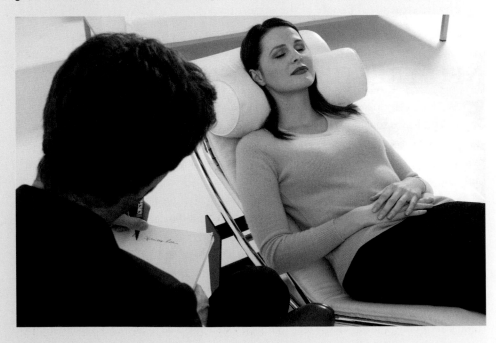

Learning Theory of Personality

Learning theory emerged as a "second force" theory. Learning theorists reacted to what they believed was the rigid focus on pathology Freudian thought emphasized. **Second force behavioral theory** sought to present behavior as a product of socialization.

The **learning theory of personality** asserts that a person is born as a *tabula rasa*, or a blank slate, and that all behavior is learned through exposure to and interaction with the environment. Learning theorists do not ascribe to the belief that personality is innate. Instead, they believe that learning experiences mold the personality. Behaviorists subsequently used learning theory and its influence on personality to predict behavior. According to learning theorists, behavior is the product of what people do, and not what they think or feel.

For this reason, behaviorists such as B. F. Skinner used learning theory to guide their experiments surrounding associations, rewards, and punishments. Skinner was a radical behaviorist who believed that personality and behaviors were a direct result of reinforcement. His most recognizable experiment, the Skinner box, was an experiment of operant conditioning. **Operant conditioning** involves therapeutic techniques that use positive and negative reinforcement to promote desired behavior while discouraging undesirable behavior.

Skinner placed a pigeon in a box with a bar that, once pressed, would release food. At first, the bird would accidentally hit the bar and be rewarded with food. As time elapsed, the bird realized that hitting the bar released food and would therefore intentionally hit the bar and receive the reward.

Skinner believed that searching either a person's personal history or the collective unconscious for behavioral motivations was a waste of time. He insisted that neither the unconscious nor personal motivation could be measured, and held that the environment was the reason for all behavior. His belief that the only evidence of personality existed in observable behaviors led the way for measurable experiments in psychology.

Albert Bandura took learning theory a bit further. He believed that the reactive predictions behind behaviorism were too simple and that humans were more self-directive than more restrictive theories allowed. Bandura believed that cognition affected learning and that social events were as important as behavioral or biological events. From this thought, both the **social learning** and **social cognitive theories** were born.

According to these perspectives, personality is the sum of all learning, including social learning, and various cultures' behaviors serve as proof that external learning is as important as internal events (i.e., certain behaviors are encouraged and rewarded in certain cultures, whereas completely different behaviors may be encouraged and rewarded in other cultures).

Bandura asserted that an observable change in behavior does not always reflect learning. He also believed that a person is less likely to engage in certain behaviors perceived to have an undesirable outcome and more likely to engage in behaviors perceived to produce a desirable outcome. Bandura believed that people learned by imitation. His famous "Bobo doll" experiment showed how children would imitate adult behavior. In this experiment, Bandura separated a group of children into an aggressive condition group and a nonaggressive condition group. Adult models in each group presented either aggressive or nonaggressive behavior toward a doll. The children in each group were more likely to imitate the behavior of the adult model than not.

SECOND FORCE BEHAVIORAL THEORY Any theory that presents behavior as a product of socialization as opposed to innate tendencies or inherited traits.

LEARNING THEORY OF PERSONALITY A theory opposing Freud's focus on pathology; it asserts that all behavior is learned through exposure to and interaction with the environment.

TABULA RASA A blank slate to be written upon; used to suggest the nature of an unformed person, uninfluenced by prior information or strong inner inclinations.

OPERANT CONDITIONING Therapeutic techniques that use positive and negative reinforcement to promote desired behavior while discouraging undesirable behavior.

SOCIAL LEARNING THEORY Bandura's theory that humans learn appropriate and inappropriate behaviors by participating in and observing social interactions with others.

SOCIAL COGNITIVE THEORY Bandura's idea that cognition affects learning.

Humanistic Theory

HUMANISTIC THEORY A theory that explains human behavior as based on the basic goodness of the person, rather than on more biologically or socially mechanistic models.

THIRD FORCE THEORISTS Those who believe that the constructs affecting personality development are more human, and thus more holistic, than previous models allowed for.

MASLOW'S HIERARCHY OF NEEDS Basic needs for food, shelter, and clothing are primary personal motivators and self-actualization as the final goal for which humans may strive; higher needs cannot be satisfied until basic needs are met.

SELF-ACTUALIZATION The desire of a person to achieve his or her full potential.

American psychologists Abraham Maslow and Carl Rogers sought to explain human nature in a less rigid way than previous psychological thinkers. **Humanistic theory** was born from their desire to explain behavior based on the basic goodness of the person and was considered the "third force" in psychology. **Third force** psychologists believed that people and personality were more holistic than previous thought allowed. Maslow and his fellow thinkers asserted that scientific research as it previously had been conducted was mechanical, oversimplified, and made the individual person less human. Humanists explain behavior as a combination of the here and now, responsibility, worth, and self-improvement.

In response to his humanistic beliefs, Maslow developed a **hierarchy of needs**. This hierarchy, generally displayed as a pyramid, lists the most basic human needs—food, shelter, and clothing—as primary, and **self-actualization**—the need to reach one's fullest potential—as what humans strive for. People encounter the need for safety, love, and esteem along the way. The inability to satisfy any one need leaves a person stuck at that level until the need is met. For instance, without the basic human requirements of food, shelter, and safety, a person cannot seek for and find love and acceptance. Only when his or her basic needs have been met can the person continue to grow. According to Maslow, few people ever fully achieve self-actualization.

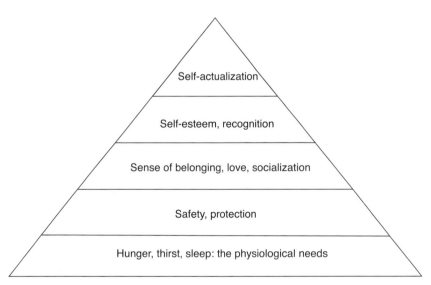

FIGURE 11.2 Maslow's Hierarchy of Needs

Maslow's hierarchy includes:
- Physiological needs: The most basic level of the hierarchy, physiological needs include the basic human needs of survival such as food, water, clothing, shelter, oxygen, and sleep.
- Safety needs: After meeting physiological needs, safety and security are a requirement of survival.
- The need for belonging and love: Once physiological and safety needs have been met, human beings search for love, acceptance, and belonging. Intimate relationships and friendships satisfy this need.
- Esteem needs: Achievement, education, competence, and respect all satisfy this need. Most people reach this level, but, according to Maslow, few move past it.

- The need for self-actualization: The highest point in Maslow's hierarchy, self-actualization signals that a person has reached his or her full potential.

Maslow's "stages" were not designed to be static. It is possible, especially at the lower levels when one is striving to satisfy basic needs, to revisit a level of the hierarchy that one has already experienced and achieved.

Carl Rogers, a humanist like Maslow, believed that healthy change is built upon certain key concepts. He called his approach **client-centered or person-centered therapy** and believed that through self-explorative therapy, a therapist could assist individual growth by practicing:

- Unconditional positive regard: A belief that people are basically good.
- Nonjudgmental attitude: A lack of personal judgment.
- Disclosure: The sharing and disclosure of personal information.
- Reflection: The mirroring of the person's thoughts and feelings.

Humanistic theory has been hailed as a way to view people as individual personalities. However, critics assert that humanism fails to address the needs of those with severe mental pathologies and that it avoids concrete treatment approaches.

CLIENT-CENTERED OR PERSON-CENTERED THERAPY A psychotherapeutic approach that seeks to reintroduce clients to their own genuine experiences so they will practice unconditional acceptance and feel valued as people.

Biological and Evolutionary Approach

The **biological theory of personality** suggests that personality is genetically determined. Genetics plays a role in appearance, for example, and studies suggest that individual appearance may affect how people view themselves and how they interact with others, both of which affect personality. While the environment also influences it, intelligence may be at least partially inherited. Likewise, research indicates that mental disorders have a genetic component, and that some aspects of temperament may also be biologically based. For instance, the theory of natural selection, on which evolutionary psychological theory is based, states that evolution is the result of the ability of an organism to exhibit traits that encourage the continued existence of the species. If this is true, then personality traits that perpetuate the continuing growth of the species exist as a form of adaptation.

BIOLOGICAL THEORY OF PERSONALITY The assertion that personality is genetically determined.

Genetic research provides much of the basis for biological theories of personality. Using twin and adopted sibling research, scientists have been able to look at inherited and environmental factors that influence personality. However, such research is time consuming and ethically restricted, so the pool of evidence is limited. Still, research has provided insight into a biological basis for intelligence, introversion-extroversion, and neuroticism.

In many ways, personality theory has come full circle. Researchers initially theorized that personality was wholly based on biology. That belief gave way to a more externally focused belief that personality was the product of several environmental factors such as parenting, socialization, and culture. Recent research has, once again, lent credibility to biology as a factor of personality. Today's research explores the roles of biology, evolution, and environmental factors on the development of human personality.

Sociocultural Perspective

The **sociocultural perspective of personality** was the brainchild of Lev Vygotsky, a Russian psychologist who practiced in the late 19th and early 20th centuries. His research and development of his sociocultural beliefs were based on his personal observations after the Russian revolution with its focus on socialism and collectivism. The sociocultural perspective highlights how social interactions with other people and the shared knowledge of a particular culture form an individual's personality.

Vygotsky believed that personality and intellectual abilities were specific to the culture in which a person is raised. To that end, children acquire both their way of thinking and their means of thinking from the culture in which they live. Simply put, the sociocultural perspective asserts that culture teaches people what to think, how to think, and gives them the means to think. Initially, thought is external to the person (the child) and then becomes internalized as the person grows and develops.

All this highlights what is known as collectivism. **Individualism** asserts that people strive to function as autonomous and unique selves. **Collectivism** is the belief that people are integrated into, and become part of, a group as a whole, incorporating the collective goals of the group as their own. The sociocultural perspective and collectivism focus on group membership as a primary aspect of identity. The goals of collectivism guide personal traits. For the collectivist, successfully fulfilling collective goals, roles, and obligations is highly prized.

Researcher Geert Hofstede helped to define individualism and collectivism, but long before Hofstede's work, people noticed that there were inherent differences among people of various cultures. For example, some Asian cultures tend to be very collectivist; people are encouraged from birth to be loyal to specific groups. On the other hand, some Western cultures are more focused on individual, rather than group, goals. A Westerner may think of an Asian person as lacking individuality. An Asian person may think of Westerners as selfish. One of the criticisms of individualism and collectivism is that this type of stereotyping has limited use in cross-cultural psychology.

MEASUREMENT

Ever since researchers first began labeling particular personality traits they have attempted to measure them and quantify the results. Personality tests have proven to be useful in a number of situations, from mental health assessment and treatment to career assessment. Most personality assessments use scales to measure traits and require a trained psychologist or psychiatrist to complete their interpretation. Objective personality tests are used to diagnose and treat mental disorders, develop counseling plans, and guide career placement.

Big Five Personality Tests

Big Five personality tests are designed to measure the Big Five personality traits: agreeableness, openness to change, extroversion, conscientiousness, and neuroticism. Big Five tests are thought to be more accurate than other personality tests

because they do not attempt to measure temperament or type, but rather they are designed to identify characteristics that may be more desirable in a given situation. For instance, if you are applying for a job as a tax accountant, your employer may test you for a high level of conscientiousness.

WHAT IS YOUR PERSONALITY TYPE?

Personality type tests are relatively simple to take. In most tests, each question is presented with multiple choice answer selections. Each question is designed to assess a particular personality trait, and each answer is assigned a point value. An example is shown below.

Look at each group of statements and select the group that best applies to you.

GROUP A	GROUP B
I am shy.	I am outgoing.
I like to be alone.	I love to be around people.
People say I am quiet.	People say I am friendly.
I like to think things over.	I tend to be impulsive.
I like quiet evenings at home with friends.	I love large parties.
I prefer to keep to myself.	I like to be the center of attention.
My idea of a great vacation is hiking alone or snorkeling.	My idea of a great vacation is spring break at the beach.

If you selected Group A, you are introverted. If you selected Group B, you are extroverted.

GROUP A	GROUP B
I do not leave anything to chance.	I go with my gut when making decisions.
I am a practical person.	I love to explore new theories.
People say I am a realist.	People say I am a philosopher.
I finish projects.	I start things, but do not always finish.
I prefer to live in the here and now.	I am always thinking about the future.

If Group A best describes you, you are the sensing type. If Group B best describes you, you are more intuitive.

GROUP A	GROUP B
I am a logical person.	I believe that instinct is important.
I am happy to share my opinion with others.	I try to focus on the positive.
People do not come to me with their problems.	People call me first when they are upset.
I think with my head.	I think with my heart.
I love a great debate.	I always do my best to avoid an argument.

If Group A best describes you, you are a thinker. If Group B best describes you, you are a feeler.

GROUP A	GROUP B
I love surprises.	I like to plan things out.
I am a multitasker.	I cannot focus on more than one thing at a time.
I thrive in chaos.	I prefer everything in its place.
I am spontaneous and flexible.	I prefer order and structure.
I am a procrastinator.	I get things done ahead of time.

If Group A best describes you, you are a perceiver. If Group B best describes you, you are a thinker.

How does it help to know your personality type? Think of it this way: If you are an introvert, you might not do well as a waitress. If you are a feeler, you might make a great nurse. If you are a thinker, you might want to consider becoming a lawyer. Personality traits can be great predictors.

Myers-Briggs Type Indicator (MBTI)

The Myers-Briggs Type Indicator (MBTI) assessment is a personality inventory intended to coordinate the personality type theory of Jung with easy to understand interpretations. The MBTI focuses on four **dichotomies**: favorite world, information, decisions, and structure. The favorite world refers to whether a person focuses on their inner world or the structure of the external world. The four dichotomies relate to Jung's research and the 16 features of personality that intertwine with those four dichotomies. The test also correlates interests, reactions, values, motivations, and skills with perception.

Along with her mother, Katherine Cook Briggs, Isabel Briggs Myers developed the MBTI in the 1940s. Since its inception, numerous scientific studies have supported the test as a valid and reliable measure of personality type. The MBTI has been used for career assessment, matching career choice and personality type, and personal growth and development.

Minnesota Multiphasic Personality Inventory (MMPI)

The **Minnesota Multiphasic Personality Inventory (MMPI)** is one of the most widely used and recognized personality tests. Developed in 1942, the MMPI was used as a clinical measure of mental illness. Because the validity of the original test, which was the creation of psychologist Starke R. Hathaway and psychiatrist J. C. McKinley, was eventually called into question, the inventory was revised and rereleased as the MMPI-2 in 1989. In the revision, many of the questions were reworded, and new questions were added to avoid test bias resulting from sexism and racism.

The MMPI, which is copyrighted by the University of Minnesota, is designed to be used on adults and includes 567 test questions. It must be administered, scored, and interpreted by a professional psychologist or psychiatrist trained in its use. In addition to being used as a clinical tool to diagnose and treat mental disorders, the MMPI is also used in the legal arena, as a professional and career assessment, and to evaluate people seeking certain high-risk employment.

The MMPI targets several different scales. These scales each highlight a different mental condition:

- Scale 1—Hypochondriasis: Designed to indicate excess concern regarding bodily functions.
- Scale 2—Depression: Depending on the score, designed to highlight depression or merely general dissatisfaction.
- Scale 3—Hysteria: Designed to measure reaction to stressful situations.
- Scale 4—Psychopathic deviate: Depending on the score, designed to indicate rebelliousness or obedience.
- Scale 5—Masculinity/femininity: This scale was designed by the original author's to identify homosexual tendencies, but was found to be largely ineffective. High scores on this scale are related to factors such as intelligence, socioeconomic status, and education. Women tend to score low on this scale. The scale has been criticized because of its blurring of sexual identity and gender.
- Scale 6—Paranoia: Designed to measure paranoid factors, such as suspiciousness, feelings of persecution, grandiose self-concepts, excessive sensitivity, and rigid attitudes.

- Scale 7—Psychasthenia: Designed to indicate obsessive-compulsive disorder.
- Scale 8—Schizophrenia: Designed to highlight schizophrenic thoughts and behavior; it is the most difficult of the 10 scales to interpret.
- Scale 9—Hypomania: Designed to highlight the elevated mood that may be a sign of hypomania.
- Scale 0—Social Introversion: Designed to measure a person's tendency to withdraw.

The MMPI also has several built-in validity scales:

- The L Scale: Designed to catch the test takers' attempts to present themselves in a more favorable light; sometimes referred to as "the lie scale."
- The F Scale: Sometimes test takers attempt to "fake good" or "fake bad" in order to make themselves look better or worse than they really are.
- The K Scale: A measure of a test taker's attempt to make himself or herself look better; sometimes referred to as "the defensiveness scale."
- The ? Scale: Also known as the "cannot say" scale, this scale refers to the number of items the test's taker left unanswered.
- True Response Inconsistency (TRIN) Scale: Designed to detect response inconsistencies, the TRIN is a set of 23 paired questions that are the opposite of each other.
- Variable Response Inconsistency (VRIN) Scale: The VRIN is also used to highlight inconsistent responses.
- The Fb Scale: The questions that make up this scale are designed to indicate whether or not the test taker has lost interest in the test and may be marking random answers.

PSYCHOLOGY & CAREERS: OFFICE MANAGER

Every office needs an experienced office manager to handle the day-to-day operations of the business. A career as an office manager is a great way for you to highlight your management, planning, and administrative skills.

Office managers for psychology or psychiatry practices may be in charge of a specific department (in a large practice or group) or for the entire practice (in a smaller group). Office managers may make appointments, process insurance forms and claims, perform new-client intakes, manage patient records, manage the group's human resources needs and finances, and implement policies.

Depending on whether you work for a large organization or a small group, your duties may be more specialized or rather broad. Degree requirements range from an associate's degree or certificate to a bachelor's degree.

SUMMARY

Writers and thinkers have tried to describe and explain human differences for a long time. Identifying and labeling personality traits is one way to determine what is normal and what is pathological, how people perceive each other, and how they use such traits to define each other.

Sigmund Freud was one of the first to categorize personality. He used the id, ego, and superego to assign understandable traits to human behavior. His psychoanalytic theory remains as one of the most hotly debated, yet pervasive, theories of personality.

Trait theory was developed as a way for psychologists to avoid the "why" behind behavior and focus on personality itself. From the Big Five to Cattell's 16 personality factors, researchers have attempted to put a name on what makes people tick.

Many of psychology's personality theories were responses to the times. Humanistic theory promotes the assumption that all human beings are essentially good. Sociocultural theories were developed from post-Russian revolution collectivism. Biological and evolutionary perspectives were a reaction to psychoanalytic theory. Interestingly, as biology sought to take free will out of the personality process, and as humanism sought to put control back into human hands, recent research indicates that personality may be more the two intertwined than either side would care to admit.

Once theorists categorized personality traits, they needed to measure them. Inventories like the MMPI and the MBTI seek to objectively measure personality. Early test versions were revised because of possible biases based on race and gender. Versions of these objective measurements are used to diagnose and treat mental disorders and to provide career counseling.

REFERENCES

Allport, G. (2008). *New World Encyclopedia*. Retrieved from http://www.newworldencyclopedia.org/entry/Gordon_Allport

Cattell, R. (2009). *The scientific analysis of personality*. Piscataway, NJ: Aldine Transaction.

Eysenck, H. J. (1997). *Dimensions of personality*. Piscataway, NJ: Transaction Publishers.

Francis, L. J., Lewis, C. A., & Ziebertz, H. G. (2006). The short-form revised Eysenck Personality Questionnaire (EPQ-S): A German edition. *Social Behavior and Personality, 34*(2), 197–204.

Hofstede, G. (n.d.). *Culture*. Retrieved from http://www.geerthofstede.nl/culture.aspx

John, O. P., Robins, R. W., & Pervin, L. A. (2008). *Handbook of personality: Theory and research* (3rd ed.). New York, NY: Guilford Press.

Kahn, M. (2002). *Basic Freud: Psychoanalytic thought for the 21st century*. New York, NY: Basic Books.

Library of Congress Public Affairs Office. (2010). Swiss psychiatrist Carl Jung's "Red Book" is focus of library exhibition opening June 17. Retrieved from http://www.loc.gov/today/pr/2010/10-052.html

MBTI Basics. (n.d.). *The Myers and Briggs Foundation*. Retrieved from http://www.myersbriggs.org/my-mbti-personality-type/mbti-basics/

McCarthy, J. (2005). Individualism and collectivism: What do they have to do with counseling? *Journal of Multicultural Counseling and Development, 33*(2), 108–117.

McCrae, R. R., & Allik, J. (2002). *The five-factor model of personality across cultures*. New York, NY: Springer.

Minnesota Multiphasic Personality Inventory-2 (MMPI-2). (2011). Product Detail. San Antonio, TX: Pearson Education. Retrieved from http://www.pearsonassessments.com/HAIWEB/Cultures/en-us/Productdetail.htm?Pid=MMPI-2

Oyserman, D., Coon, H. M., & Kemmelmeier, M. (2002). Rethinking individualism and collectivism: Evaluation of theoretical assumptions and meta-analyses. *Psychological Bulletin, 128*(1), 3–72.

Turner, F. J. (1996). *Social work treatment* (4th ed.). New York, NY: Free Press.

Voronov, M. & Singer, J. A. (2002). The myth of individualism-collectivism: A critical review. *The Journal of Social Psychology, 142*(4), 461–480.

Wrightsman, L. S. (1994). *Adult personality development* (Vol. 1, theories and concepts). Thousand Oaks, CA: Sage Publications.

CHAPTER 12

Social Psychology

"The ultimate measure of a man is not where he stands in moments of comfort, but where he stands at times of challenge and controversy."

— Martin Luther King, Jr.

WHAT IS SOCIAL PSYCHOLOGY?

At some point in your life, you have done someone a favor when you did not have to. You have probably also bought something you knew you did not need, just because you wanted to. Social psychology can help us understand why we do things like this. Social psychology examines how people respond to groups and social issues.

SOCIAL PSYCHOLOGY The branch of psychology that investigates social relationships, from relationships between two individuals to group dynamics.

Social psychology is the subdiscipline of psychology that investigates how being aware of other people affects a person's conscious and unconscious behaviors, thoughts, and feelings. Two primary themes underlie the discussion of social psychology today. First, human beings are highly social animals, acutely sensitive to the presence of others. They form groups easily and behave differently when they perceive themselves to be part of a group. Second, people use both automatic and controlled psychological processes to negotiate social relationships.

SCIENTIFIC METHOD A method of obtaining objective knowledge about the world through systematic, empirical, and replicable observations.

As with other subdisciplines of psychology, social psychology researchers use the **scientific method**, a system of proposing and testing hypotheses, to formulate theories about the factors that influence behavior, thought, and feeling. The first social psychology experiment took place in the late 19th century, when psychologist Norman Triplett investigated how the presence of others affected performance on a simple task. Triplett timed children as they wound fishing line around a pole. Some of the children in the group performed the task alone, while some performed the task while other children watched. Of those who were watched, half performed much faster than those who worked unobserved.

SOCIAL FACILITATION The tendency of an awareness of others to affect one's performance on a task.

This result led Triplett to conclude that the presence of others improved individual performance on a task. The term **social facilitation** was later used to describe Triplett's observation that people change their behavior when they know that others are watching them.

In the early decades of the 20th century, most social psychology research explored different aspects of social facilitation. After the Great Depression in the United States and the social and political upheavals in Europe generated by World Wars I and II, social psychologists focused on topics that reflected political and social concerns of the times, such as conflict, obedience to authority, and conformity to group behavior.

TRY IT!

Read the following scenarios and make a prediction about the probable outcome of each. Each situation has been tested in social psychology research and is discussed in this chapter, and the answers appear at the end of the chapter.

1. After repeated exposures to the same stimulus, such as a painting, a person, or a song, will you like the stimulus more or less?
2. If you initially agree to a small request from another person, will you be more or less likely to agree to a large request from the same source?

KEY CONCEPTS

1. Social psychology addresses how groups affect individual behavior, thought, and feeling. See page 219.

2. The effectiveness of persuasive communication depends on the source of the message, the message, the recipient, and the situation in which the message is received. See page 224.

3. Milgram's obedience to authority experiment concluded that the majority of people will obey authority, even against their best judgment. See page 227.

4. The situational theory of leadership contends that the particular time or situation determines who will be a leader. See page 229.

5. Prejudice is a hostile or negative attitude toward a distinct group of people. See page 232.

6. Stereotyping is making a generalization about a group without recognizing that the members are individuals. See page 231.

7. Discrimination is unjustified negative or harmful action based on a person belonging to a particular group. See page 231.

8. Attribution theory refers to how people explain why they behave the way they do. See page 235.

9. Sternberg proposed three elements of love: passion, intimacy, and commitment. See page 238.

10. Aggression is associated with the amygdala and hormone levels in the brain. See page 240.

11. Altruism is providing help when there is no reward for doing so. See page 241.

Social psychology also overlaps to some degree with other social sciences, including economics, political science, and sociology, as all of these fields are concerned with the behavior of people in groups. The difference between social psychology and these social science disciplines is the level of analysis. The social science fields focus on broad social, economic, political, and historical factors. In contrast, social psychology focuses on people in their social world.

Contemporary research in social psychology investigates basic research questions, such as those that examine social facilitation, group dynamics, interpersonal attraction, and stereotypes. Applied research in social psychology investigates how basic psychological principles of social behavior affect the function of organizations, the development of leaders, and the reduction of stereotypes and discrimination. In fact, social psychology has applications to all forms of human endeavor, as social relationships are part of the fabric of every society. Your study of social psychology will help you recognize and understand systematic mental processes that you might never have thought existed. Understanding the psychological forces that create (and discourage) social relationships is an invaluable part of your education.

GROUP DYNAMICS

GROUP Two or more people who interact with each other and whose needs and goals influence each other.

INNATE Inborn traits, characteristics, or tendencies.

EVOLUTIONARY PSYCHOLOGISTS Psychologists who investigate how the course of human evolution may have shaped contemporary human characteristics.

How many groups do you belong to? In addition to groups with explicit rules, such as service organizations or athletic clubs, you may belong to many less structured groups, such as students in the same psychology class or groups of friends who went to high school together. Social psychologists define a **group** as two or more people who influence each other's needs and goals.

Groups are more than the sum of their parts. Although groups are composed of people with their own ideas, beliefs, and attitudes, group membership can influence group members to behave in ways they would be unlikely to endorse when acting alone. Groups also exert social influence on people who are outside of their bounds.

People may possess an **innate**, or inborn, need to belong to groups. Some **evolutionary psychologists**—those who investigate how the course of human evolution may have shaped contemporary human characteristics—argue that group membership helped humans survive over the millennia. People who were bonded together could hunt for and grow food, find mates, and care for children. Consequently, evolutionary psychologists argue, the need to belong has become innate and occurs in all societies.

Benefits of Group Membership

There are many benefits to belonging to a group. This is true in **collectivistic cultures**, in which the well-being of the group is valued over the autonomy of the person, as well as in **individualistic cultures**, which value the individual's ability to

pursue their own goals free from the influence of others. In both collectivistic and individualistic cultures, other people act as valuable sources of social information. Groups also establish **social norms**, or implicit or explicit rules of conduct, thereby educating their members about what types of behavior are acceptable in that particular social world.

Groups also provide a social identity. **Social identity theory** investigates how group membership contributes to a person's sense of self. According to social identity theory, people are motivated to maintain an overall positive self-evaluation. In trying to see themselves in a positive light, they often compare themselves to others. When you consider yourself to be a member of a particular group—psychology students, or members of the school marching band, perhaps—you may integrate characteristics of typical group members into your own identity. The social identity gained through group membership expands your feeling of self-worth, giving you a way to compare yourself with others.

Social Cognition

Groups influence how people think, feel, and act. **Social cognition** is the thought processes that people use to select, interpret, remember, and use social information to make judgments and decisions. In order to understand how groups influence people, it is helpful to review some basic assumptions of **cognitive psychology**. One underlying tenet of cognitive psychology is that the human mind actively attempts to make sense of the world, using both **automatic** and controlled **thinking processes**. Automatic thinking processes occur without your conscious awareness; controlled thinking processes require conscious effort.

Ingroup/Outgroup Categorization

One cognitive process that plays a major role in social thinking is **categorization**, the process of grouping objects (ideas, things, or people) into categories by virtue of their shared properties. Categorization can be an automatic or a controlled thinking process. Categorization contributes to the efficiency of your thinking processes by reducing the amount of information you must hold in your memory.

Group members categorize others according to whether or not they are members of their own group, or **ingroup**, or whether they are **outgroup** members. Group members tend to develop strong positive biases toward ingroup members and negative biases toward outgroup members. They may also tend to think of ingroup members as unique people with diverse opinions and outgroup members as less defined and more similar to each other. This way of thinking is called the **outgroup homogeneity effect**.

COLLECTIVISTIC CULTURE A culture in which the well-being of the group is valued over the autonomy of the individual.

INDIVIDUALISTIC CULTURE A culture that values the individual's ability to pursue his or her own goals free from the influence of others.

SOCIAL NORMS The implicit or explicit rules a group has for the behavior of its members.

SOCIAL IDENTITY THEORY A social psychological theory that investigates how group membership affects a person's social identity.

SOCIAL COGNITION The processes of perceiving and ascribing meaning to the presence of others.

COGNITIVE PSYCHOLOGY A field of psychology that investigates processes related to thinking, including memory, reasoning, and decision making.

AUTOMATIC THINKING PROCESS Thinking that is nonconscious, unintentional, involuntary, and effortless.

CATEGORIZATION The process of grouping objects (ideas, things, or people) into categories by virtue of their shared properties.

INGROUP A group to which one perceives oneself as belonging, toward whom one has positive biases.

OUTGROUP Those outside a group to which one belongs, toward whom one has negative biases.

OUTGROUP HOMOGENEITY EFFECT The tendency to think of ingroup members as unique people with diverse opinions and of outgroup members as less defined and more similar to each other.

Schemas

The human memory system uses information from past experiences to anticipate new encounters with people and objects in the world. The brain unconsciously creates **schemas**, or mental structures that organize information about the world. Schemas often prescribe **social roles**, or expectations about how particular people should behave. Some schemas are related to **gender roles**, or behavior that is considered acceptable for males or females.

Schemas also describe actions in the world. You probably have a schema for the sequence of events that unfold when you go to a restaurant. This schema prepares you to wait to be seated at a table by a host or hostess who will give you a menu, rather than you just walking up to a waiter or waitress and placing an order.

The automaticity of social cognitive processes, as seen in the outgroup homogeneity effect and the formation of schemas, has obvious benefits: You do not have to overload your memory or reprogram your actions each time you encounter a situation that reminds you of something you encountered in the past. However, there is a downside to automatic thinking in social situations. Schemas and other automatic thinking processes can prevent people from carefully evaluating the facts of a situation or considering each person's individuality.

Not all social cognitive processes are automatic. Controlled thinking functions in some social situations, such as when you think carefully about the content of persuasive messages. It is important to recognize automatic thinking processes in social cognition because these processes exert a strong influence on how people perceive and react to their own social world.

SCHEMAS Mental structures that people use to organize their knowledge about the social world around themes or subjects and that influence the information people notice, think about, and remember.

SOCIAL ROLE A schema related to expectations about how particular people are expected to behave.

GENDER ROLES Behavioral patterns and expectations shared by a culture based on maleness and femaleness.

Cognitive Dissonance

Human beings have a natural need to see themselves as competent, reasonable, and moral people. When you express an idea or behave in a way that conflicts with your own self-concept, you may experience the feeling of discomfort known as **cognitive dissonance**.

Cognitive dissonance always makes us uncomfortable, and people take active steps to reduce this feeling of discomfort. There are three basic ways that people attempt to reduce the discomfort of cognitive dissonance:

- by changing their behavior to bring it in line with their self-concept
- by changing one of their thoughts that conflict with the behavior
- by adding new thoughts about their behavior

For example, any smoker who lives in the United States is probably aware that the surgeon general has determined that smoking is hazardous to one's health. Acknowledging the dangers of smoking would probably cause a smoker to experience cognitive dissonance. To relieve the discomfort of cognitive dissonance, the smoker could:

- change the behavior by giving up smoking
- justify smoking by denying that smoking causes cancer

COGNITIVE DISSONANCE A feeling of internal discomfort that occurs when a person is aware of a conflict between two attitudes, or between an attitude and a behavior.

■ justify smoking by adding new thoughts about it, such as "All things considered, smoking is worthwhile because it helps me relax"

PERSUASION

Persuasion begins with the attitudes you have about the world. These attitudes can be changed. First, how can attitudes be defined, and what are the characteristics of an attitude? Second, how do attitudes change, and what techniques are involved? These are the questions addressed in the following sections.

Attitudes

People are not neutral observers of the world. They form **attitudes**, evaluations about the other people, objects, events, and ideas they encounter in the world. Psychologists have identified three characteristics of attitudes:

■ Attitudes are always directed at a target with identifiable characteristics, and are always evaluative (positive or negative).

■ Attitudes are stored in memory and differ with respect to their **accessibility**, the ease or speed with which they can be retrieved from memory.

■ Finally, attitudes can be developed from cognitive, affective, and/or behavioral information.

Often, attitudes are formed from all three of these sources of information.

ATTITUDE A positive or negative evaluation of an object, event, idea, or person.

ACCESSIBILITY The ease or speed with which attitudes can be retrieved from memory.

Attitude Formation

Attitudes can be based on cognitive information or on emotional information. People form attitudes based on personal experience and others' input. A person may be consciously aware of some attitudes, but not all of them. The next section examines each of the ways that people form attitudes.

Attitudes Based on Cognitive Information

Attitudes that are based on cognitive information develop either from direct personal experience or from indirect information obtained from other people. Many beliefs are derived from personal experience. For example, you probably learned that hot fudge sundaes are sweet and gooey, and that ice-covered sidewalks are slippery, so you may ascribe positive and negative evaluations, respectively, to these experiences.

People also form beliefs based on others' input. Parents are often the first source of indirect information about the world. Friends and peers can influence those around them. Societal institutions, such as schools, religious institutions, and the media, can also have an influence.

Attitudes Based on Emotional Information

People can also develop attitudes by linking emotional information with particular objects. There are two primary ways that affect, or emotion, becomes associated with objects: through the mere exposure effect and through classical conditioning.

Classical conditioning occurs when a stimulus comes to evoke a response that it did not previously evoke simply by being paired with another stimulus that naturally evokes the response. For example, if an animal is given a food treat every time its owner says "treat," then this word alone will cause salivation and excitement. Many human attitudes contain some classically conditioned affect. You may feel affection for people, places, and things that you associate with happy experiences. You probably dislike things associated with negative past experiences.

Attitudes Based on Behavioral Information

SELF-PERCEPTION THEORY Theory suggesting that attitudes are based on people's perception of how they behave toward an object or situation.

Sometimes you may not know how you feel about a person until you encounter them directly. According to **self-perception theory**, under certain circumstances people do not know how they feel until they see how they behave. People develop behaviorally based attitudes, founded on their own observations of how they act toward another person when they first encounter them. Behaviorally based attitudes develop only under certain conditions. First, a person's initial attitude toward an object has to be weak or ambiguous. Second, people infer their attitudes from their behavior only when there are no other plausible explanations for their behavior.

Of course, attitudes and social perceptions are not completely accurate all the time, and as a result, erroneous judgments or logical fallacies can occur. For example, stereotypes are created by a person's broad and generalized assumptions, and conclusions are made about groups in which all people in that group are believed to have the same characteristics. Human beings also make selective perceptions by which they selectively obtain, retain, and use information that is consistent with their existing values, beliefs, emotions, and worldviews.

Another fallacy in social perceptions is the concept of a self-fulfilling prophecy. Individuals' social expectations influence how they interact with the others in such a way that elicits the very behaviors they expect. Fundamental attribution errors or actor–observer biases can also result. Actors perceive their own actions or behaviors as situationally determined; however, when people observe the behaviors of others, they tend to attribute those behaviors as being dispositionally determined.

Implicit and Explicit Attitudes

EXPLICIT ATTITUDE An attitude that a person is aware of and can report.

IMPLICIT ATTITUDE An attitude that is involuntary, uncontrollable, and at times unconscious.

You are probably aware of some of the attitudes you hold and unaware of others. **Explicit attitudes** are the ones you consciously endorse and can easily report. For example, if you say you like bicycling, you are stating your explicit attitude toward it. There may also be many **implicit attitudes** that influence your feelings on an unconscious level. Implicit attitudes are accessed from memory, using little conscious effort or control.

Changing Attitudes through Persuasion

PERSUASION Active, conscious attempt to change attitudes through a message.

When attitudes change, it is often in response to social influence. People and groups use **persuasion**, the active and explicit use of messages to encourage others to change their attitudes. Persuasion plays a major role in advertising, marketing, politics, and personal relationships. Yale University researchers who conducted the first systematic study of persuasive communications in the 1950s identified four key factors that contribute to the effectiveness of persuasive communications:

- Source of the persuasive message
- The message itself
- Recipients of the message, whether a person or a larger audience
- Situation or context in which the message is received

Researchers now agree that persuasive messages reach people through two fundamentally distinct processes: a **cognitive process**, in which the recipient uses rational thinking to consider the arguments of a persuasive message, and by relying on **heuristics**, or mental shortcuts that allow people to make rapid judgments.

People differ in the extent to which they enjoy, or have time for, effortful thinking. Those who enjoy thinking are more likely to use cognitive processes to consider persuasive messages even when the message is not personally relevant. Persuasive communications that reach recipients through cognitive processes lead to the formation of strong attitudes that last over time and are resistant to change.

Who is most likely to use heuristics in response to persuasive communications? Usually, a heuristic user is someone who does not have the time to use, or who does not enjoy using, effortful thinking. When a person uses a heuristic, he or she makes an association with a surface feature of the persuasive message.

- For example, someone who is choosing among several brands of a new product might choose the one with the most appealing packaging. In this case, the person would be relying on the **attractiveness heuristic**. ("The package is impressive—it must be a good product.") Attitudes that are formed in this way can lead to impulsive actions and the formation of short-lived attitudes.
- The **expertise heuristic** is used when evaluating a persuasive message. ("If the expert likes it, it must be a good thing.")
- The **familiarity heuristic** is used when a person is persuaded based on the fact that the idea is familiar to them. ("I've heard this idea before. I like this idea because it is familiar.")
- A person's mood can also influence persuasion. For example, when someone is not inclined to use effortful thinking, their mood can serve as a simple peripheral cue. ("I feel good, so I must agree with the message.")

A model of persuasion that accounts for both the cognitive and heuristic routes to persuasion and attitude change is the **elaboration likelihood model**. In this model, the use of cognitive processes is considered the **central route to persuasion**, and the use of heuristics is considered the **peripheral route to persuasion**.

Methods of Persuasion

In addition to studying the internal mechanisms of persuasion, researchers have examined explicit methods used to persuade others. Foot-in-the-door and door-in-the-face are some of the best known of these techniques.

COGNITIVE PROCESS A process in which the recipient uses rational thinking to consider the arguments of a persuasive message.

HEURISTICS Mental shortcuts that allow people to make rapid judgments.

ATTRACTIVENESS HEURISTIC Idea that an object that is visually impressive must be good.

EXPERTISE HEURISTIC Idea that expert approval makes something good.

FAMILIARITY HEURISTIC Assumption that familiarity means something is good.

ELABORATION LIKELIHOOD MODEL A model that proposes two ways in which persuasive communications can cause attitude change, through the central route to persuasion and the peripheral route to persuasion.

CENTRAL ROUTE TO PERSUASION The process by which people rationally consider the arguments in an attempt at persuasive communication.

PERIPHERAL ROUTE TO PERSUASION The process by which people are persuaded by peripheral heuristics and cues rather than rational arguments.

Foot-in-the-Door Technique

Door-to-door salespeople are famous for this technique. First, the salesperson asks for a small favor. ("Might I have a glass of water?") Then, he or she requests a larger favor. ("Did you know that you can get this entire set of CDs for only $19.95?") If salespeople gain compliance for the small favor, compliance for the larger request that follows is more likely to occur. This phenomenon is known as the **foot-in-the-door technique**.

In one of the first scientific tests of the foot-in-the-door technique, researchers J. L. Freedman and S. C. Fraser conducted an experiment. They went door-to-door in a northern California suburb asking homeowners to put a small sign in their windows that said "Be a safe driver." Two weeks later, a different researcher made a larger request, to put a large, ugly sign on the lawn: "Drive Carefully." The researchers knew that most homeowners would not want a large, ugly sign on their lawns because when they made this request to a different set of homeowners, only 17 percent said yes. However, when they made this request to the homeowners who agreed two weeks earlier to put the small "Be a safe driver" sign in their windows, 76 percent said yes. The foot-in-the-door caused an increase in compliance of more than 400 percent.

Psychologists have proposed a number of theories about how the foot-in-the-door technique works. One theory suggests the act of compliance with the small request changes a person's self-image. In the Freedman and Fraser study, for example, when homeowners agreed to display the small sign, they started to perceive themselves as having concern for road safety. A person who cares about road safety would probably be willing to display a large "Drive Carefully" sign, even if it was an unattractive sign.

Door-in-the-Face Technique

The **door-in-the-face technique** is based on the following idea: If you want to make a request of someone but you are worried that they might say no, get them to say no to a larger request first.

In one of the first scientific demonstrations of the door-in-the-face technique, researcher Robert Cialdini conducted an experiment in which university students were approached and asked to spend a day chaperoning juvenile delinquents on a trip to the zoo. Only 13 percent agreed. The researcher made the same request to another set of students. With the second group, the researcher first asked if they would be willing to act as counselors for juvenile delinquents for two hours a week for two years. When the students said no, the researcher asked if, instead, they would chaperone the juvenile delinquents to the zoo for a day. This time, 50 percent agreed.

Cialdini proposed that two mechanisms were at work the door-in-the-face technique. The first mechanism is the **rule of reciprocity**, which states that if someone does something for you, you feel obligated to do something for them in return. If a friend asks to borrow $100 and you say no, you are more likely to comply with his or her request for a smaller amount. The friend has done something for you (lowering the amount of the request). In return, you do something for your friend (you agree to the request). The second explanation for effectiveness of the foot-in-the-door technique is the **contrast effect**. In contrast to $100, $25 does not seem like much money at all.

SOCIAL INFLUENCE

How do groups influence their members to say and do things that are contrary to the individual member's best judgment? **Social influence** refers to the phenomenon of being influenced by the presence of others.

Obedience to Authority

During the highly publicized Nuremberg trials following World War II, German guards who served as executioners in concentration camps were placed on trial for crimes against humanity. The guards claimed innocence on the grounds that they were merely following orders. In response to the Nuremberg trials, psychologist Stanley Milgram was motivated to investigate whether most people would obey the orders of an authority figure even if they knew that they would harm others in the process.

In Milgram's famous **obedience** experiments, participants were recruited for experiments that were advertised as "learning studies." In this scenario, "learners" were **confederates** of the experimenter, meaning they were told of the real purpose of the experiment, unlike the participants of the study. The learners were asked to memorize word-pairs read by the naïve participant, who assumed the role of "teacher." When the learner missed a word pair, the experimenter instructed the teacher (the naïve participant) to administer an "electric shock" to the learner via a device intended to simulate an electrical generator. In reality, no shocks were administered. Many of the participants objected to administering the shocks, particularly when they heard cries of pain (prerecorded by an actor) from the learner. However, more than 65 percent of the participants obeyed the authority figure (the experimenter) and gave what they thought was the maximum level of electrical shock—450 volts.

Compliance

Compliance refers to an overt, public action performed in accordance with a request from an external source. The request can be from another person(s) or from an object, such as a billboard or television advertisement.

Researcher S. E. Asch conducted one of the best-known compliance studies. In this experiment, a single participant joined others (who were confederates) in what was purported to be a study of visual perception. The criterion task was simply to compare the lengths of lines displayed on two cards. The first card showed a single target line, approximately eight inches in length. The second card had three lines. One line was clearly the same length as the target, while the two others were considerably shorter.

For the first few trials, each member of the group chose the obviously correct answer. After a few trials, however, the confederates chose lines that were clearly shorter than the target, and naïve participants began to conform to the group's obviously incorrect answers. Over multiple experiments, naïve participants conformed with the group's incorrect answer in more than 30 percent of trials when they knew that their own answer was correct. Only about 25 percent of the naïve participants performed without succumbing to group pressure.

Decision Making as a Group

As described in the Asch compliance study, being a member of a group can change the decision a person would make on his own. Group dynamics can lead groups to make extreme and even disastrous decisions.

Groupthink describes a process in which groups of people make poor decisions despite the competence of individual group members. Psychologists believe that groupthink arises when the desire to achieve consensus overrides a group's consideration of evidence that might threaten group cohesiveness.

The groupthink model is used to understand poor decision making in public and corporate life. The ill-fated launch of the space shuttle *Challenger* in 1986 is often cited as an example of groupthink. The spacecraft disintegrated within minutes after launch, killing all seven astronauts aboard. A presidential commission investigating the disaster revealed that a group decision was made to launch the spacecraft in conditions known to be unsafe. Psychologists who examined the commission's transcript identified characteristics of overconfidence, rationalization, and self-censorship in the group's decision-making process.

Abilene Paradox

The term **Abilene paradox** refers to a breakdown of group communication in which people refrain from objecting to a group decision because they mistakenly believe that their own preferences conflict with those of the group. Management consultant Jerry Harvey coined this term to describe a personal experience in which he and four family members agreed to drive 53 miles to dinner on a dusty road in searing heat. After the trip, Harvey discovered that each person had agreed to the journey merely because they sensed that someone else in the group wanted to go.

Mob Behavior

Mob behavior refers to the tendency for groups to behave in extreme ways. Mob behavior might be benign, such as a collective "wave" at a sporting event. At other times, mobs behave in destructive and violent ways. The process of deindividuation is a partial explanation for the conduct of a mob, whether harmless or destructive. **Deindividuation** means that people in a large group lose their sense of individuality: crowd membership confers anonymity and reduces a person's inhibitions and sense of personal responsibility. The presence of large numbers of people also encourages heightened physiological arousal, putting people at risk for impulsive and emotional behavior.

GROUPTHINK The process in which groups of people make poor decisions despite the individual competence of group members.

ABILENE PARADOX The tendency for a group to act in a way that is counter to the preferences of any single member of the group.

MOB BEHAVIOR The tendency for crowds to behave in more extreme ways than the people who compose them normally do.

DEINDIVIDUATION The process of losing one's sense of personal identity in a group.

LEADERSHIP

In any group, some people exert more social influence and power than others. **Leaders** can use democratic or autocratic styles to exert their influence to achieve positive or negative ends. What makes someone a leader? How does a political or social situation affect the development of leaders? These are some of the questions that motivate the development of theories of leadership.

Trait Theories of Leadership

In the early 20th century, research on leadership focused on determining the specific traits that differentiated leaders from followers. **Trait theories of leadership** propose that the personal characteristics of a group's leader(s), rather than situational factors (political and historical issues), determine a group's success. An assumption of the trait approach to leadership is the adage "leaders are born, not made." Early trait theorists proposed that key events in history were the result of the heroism of great men who led society in the directions they believed to be important. For this reason, trait theories of leadership are also called "great men" theories of leadership.

Critics of trait theories of leadership cite methodological and theoretical limitations to this approach. One criticism is that there is no clear consensus among psychologists on the definition of leadership, nor on the most appropriate tools, models, and processes with which to investigate it.

Hundreds of studies have shown that leaders tend to have distinctive cognitive, personal, and interpersonal traits. The cognitive traits associated with leadership are high intelligence and **expertise**, or a deep understanding and knowledge of a specific domain. Personality traits associated with leaders include high levels of energy, tolerance to stress, and self-confidence. Interpersonal traits associated with leadership include integrity and motivation. Authoritarian leaders, those who stress authority and power in relationships, may also use Machiavellian means to deceive and manipulate others for personal gain. **Machiavellian** leaders may use unethical principles to achieve their goals.

Situational Theories of Leadership

In contrast to trait theories, situational theories argue that there is no perfect combination of personality traits that predict leadership, nor any single best style of leadership. Instead, **situational theories of leadership** propose that a variety of situational factors determines who will become the leader. Crises seem to cause people to rally around their leader. Other situational factors that can affect leadership include intragroup competition. Groups facing competition or threat are more likely to accept an authoritarian leader than groups not facing such difficulties.

The point has been made that if Adolf Hitler had espoused his doctrine in the United States rather than in Germany, he probably would have

LEADER The person who exerts the most influence and power in a group.

TRAIT THEORY OF LEADERSHIP The theory that the qualities of the particular person in a leadership position shape a group's behavior.

EXPERTISE A high degree of competency in a given field.

MACHIAVELLIAN Authoritarian and concerned with achieving ends, often at the expense of ethical principle.

SITUATIONAL THEORY OF LEADERSHIP The theory that a particular situation determines who will become a leader.

been thrown in jail or committed to a mental institution. In pre–World War II Germany, however, the time and situation were right for people to follow the lead of such a person.

Contingency Theories of Leadership

Social psychologists have abandoned the debate between trait and situational approaches to leadership. Social psychologists currently espouse theories that integrate both points of view, called contingency theories.

Fred Fiedler was one of the first social psychologists to propose **contingency theories of leadership**. His model identifies two different leadership styles. One is the task-oriented leader who is concerned primarily with getting the job done. The other is the relationship-oriented leader who is more concerned with feelings and relationships in the group. The key idea in Fiedler's contingency model is that whether the task-oriented or relationship-oriented leadership style is most effective will depend on the situation the leader faces.

Fiedler's theory is complex. Situations can be classified according to how favorable they are to the leader, and favorability of the situation depends on three factors. The first is the quality of leader-group relationships. The situation is favorable to the leader if these relationships are good; in other words, if the leader is trusted, admired, and respected. The second factor is task structure. Here the situation is favorable to the leader if the task is clear and everyone knows who needs to do what. The third factor is the leader's position power. If the leader has a position with a great deal of power (for example, a head of state with no legislature), the situation is more favorable for that leader.

Theory X versus Theory Y

Theories of leadership have practical applications in many fields, including human resource management and organizational behavior. Theories of management investigate the attitudes of managers and employees toward each other. In the 1960s, Douglas McGregor identified and contrasted two very different theories or attitudes toward workforce motivation that he called **Theory X versus Theory Y**.

Theory X proposes an assumption on the part of the manager that employees are inherently lazy and will avoid work whenever possible. A corollary of this assumption is that workers need to be closely supervised and comprehensive systems of controls need to be developed. A hierarchical structure is needed, with a narrow span of control at every level. According to this theory, employees will show little ambition without an enticing incentive program and will avoid responsibility whenever they can. The conventional conception of management's task is one of harnessing human energy.

Theory Y, on the other hand, proposes that employees are not inherently lazy, but rather that they have become passive as a result of socialization in organizations. According to Theory Y, every person has the potential to develop and assume responsibility and to work toward organizational goals.

CONTINGENCY THEORY OF LEADERSHIP The theory that both trait and situational factors contribute to leadership.

THEORY X VERSUS THEORY Y Two opposing theories of management: Theory X assumes that employees of an organization are inherently lazy and that management must tightly control an organization. Theory Y proposes that employees have the potential to become productive and that the responsibility of management is to make it possible for people to achieve their best.

McGregor felt that companies followed either one or the other approach, and believed that the level of trust between subordinates and their managers was key in connecting self-actualization with work. McGregor proposed that management was responsible for enabling people to recognize and develop their potential. Organizations could support employees by creating opportunities, removing obstacles, encouraging growth, and providing guidance. In summary, Theory X takes a pessimistic view of human motivation in organizations and emphasizes the external control of human behavior by management. In contrast, Theory Y emphasizes that employees have an innate drive for self-direction and performance, which management can encourage and support.

CASE STUDY: COLIN POWELL AS AN EXAMPLE OF LEADERSHIP

Leadership is the art of accomplishing more than the science of management says is possible.
—Colin Powell

Colin Powell, a retired four-star general in the U.S. Army, served as the 65th U.S. secretary of state from 2001 to 2005 and was the first African American ever appointed to that position. During his military career, Powell served as National Security Advisor (1987–1989), as commander of the U.S. Army Forces Command (1989), and as chairman of the Joint Chiefs of Staff (1989–1993), holding the latter position during the Gulf War.

Despite his parents' encouragement to get a good education, Powell has admitted that he was an indifferent student until he joined the Reserve Officers' Training Corps (ROTC) while enrolled at the City College of New York (CCNY). His experience in the ROTC offered him structure and a sense of purpose. He received a commission as an army second lieutenant upon his graduation in June 1958.

After his retirement from military and government service, Powell served on the boards of many corporations, including America Online and Howard University. He is also involved in the Colin Powell Center for Policy Studies at CCNY. The center focuses its efforts in the areas of community and economic development, education, health care, environmental concerns, international development, and global security issues.

According to those who have worked closely with Powell, one of his strengths is his ability to connect with people at any level, from maintenance workers to career diplomats. Powell himself has characterized his leadership style as "a very open, collegial kind of style . . . but with high standards and high expectations for performance."

PREJUDICE, STEREOTYPING, AND DISCRIMINATION

There are differences between prejudice, stereotyping, and discrimination. Stereotyping is making a generalization about a group. Prejudice is an attitude, usually a negative one. Discrimination is most often an action taken against a person or group. Each of these will be examined in the next section.

Prejudice

Prejudice is an attitude. Social psychologists use the word primarily to refer to *negative* attitudes about others. When a person is prejudiced against a group, the person may be distant or hostile toward members of that group, or feel that all members of the group are basically the same.

Stereotypes

A **stereotype** is a generalization about a group of people in which identical characteristics are assigned to virtually all members of the group regardless of variation among members. Once formed, stereotypes are resistant to change.

Stereotyping is not always emotional and does not always lead to acts of abuse. Often stereotyping is merely a technique used to simplify one's world view; all people do it to some extent. According to American social psychologist Gordon Allport, who conducted research in the early and mid-20th century, the world is too complicated for people to maintain a highly differentiated attitude about everything. Instead, they maximize their cognitive energy by developing elegant, accurate attitudes about some things while relying on sketchy beliefs for others.

Discrimination

Discrimination refers to unjustified negative or harmful actions toward people simply on the basis of their membership in a particular group. Discrimination often results from stereotypical beliefs. The link between stereotypical beliefs and discrimination has been demonstrated in laboratory experiments.

In one such experiment, a group of 155 Caucasian men were asked to evaluate resumes of male job applicants for low-status and high-status jobs. The resumes included the applicant's name (in bold letters), education, employment history and experience, and activities and interests. The experimenter made up fictitious names that are generally stereotyped as being Asian American, African American, Hispanic, and Caucasian for the group of "job candidates."

After reading the resumes, participants evaluated each job applicant by responding to scale questions, such as, "How intelligent do you think this person is?" and, "How likely would you be to hire this person for a high-status/low-status job?" Fictitious "Asian American" applicants received the strongest evaluations for high-status jobs, regardless of the content of their resumes. "Caucasian" and "Hispanic" applicants both benefited from a high-quality resume, but "African American" applicants were evaluated negatively, even if they had strong credentials. These results suggested that stereotypes related to race and occupation could lead to job discrimination.

PREJUDICE A hostile or negative attitude toward a distinguishable group of people, based solely on their membership in that group.

STEREOTYPE A generalization about a group of people in which certain traits are assigned to all members of the group without regard for its members' individuality.

DISCRIMINATION Inappropriate and unjustified treatment of people based solely on their group membership.

Foundations of Prejudice

Most social psychologists believe that the specifics of prejudice have to be learned. In 1968, a third-grade Ohio schoolteacher named Jane Elliot tested this hypothesis. Shaken by the recent murder of Dr. Martin Luther King Jr., Elliot devised a novel exercise to demonstrate the effects of discrimination to her third-graders. After discussing King's murder, she asked her class if they wanted to participate in an experiment. With their consent, she divided the class into two groups: blue-eyed people and brown-eyed people. Over the next three days, her students experienced the effects of discrimination based on an arbitrary criterion: eye color.

On the first day, Elliot told her students that blue-eyed people were smarter, more trustworthy, and generally superior to brown-eyed people. The brown-eyed children were required to wear scarves around their necks to identify them as members of the inferior group. The blue-eyed children could play longer during recess, have second helpings for lunch, and were praised in the classroom. After a few hours, the atmosphere of cooperation that had existed in Elliot's classroom evaporated. The blue-eyed kids made fun of the brown-eyed kids, refused to play with them, tattled on them to the teacher, and even started a fistfight. The brown-eyed kids became self-conscious and depressed and performed poorly on tests.

The next day, Elliot told the students that she had made a mistake: the brown-eyed people were really the superior group. Immediately, the brown-eyed children began to take their revenge on the blue-eyed group. On the third day, Elliot explained to her students that the exercise was intended to teach them about prejudice and discrimination. The children discussed the two-day experience and clearly understood its message. At a reunion years later, the students, by then adults, met with Elliot and reported that the experience had had a lasting impact on them.

Prejudice may be an inevitable byproduct of the human tendency to categorize. The first step in prejudice is the creation of groups—putting some people into one group based on certain characteristics and others into another group based on different characteristics. Early laboratory studies on group formation investigated how easily people form groups.

In 1971, social psychologist Henri Tajfel and his colleagues demonstrated that a group could form in the absence of face-to-face contact between members, when none of the people knew each other, and when their "group" behavior had no practical consequences. Tajfel and his colleagues recruited 14- and 15-year-old boys for the experiment. The boys were brought into the lab individually and shown slides of paintings by two artists. The participants were told their preferences for the paintings would determine which group they would join. This explanation was a cover story, intended to encourage the boys to form ingroup and outgroup identities. The experimenters wanted two groups of boys who had no idea who was in their own group or what the grouping meant.

After this setup, the boys were taken to a cubicle one at a time and asked to distribute virtual money to the other members of both groups. The only information each boy had about the others was a code number for each boy and that boy's group membership. From the way the boys distributed the virtual money, they demonstrated classic behavioral markers of group membership: they favored their own group over the other. This pattern was consistent over many trials and has been replicated in other experiments. The boys had no idea who was in their group or who was in the other group, and had nothing to gain from favoring their own group.

Tajfel argued, however, that there *was* something very subtle, yet incredibly profound riding on the decisions the boys made. Tajfel proposed that people build their identities from their own group memberships. It is only natural to want to be part of groups that have high status and a positive image. Crucially though, groups only have high status when compared to other groups. In other words, knowing your group is superior requires looking down on a group with lower status. Selfishness allowed the boys in the experiment to boost their own identities through making their own group look better.

Measuring Prejudice

Prejudice often results from unconscious, or implicit, attitudes toward particular groups. Such attitudes can form as the result of exposure to the prejudicial attitudes of others. Implicit attitudes surface from memory with little conscious effort or control.

Implicit prejudice can be difficult to measure. People may not know they hold prejudices until their attitudes surface in social situations. People may also be reluctant to admit to themselves or others that they hold prejudices against certain groups. In recent years, psychologists devised a powerful way to measure implicit prejudice by leveraging the automaticity of unconscious attitudes. Because people respond automatically to their own unconscious attitudes, reaction time, or a measure of how quickly a person reacts to a stimulus in a laboratory experiment, can be used to assess unconscious attitudes. The Implicit Association Test (IAT) is a computer-based test that uses reaction time (measured in thousandths of a second) to measure how quickly people associate concepts or objects with positive or negative words. For example, responding more quickly to the association of *Asian American* with positive words than with negative words indicates an implicit positive attitude toward Asian Americans.

One way to better understand how implicit prejudices enter into your thoughts and feelings is by visiting the Project Implicit website (use a search engine, such as Google, to locate the site's address). There, you can assess your conscious and unconscious preferences for more than 90 different topics, ranging from pets to political issues, ethnic groups, and styles of music. Participation is anonymous. Data collected by Project Implicit contributes to ongoing research on prejudice.

Prejudice Reduction

Is prejudice an essential aspect of human interaction? Will prejudice always be with us? Despite the automaticity of some social cognitive processes, such as schema and stereotype formation and ingroup/outgroup biases, social psychologists believe that there are antidotes to the prejudice and stereotypes.

Contact Hypothesis

CONTACT HYPOTHESIS
Hypothesis that interaction between members of different groups will reduce intergroup prejudice.

In 1954, Gordon Allport proposed the **contact hypothesis**, which states that interaction between members of different groups will reduce intergroup prejudice. There are two contingencies in Allport's theory. Both groups must be of equal status, and both must share a common goal.

Additional research has identified factors that contribute to the reduction of stereotypes and prejudice. Intergroup prejudices tend to diminish when contact occurs in a friendly, informal setting where ingroup and outgroup members can interact on a one-on-one basis. Furthermore, contact with multiple members of an outgroup can help diminish ingroup members' stereotypes. If an ingroup member meets only one member of an outgroup, the outgroup member could be perceived as an exception to the stereotype. Finally, contact is most likely to lead to prejudice reduction when social norms promoting equality among groups are endorsed.

SOCIAL PERCEPTION

Social perception refers to the processes by which humans make sense of their own and others' behavior. Social perception theory also investigates the factors that create attraction, friendships, and romantic attachments between people.

Attribution Theory and Biases

It is human nature to be curious about what makes other people "tick." An **attribution** is an inference made about the causes of one's own, or another's, actions. **Attribution theory** attempts to identify predictable ways in which humans make inferences about the behavior of others and themselves.

Social psychologists who study attribution use the word **disposition** to refer to the personal qualities or traits that vary across people. For example, you may consider one of your friends to be highly conscientious, while you think that another is careless. Conscientiousness and carelessness are examples of dispositions you have ascribed to these two friends.

Social psychologists describe two types of attributions: If you explain someone's behavior in terms of dispositional factors, such as a mood, an attitude, or personality traits, you are making an **internal attribution**. If you explain someone's behavior in terms of an environmental or situational factor, such as weather, traffic, or the economy, you are making an **external attribution**.

For example, imagine that you are driving down a country road. You round a corner and notice a swerving car ahead. If you think to yourself: "That driver is either drunk or texting," you are using an internal attribution to understand what you see. If you think: "There may be something wrong with that car," you are using an external attribution.

Do humans make internal and external attributions with equal frequency? A large body of research argues that in Western cultures, people are more likely to use internal, rather than external, attributions to explain the behavior of others. There is related evidence that people tend to conflate a person's behavior with his or her disposition, a

SOCIAL PERCEPTION The processes by which humans make sense of their own and others' behavior.

ATTRIBUTION An inference about the underlying causes for one's own behavior, or the behavior of others.

ATTRIBUTION THEORY A description of the way in which people explain the causes of their own and other people's behavior.

DISPOSITION The personal traits that distinguish one person from another.

INTERNAL ATTRIBUTION The inference that a person is behaving in a certain way because of an internal disposition.

EXTERNAL ATTRIBUTION The inference that a person is behaving in a certain way because of an environmental or situational factor.

tendency that is called the **correspondence bias**. For example, if you witnessed a noisy argument between a customer and a department store salesperson, you have fallen prey to the correspondence bias if you assumed that both parties' angry personalities caused the argument. Another explanation for the argument might simply be that the salesperson refused to give the customer a refund on returned merchandise.

Humans make attributions not only about other people but also about themselves. The **actor-observer bias** is the tendency to attribute one's own behavior to a given environment or situation, rather than to one's disposition. Students who procrastinate instead of studying for an exam commit the actor-observer bias when they attribute their low test scores to the instructor's harsh grading policies, rather than to their own lack of preparation.

CORRESPONDENCE BIAS The tendency to infer that a person's behavior corresponds to, or matches, their personality.

ACTOR-OBSERVER BIAS The tendency for people to attribute their actions to situational factors and the actions of others to the person's character.

Individual differences, such as socioeconomic class and gender, can determine how people attribute responsibility and punishment when evaluating the behavior of others. For example, there is evidence that people are generally biased against the poor when evaluating social interactions. Another example is that women are more likely than men to judge as a criminal act a scenario in which there is forced sexual intercourse between a dating couple—otherwise known as "date rape."

Date rape is an appropriate subject for studying attribution of blame because there is ambiguity in how people define and report forced sexual intercourse between acquaintances. Victims of date rape do not always characterize their experience as rape. Even for those who do recognize their experience as rape, many do not report it to the police because they feel personally responsible for the rape, and they fear they will be blamed or otherwise judged negatively.

A recent laboratory study investigated how people attribute blame and punishment in hypothetical scenarios describing date rape. Researchers asked 160 college students (80 men and 80 women) to read four versions of a fictitious scenario that described sexual intercourse between a man and a woman that occurred without the woman's consent. The perpetrator's socioeconomic status varied in the different versions of the story. In some conditions, the perpetrator was a bus driver, and in other conditions, a doctor. The victim's level of resistance was also varied. In some conditions the woman resisted verbally, while in others she resisted verbally and physically. After reading the scenarios, experiment participants judged who was at fault and what the consequences should be.

In general, men assigned more blame to the victim and less blame to the perpetrator than did women. However, men assigned more blame to the bus driver than to the doctor. Women, on the other hand, assigned more blame to the bus driver's victim than the doctor's. The results also indicated that participants recommended harsher punishments for the perpetrator when the victim resisted verbally only, rather than verbally and physically.

SOCIAL BEHAVIORS

Relationships are the glue that keeps people together. Conflict and aggression are forces that push them apart. Psychologists refer to behaviors that promote social

relationships as **prosocial behaviors**, and to behaviors that create conflict as **antisocial behaviors**.

Interpersonal Attraction and Relationships

How did you meet your best friend? Perhaps she sat next to you in chemistry class. Maybe similar tastes in music drew you together. Some of the factors that cause us to be attracted to others are situational, or related to external events.

Proximity

One situational factor that promotes friendships among people is **proximity**, or geographical closeness. The proximity effect was first explored in the 1950s, when researchers investigated friendships among students living in a large college housing complex with many separate buildings. The students had been assigned their rooms at random. When asked to name their three closest friends in the housing project, 65 percent of the students mentioned people who lived in the same building, despite the fact that other buildings were not far away.

Similarity

Do birds of a feather really flock together? Research conducted over the last 40 years in laboratories and natural settings indicates that this is the case. In early laboratory studies on the **similarity–attraction hypothesis**, people were asked to fill out a 12-item attitude scale and then evaluate the profile of a fictional stranger. Participants liked the stranger more when they shared similar political, economic, or religious attitudes. People also tend to form intimate relationships with others who are similar to them in values, preferences, and personality traits.

Mere Exposure Effect

Human beings tend to prefer familiar, rather than unfamiliar, people and things. The appeal of the familiar is known as the **mere exposure effect**. This phenomenon has been demonstrated in dozens of experimental studies.

In one study, three attractive female confederates of the experimenters pretended to be students in a university psychology class. (Note that prior to the study, neutral raters judged the women as equally attractive.) Each female confederate attended a different number of classes over the semester. The women sat in visible locations in a large lecture hall and refrained from interacting with the students. At the end of the term, students were shown slides of the women and completed measures of rating each woman's perceived attractiveness. There were strong relationships between each woman's perceived attractiveness and the number of times she had attended the class.

Physical Attractiveness

What attracted you to your significant other? It should come as no surprise that physical attractiveness plays an important role in forging intimate relationships. Social psychologists have investigated the role of physical attraction in mate selection and intimate relationships.

PROSOCIAL BEHAVIORS Behaviors that tend to benefit others.

ANTISOCIAL BEHAVIORS Behaviors that cause harm to others.

PROXIMITY Geographical nearness.

SIMILARITY–ATTRACTION HYPOTHESIS The theory that in friendships and intimate relationships, people are attracted to others with similar values and attitudes.

MERE EXPOSURE EFFECT The phenomenon of developing a positive attitude toward a person or an object simply as a function of frequent exposure to the person or object.

In one study, experimenters randomly matched incoming university freshmen for a blind date at a dance. After the couples spent a few hours together dancing and chatting, they were asked to evaluate their date and to indicate how much they wanted to see them again. Of the many possible characteristics that could have determined whether the partners liked each other, such as intelligence, independence, sensitivity, or sincerity, the strongest determinant was physical attractiveness.

Baby-Faced Features

How do you define physical attractiveness? Some standards of beauty, such as preferences for particular body types, appear to change over time and across cultures, while other standards seem to be consistent across all cultures. Researcher Michael Cunningham and his colleagues proposed a comprehensive model of attractiveness, which they called the multiple fitness model. One of the tenets of this model is that the perception of fitness of an ideal romantic partner involves a combination of features that simultaneously convey youthfulness, sexual maturity, an absence of signs of advanced age, friendliness, and cultural similarity. This model suggests that facial features that are characteristic of newborns, such as large eyes, a small nose, round cheeks, smooth skin, and glossy hair, may convey an exaggerated sense of youthfulness, freshness, naïveté, and openness. **Baby-faced features** are thought to be attractive because they elicit feelings of warmth and nurturance in perceivers.

This prediction was supported in studies in which male and female students rated the attractiveness of photographs of opposite sex people. The researchers measured the relative size of the facial features in each photograph. For both sexes, high attractiveness ratings were associated with faces with large eyes, a small nose, a small chin, prominent cheekbones and narrow cheeks, high eyebrows, large pupils, and a big smile.

Types of Love

Social psychologists began scientific studies of love in the mid-20th century. Some psychologists have drawn a distinction between **companionate love** and **passionate love**. According to cognitive psychologist Robert J. Sternberg, companionate love consists of feelings of affection that are not accompanied by feelings of sexual arousal. People can experience companionate love in nonsexual relationships, such as close friendships. **Passionate love** refers to the arousal you experience toward your partner, including sexual arousal. People who are passionately in love feel an overwhelming urge to be together. Although most people experience passionate love early in relationships, in most enduring relationships it evolves into a more companionate love, in which intimacy and commitment dominate. Others have classified love into conditional and unconditional love. Unconditional love refers to love given to another person regardless of his or her qualities and/or actions, while conditional love is contingent on what the other person can give.

Dr. John Gottman is a psychologist known for his research on love, marriage, and divorce. Basing his work on Paul Ekman's microexpressions, Gottman developed his own coding system, which he termed the specific affect coding system (SPAFF). The SPAFF attempted to classify a range of positive and negative emotional behaviors. Using the SPAFF, Gottman's research focused on developing a predictive model that would reveal what couples would be more likely to stay married.

After observing couples and their behaviors with the SPAFF, Gottman argued that the patterns of and amount of positive (i.e., interest, humor, affection) and negative (i.e, anger, sadness, contempt) emotional behavior influence the reciprocity

BABY-FACED FEATURES Features that are characteristic of newborns or young children, such as large eyes, a small nose, round cheeks, smooth skin, and glossy hair; these features may convey an exaggerated sense of youthfulness, freshness, naïveté, and openness.

COMPANIONATE LOVE Feelings of intimacy and affection that are not accompanied by passion and physiological arousal.

PASSIONATE LOVE An intense longing felt for another accompanied by physiological arousal.

of behaviors, which then can be used to predict levels of marital satisfaction. In other words, when one spouse expresses negative affect, the other spouse reciprocates with negative affect, triggering a pattern called negative affect reciprocity.

Gottman also introduced the concept of love maps, which are storing places in the brain where spouses house important information about their life partners, such as their likes, dislikes, needs, frustrations, and joys, as well as important dates and events. These love maps are updated continually; Gottman found that couples with extensive love maps have stronger marriages and undergo stress more effectively.

Sternberg's **triangular theory of love** proposed that love consists of three elements: passion, intimacy, and commitment. Intimacy refers to the feelings of being close to and bonded with a partner. Commitment consists of two decisions: the short-term decision that you love your partner and the long-term decision to maintain that love and stay with your partner.

TRIANGULAR THEORY OF LOVE Theory that states that love consists of three distinct ingredients: intimacy, passion, and commitment.

SELECTED QUESTIONS FROM STERNBERG'S INTIMACY AND PASSION QUIZ

Use this scale to evaluate your relationship with someone you love. Write the person's name in the first blank of each line, then rate the degree to which you agree with the statement, on a scale of 1 to 9 (with 9 signifying strong agreement). Add up your totals for each component and divide the number by five to obtain a rough score for that component. To view the complete Sternberg scale and assess a relationship, use a search engine, such as Google, to find a link to a Sternberg scale.

Intimacy Component

I have a warm relationship with _____.   ____

_____ is able to count on me in times of need.   ____

I receive considerable emotional support from _____.   ____

I give considerable emotional support to _____.   ____

I communicate well with _____.   ____

Intimacy Total   ____

Passion Component

Just seeing _____ excites me.   ____

I find myself thinking about _____ frequently during the day.   ____

My relationship with _____ is very romantic.   ____

I find _____ to be very personally attractive.   ____

I cannot imagine another person making me as happy as _____ does.   ____

Passion Total   ____

Decision/Commitment Component

I am committed to maintaining my relationship with _____.   ____

Because of my commitment to _____, I would not let other people
come between us.   ____

(*Continued on next page*)

I have confidence in the stability of my relationship with _____.   _____

I expect my love for _____ to last for the rest of my life.   _____

I will always feel a strong responsibility for _____.   _____

Decision/Commitment Total   _____

Aggression

AGGRESSION Any behavior or action that involves the intention to harm someone.

Psychologists define **aggression** as any behavior or action that involves the intention to harm someone. Acts of aggression are pervasive across recorded history. Over the centuries, thinkers have debated whether aggressiveness is primarily instinctive or learned. Given the universality of aggression, psychologists have tried to understand the biological, social, and cultural factors that cause aggressive behavior.

Biological Factors

AMYGDALA Part of the brain that pairs emotion and memory; it is part of the limbic system.

SEROTONIN A neurotransmitter.

TESTOSTERONE Male sex hormone that regulates the growth of male sex organs and influences sex drive in males and human females.

In research with human and nonhuman subjects, psychologists have observed that stimulating certain brain regions or altering neurochemicals can lead to substantial changes in aggressive behavior. Stimulation of the **amygdala**, an area in the core of the brain, is associated with aggressive behaviors.

The neurotransmitter **serotonin** is important in inhibiting aggressive behavior. Researchers have found that violent criminals have particularly low levels of naturally produced serotonin. High levels of **testosterone**, a male sex hormone, can also lead to increases in aggression. Naturally occurring testosterone levels are significantly higher among prisoners convicted of violent crimes than among those convicted of nonviolent crimes. Also, once incarcerated, prisoners with higher testosterone levels have been shown to violate more prison rules, especially those involving overt confrontation.

Social Factors

FRUSTRATION-AGGRESSION THEORY The theory that frustration can contribute to aggressive behavior.

Aggression can be caused by unpleasant social situations. Imagine, for example, that your friend Jack has offered to drive you to the airport for spring break. Jack arrives at your apartment later than promised but assures you that he knows the route to

the airport well, so you will arrive with time to spare. Halfway to the airport, you find yourself stuck in bumper-to-bumper traffic. Jack assures you that there is still plenty of time. You get out of the car and notice that not a car is moving as far as you can see. You get back in the car, slam the door, and glare at Jack. He smiles lamely and says, "How was I supposed to know there would be so much traffic?" Should Jack be prepared to duck?

The **frustration-aggression theory** proposes that frustration leads to aggression. According to this theory, the more a person's goals are blocked, the likelier he or she is to respond with aggression. Several things can increase frustration. One factor is the closeness to the goal of a person's object of desire. The closer the goal, the greater the expectation of pleasure is thwarted; the greater the expectation, the more likely the aggression.

Cultural Factors

Murder rates are far higher in some countries than in others. The expression of aggressive behaviors varies widely depending on the culture. Researcher Richard Nisbett showed that homicide rates for white southern males are substantially higher than those for white northern males, particularly in rural areas where homicide was often related to an argument. Nisbett attributed this to the phenomenon of a **culture of honor**, a belief system in which men are expected to protect their reputations through physical aggression.

Helping Others

Prosocial behaviors include doing favors, offering assistance, paying compliments, or simply being cooperative. Situational factors influence the extent to which people will conduct prosocial behaviors. This section examines the social psychology of helping, which includes altruistic behavior and the bystander effect.

Altruism

Altruism is the act of providing help when it is needed, without the expectation of any reward. According to the **model of inclusive fitness**, people are altruistic to those with whom they share genes, a phenomenon known as kin selection. However, people also help those to whom they are not related. This is called **reciprocal helping**.

Diffusion of Responsibility

People are less likely to help others when there are personal risks involved and when responsibility is diffused, meaning that there are other people present who might be able to help. This is referred to as the **bystander effect**.

The widely publicized 1964 murder of Kitty Genovese motivated research into the diffusion of responsibility. The young woman was walking home alone at three a.m. from the bar where she worked. She was in a relatively safe area of New York when she was brutally attacked. Genovese ultimately died from her injuries. According to newspaper reports of the time, 38 witnesses heard the young woman's screams for help during the attack, but most ignored the screams. Media reports of the incident created a national conversation about the responsibility to aid others in need.

Decision to Give Aid

Following the wide publication of the Kitty Genovese story, some social psychologists investigated the conditions under which people give aid to others in need. In one set of experiments, researchers asked male college students to fill out questionnaires as they sat in a room that gradually filled with annoying, but not suffocating, smoke. In a number of different conditions, the researchers varied the number of participants versus confederates who were present in the smoky rooms. When participants were on their own, most went for help. When three naïve participants were together, few initially went for help. When in the company of the two calm confederates, 10 percent of the participants went for help within the first six minutes, while the other 90 percent appeared to be uncomfortable but did not report the smoke.

Getting Help

Social psychologists Bibb Latané and John Darley also studied the phenomenon of witnesses failing to get involved in a crisis. Their studies found that the greater the number of people who witness an event, the less likely any one person would be to step forward. People may hesitate to help because they fear making social blunders in ambiguous situations, such as in cases of domestic disputes. People are less likely to help when they are anonymous and can remain so. People also pause to weigh how much harm to themselves they will risk by helping against the benefits of helping someone.

SUMMARY

Social psychology addresses how groups affect individual behavior, thought, and feeling. In some cultures, the well-being of the group is valued over the autonomy of the individual. People tend to think of the groups they belong to as unique and diverse and believe that outgroup members are more similar to each other.

The effectiveness of persuasive communication depends on the source of the message, the message, the recipient, and the situation in which the message is received. Heuristics are mental shortcuts that allow people to make rapid decisions. Types of heuristics include attractiveness, expertise, and familiarity. The peripheral route to persuasion is when a person is persuaded by heuristics and cues rather than rational arguments. The foot-in-the-door technique is a form of persuasion based on asking for a small favor before asking for a larger favor, whereas in the door-in-the-face technique you ask for a large favor before "compromising" to ask for the smaller favor you really want.

Milgram's obedience to authority experiment concluded that the majority of people will obey authority, even against their best judgment. Groupthink is when an entire group makes a poor decision despite the competence of individual members.

Theories of leadership attempt to explain the qualities that make a person a leader who can shape group behavior. The situational theory of leadership contends that the particular time or situation determines who will be a leader.

Prejudice is a hostile or negative attitude toward a distinct group of people. Stereotyping is making a generalization about a group without recognizing that the members are individuals. Discrimination is unjustified negative or harmful action based on a person belonging to a particular group. Interaction between members of different groups reduces prejudice.

Attribution theory refers to how people explain why they behave the way they do. Geographical closeness to someone can breed friendship; this is the proximity effect. The appeal of the familiar is referred to as the mere exposure effect.

Types of love include companionate love and passionate love. Sternberg proposed three elements of love: passion, intimacy, and commitment.

Aggression is associated with the amygdala and hormone levels in the brain. Social and cultural factors also contribute to aggression. Altruism is providing help when there is no reward for doing so. The bystander effect is the failure to help someone who is in obvious need of help.

REFERENCES

Allport, G. W. (2000). The nature of prejudice. In C. Stangor & C. Stangor (Eds.), *Stereotypes and prejudice: Essential readings* (pp. 20–48). Philadelphia, PA: Taylor & Francis Group.

Asch, S. (1951). Effects of group pressure upon the modification and distortion of judgments. In H. Guetzkow (Ed.), *Groups, leadership and men: Research in human relations* (pp. 177–190). Pittsburgh, PA: Carnegie Press.

Barelds, D. P. H., & Barelds-Dijkstra, P. (2007). Love at first sight or friends first? Ties among partner personality trait similarity, relationship onset, relationship quality, and love. *Journal of Social and Personal Relationships, 24*(4), 479–496. doi: 10.1177/0265407507079235

Baumeister, R. F., & Leary, M. R. (1995). The need to belong: Desire for interpersonal attachments as a fundamental human motivation. *Psychological Bulletin, 117*(3), 497–529. Retrieved from http://blog.lib.umn.edu/stei0301/sp_bbk/BandM%20Need%20to%20Belong.pdf

Beeler, C. K. (2010). Leader traits, skills, and behaviors. In M. D. Mumford (Ed.), *Leadership 101* (pp. 87–116). New York, NY: Springer Publishing.

Bem, D. J. (1967). Self-perception: An alternative interpretation of cognitive dissonance phenomena. *Psychological Review, 74*(3), 183–200. Retrieved from http://psycnet.apa.org/index.cfm?fa=buy.optionToBuy&id=1967-13584-001

Berkowitz, L. (1989). Frustration-aggression hypothesis: Examination and reformulation. *Psychological Bulletin, 106*(1), 59–73. Retrieved from http://robertmijas.com/blog/wp-content/uploads/2011/03/frustration-aggression.pdf, 0033-2909/89/$00.75

Berscheid, E. (2010). Love in the fourth dimension. *Annual Review of Psychology, 61*, 1–25.

Black, K., & Gold, D. (2008). Gender differences and socioeconomic status biases in judgments about blame in date rape scenarios. *Violence and Victims, 23*(1), 115–128.

Byrne, D. D. (1971). The ubiquitous relationship: Attitude similarity and attraction: A cross-cultural study. *Human Relations, 24*(3), 201–207.

Carstensen, L. L., Gottman, J. M., & Levenson, R. W. (1995). Emotional behavior in long-term marriage. *Psychology and Aging, 10(1)*, 140–149.

Cialdini, R. B., Vincent, J. E., Lewis, S. K., Catalan, J., Wheeler, D., & Darby, B. (1975). Reciprocal concessions procedure for inducing compliance: The door-in-the-face technique. *Journal of Personality and Social Psychology, 31*(2), 206–215. Retrieved from http://www.psychology.uiowa.edu/Classes/31015sca/Cialdini%20Door%20in%20Face.pdf

Cunningham, M. R., Barbee, A. P., & Philhower, C. L. (2001). Dimensions of facial physical attractiveness: The intersection of biology and culture. In G. Rhodes & L. A. Zebrowitz (Eds.), *Facial attractiveness: Evolutionary, cognitive, and social perspectives* (pp. 193–238). London, UK: Ablex Publishing.

Dabbs, J. M., Carr, T. S., Frady, R. L., & Riad, J. K. (1995). Testosterone, crime, and misbehavior among 692 male prison inmates. *Personality and Individual Differences, 18*(5), 627–633.

Darley, J. (2004). Social comparison motives in ongoing groups. In M. B. Brewer & M. Hewstone (Eds.), *Emotion and motivation* (pp. 281–297). Malden, UK: Blackwell Publishing.

Davidson, R. J., Putnam, K. M., & Larson, C. L. (2000). Dysfunction in the neural circuitry of emotion regulation—A possible prelude to violence. *Science, 289*(5479), 591–594.

Dollard, J., Doob, L., Miller, N., Mowrer, Q., & Sears, R. (1939). *Frustration and aggression.* New Haven, CT: Yale University Press.

Festinger, L. (1962). Cognitive dissonance. *Scientific American, 207*(4), 93–107.

Festinger, L., Schachter, S., & Back, K. (1950). *Social pressures in informal groups: A study of human factors in housing.* Oxford, England: Harper.

Fiedler, F. (1967). *A theory of leadership effectiveness.* New York, NY: McGraw-Hill.

Foley, L. A., Evancic, C., Karnik, K., King, J., & Parks, A. (1995). Date rape: Effects of race of assailant and victim and gender of subjects on perceptions. *Journal of Black Psychology, 21*, 6–18.

Freedman, J. L., & Fraser, S. C. (1966). Compliance without pressure: The foot-in-the-door technique. *Journal of Personality and Social Psychology, 4*(2), 195–202.

Friel, B. (2001). The Powell leadership doctrine. *Government Executive, 33*(7), 22–28.

Frontline. (1995–2011). A class divided. Retrieved from http://www.pbs.org/wgbh/pages/frontline/shows/divided/

Gibbons, F. X., Eggleston, T. J., & Benthin, A. C. (1997). Cognitive reactions to smoking relapse: The reciprocal relation between dissonance and self-esteem. *Journal of Personality and Social Psychology, 72*(1), 184–195.

Gottman, J. M., & Krokoff, L. J. (1989). The relationship between marital interaction and marital satisfaction: A longitudinal view. *Journal of Consulting and Clinical Psychology, 57*, 47–52.

Greenwald, A. G., Banaji, M. R., Rudman, L. A., Farnham, S. D., Nosek, B. A., & Mellott, D. S. (2002). A unified theory of implicit attitudes, stereotypes, self-esteem, and self-concept. *Psychological Review, 109*(1), 3–25. Retrieved from http://faculty.washington.edu/agg/pdf/UnifiedTheory.2002.pdf

Greenwald, A. G., McGhee, D. E., & Schwartz, J. K. (1998). Measuring individual differences in implicit cognition: The Implicit Association Test. *Journal of Personality and Social Psychology, 74*(6), 1464–1480. Retrieved from http://faculty.washington.edu/agg/pdf/Gwald_McGh_Schw_JPSP_1998.OCR.pdf

Harari, O. (2002). *The leadership secrets of Colin Powell.* New York, NY: McGraw-Hill Professional.

Harvey, J. B. (1988). The Abilene paradox: The management of agreement. *Organizational Dynamics, 17*(1), 17–34.

Heine, S. J., Foster, J. B., & Spina, R. (2009). Do birds of a feather universally flock together? Cultural variation in the similarity-attraction effect. *Asian Journal of Social Psychology, 12*(4), 247–258. doi: 10.1111/j.1467-839X.2009.01289.x

Hoffman, M. L. (1981). Is altruism part of human nature? *Journal of Personality and Social Psychology, 40*(1), 121–137. doi: 10.1037/0022-3514.40.1.121

Hovland, C. I., Janis, I. L., & Kelley, H. H. (1953). *Communication and persuasion.* New Haven, CT: Yale University Press.

Janis, I. L. (2007). Groupthink. In R. P. Vecchio (Ed.), *Leadership: Understanding the dynamics of power and influence in organizations* (2nd ed., pp. 157–169). Notre Dame, IN: University of Notre Dame Press.

Jones, E. E., & Nisbett, R. E. (1987). The actor and the observer: Divergent perceptions of the causes of behavior. In E. E. Jones, D. E. Kanouse, H. H. Kelley, R. E. Nisbett, S. Valins, & B. Weiner (Eds.), *Attribution: Perceiving the causes of behavior* (pp. 79–94). Hillsdale, NJ: Lawrence Erlbaum Associates.

King, E. B., Mendoza, S. A., Madera, J. M., Hebl, M. R., & Knight, J. L. (2006). What's in a name? A multiracial investigation of the role of occupational stereotypes in selection decisions. *Journal of Applied Social Psychology, 36*(5), 1145–1159. doi: 10.1111/j.0021-9029.2006.00035.x

Koss, M. P., & Cook, S. L. (2005). More data have accumulated supporting date and acquaintance rape as significant problems for women. In D. R. Loseke, R. J. Gelles, & M. M. Cavanaugh (Eds.), *Current controversies on family violence* (pp. 97–116). Thousand Oaks, CA: Sage Publishing.

Koss, M. P., Dinero, T. E., Seibel, C. A., & Cox, S. L. (1988). Stranger and acquaintance rape: Are there differences in the victim's experiences? *Psychology of Women Quarterly, 12*, 1–24.

Latané, B., & Darley, J. M. (1968). Group inhibition of bystander intervention in emergencies. *Journal of Personality and Social Psychology, 10*(3), 215–221.

Lewin, K. (1948). *Resolving social conflicts: Selected papers on group dynamics.* Oxford, England: Harper.

Manning, R., Levine, M., & Collins, A. (2007). The Kitty Genovese murder and the social psychology of helping: The parable of the 38 witnesses. *American Psychologist, 62*(6), 555–562.

McGregor, D. (2005). *The human side of enterprise.* New York, NY: McGraw-Hill. (Original work published 1960)

Miller, N. E., Mowrer, O. H., Doob, L. W., Dollard, J., & Sears, R. R. (1958). Frustration-aggression hypothesis. In C. L. Stacey & M. DeMartino (Eds.), *Understanding human motivation* (pp. 251–255). Cleveland, OH: Howard Allen Publishers.

Moorhead, G., Ference, R., & Neck, C. P. (1991). Group decision fiascoes continue: Space shuttle *Challenger* and a revised groupthink framework. *Human Relations, 44*(6), 531–550.

Moreland, R. L., & Beach, S. R. (1992). Exposure effects in the classroom: The development of affinity among students. *Journal of Experimental Social Psychology, 28*(3), 255–276.

Nisbett, R. E. (1993). Violence and US regional culture. *American Psychologist, 48*(4), 441–449.

Ostrom, T. M., & Sedikides, C. (1992). Out-group homogeneity effects in natural and minimal groups. *Psychological Bulletin, 112*(3), 536–552.

Petty, R. E. (1994). Two routes to persuasion: State of the art. In G. d'Ydewalle, P. Eelen, & P. Bertelson (Eds.), *International perspectives on psychological science: Vol. 2. The state of the art* (pp. 229–247). Hillsdale, NJ: Lawrence Erlbaum Associates.

Project Implicit. (n.d.). Retrieved from http://implicit.harvard.edu/implicit/research/

Selfhout, M., Denissen, J., Branje, S., & Meeus, W. (2009, June). In the eye of the beholder: Perceived, actual, and peer-rated similarity in personality, communication, and friendship intensity during the acquaintanceship process. *Journal of Personality and Social Psychology, 96*(6), 1152–1165.

Sternberg, R. J. (1986). A triangular theory of love. *Psychological Review, 93*(2), 119–135.

Tajfel, H., Billig, M. G., Bundy, R. P., & Flament, C. (1971). Social categorization and intergroup behavior. *European Journal of Social Psychology, 1*(2), 149–178. Online publication (2002) doi: 10.1002/ejsp.2420010202

Tajfel, H., & Turner, J. C. (2004). The social identity theory of intergroup behavior. In J. T. Jost & J. Sidanius (Eds.), *Political psychology: Key readings* (pp. 276–293). New York, NY: Psychology Press. (Original work published 1986)

Takooshian, H. (2009, March 11). The 1964 Kitty Genovese tragedy: Still a valuable parable. *PsycCRITIQUES, 54*(10), Article 2. Retrieved from http://psqtest.typepad .com/blogPostPDFs/200900817_psq_54-10_The1964KittyGenoveseTragedyStillAValuable Parable.pdf

Thompson, A. D., & Riggio, R. E. (2010). Introduction to special issue on defining and measuring character in leadership. *Consulting Psychology Journal: Practice and Research, 62*(4), 211–215.

Triplett, N. (2007). The dynamogenic factors in pacemaking and competition. In D. Smith & M. Bar-Eli (Eds.), *Essential readings in sport and exercise psychology* (pp. 2–12). Champaign, IL: Human Kinetics.

Vroom, V. H., & Jago, A. G. (2007). The role of the situation in leadership. *American Psychologist, 62*(1), 17–24.

Walster, E., Aronson, V., Abrahams, D., & Rottman, L. (1966). Importance of physical attractiveness in dating behavior. *Journal of Personality and Social Psychology, 4*(5), 508–516. Retrieved from http://www2.hawaii.edu/~elaineh/13.pdf

Wilder, D. A. (1984). Predictions of belief homogeneity and similarity following social categorization. *British Journal of Social Psychology, 23*(4), 323–333.

Wilder, D. A. (2001). Intergroup contact: The typical member and the exception to the rule. In M. A. Hogg & D. Abrams (Eds.), *Intergroup relations: Essential readings* (pp. 370–382). New York, NY: Psychology Press. (Original work published 1984, *Journal of Experimental Social Psychology, 20*(2), 177–194.) doi:10.1016/0022-1031(84)90019-2

Zajonc, R. B. (1965). Social facilitation. *Science, 149*(3681), 269–274.

Psychological Disorders

"No one who, like me, conjures up the most evil of those half-tamed demons that inhabit the human breast, and seeks to wrestle with them, can expect to come through the struggle unscathed."

—Sigmund Freud

MENTAL ILLNESS: DIAGNOSIS

Crime dramas have made a business out of depicting psychological disorders. In fact, some propose that movies and television shows actually teach people about psychological disorders. Whenever a tragic crime occurs or a celebrity's life falls apart, news organizations race to assign a **diagnosis**. A diagnosis is a description of a pathological state, located within a range of norms and providing an assessment of its cause that may also assist in treating or curing the problem. There is a collective fascination with what happened and what might have caused it to happen—an abusive childhood, too much stress, not taking medication as prescribed, or using illegal drugs, for example. Yet this fascination may turn to discomfort and avoidance when the topic of mental illness is brought up at the dinner table about a loved one. Stigma surrounds psychological disorder.

DIAGNOSIS Description of a pathological state, locating it within a range of norms and providing an assessment of its cause that may also assist in treating or curing the problem.

MENTAL ILLNESS An issue that brings people mental or physical discomfort and causes them to perceive and behave outside of the norms for that culture.

What exactly is mental illness? **Mental illnesses** can be defined as issues that bring people mental or physical discomfort, causing them to have perceptions and exhibit behavior outside of the norms of their culture.

Defining Abnormality and Normality

Thoughts and behaviors that are outside of the **normal**, or what is expected in a given society, are considered **abnormal**. The criteria for normal and abnormal behaviors are based on cultural and developmental norms within a society. What might seem normal to someone in the United States might not seem normal in another part of the world; likewise, what seems abnormal at one time may become accepted later.

NORMAL The behaviors, attitudes, and approaches to life expected for a given society.

ABNORMAL The thoughts and behaviors that stand outside of what is expected for a given society.

Society also shapes perceptions of what is normal, based on current trends in thought. In the United States, for example, homosexuality was once considered a psychological disorder rather than a sexual orientation. As society became more accepting of homosexuality, the designation changed. Thus, the specific definition of what constitutes abnormal thought and behavior varies by place and time.

Perspectives

The determination of what is normal and abnormal does not begin and end with a society's norms. Labels of normalcy also describe a person's ability to function in society and his or her ability to cope with problems and mishaps. Diagnosis of psychological disorders varies based on the perspective or theoretical model that a particular clinician uses. Physicians tend to rely more heavily on biological components (physical symptoms) while a behavior specialist might focus on the observable behaviors a patient exhibits. Each perspective looks at a part of the puzzle of mental illness.

KEY CONCEPTS

1. Both culture and environment have a role in psychological diagnoses. See page 247.

2. Current trends in diagnosis and treatment suggest that blended methods based on more than one diagnostic theory and using more than one approach to treatment may be most successful. See page 247.

3. Theoretical perspectives on psychological disorders have moved from moral and spiritual castigation and blame to an effort to understand, describe, and treat the human individuals suffering from such disorders. See page 253.

4. Misconceptions about mental health are common when knowledge of brain health and brain functioning are rudimentary and when symptomatic behaviors are wrongly attributed. See page 248.

5. Controversies and debate in treatment approaches to the mentally ill have continued in the past two centuries, but progress has been made in understanding and describing possible causes and treatment programs. See page 253.

Medical Perspective

MEDICAL PERSPECTIVE ON MENTAL ILLNESS
A perspective that seeks to determine the root of issues based on physical symptoms and causes. It proposes that a physical examination of the individual will reveal physical abnormalities, injury, or imbalances that explain the mental illness.

The **medical perspective** seeks to determine the root of a person's mental issues based on his or her physical symptoms and causes. It proposes that a physical examination of a person will reveal physical abnormalities, injury, or imbalances that explain the mental illness. In fact, many terms associated with psychological disorders are rooted in medical diagnosis. The terms mental *illness*, behavioral *symptoms*, and psychological *pain* all stem from the medical or biological basis of mental diagnosis that was used for years.

This medical basis does have merit. Many psychological disorders have some element of biological dysfunction that is contributing to the problem. For example, fear is an emotional response that begins with biological components. The onset of fear and physical responses to unsettling situations are integral to the function of the amygdala and hippocampus, and they are also the primary concern in most anxiety disorders. Some studies have indicated that as physical responses to fear are processed in the body, a neural mechanism may begin to malfunction, causing the fear response to become more severe than warranted for the situation. Genetic factors have also been implicated, as new studies have shown an inherited component of depression, schizophrenia, and certain anxiety disorders.

The medical perspective, then, has some validity: There is an observable biological basis to psychological disorders, and some disorders require medical intervention as part of the treatment process. Yet the medical perspective does not provide a complete picture of a psychological disorder. The influence of environmental factors, for example, is undeniable—even among those who are trying to manage mental health symptoms without medical intervention. Additionally, some

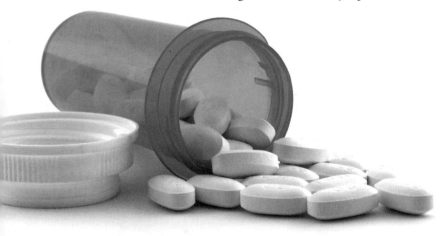

fear that using the medical perspective as the sole approach removes people's responsibility for their thoughts and behaviors and creates a reliance on medical methods as a cure-all.

While the medical perspective focuses on the biological issues that might be involved in abnormal behavior, additional issues affect how people think and act. These perspectives cover areas of thought and behavior and present options for identification and treatment.

Psychoanalytic Perspective

PSYCHOANALYTIC PERSPECTIVE ON MENTAL ILLNESS A perspective holding that psychological disorders stem from unresolved childhood issues pertaining to sex drive and aggression. It deals with subconscious impulses and influences on conscious thought and behavior.

The **psychoanalytic perspective** proposes that psychological disorders stem from unresolved childhood issues pertaining to sex drive and aggression. It focuses on subconscious impulses and their influences on conscious thought and behavior. This perspective has its basis in the work of Sigmund Freud, who theorized that sex drives create tension and aggression as children develop into adolescence. These early-childhood conflicts cause psychological trauma that is stored in the subconscious, influencing thoughts and behaviors throughout life.

Freud believed that the mind has three subdivisions: the id, the ego, and the superego. The id acts to create tension that forces an individual to act to satisfy instinctual needs. The ego acts through the reality principle to satisfy the needs of the id. The superego acts as a conscientious overseer that prevents the ego from simply satisfying its needs without regard for right and wrong.

The id and the superego, therefore, do not always get along, leaving the ego to try to work to satisfy needs and values at the same time. This causes anxiety in the ego as it works to resolve conflict. If rational approaches to easing anxiety do not work, an individual might revert to defense mechanisms to resolve these tensions more superficially.

Defense mechanisms are unconscious methods of resolving anxiety. Denial is a defense mechanism that occurs when a person fails to recognize a negative situation. In general, defense mechanisms are negative methods of coping with problems and anxiety-provoking situations. Everyone uses them at some point to avoid confronting an undesirable issue.

The psychoanalytic perspective has its criticisms. Some propose that it overemphasizes drives and subconscious impulses and therefore takes responsibility away from the individual. Some critics believe the psychoanalytic perspective may be less about achieving happiness and more about learning to live with symptoms. However, the psychoanalytic perspective brings to the surface those buried or repressed emotions or events that affect behaviors and emotions. This can provide a patient with new options for dealing with these challenges.

DEFENSE MECHANISMS
Unconscious methods of working with anxiety issues.

Behavioral Perspective

The medical and psychoanalytic perspectives look at behaviors as the overt symptoms of underlying issues. The **behavioral perspective** works with the abnormal behaviors more directly, when they present in the patient's responses to problems. The emotional content is not central to the behavioral perspective. Instead, behaviorism concentrates on altering behaviors, first by observing the situations in which the behaviors occur, and then by recording their frequency and severity and determining ways to alter them.

The behavioral perspective works with what is measurable and tangible: It uses overt behaviors to determine what is to be considered normal and abnormal in the patient's life. This focus on behavior leaves out key elements, such as emotion, thought, and underlying issues from the environment. These are all important factors that must be considered in addition to the behaviors.

BEHAVIORAL PERSPECTIVE ON MENTAL ILLNESS
A perspective that works with the abnormal behaviors themselves, as they present, without looking at the emotional content.

SOCIOCULTURAL PERSPECTIVE ON MENTAL ILLNESS A perspective proposing that normal and abnormal behaviors are the result of the interaction of the family, society, and culture a person is a part of.

Sociocultural Perspective

The **sociocultural perspective** proposes that normal and abnormal behaviors result when the combined expectations of family, society, and culture interact on an individual. Environmental factors shape how people think and behave. These daily stressors and larger problems that may arise at home, work, or school could set a person up for either normal or abnormal behavior, depending on the positive or negative circumstances.

This perspective also accounts for contributing factors, such as socioeconomic status (SES) and race. For example, some mental health disorders—such as depression, anxiety, substance abuse, and alcohol abuse—are more prevalent in lower-SES neighborhoods. The combination of increased daily stressors, fewer resources, poor

nutrition, and a smaller effective support system presents individuals with lower SES with few ways to solve basic problems that many people take for granted.

Mental illness is also more prevalent in lower SES neighborhoods because people who have psychological disorders are more likely to end up in negative sociocultural circumstances. They may have trouble holding better-paying jobs and are therefore more likely to live in lower-SES neighborhoods. Sociocultural factors are sometimes the result of mental health issues rather than the cause.

Biopsychosocial Perspective

BIOPSYCHOSOCIAL PERSPECTIVE A comprehensive perspective on mental illness that covers all aspects of an individual's life, including biological/medical components, emotional history, behaviors, and environmental circumstances.

Each perspective—biological/medical, psychological, and social—has an effect on normal and abnormal behaviors. Each perspective also provides a different approach to treatment. Many professionals responsible for classifying (diagnosing) a person's abnormal behavior have adopted a biopsychosocial approach, which encompasses all the perspectives discussed. The **biopsychosocial perspective** is a comprehensive perspective that covers all aspects of a person's life, including biological/medical components, emotional history, behaviors, and environmental circumstances. This perspective looks at a person's entire life circumstances in order to provide a diagnosis based on all information available.

Classifying Abnormal Behavior

Definitions of normal and abnormal behavior vary based on culture and circumstance, which makes it harder to diagnose a psychological disorder. What might be viewed as depression in one person might simply be seen as natural reservation or shyness in another. One clinician might believe quietness is a sign of depression while another might think it is a sign of an anxiety disorder. Yet another clinician might see quietness as a normal characteristic of an inherently introverted person. Interpretation of behaviors is subject to the perceptions of the person who is evaluating them. Different evaluators might well have different perceptions.

How can clinicians evaluate patients more coherently so that a depression diagnosis is essentially the same from one evaluator to the next? A uniform set of diagnostic criteria enables clinicians to offer more consistent classifications in individual cases.

DIAGNOSTIC AND STATISTICAL MANUAL OF MENTAL DISORDERS (DSM) Published descriptive system for use in the diagnosis of, communication about, and standardization of treatment for psychological disorders.

The *Diagnostic and Statistical Manual of Mental Disorders (DSM)* was created to present a uniform set of criteria for diagnosis of disorders. The DSM, as of 2013, is now in its fifth edition (DMS-5). The DSM-5 provides information, diagnostic criteria, and definitions for more than 200 disorders in 22 categories. Diagnosis is based on diagnosis criteria that replaces the Five-Axis system from the DSM-IV. The past 5-axial diagnostic system has been removed from DSM-5, and been replaced by alpha designations (A, B, C, etc.) to document diagnoses. The new approach will combine the former axes I, II, and III with separate notations for psychosocial and contextual factors (formerly axis IV) and disability (formerly axis V). Another important change is the change from "not otherwise specified" (NOS) to "not elsewhere defined" (NED). The DSM-5 was updated to harmonize between the **International Publication of Diseases** (ICD-11) to aide in global applicability of diagnoses that, in turn, may align treatment strategies.

The *DSM* provides a consistent descriptive system for use in diagnosis. The uniformity of diagnosis between the DSM-5 and ICD-11 allows mental health professionals to communicate with each other more effectively. It also provides a basis for research into the various disorders as reliable descriptions are used and studied.

Some basic terminology was changed from DSM-IV to DSM 5. For example, "general medical condition" was replaced with "another medical condition"; this change was made across all of the disorders. The table below lists some of the major DSM categories, highlighting the changes made from DSM-IV to the DSM 5. This is only a partial list, and definitions and, or criteria are not complete.

DISORDER CATEGORY	DISORDER	DEFINITION	CRITERIA FOR DIAGNOSIS
Anxiety Disorders	Social Anxiety Disorder (One major change from the DSM-IV to DSM -5 is that obsessive-compulsive disorders has been removed and moved to category Obsessive-compulsive and Related Disorders)	Individuals with marked, or intense, fear or anxiety of social situations in which the individual may be scrutinized by others	A. Marked fear or anxiety about one or more social situations in which the individual is exposed to possible scrutiny by others. B. The individual fears that he or she will act in a way or show anxiety symptoms that will be negatively evaluated. C. The social situations almost always provoke fear or anxiety. D. The social situations are avoided or endured with intense fear or anxiety E. The fear or anxiety is out of proportion to the actual threat posed by the social situation.
Somatic Symptom and Related Disorders (This was changed from Somatoform Disorders in the DSM-IV)	Conversion Disorder	The prominence of somatic symptoms associated with significant distress and impairment.	A. One or more symptoms of altered voluntary motor or sensory function. B. Clinical findings provide better evidence of incompatibly between the symptom and recognized neurological or medical conditions. C. The symptom or deficit is not better explained by another medical or mental disorder. D. The symptom or deficit causes clinically significant distress or impairment in social, occupational, or other important areas of functioning, or warrants medical evaluation.

(*Continued on next page*)

	Factitious Disorder (Diagnoses of somatization disorder, hypochondriasis, pain disorder, and undifferentiated somatoform disorder have been removed from the previous edition)		A. Falsification of physical or psychological signs or symptoms, or induction of injury or disease associated with identified deception. B. The individual presents himself or herself to others as ill, impaired, or injured. C. The deceptive behavior is evident even in the absence of obvious external rewards. D. The behavior is not better explained by another mental disorder, such as delusional disorder or another psychotic disorder.
Dissociative Disorders	Dissociative Identity Disorder (DID) (Major changes in Dissociative disorders include the following: 1) derealization is included in the name and symptom structure of what previously was called depersonalization disorder and is now named depersonalization and, or derealization disorder. 2) dissociative fugue is not a specifier of dissociative amnesia rather than a separate diagnosis and 3) the criteria for dissociative identity disorder have been changed to indicate that symptoms of disruption of identity may be reported as well as observed, and that gaps in recall of events may occur for everyday and not just traumatic events.)	These disorders are characterized by a disruption of and, or discontinuity in the normal integration of consciousness, memory, identity, emotion, perception, body representation, motor control, and behavior.	A. Disruption of identity characterized by two or more distinct personality states that may be described in some cultures as an experience of possession. The disruption in identity involves marked discontinuity in sense of self and sense of agency, accompanied by related alterations in affect, behavior, consciousness, memory, perception, cognition, and, or sensory-motor functioning. B. Recurrent gaps in the recall of everyday events, important personal information, and, or traumatic events that are inconsistent with ordinary forgetting.
Bipolar and Related Disorders (This was changed from Mood Disorders in the DSM-IV)	Bipolar I Disorder (Bipolar and related disorders were separated from depressive disorders and placed between chapters on schizophrenia spectrum and other psychotic disorders to help in diagnosis)	A condition that consists of both mania and depression in varying degrees of intensity	A. Criteria have been met for at least one manic episode. B. The occurrence of the manic and major depressive episode(s) is not better explained by schizoaffective disorder, schizophrenia, schizophreniform disorder, delusional disorder, or other specified or unspecified schizophrenia spectrum and other psychotic disorder.

Schizophrenia Spectrum and other Psychotic Disorders. (Spectrum was added in the new edition)	Schizophrenia (Two changes were made for schizophrenia the first being the elimination of the special attribution of bizarre delusions and Schneiderian first-rank auditory hallucinations, (two or more voices conversing). The second change is the addition that individuals must have at least one of these three symptoms: delusions, hallucinations, and disorganized speech.)	Defined as the abnormalities in one or more of the five following domains: delusions, hallucinations, disorganized thinking, (speech), grossly disorganized or abnormal motor behavior, (including catatonia), and negative symptoms.	A. Two (or more) of the following, each present for a significant portion of time during a 1 month period (or less if successfully treated). At least one of these must be (1), (2), or (3): 1. Delusions 2. Hallucinations 3. Disorganized speech 4. Grossly disorganized or catatonic behavior 5. Negative symptoms
Personality Disorders	Antisocial Personality Disorder (No changes in description were changed from the previous edition)	An enduring pattern of inner experience and behavior that deviates markedly from the expectations of the individual's culture, is pervasive and inflexible, has an onset in adolescence or early adulthood, is stable over time, and leads to distress or impairment.	A. A pervasive pattern of disregard for and violation of the rights of others, occurring since age 15 years, as indicated by three (or more) of the following: 1. Failure to conform to social norms with respect to lawful behaviors, as indicated by repeatedly performing acts that are ground for arrest. 2. Deceitfulness, as indicated by repeated lying, use of aliases, or conning others for personal profit or pleasure. 3. Impulsivity or failure to plan ahead. 4. Irritability and aggressiveness, as indicated by repeated physical fights or assaults. 5. Reckless disregard for safety of self or others. 6. Consistent irresponsibility, as indicated by repeated failure to sustain consistent work behavior, or honor financial obligations. 7. Lack of remorse, as indicated by being indifferent to or rationalizing having hurt, mistreated, or stolen from another.
Obsessive-Compulsive and Related Disorders	Hoarding Disorder (This is a new diagnosis in the DSM-5, possibly a symptom of obsessive-compulsive personality disorder.)	Reflects persistent difficulty discarding or parting with possessions due to a perceived need to save the items and distress associated with discarding them.	A. Persistent difficulty discarding or parting with possessions, regardless of their actual value. B. This difficulty is due to a perceived need to save the items and the distress associated with discarding them. C. The difficulty discarding possessions results in the accumulation of possessions that congest and clutter active living areas, and substantially compromises the areas' intended use. D. The hoarding causes clinically significant distress or impairment in social, occupational, or other important areas of functioning.

FIGURE 13.1 Selected List of Major Psychological Disorders

INTERVENTION AND TREATMENT METHODS

From exorcisms through institutionalism to psychoanalysis and drug therapy, many treatment methods for psychological disorders have been used over the centuries.

A History of Treatment Methods

Earlier views that molded perceptions of abnormal psychological behaviors included demonology, asylums, mental hospitals, and community mental health.

Demonology

Early references in ancient Chinese, Egyptian, Hebrew, and Greek literature attribute abnormal behaviors to demonic possession. In settings where such speech or behaviors were interpreted as religiously significant, an afflicted person was thought to be possessed by a beneficial spirit or god, and thus he or she was treated well. However, if the person was thought to be possessed by an evil spirit, he or she faced various unpleasant methods to get rid of the spirit.

These beliefs fell out of favor over time as philosophers and physicians began to understand abnormal behavior. Cognitive explanations made older demonic ideologies obsolete. Removing people with abnormal behavior from society, rather than getting rid of the demons within, became the more common method of dealing with people with mental illness.

Asylums

Asylums were developed in Europe around the sixteenth century to house people with abnormal behaviors, isolating them from the general public. The institutions often exploited their patients, placing them on display and publicly exhibiting them for a fee. Some patients were shackled to walls in dark cells. They lived like animals and were left unattended except for being fed.

In the United States a more proactive type of asylum became commonplace in the eighteenth and nineteenth centuries. Treatments at these asylums included drugs, bleeding, blistering, and electric shock treatment (EST), but most of these treatment methods had little to do with helping or easing symptoms.

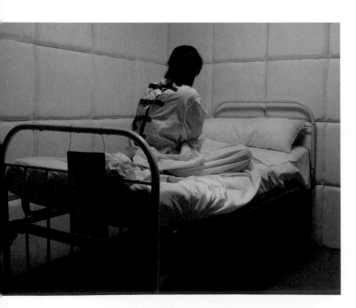

Mental Hospitals

The mental hospital is the successor of the asylum. Humanitarian efforts to provide care and treatment began in the late 18th century. While this practice began as well-intentioned, mental hospitals evolved into overcrowded institutions that provided little in the way of good care. Straitjackets replaced chains and torture devices, but basic comforts and humane treatment were still absent. The buildings themselves, which used extensive security measures to separate "well" and "ill" populations, were fortress-like in appearance, adding to the stigma of mental illness. As the twentieth century progressed, authors and journalists exposed the conditions within the hospitals, which incited change and led to deinstitutionalization.

PSYCHOLOGY & CAREERS: NURSING

Nurses often work with people with psychological disorders. Registered nurses may work with patients, families, and groups to develop nursing treatment plans and plans of care. A registered nurse who wishes to have a greater role in the mental health treatment process may pursue an advanced nursing degree and become a psychiatric nurse. Psychiatric nurses must often earn at least a master's degree, and most obtain a doctoral degree. They assess, diagnose, and treat mental health disorders and can practice independently.

The Community Mental Health Movement

The plight of patients within mental hospitals became a focus of public interest as the need for reform became more evident. Books, articles, and movies chronicled the conditions in many U.S. institutions and by the 1950s and 1960s professional attention had turned toward improving the state of mental hospitals. The development of effective medications for psychological disorders helped move people with psychological disorders out of the hospital environment and back into the community. **Deinstitutionalization** is the process of discharging and reintegrating mental health inpatients into the community.

DEINSTITUTIONALIZATION
The process of discharging and reintegrating mental health inpatients into the community.

Many patients benefited from deinstitutionalization. The new medications helped some patients function better and live more productive lives. Many people had supportive families to help them along and make sure they took their medications.

Others, however, were released to fend for themselves. They could not care for themselves and had no one to help them. Many formerly institutionalized people became homeless. The effect of deinstitutionalization is a current area of research. Some research shows a trend of placing people with mental illness in jail for lack of other options.

Biomedical Therapy

Biomedical therapy focuses treatment of abnormal behavior on brain chemistry and neurological factors rather than on environmental factors or past traumas. Biomedical therapy may involve drugs, electric shock, and neurosurgery in working with psychological disorders.

Psychopharmacology

Psychopharmacology is the use of prescription medications to treat psychological disorders. Medical advances in psychopharmacology are continuing, and new medicines are easing the symptoms of many people with psychological disorders. For example, antipsychotic drugs are very successful in treating psychotic disorders and schizophrenia. Antidepressant medications have become significantly safer and better tolerated in the past thirty years. Antianxiety drugs ease anxiety symptoms, although it is uncertain whether these medications treat the problem or simply mask it. Psychopharmacology is often paired with psychotherapy for a more effective treatment program.

PSYCHOPHARMACOLOGY
The use of medications to treat psychological disorders.

Electroconvulsive Therapy

Electroconvulsive therapy (ECT) is a treatment method that sends an electric current of between 70 and 150 volts to electrodes attached to a patient's head in order to ease severe depression. This form of therapy has become a last resort. ECT can produce loss of consciousness, seizures, disorientation, confusion, and potential memory loss, but it works quickly and is sometimes used to prevent suicide. While this form of therapy is not widely used, it has seen a resurgence in recent years, as alternative treatments are sought.

Transhemispheric Magnetic Stimulation

Transhemispheric magnetic stimulation, or **transcranial magnetic stimulation (TMS)**, is a form of brain imaging that interrupts brain activity in a given location. It has been used to treat major depressive disorder and bipolar disorder. The noninvasive procedure emits a pulsed magnetic field outside the cranium to induce changes inside it. It is thought to disrupt maladaptive function, allowing for a new pattern of activation that could restore interhemispheric equilibrium (balance between the hemispheres of the brain). While it has shown some success, the positive effects have proven thus far to be only short-term. As advances continue, TMS could become more widely used for both scanning and treating mood and cognitive disorders.

Psychosurgery

Psychosurgery is a form of brain surgery used to reduce symptoms of psychological disorders. This form of therapy, which involves removing parts of a patient's brain, is more drastic than ECT and rarely used today. While this method may ease symptoms, it also produces side effects, including personality changes, increased aggression, and even death in some cases.

One early form of psychosurgery was the **prefrontal lobotomy**: the surgical destruction or removal of parts of the frontal lobes. Doctors believed that the frontal lobes controlled the emotions and thought that their removal would reduce the more erratic behavioral symptoms of those with mental disorders. Unfortunately, more severe side effects often occurred. Some patients experienced personality changes ranging from a loss of affect to increased aggression. Some patients died as a result of the invasive procedures used.

Psychotherapy

Psychotherapy is a general form of treatment that addresses psychological disorders through different approaches that help patients modify their behaviors and increase self-understanding and acceptance. A variety of psychotherapy options exist; some focus on past experiences and traumas, while others focus on thoughts and behaviors.

ELECTROCONVULSIVE THERAPY (ECT) A treatment method that delivers an electric current of between 70 and 150 volts to electrodes placed on a patient's head in order to ease severe depression symptoms.

TRANSHEMISPHERIC MAGNETIC STIMULATION/ TRANSCRANIAL MAGNETIC STIMULATION (TMS) A form of brain imaging that interrupts current brain activity in a given location.

PREFRONTAL LOBOTOMY A form of psychosurgery in which parts of the frontal lobes are destroyed or removed.

PSYCHOTHERAPY A general form of treatment that uses different approaches to work on psychological disorders through modifying behaviors and increasing self-understanding and acceptance.

Psychodynamic Approaches

Psychodynamic approaches to therapy use an in-depth process to explore past trauma and relationships that may have produced feelings that lie buried in the subconscious. As these feelings manifest, they can create negative behaviors. The psychodynamic approach explores life history and relationships in an effort to narrow down the source of the negative content in the subconscious.

Psychoanalysis is a form of psychodynamic therapy that Sigmund Freud developed and introduced in his efforts to explore hidden unconscious thoughts and feelings and alter the behaviors they cause. This form of therapy requires meeting often for sessions that last up to an hour over an extended period of years.

In **free association**, a technique often used in psychoanalysis, patients are instructed to say whatever comes to mind. No patterns are necessary and thoughts do not have to be complete. The therapist then tries to connect this information to possible unconscious issues. Therapists might also have patients write down their dreams, making it possible to search for clues to their difficulties within the subconscious.

This process is not always simple, because defense mechanisms can interfere. The patient may unconsciously use a defense mechanism such as repression to bury negative thoughts or memories about traumatic life experiences. These experiences are then blocked from conscious thought. They are not easily retrieved and often require the proper cue in order to emerge.

Transference is another defense mechanism that can affect treatment in psychoanalysis. The length of time and the emotion and vulnerability inherent in psychoanalysis create close relationships between therapists and patients. A patient who unconsciously uses transference as a defense mechanism transfers feelings originally directed to a parent or other authority figure to the therapist. **Countertransference** can be used to create a type of role-play situation in which the therapist takes on the role of the person at whom the patient's original feelings were directed.

Psychodynamic approaches have been updated to keep up with current research and therapy trends. Today's sessions are shorter in length, and therapy takes place over months instead of years. Therapists take a more active role in the process and offer more prompt and direct support and feedback.

The main criticism of psychodynamic approaches is the length of the process. Few people can afford the cost of therapy for as often and as long as effective psychoanalysis takes. Because the results of psychodynamic therapy are to some degree subjective, it is also questionable whether or not such approaches actually work; one must rely on the patients' and therapists' own reports to gauge success.

Behavioral Approaches

Behavioral approaches contrast sharply with psychodynamic approaches. Behavioral approaches look at observable behaviors and propose that both normal and abnormal behaviors are learned. Abnormal behaviors are viewed as the result

PSYCHOANALYSIS Originated by Sigmund Freud, the clinical practice that attempts to bring an individual's unconscious conflicts into conscious awareness.

FREE ASSOCIATION A psychoanalytic technique in which patients say whatever occurs to them, or relate remembered dreams, after which the therapist works to find connections between such raw subconscious production and other presenting issues.

TRANSFERENCE In psychotherapy, when patients project feelings, thoughts, and behaviors characteristic of early formative relationships onto the therapist.

COUNTERTRANSFERENCE The therapist's response to the patient's transference, which may be useful in helping the patient to reenact earlier scenes and replay them in different ways.

BEHAVIORAL APPROACHES TO PSYCHOTHERAPY An approach that looks at observable behaviors and proposes that both normal and abnormal behaviors are learned.

of faulty problem solving and coping skills acquired through interaction with and reinforcement by others. Thus, in order to change abnormal behaviors individuals must first learn new behaviors and unlearn the maladaptive behaviors and reactions that initially contributed to the problems.

The behavioral approach does not delve into family history or traumatic experiences. It deals only with behaviors, not emotions. This is accomplished through the use of classical and operant conditioning techniques and dialectical behavior therapy.

Classical Conditioning

Classical conditioning acts to revise automatic processes by creating new automatic responses based on the introduction of a stimulus. Classical conditioning pairs a stimulus with another, unrelated stimulus to create a different response. In some cases, classical conditioning is undertaken to alter undesirable behavior, and in others, to reduce fear and avoidance of certain events or objects. Two general forms of classical conditioning are aversive conditioning and operant conditioning.

With **aversive conditioning**, undesired behaviors are paired with unpleasant stimuli designed to reduce or remove the unwanted behavior. For example, people with alcoholism are sometimes given drugs such as disulfiram that cause them to become sick when they drink. The goal is to create a relationship between drinking and getting very sick. As the patients associate the feelings of nausea and vomiting with the smell of alcohol, they become averse to drinking. This process is used in the initial stages of therapy to get the patient to stop drinking, but it is not used as the sole form of therapy or expected to last indefinitely, as the efficacy of the drug can wear down over time, particularly if the user continues to drink and becomes used to the sensations of the medication.

Another form of classical conditioning is **exposure therapy**. This therapy is often used in phobic situations to slowly expose patients to the object or situation that causes their fear. Systematic desensitization gradually introduces the fear object or situation to patients to help them become used to it. For example, if a patient is afraid of spiders and receives exposure therapy, he would be exposed to spiders gradually and indirectly at first. His therapy might begin with looking at pictures of spiders and learning more about them. The next step might be to enter a room that contains a spider in a glass container. Next, he would be asked to open the lid of the container, then to stick his hand in, and then to touch the spider. This series would be performed over a period of time, along with exercises in relaxation.

Operant Conditioning

Operant conditioning techniques use positive and negative reinforcement to promote desired behaviors while discouraging undesirable behaviors. This process is often used in elementary schools to help children learn proper school behaviors. Teachers may give out stickers to reward good behavior and give check marks to punish undesirable behavior. At the end of a day or week, students with more stickers than check marks get a prize or privilege. Students with more check marks than stickers review with the teacher what can be done differently in the coming week.

CLASSICAL CONDITIONING A form of therapy that acts to revise automatic processes by creating new automatic responses based on the introduction of a stimulus.

AVERSIVE CONDITIONING A therapy in which the undesired behaviors are paired with an unpleasant stimulus designed to reduce or remove the unwanted behavior.

EXPOSURE THERAPY A form of therapy often used in fear or phobic situations to slowly expose an individual to the fear.

OPERANT CONDITIONING Therapeutic techniques that use positive and negative reinforcement to promote desired behavior while discouraging undesirable behavior.

Dialectical Behavior Therapy

Dialectical behavior therapy focuses on self-acceptance regardless of circumstance. It is often used with patients who have borderline personality disorders, notably those with negative moods and self-perception issues. These patients find significant difficulty in accepting negative situations without engaging in self-destructive behaviors. Dialectical behavior therapy requires the patient to choose between remaining unhappy or changing. The patient must learn to live with less-than-perfect circumstances and find ways to keep unhappy experiences from too strongly affecting his or her behavior.

Cognitive Approaches

Cognitive approaches to therapy address faulty thought processes that tend to elicit improper behavioral and emotional responses. The cognitive approach proposes that thoughts influence emotion, motivation, and behavior. By changing the faulty thoughts, faulty behaviors can also be changed. Most cognitive approaches are paired with behavioral approaches because they work on both thoughts and behaviors.

Rational Emotive Behavior Therapy

Psychologist Albert Ellis is the founder of **rational emotive behavior therapy (REBT)**, a cognitive–behavioral therapeutic approach to coping with stress. He developed the ABC (activating event, belief, and consequence) model. When faced with adversity, some people immediately shift into negative thought patterns and then feel stress, worry, or other unpleasant emotions (the consequence) resulting from those irrational beliefs or judgments about the adversity.

REBT, which has a behavioral orientation, seeks to identify and change unhelpful thought processes that promote maladaptive emotional and behavioral responses. Ellis theorized that when people develop unrealistic beliefs and perfectionist values, they end up expecting too much of themselves and set themselves up for failure. This process results in irrational behaviors.

REBT looks at the shoulds and musts found in self-talk. For example, consider a student who believes she should get a perfect score on every test in order to feel smart and ultimately to feel worthwhile. When she does not get a perfect score, she feels like a failure and views herself as worthless. Faulty behaviors, such as cheating on tests or avoiding them altogether, could be the result. The student might fail the course by choosing not to take tests or turn in required work—thus avoiding feelings of worthlessness that might accompany anything less than a perfect score, but achieving certain failure.

REBT uses confrontation to challenge the patient's faulty beliefs: "Why does getting less than a perfect score mean you are a failure?" Therapists who use REBT often give patients homework—for example, to write down every time the "should" thinking occurs and then record a rational thought in response, or a question that challenges the original "should" thought. REBT uses an ABCDE model for recording and understanding the impact of thoughts on behavior and emotions. A is the activating event that leads to B, the faulty belief. Faulty beliefs set up C,

DIALECTICAL BEHAVIOR THERAPY A form of therapy that focuses on self-acceptance regardless of circumstances.

COGNITIVE APPROACHES Approaches to therapy that work to revise faulty or maladaptive thought processes that tend to elicit improper behavioral and emotional responses.

RATIONAL EMOTIVE BEHAVIOR THERAPY (REBT) A cognitive–behavioral therapeutic approach to coping with stress using an ABC model—activating event, belief, and consequence—based on the idea that negative thought patterns when facing adversity lead to negative feelings.

an emotional consequence that may produce anxiety or misunderstanding. The letter D stands for dispute of the faulty belief, B, which is then replaced with E, an effective new alternative belief. See Figure 13.2.

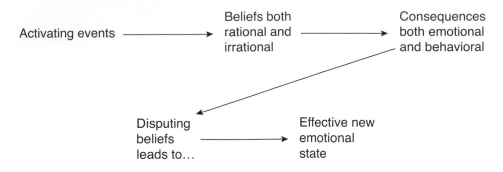

FIGURE 13.2 Ellis's ABC Model

Beck's Cognitive Therapy

Psychiatrist Aaron T. Beck's model of cognitive therapy is designed to correct faulty information processing. This form of therapy assumes that behavior problems are the result of distorted or biased processing of external events or internal thoughts—a patient processes information based on dysfunctional beliefs that lead to faulty interpretations of the information. These patterns of thinking then lead to emotional responses that create abnormal behaviors.

Patients who are in cognitive therapy identify and record their automatic thoughts and their reactions to such thoughts. During the next session, therapist and patient go over the log together to identify errors in logic that lead to cognitive distortions such as overgeneralizing, all-or-nothing thinking, and catastrophizing.

While this sounds very similar to REBT, Beck's cognitive therapy does not use debate and persuasion to help the patient recognize faulty thoughts. Cognitive therapy focuses on the patient determining why their faulty beliefs exist at all.

Both cognitive approaches have been successful in helping people work through faulty thought processes and in helping patients who have anxiety disorders, personality disorders, or depression. Both approaches are widely used in substance abuse treatment. When cognitive and behavioral approaches are combined, results seem generally positive, but emotional responses and underlying issues still need to be addressed.

Humanistic Therapy

Humanistic therapy approaches propose that abnormal behaviors occur in many cases as a result of feelings of alienation, depersonalization, loneliness, and failure to find meaning and fulfillment in life. These therapeutic approaches assume that all people can control their own present behaviors. The approaches focus on expanding the patient's awareness of and responsibility for personal direction in life. Humanistic therapies include person-centered therapy, group therapy, family therapy, and couples therapy.

Person-Centered Therapy

Psychologist Carl Rogers introduced person-centered therapy, a form of therapy designed to free patients from self-imposed restrictions and demands. **Person-centered therapy** seeks to reintroduce patients to their own genuine experiences. Patients learn to accept and be themselves through unconditional acceptance, as

HUMANISTIC THERAPY An approach to psychotherapy proposing that abnormal behaviors occur in many cases as a result of feelings of alienation, depersonalization, loneliness, and failure to find meaning and fulfillment in life.

PERSON-CENTERED THERAPY A psychotherapeutic approach that seeks to reintroduce patients to their own genuine experiences so they will accept and be themselves through unconditional acceptance, understanding, and feeling valued as an individual.

they experience understanding and feeling valued as an individual. Patients learn this self-acceptance through techniques such as empathic reflecting, or restatement of perceived life difficulties. Restatements help patients clarify their own feelings more completely and learn to acknowledge them. Patients learn more about what they are feeling as the therapist restates what was just said.

The person-centered process provides an important element of unconditional acceptance, as patients' thoughts are reflected back to them in a safe environment. Yet as a therapeutic procedure, it lacks structure and consistency. Research suggests that this treatment approach may be helpful, but it is not clear to what extent.

Group Therapy

Group and couples therapies seek to increase participants' levels of interactive functioning and include other peoples' perspectives on their issues. In **group therapy**, patients meet with one or more therapists to discuss issues or a given topic. Groups are usually focused around a specific issue or situation, such as substance abuse, coping with grief, or working on self-achievement.

GROUP THERAPY Therapy in which patients meet in a group to discuss issues or a given topic with a therapist or therapists.

Unlike individual therapies, where patient and therapist determine the length of therapy based on progress, group sessions are for a set number of weeks. The people in the group work together to talk about their own issues, including taking part in exercises and activities designed to create group cohesiveness and facilitate greater understanding of the issues or topics under consideration.

Family Therapy

Family therapy is conducted with members of a family in which one or more members are having a problem, whether emotional, behavioral, or of another type. The family is seen as a system, with people interacting together to make up a single family unit. Therapists meet with all participating members simultaneously to gain an understanding of the system's function. Family members often take on certain roles within the family system, such as hero (the family member who must do everything right and affirm to the family that all is well) and scapegoat (the family member who most exhibits the symptoms of the malfunctioning family). The therapist works with all family members to help them recognize the roles they have taken on within the family and how their interactions within these roles cause greater conflict.

FAMILY THERAPY Therapy conducted with members of a family in which one or more members are having a problem, often an emotional or behavioral one.

Group therapies are effective in helping with social and group interaction skills. They provide individuals with similar issues a support group and new ideas. Group therapies are attractive to insurance providers because they treat multiple individuals at the same time, cutting down on cost. However, group therapy does not provide individualized care, which may be necessary for some people.

It is the therapist's responsibility to ensure that all members of a group have the opportunity to participate. Members who are shy might not receive as much attention if they are allowed to sit quietly. In many cases, group therapy coupled with individual therapy provides patients with a well-rounded treatment system.

Couples Therapy

Couples therapy addresses problems that arise in the context of an intimate relationship. These problems often pertain to infidelity, the threat of a break-up, disagreements regarding childrearing or financial practices, or ineffective communication patterns that are causing an imbalance in the relationship. Therapy

COUPLES THERAPY Therapy centered on conflicts between persons in a relationship with each other.

occurs in joint sessions, with a therapist working with both parties at the same time to help them work through issues and to work together as a couple.

Clinical Hypnosis

Clinical hypnosis is a form of treatment in which patients are placed in a state of consciousness that is different from the normal waking state. The therapist induces a trancelike state in the patient, making them more open to suggestion. Clinical hypnosis is used to treat psychological disorders and to help patients relax and become more receptive to changing maladaptive thought patterns. Hypnosis is used in a wide range of fields, including psychology, medicine and health care, forensics, education, physical therapy, and rehabilitation. It is used for a wide range of issues, including, but not limited to, smoking cessation, controlling pain, improving post-surgery recovery, and weight loss.

CLINICAL HYPNOSIS A form of psychotherapeutic treatment in which patients are placed in a trancelike state of consciousness that is different from the normal waking state.

CASE STUDY: CATHERINE ZETA-JONES

Catherine Zeta-Jones, an Academy Award-winning Welsh singer, dancer, and actress born in 1969, was recently diagnosed with bipolar II disorder. In November 2000, Zeta-Jones and actor Michael Douglas were married in New York City, and today they have two children—a son, Dylan, and a daughter, Carys. Recently, Zeta-Jones announced that she had been diagnosed with bipolar II disorder. Bipolar disorders are mood disorders characterized by episodes of depressive, sad moods alternating with episodes of elevated moods.

These disorders can be categorized as bipolar I or bipolar II disorder. People with bipolar I disorder have full-blown manic and also major depressive episodes. For example, a person with bipolar I disorder may experience several weeks characterized by elevated mood, inflated self-esteem, pressured talking, racing thoughts, and increased activity. This period may be followed by weeks during which the patient experiences no symptoms at all, followed by weeks in which he or she experiences severe depressive symptoms.

On the other hand, individuals with bipolar II disorder, like Zeta-Jones, have milder forms of mania (called hypomania) followed by depressive episodes. In media reports, Zeta-Jones indicated that she had experienced intermittent depression for many years, but these feelings peaked around the time her husband was diagnosed with throat cancer and continued throughout his treatment for the disease. She knew something was wrong when, after the completion of Douglas's treatment and subsequent clean bill of health, the depression continued. Zeta-Jones checked herself into a mental health facility, and it was during that stay that she was given the diagnosis of bipolar disorder.

Like many mental illnesses, bipolar disorders have both a biological predisposition as well as an environmental component. Bipolar disorders, for example, tend to run in families. Stress can also contribute to bipolar disorders, because it can trigger an underlying predisposition to the illness.

At the time of her diagnosis, Zeta-Jones had multiple stressors in her life, including her husband's cancer, her stepson's incarceration, and a pending lawsuit from her husband's former wife. Since her diagnosis, Zeta-Jones has been open about her bipolar disorder, hoping that her celebrity can help create an open dialogue about the illness.

SUMMARY

Psychological disorders are receiving more attention and understanding as research continues to pinpoint their biological, psychological, and social causes and as treatment options show greater success. The biological components of psychological disorders interact with the social and psychological components to create mental health issues that need treatment. Historically, people with psychological disorders were treated with harsh measures designed to remove them from mainstream society. As treatment methods improved, the therapeutic focus slowly shifted away from confinement and toward help.

The perspectives discussed in this chapter are often used in combination to present an integrative approach designed to meet each patient's present needs. This allows for greater flexibility in treatment and often a stronger likelihood of success in understanding of the issues at hand. Medical advances in brain imaging, especially those showing which parts are active during different tasks, have yielded much information on how the brain works.

Therapy has also moved away from traditional psychoanalysis to keep up with the growing body of research. Today, there are many ways of working in group therapy, and new and innovative methods in individual therapy help people learn to live fulfilling, productive lives.

People with psychological disorders have historically suffered societal stigma and shame, a problem that still holds true to some extent today. As more discoveries about these disorders occur, and as more people with mental illness find ways to live satisfying, more productive lives, there is hope that fewer stigmas—and more understanding—will be associated with mental illness.

REFERENCES

American Psychiatric Association. (2000). *Diagnostic and statistical manual of mental disorders* (4th ed., Text rev.). Washington, DC: American Psychiatric Publications.

American Psychiatric Association. (2013). *Diagnostic and statistical manual of mental disorders* (5th ed.). Arlington, VA: Author.

Bloom, J. D. (2010). The incarceration revolution: The abandonment of the seriously mental ill to our jails and prisons. *Journal of Law, Medicine and Ethics, 38*(4), 727–734. doi: 10.1111/j.1748-720X.2010.00526.x

Carr, D. (2008, April 20). Been up, been down. Now? Super. *The New York Times.* Retrieved from http://www.nytimes.com/2008/04/20/movies/20carr.html

Cheng, A. A. (2009). Psychoanalysis without symptoms. *Differences: A Journal of Feminist Cultural Studies, 20*(1), 87–101. doi: 10.1215/10407391-2008-017

Cortina, M. (2010). The future of psychodynamic psychotherapy. *Psychiatry, 73*(1), 43–56.

Doerfler, L. A., Moran, P. W., & Hannigan, K. E. (2010). Situations associated with admission to an acute care inpatient psychiatric unit. *Psychological Services, 7*(4), 254–265. doi: 10.1037/a0020642

Farb, N. A., Anderson, A. K., Mayberg, H., Bean, J., McKeon, D., & Segal, Z. V. (2010). Minding one's emotions: Mindfulness training alters the neural expression of sadness. *Emotion, 10*(1), 25–33. doi: 10.1037/a0017151

Haftgoli, N., Favrat, B., Verdon, F., Vaucher, P., Bischoff, T., Burnand, B., & Herzig, L. (2010). Patients presenting with somatic complaints in general practice: Depression, anxiety and somatoform disorders are frequent and associated with psychosocial stressors. *BMC Family Practice, 11*(67), 1–8. doi:10.1186/1471-2296-11-67

Mark, T. L. (2010). For what diagnoses are psychotropic medications being prescribed? *CNS Drugs, 24*(4), 319–326. doi: 10.2165/11533120-000000000-00000

McAllister, M. (2010). Solution focused nursing: A fitting model for mental health nurses working in a public health paradigm. *Contemporary Nurse, 34*(2), 149–157.

Miniussi, C., Cappa, S. F., Cohen, L. G., Floel, A., Fregni, F., Nitsche, M. A., ... Walsh, V. (2008). Efficacy of repetitive transcranial magnetic stimulation/transcranial direct stimulation in cognitive neurorehabilitation. *Brain Stimulation, 1*(4), 26–36.

Morin, D., Cobigo, V., Rivard, M., & Levine, L. (2010). Intellectual disabilities and depression: How to adapt psychological assessment and intervention. *Canadian Psychology/Psychologie Canadienne, 51*(3), 185–193. doi: 10.1037/a0020184

Oyebode, F. (2006). History of psychiatry in West Africa. *International Review of Psychiatry, 18*(4), 319–325. doi: 10.1080/09540260600775397

Sanislow, C. A., Pine, D. S., Quinn, K. J., Kozack, M. J., Garvey, M. A., Heinssen, R. K., ... Cuthbert, B. N. (2010). Developing constructs for psychopathology research: Research domain criteria. *Journal of Abnormal Psychology, 119*(4), 631–639. doi: 10.1037/a0020909

Schoevers, R. A., Van, H. L., Koppelmans, V., Kool, S., & Dekker, J. J. (2008). Managing the patient with co-morbid depression and an anxiety disorder. *Drugs, 68*(12), 1621–1634.

Shorter, E., & van Praag, H. M. (2010). Disease versus dimension in diagnosis. *The Canadian Journal of Psychiatry/Revue canadienne de psychiatrie, 55*(2), 59–64.

Snowden, A. (2009). Classification of schizophrenia, part 2: The nonsense of mental health illness. *British Journal of Nursing, 18*(20), 1228–1232.

Snyder, E. K. (2010). Psychiatric nursing: Nurse faulted, discharged patient without full mental health evaluation. *Legal Eagle Eye Newsletter for the Nursing Profession, 18*(7). Retrieved from http://www.nursinglaw.com/fullmentalhealth.pdf

Stanford, M. S. (2007). Demon or disorder: A survey of attitudes toward mental illness in the Christian church. *Mental Health, Religion and Culture, 10*(5), 445–449. doi: 10.1080/13674670600903049

Stern, S. (2009). Session frequency and the definition of psychoanalysis. *Psychoanalytic Dialogues, 19*, 639–655. doi: 10.1080/10481880903232058

APPENDIX A

LIST OF PSYCHOLOGICAL ASSOCIATIONS AND ORGANIZATIONS

A
AboutOurKids.org

AboutOurKids.org is the website of the NYU Child Study Center. The center is dedicated to increasing the awareness of child mental health issues and improving the treatment of child psychiatric illnesses through scientific practice, research, and education. The center seeks to bridge the gap between science and practice by integrating the finest research with patient care. AboutOurKids.org provides scientifically based child mental health and parenting information for parents, pediatricians, educators, mental health professionals, and anyone who cares about kids. Drawing on the perspectives of the nation's experts and the resources of the Child Study Center, the site provides a continually expanding store of practical and accessible articles based on the latest research in child psychiatry, psychology, and development. AboutOurKids.org is a reliable resource for both common challenges, such as toilet training, and more serious problems, such as depression and developmental disorders.

E-mail Address: webmaster@aboutourkids.org
Web Address: www.aboutourkids.org/
Mailing Address: New York University Child Study Center, 577 First Ave., New York, NY 10016
Phone: 212-263-6622

American Academy of Child and Adolescent Psychiatry (AACAP)

The American Academy of Child and Adolescent Psychiatry, formerly the American Academy of Child Psychiatry, was founded in 1953 to further the diagnosis, research, and treatment of mental illnesses affecting children, adolescents, and their families. It provides information for both the public and mental health professionals. The academy also works with a network of mental health groups to improve mental health care and with government agencies to influence public policy. It also holds scholarly institutes on such subjects as epidemiology and psychiatry and the law.

E-mail Address: executive@aacap.org
Web Address: www.aacap.org
Mailing Address: 3615 Wisconsin Ave., NW, Washington, DC 20016
Phone: 800-333-7636, 202-966-7300
Fax: 202-966-2891

American Association for Geriatric Psychiatry (AAGP)

The American Association for Geriatric Psychiatry (AAGP) is a national nonprofit organization dedicated to promoting the mental health and well-being of older people and improving the care of those with late-life mental disorders. AAGP's mission is to enhance the knowledge base and standard of practice in geriatric psychiatry through education and research and to advocate for meeting the mental health needs of older Americans.

E-mail Address: main@GMHFonline.org
Web Address: www.aagponline.org
Mailing Address: 7910 Woodmont Ave., Ste. 1050, Bethesda, MD 20814-3004
Phone: 301-654-7850
Fax: 301-654-4137

American Association for Marriage and Family Therapy (AAMFT)

The American Association for Marriage and Family Therapy (AAMFT) is the national association of marriage and family therapists. A principal goal of the AAMFT is to increase understanding, research, and education of the discipline and to ensure that public needs for marriage and family therapy are met by well-trained, qualified practitioners. The organization accredits graduate degrees and postgraduate training institutes throughout the United States and Canada; represents member concerns on legislative and policy matters; and promotes research and education in the field of marriage and family therapy. Services to the general public include a brochure about marriage and family therapy and an online directory of AAMFT clinical members.

E-mail Address: central@aamft.org
Web Address: www.aamft.org
Mailing Address: 112 South Alfred St., Alexandria, VA 22314-3061
Phone: 703-838-9808
Fax: 703-838-9805

American Counseling Association (ACA)

In 1952, four independent associations established the American Personnel and Guidance Association to provide a stronger voice for related counseling professions. In 1983, the association became the American Association for Counseling and Development, and in 1992, it became the American Counseling Association. Today, ACA includes 19 divisions, 56 branches, and four regions in the United States, Europe, Latin America, Puerto Rico, the Virgin Islands, and the Philippines. Branches allow members to network with peers and advocate for professional and government relations issues at a local level. ACA's mission is to enhance the quality of life in society by promoting the development of professional counselors, advancing the counseling profession, and using the profession and practice of counseling to promote respect for human dignity and diversity.

E-mail Address: webmaster@counseling.org
Web Address: www.counseling.org
Mailing Address: 5999 Stevenson Ave., Alexandria, VA 22304-3300
Phone: 800-347-6647, 703-823-9800
Fax: 800-473-2329, 703-823-0252

American Psychiatric Association (APA)

The American Psychiatric Association (APA) was established in 1844 as the Association of Medical Superintendents of American Institutions for the Insane. It became the American Medico-Psychological Association in 1892, and adopted its present name in 1921. The goals of the Association are to improve the treatment of the mentally ill; to promote research, professional education in psychiatry and related fields, and the prevention of psychiatric disabilities; to advance the standards of all psychiatric services and facilities; to foster the cooperation of all who are concerned with the medical, psychological, social, and legal aspects of mental health and illness; and to make psychiatric knowledge available to other medical practitioners, other scientists, and the public. The APA maintains a library of 6,000 volumes and 75 journal titles that is open to members of the Association and mental health researchers by appointment. The APA serves as an educational organization at the federal level.

E-mail Address: apa@psych.org
Web Address: www.psych.org
Mailing Address: 1000 Wilson Blvd., Ste. 1825, Arlington, VA 22209
Phone: 1-888-35-PSYCH, 703-907-7300

American Psychological Association (APA)

The American Psychological Association (APA) was founded in 1892 as a professional organization for psychologists. It exists to advance psychology as a science, as a profession, and as a means of promoting human welfare. The APA promotes research, establishes professional standards, maintains a personnel placement service, conducts meetings, holds an annual convention, and provides information to members, the media, students, and the public. Information services include the publication of 18 journals, an abstracting and indexing service, and responding to mail and telephone requests for information. DATABASE: the PsycINFO and PSYCHLIT database abstracts and indexes psychological literature published since 1967. It is the online version of Psychological Abstracts. Sources indexed by this database include books, periodicals, technical reports, and instructional media such as films and audiotape recordings. The information can be accessed using one of several commercial database vendors, by leasing computer disks, or by requesting a search from the Association's PASAR service. Each year, records from over 1,000 periodicals and 1,500 books and monographs are added. The Thesaurus of Psychological Index Terms has been developed to aid in indexing and retrieving information, and is available for purchase from APA.

E-mail Address: public.affairs@apa.org
Web Address: www.apa.org
Mailing Address: 750 First St., NE, Washington, DC 20002-4242
Phone: 800-374-2721, 202-336-5500
TDD/TTY: 202-336-6123

Anxiety Disorders Association of America (ADAA)

Anxiety Disorders Association of America (ADAA), a nonprofit organization, was founded in 1980. The Association is dedicated to educating the public and professionals about the nature of phobias and anxiety disorders and their treatment, as well as assisting people in locating treatment in their area. ADAA serves as a national clearinghouse for information on resources and referrals and helps in the exchange of information and ideas on phobia and related anxiety disorders treatment. The organization answers inquiries, provides reference services, provides information on research in progress, and conducts an annual national conference with workshops. ADAA is supported by membership dues from its more than 1,000 members, contributions, grants, and the sale of materials.

E-mail Address: information@adaa.org
Web Address: www.adaa.org
Mailing Address: 8730 Georgia Ave., Silver Spring, MD 20910
Phone: 240-485-1001
Fax: 240-485-1035

Asian American Psychological Association (AAPA)

The Asian American Psychological Association (AAPA) is a national organization for psychologists serving the Asian American community. The association's goals include advancing the welfare of Asian Americans by encouraging, assisting, and advocating research about, and service to, Asian Americans and providing a network and forum for Asian American psychologists and psychological professionals working with Asian Americans.

E-mail Address: gisela@scs.tamu.edu
Web Address: www.aapaonline.org
Mailing Address: PMB #527, 5025 North Central Ave., Phoenix, AZ 85012
Phone: 602-230-4257

Association of Black Psychologists (ABPsi)

This association serves as the leader and international resource for addressing the psychological needs of African people in the Diaspora. ABPsi works in collaboration with other Afrocentric associations in social work, law, medicine, and related social service disciplines to formulate or influence the development of policy to ensure positive solutions to the challenges that impact people of African descent.

E-mail Address: abpsi_office@abpsi.org
Web Address: www.abpsi.org
Mailing Address: PO Box 55999, Washington, DC 20040-5999
Phone: 202-722-0808
Fax: 202-722-5941

C

Center for Mental Health Services, Substance Abuse and Mental Health Services Administration (CMHS)

This office, in partnership with states, leads national efforts to demonstrate, evaluate, and disseminate service delivery models to treat mental illness, promote mental health, and prevent the development or worsening of mental illness when possible. CMHS oversees a variety of service-related programs and conducts several new programs mandated by Congress. Among them are the Mental Health Services Block Grant to the States and programs for children needing mental health services.

Web Address: http://www.samhsa.gov/about/cmhs.aspx
Phone: 240-276-1310
Fax: 240-276-1320

Center for Psychiatric Rehabilitation

The Center for Psychiatric Rehabilitation (CPR) is a research, training, and service organization dedicated to improving the lives of persons who have psychiatric disabilities by improving the effectiveness of people, programs, and service systems. The center's mission is to increase knowledge in the field of psychiatric rehabilitation; to train treatment personnel; to develop effective rehabilitation programs; and to assist in organizing both personnel and programs into efficient and coordinated service delivery systems. The center is affiliated with Sargent College of Health and Rehabilitation Sciences and the Department of Rehabilitation Counseling at Boston University.

E-mail Address: psyrehab@bu.edu
Web Address: www.bu.edu/sarpsych
Mailing Address: 940 Commonwealth Ave., West, Boston, MA 02215
Phone: 617-353-3549
Fax: 617-353-7700
TTY: 617-353-7701

Center for Substance Abuse Treatment (CSAT), Substance Abuse and Mental Health Services Administration

This office was created in October 1992 with the congressional mandate to expand the availability of effective treatment and recovery services for alcohol and drug problems. SAMHSA/CSAT works cooperatively across the private and public treatment spectrum to identify, develop, and support policies, approaches, and programs that enhance and expand treatment services for individuals who abuse alcohol and other drugs and that address individuals' addiction-related problems.

E-mail Address: info@samhsa.gov
Web Address: http://www.samhsa.gov/about/csat.aspx
Phone: 240-276-1660
Fax: 240-276-1670
TDD: 800-487-4889

I

Institute for the Advancement of Human Behavior (IAHB)

Founded in 1977, the Institute for the Advancement of Human Behavior (IAHB) is a nonprofit educational organization begun with the primary objective of knowledge dissemination in the biobehavioral sciences. IAHB is a provider of continuing education for health care professionals and provides seminars and workshops for physicians, psychologists, social workers, nurses, certified counselors, and other mental health professionals.

E-mail Address: staff@iahb.org
Web Address: www.iahb.org
Mailing Address: 4370 Alpine Rd., Ste. 209, Portola Valley, CA 94028
Phone: 800-258-8411, 650-851-8411
Fax: 650-851-0406

International OCD Foundation (OCF)

The Obsessive Compulsive Foundation, founded in 1986, is a national, nonprofit organization dedicated to increasing public awareness of obsessive-compulsive disorder, as well as providing support and information to those who have OCD, their families and friends, and medical professionals. The foundation provides referrals to both treatment centers and mental health professionals, and helps coordinate support groups, at the community level, throughout the country. It holds bimonthly support group meetings. Public education is conducted through distribution of literature, lectures, and presentations. The scientific advisory board monitors research and developments in the treatment of OCD. The foundation distributes scientific article reprints, books, videotapes, and audiocassettes for a fee. Materials are available in Spanish.

E-mail Address: info@ocfoundation.org
Web Address: www.ocfoundation.org
Mailing Address: PO Box 961029, Boston, MA 02196
Phone: 617-973-5801

M

Mental Health America

Mental Health America (formerly known as the National Mental Health Association) is the country's leading non-profit dedicated to helping ALL people live mentally healthier lives. With our more than 320 affiliates nationwide, the organization represents a growing movement of Americans who promote mental wellness for the health and well-being of the nation.

Web Address: www.mentalhealthamerica.net
Mailing Address: 2000 N. Beauregard St., 6th Floor, Alexandria, VA 22311
Phone: 800-969-6642, 703-684-7722
Fax: 703-684-5968
TTY: 800-433-5959

Mental Help Net

Mental Help Net is a comprehensive guide to mental health online, featuring over 6,000 individual resources. The site covers information on disorders such as depression, anxiety, panic attacks, chronic fatigue syndrome, and substance abuse, to professional resources in psychology, psychiatry and social work, journals, and self-help magazines.

E-mail Address: info@centersite.net
Web Address: www.mentalhelp.net
Mailing Address: CenterSite, LLC, PO Box 20709, Columbus, OH 43220
Phone: 614-448-4055

The Mind and Life Institute

The Mind and Life Institute is devoted to studying the connections between Buddhism and science and using them to better understand the mind and human understanding of reality. The Dalai Lama sits on the organization's board of directors.

Web Address: www.mindandlife.org
Mailing Address: 7007 Winchester Cir., Suite 100, Boulder, CO 80301
Phone: 303-530-1940

N

National Alliance on Mental Illness (NAMI)

The National Alliance on Mental Illness (NAMI) is a network of local support groups for the mentally ill and their families. It provides information on severe mental illness and its effects on families, support for the rights of patients and families, and help in starting local groups. It advocates for research and quality services works to educate the public and public officials on the needs of the mentally ill.

Web Address: www.nami.org
Mailing Address: 3803 N. Fairfax Dr., Ste. 100, Arlington, VA 22203
Phone: 800-950-6264 (Information Helpline), 888-999-6264 (Member Services), 703-524-7600
Fax: 703-524-9094
TDD: 703-516-7227

National Center for PTSD

The National Center for PTSD is a program of the U.S. Department of Veterans Affairs. The center has seven divisions across the country and carries out a broad range of activities in research, education, and training on traumatic stress and PTSD (posttraumatic stress disorder). Advancing science and promoting understanding of traumatic stress, the NCPTSD works to understand, prevent, diagnose, and treat PTSD in veterans and others following exposure to traumatic stress. NCPTSD cooperates with other agencies and organizations concerned with the impact of traumatic events on mental health. A variety of information resources, for both the general public and health professionals, are produced and disseminated by the center.

E-mail Address: ncptsd@va.gov
Web Address: www.ptsd.va.gov
Mailing Address: National Center for PTSD (116D), VA Medical Center, 215 N. Main St., White River Junction, VT 05009
Phone: 802-296-5132, 802-296-6300 (PTSD Information Line)
Fax: 802-296-5135

National Council for Community Behavioral Healthcare (NCCBH)

The National Council for Community Behavioral Healthcare is the oldest and largest national community behavioral health care advocacy organization in the country. It was formed in 1970 and represents the interests of community behavioral health care organizations nationwide. The National Council conducts federal advocacy activities, representing the industry on Capitol Hill and before federal agencies, and offers a national consulting service program, publications, and an annual training conference.

E-mail Address: communications@thenationalcouncil.org
Web Address: www.thenationalcouncil.org
Mailing Address: 1701 K St. NW, Ste. 400, Washington, DC 20006
Phone: 202-684-7457
Fax: 202-684-7472

National Institute of Mental Health (NIMH)

The National Institute of Mental Health (NIMH), a component of the National Institutes of Health, seeks to reduce the burden of mental illness and behavioral disorders through research on the mind, the brain, and human behavior. NIMH provides a wide range of information based on that research. Publications are available through the NIMH website or by calling the NIMH information center.

E-mail Address: nimhinfo@nih.gov
Web Address: www.nimh.nih.gov
Mailing Address: National Institutes of Health, 6001 Executive Blvd., Room 8184, MSC 9663, Bethesda, MD 20892-9663
Phone: 866-615-6464, 301-443-4513
Fax: 301-443-4279
TTY: 866-415-8051

National Register of Health Service Providers in Psychology

The National Register of Health Service Providers in Psychology, a national nonprofit organization since 1974, is committed to advancing psychology as a profession and improving the delivery of high-quality health services to the public. The organization strives to disseminate standards for evaluating the education and training of licensed psychologists; evaluate programs that enhance the education, training, and delivery of services by psychologists; review the practices and ethics of psychologists to ensure integrity in the profession and quality of patient care; and provide information on psychologists to the health care community and to the general public.

E-mail Address: support@nationalregister.org
Web Address: www.nationalregister.org
Mailing Address: 1120 G St. NW, Ste. 330, Washington, DC 20005
Phone: 202-783-7663
Fax: 202-347-0550

National Suicide Prevention Lifeline

The National Suicide Prevention Lifeline—1-800-273-TALK (8255)—is a 24-hour, toll-free, confidential suicide prevention hotline available to anyone in suicidal crisis or emotional distress. When a person dials 1-800-273-TALK, the call is routed to the nearest crisis center in the lifeline's national network of more than 140 crisis centers. The lifeline's network members provide crisis counseling and mental health referrals day and night. The National Suicide Prevention Lifeline is administered by Link2Health Solutions, Inc., a wholly owned subsidary of the Mental Health Association of New York City. Lifeline's grant is funded by the Substance Abuse and Mental Health Services Administration (SAMHSA).

E-mail Address: ckelly@mhaofnyc.org
Web Address: www.suicidepreventionlifeline.org/default.aspx
Mailing Address: Link2Health Solutions, Inc., 666 Broadway, Ste. 200, New York, NY 10012
Phone: 800-273-8255
TTY: 800-799-4889

O
Office of Applied Studies, SAMHSA

The Substance Abuse and Mental Health Services Administration (SAMHSA) Office of Applied Studies collects and reports on national and state data to help policymakers, treatment providers, and patients make informed decisions regarding the prevention and treatment of mental and substance use disorders.

Web Address: oas.samhsa.gov
Mailing Address: 1 Choke Cherry Rd., Room 7-1044, Rockville, MD 20857
Phone: 240-276-1212

P
Postpartum Support International (PSI)

Postpartum Support International (PSI) was formed to increase awareness in our communities about the emotional changes often experienced during pregnancy and after the arrival of the baby. Objectives of PSI are to facilitate the exchange of information between members, encourage formation of new postpartum support groups, encourage health care professional participation, address legislative issues, encourage research and collaboration with other related organizations, establish criteria for training and for supervision and evaluation of volunteers, and address insurance coverage issues. The organization's mission is to promote international awareness, prevention, and treatment of mental health issues related to childbearing.

E-mail Address: psiofficc@postpartum.net
Web Address: www.postpartum.net
Mailing Address: 6706 SW 54th Ave., Portland, OR 97219
Phone: 503-894-9453
Fax: 503-894-9452

S
Sidran Institute

The Sidran Institute is a nonprofit organization devoted to helping people who have experienced traumatic life events. The institute provides education and advocacy related to traumatic stress. The organization's programs and activities focus on the early recognition and treatment of trauma-related stress in children to promote healthy growth and development; the understanding and treatment of adults suffering from traumatic stress to promote psychological health and recovery; and the promotion of trauma-informed systems of care in agencies providing mental health, counseling, substance abuse, or rehabilitative services to improve care and outcomes. Sidran Education and Training Services, a program, provide conference speakers, consultation, and technical assistance on all aspects of traumatic stress, including public education workshops on understanding PTSD and the psychological outcomes of severe childhood trauma for a variety of audiences. The institute provides resources for survivors through the Trauma Resource Specialists Center, which helps victims find a therapist, reading matter, and other resources to aid progress toward recovery.

E-mail Addresses: consulting@sidran.org, info@sidran.org
Web Address: www.sidran.org
Mailing Address: PO Box 436, Brooklandville, MD 21022-0436
Phone: 410-825-8888
Fax: 410-560-0134

Society for Neuroscience

The Society for Neuroscience is devoted to advancing the understanding of the brain and the nervous system; providing professional development activities, information, and educational resources; promoting public information and general education about the nature of scientific discovery; and informing legislators and other policymakers about new scientific knowledge and recent developments in neuroscience research.

Web Address: www.sfn.org
Mailing Address: 1121 14th Street, NW, Suite 1010, Washington, DC 20005
Phone: 202-962-4000

Substance Abuse and Mental Health Data Archive (SAMHDA)

The goal of the archive is to distribute and promote the usage of research data on substance abuse and mental health problems and the impact of related treatment systems. Data collections distributed by SAMHDA are available for free download from the archive's website in a standard format that is readable by most statistical applications. The project also maintains an online analysis system that permits users to conduct rapid statistical analysis without requiring a download of large data files or use of specialized statistical software. SAMHDA's major holdings include the National Household Survey on Drug Abuse series, the National Comorbidity Survey (Baseline and Replication), the Monitoring the Future series, and many others. SAMHDA is an initiative of the Office of Applied Studies at the Substance Abuse and Mental Health Services Administration (SAMHSA), U.S. Department of Health and Human Services.

E-mail Address: samhda-support@icpsr.umich.edu
Web Address: www.icpsr.umich.edu/SAMHDA
Mailing Address: SAMHDA, ICPSR/University of Michigan, Institute for Social Health Research, PO Box 1248, Ann Arbor, MI 48106-1248
Phone: 888-741-7242 (SAMHDA Helpline), 734-615-9524
Fax: 734-647-8200

Suicide Prevention Resource Center (SPRC)

The Suicide Prevention Resource Center (SPRC) supports suicide prevention skills and practice to advance the National Strategy for Suicide Prevention (NSSP). SPRC provides prevention support, training, and resources to assist organizations and individuals to develop suicide prevention programs, interventions, and policies, and to advance the NSSP. SPRC creates publications and web content on suicide and suicide prevention; identifies and disseminates best practices; facilitates informational exchanges and peer-to-peer mentoring using listservs and other technologies; and promotes suicide prevention as a component of mental health transformation.

E-mail Address: info@sprc.org
Web Address: www.sprc.org
Mailing Address: 55 Chapel St., Newton, MA 02458
Phone: 877-438-7772

APPENDIX B

COMMON THEORIES DISCUSSED IN THE TEXT

CHAPTER	THEORY	THEORIST OR RESEARCHER	DEFINITION
1, 6	Psychodynamic theory	Sigmund Freud	Behavior satisfies innate drives of the id, ego, and superego. Consciousness and unconsciousness is a hierarchy of memory and thought storage, sort of like the layers of an onion. The conscious mind is at the top of the hierarchy (the onion peel), housing everything we are aware of. ■ Id: Primitive sexual and aggressive energy; corresponds to the deepest part of the unconscious mind ■ Superego: Higher ideals and standards of maturity and morality, as embodied by parents and society ■ Ego: Responsible for balancing the drives of the id with the ideals of the superego ■ Defense mechanisms: Used to protect oneself from the distress of unacknowledged feelings and experiences ■ Neurosis: Emotional problems in everyday living ■ Projection: A type of defense that attributes one's unacknowledged feelings to another person ■ Repression: A force that buries painful thoughts and emotions in the unconscious mind
1	Object-relations theory	Donald Winnicott	This neo-Freudian theory is a modification of Freud's psychodynamic approach. Object relations theory emphasizes the importance of a nurturing parental relationship to a young child's developing personality.

CHAPTER	THEORY	THEORIST OR RESEARCHER	DEFINITION
6	Theory of cognitive development	Jean Piaget	This theory rests on an understanding of three concepts: assimilation, accommodation, and equilibration. ■ Assimilation: The process by which an individual incorporates external stimuli or observations into a previously developed framework for understanding the world ■ Accommodation: The process by which an individual modifies his or her understanding of a concept to include newly acquired information or experiences ■ Equilibration: The concept that individuals want to bring their understandings of their environments into balance
6	Sex role development: The stages of the ethic of care	Carol Gilligan	Includes three stages of morality. Females progress from one stage to the next as the result of changes in identity rather than cognitive developments. In the preconventional stage of morality, the goal is for individual survival. The main task for the girl moving forward from this stage is to move from making decisions based on selfishness to making them based on responsibility for others. Conventional morality is the belief that self-sacrifice is equivalent to goodness. Girls and women at this stage progress to postconventional morality by letting go of a desire to be good through self-sacrifice to realizing that she, too, is a person of importance. Postconventional morality is reached when a woman adopts a belief in nonviolence toward others as well as toward herself.
6	Stage theory of human development	Jean Piaget	Children must accomplish the cognitive tasks of one stage before moving on to the next. The theory includes four stages: sensorimotor, preoperational, concrete operational, and formal operational. ■ The sensorimotor stage, from birth to age 2, is marked by using the senses to understand the environment. Infants and toddlers develop their cognitive schemes, or mental frameworks, based on what they experience and observe. According to Piaget, the most integral task of this stage is acquiring object permanence. Object permanence is understanding that an object continues to exist even when it cannot be seen. ■ The preoperational stage, from age 2 until approximately age 7, is marked by egocentrism and improved use of symbolic thought. ■ The concrete operational stage, from approximately age 7 through age 11, is when a child develops the ability to perform mental operations without visual cues. ■ The formal operational stage begins at age 11 and continues throughout adulthood, when individuals begin to use abstract thought.

(Continued on next page)

CHAPTER	THEORY	THEORIST OR RESEARCHER	DEFINITION
6	Stage theory of socioemotional development	Erik Erikson	This theory includes eight stages, beginning at birth and ending in old age. Each stage includes a crisis that requires a resolution. Individuals can resolve the crisis at each stage successfully or unsuccessfully. ■ Trust vs. mistrust: Lasts from birth through 18 months of age ■ Autonomy vs. self-doubt: Lasts from 18 months of age until age 3 ■ Initiative vs. guilt: From ages 3 to 6, children begin mental and physical activities that develop self-confidence ■ Competence vs. inferiority: From age six through puberty, children develop social and intellectual skills and become confident in their talents and competencies ■ Identity vs. role confusion: Adolescents and adults understand themselves in many dimensions and take on many roles in life ■ Intimacy vs. isolation: Individuals learn to maintain intimate relationships ■ Generativity vs. stagnation: Adults widen their focus to include the welfare of others, typically their families and communities ■ Ego integrity vs. despair: Occurs in older adulthood and is marked by an individual's integration of life experiences into a coherent whole
6	Theory of moral development	Lawrence Kohlberg	This is a three-level, seven-stage theory of moral reasoning. Individuals functioning at the lower levels are motivated by self-interest, while those operating at higher levels focus on serving the common good, regardless of personal outcomes. ■ Level 1, preconventional morality, includes the pleasure/pain orientation and the cost-benefit orientation. Children make decisions based on seeking pleasure and avoiding pain. ■ Level 2, conventional morality, is exhibited by adolescents. Stage three is the good child orientation, and stage four is the law and order orientation. In the good child orientation, children behave morally in order to be accepted by their caregivers or peers and to avoid criticism. In the law and order orientation, children are motivated by rules and regulations. Many people remain in stage four throughout adolescence and adulthood, continuing to be externally motivated to act morally. ■ Level 3, principled morality, includes three stages. In level three, the motivations behind moral behavior have become internal. Individuals in level three make moral decisions based on what they believe to be right rather than what the possible outcome of their choice may be. Stage five is the social contract orientation—individuals desire to promote the common good and make moral decisions that reflect that value.

CHAPTER	THEORY	THEORIST OR RESEARCHER	DEFINITION
			Stage six is the ethical principle orientation, in which the goal is adhere to a few specific values that guide the individual's moral choices. These values can include a desire to promote justice, equality, or human dignity. Stage seven is a hypothetical stage called the cosmic orientation or transcendental morality. This stage links moral decision-making to a desire to "be true to universal principles and feel oneself part of a cosmic direction that transcends social norms."
6	Social world in late adulthood	Bernice Neugarten	Neugarten challenged social myths about older adults, debunking the belief that "empty nesters" were miserable without their children and that menopausal women were devastated by the "change of life." Her social clocks concept challenged the conventional concept of biological clocks for influencing individuals' behaviors. People respond to social clocks that are governed by cultural norms. Adults judge whether they are socially "on time" or "off time" based on cultural cues about age-appropriate behaviors. Neugarten recognized and defended the diversity present in adult life, honoring the process of aging and highlighting continued human development across the lifespan.
6	Death and dying	Elisabeth Kübler-Ross	Kübler-Ross studied how individuals cope with the knowledge of their imminent death. She developed a stage theory to explain the coping process: denial, anger, bargaining, depression, and acceptance.
7	Theory of multiple intelligences	Howard Gardner	Gardner's multiple intelligences include linguistic, logical–mathematical, spatial, musical, bodily–kinesthetic, interpersonal, intrapersonal, naturalistic, and existential.
7	Triarchic theory of intelligence	Robert Sternberg	Categorizes intelligence into analytical, creative, and practice. Analytical intelligence is normally assessed in intelligence tests and standardized tests. Creative intelligence addresses how well an individual reacts and adapts to novel situations and ideas. Practical intelligence refers to an ability to think through and complete everyday tasks.
7	Creativity	Robert Sternberg	Six interrelated resources produce creativity: intellectual abilities, knowledge, styles of thinking, personality, motivation, and environment.
7	False memory, eye-witness testimony	Elizabeth Loftus	Influential exposure to misinformation can create false memories. When people are suggestively interrogated or provided with information about an event they experienced, they may mistakenly incorporate the new information.

(Continued on next page)

CHAPTER	THEORY	THEORIST OR RESEARCHER	DEFINITION
7	Language and culture	Noam Chomsky	The nativist approach to language acquisition suggests that language is an innate skill. All languages share a universal grammar, or common underlying structure. Chomsky described a language-acquisition device that is part of the neural system in the brain used to allow us to learn language. This is confirmed by some research and brain imaging studies that suggest that certain genes may be specific to certain aspects of language.
8	Classical conditioning	Ivan Pavlov	Classical conditioning occurs when a stimulus is used to train someone to perform a behavior. Pavlov's famous experiments with dogs tested how they responded to different stimuli before and after conditioning. Through conditioning, the dogs were trained to salivate in response to different stimuli. ■ Unconditioned stimulus: a stimulus that occurs naturally, eliciting a reflexive, or unconditioned, response in an organism ■ Unconditioned response: a response that is reflexive, not learned ■ Conditioned stimulus: a stimulus that becomes associated with a particular response through learning ■ Conditioned response: a learned response to a conditioned stimulus
8	Classical conditioning	John Watson and Rosalie Rayner	An infant named Little Albert was used in the study of fear responses. This was done by changing Little Albert's emotional associations with a white rat. Little Albert was fond of the rat before Watson and Rayner began their experiment. The white rat became the conditioned stimulus. Each time they presented the rat to Little Albert, they also banged a large steel bar with a hammer. This loud noise, the unconditioned stimulus, terrified the baby. His distressed response was initially unconditioned because it was the result of being upset by the loud bang, but soon, just the sight of the white rat sent Little Albert into a fearful and distressed state. In fact, it only took seven trials to elicit the conditioned response from the baby. His response then generalized to other furry animals and objects, including dogs, rabbits, and a Santa Claus mask. Watson's famous experiment would lead to discoveries in generalization and discrimination.
8	Operant conditioning	Edward Thorndike	The connection between a behavior and a behavior's outcome is the law of effect. This law was demonstrated using cats trapped in a puzzle box. Once they learned the association between the stimulus (the puzzle box) and the response (swiping at a loop that temporarily released them from the box), the cats performed that behavior over and over to release themselves from their confinement.
9	James-Lange theory of emotion	William James, Carl Lange	Both James and Lange independently proposed the theory that emotional experiences follow physiological arousal in response to environmental stimuli. Emotions are experienced only after perception of an event and physical reaction to the perception.

CHAPTER	THEORY	THEORIST OR RESEARCHER	DEFINITION
9	Cannon-Bard theory of emotion	Walter Cannon, Philip Bard	This theory suggests that emotions and physiological responses occur simultaneously. A frightening experience causes both the emotion of fear and the physiological response. Cannon and Bard did not think that physiological responses by themselves were enough to generate emotions such as fear, anger, or love.
9	Two-factor theory of emotion	Stanley Schachter, Jerome Singer	This theory proposes that emotions develop from a physiological response and also a cognitive label or thought that describes or defines the physical arousal.
9	Facial recognition program	Paul Ekman	Ekman suggested that emotional expression is influenced by culture. Ekman studied emotions and human facial expressions. He researched the ability to recognize facial clues indicating emotion and formulated a system called a facial recognition program, which is a universal tendency to equate certain facial expressions with particular emotions. When you feel happy, the muscles of your face contract in a certain way, and people around you recognize from your facial expression that you are happy. The same pattern of facial expression recognition exists for a range of emotions.
10, 11	Hierarchy of needs	Abraham Maslow	This humanistic theory focuses on people's need for self-actualization (achieving one's full potential) and the importance of intentionality and ethical values. He developed a hierarchy of human needs that includes (in order of priority): physiological needs, safety, love/belonging, esteem, and self-actualization.
10	Drive-reduction theory	Michael Lowe, Allen Levine	This theory suggests that needs create drives. Basic drives include hunger, thirst, sex, and escape from pain. A physiological need results in an aroused state that motivates behavior to reduce the need and maintain a stable state called homeostasis. Lowe and Levine call this theory the homeostatic–hedonistic model of hunger. Their research focuses on the concept of dieting to limit food intake and reasons that people eat when they are not hungry. Lowe and Levine argue that the modern trend of dieting to achieve thinness by normal-weight people contributes to eating disorders and obesity.
10	Sexual response	William Masters, Virginia Johnson	Masters and Johnson studied the physiological responses of sexually aroused volunteers. They described a cycle of sexual response with four stages—excitement, plateau, orgasm, and resolution. The physiological elements of sexual response are vasocongestion (increased blood flow) and muscle tension.
10	Motivation–hygiene theory	Frederick Herzberg	Motivation–hygiene theory is also called the two-factor theory. It suggests that job satisfaction is generated by motivators such as achievement, recognition, the nature of the work, responsibility, advancement, and growth. It is also affected by hygiene factors, including company policies, supervision and relationship with management, work conditions, salary, and relationship with peers. Herzberg believed that motivators are the primary causes of job satisfaction, while hygiene factors are the causes of unhappiness.

(Continued on next page)

(*Continued from previous page*)

CHAPTER	THEORY	THEORIST OR RESEARCHER	DEFINITION
10	Three needs theory	David McClelland	This theory suggests that human motivation is dominated by three needs: ■ Achievement—the need to succeed, achieve, and excel ■ Affiliation—the need for human interaction and positive relationships with others ■ Power—the need to make an impact and lead others
10	Sex drive	Alfred Kinsey	The Kinsey Reports covered topics such as nudity, masturbation, fantasy, petting, sexual practices and orientation, and marital and extramarital sex. The research was controversial because the findings openly reported sexual behavior. In Kinsey's words, the report was "an objectively determined body of fact about sex." The work was criticized for being misleading and unscientific due to nonrandom sampling and leading questions.
11	Operant conditioning	B. F. Skinner	Skinner identified four factors that served as the foundation for his model of operant conditioning: behavior, past learning, present conditions, and genetic endowment.
	Skinner learning theory of personality (behaviorist)		The operant chamber, also known as a Skinner Box, reinforces certain observed behaviors with food. For example, when a rat presses the middle button in a series of three buttons, it gets a food pellet. The positive reinforcement of the food pellet will shape the rat's future behavior. Once the animal learns that pressing the middle button results in the presentation of a food pellet, it is highly likely that the rat will consistently press the middle button rather than one of the other buttons.
11	Sixteen personality factors	Raymond Cattell	These 16 traits are the source of all human personality. There are several types of personality traits: temperament (how a person behaves), motivation, and ability. Second-order traits include extraversion/introversion and anxiety. Dynamic traits include attitudes about a particular action or in response to a situation. Other dynamic traits are innate drives such as sex, hunger, and loneliness.
			This theory considers 16 traits, developed in response to Eysenck's scale: warmth, reasoning, personal stability, dominance, liveliness, rule conscious, social boldness, sensitivity, vigilance, abstractedness, privateness, apprehension, openness to change, self-reliance, perfectionism, and tension.
11	Humanistic theory of personality: client-centered therapy	Carl Rogers	Human behaviors as based on the basic goodness of the individual, rather than on more biologically or socially mechanistic models. Rogers's work focused on client-centered therapy, with the therapist expressing unconditional acceptance of the client's subjective experience.

CHAPTER	THEORY	THEORIST OR RESEARCHER	DEFINITION
8, 11	Cognitive approach to learning	Albert Bandura	Bandura's famous Bobo doll experiment investigated the link between observing an aggressive behavior and acting aggressively. His research marked the beginning of a new focus in the field of psychology called social learning theory. Social learning theory postulates that humans learn appropriate and inappropriate behaviors by participating in and observing social interactions with others.
	Observational learning and social cognitive theory		Bandura believed that cognition affected learning and that social events were as important as behavioral or biological events. Social cognitive theory is Bandura's idea that cognition affects learning.
11	Trait theory of personality	Hans Eysenck	Eysenck theorized that human personality was comprised of variations of intelligence, neuroticism, introversion/extroversion, and psychoticism. Everyone possesses each of these traits in varying degrees.
11	Neo-Freudian personality theory	Karen Horney	Horney believed that the differences that exist between male and female personalities are due more to society and culture than biology. Horney countered many of Freud's concepts with those of her own, countering penis envy with womb envy, the male envy of the female's ability to bear children.
11	Five-factor model of personality (the Big Five)	Raymond Cattell and Hans Eysenck	A merging of Cattell's sixteen personality factors and Eysenck's trait theories, this model focuses on extroversion, agreeableness, conscientiousness, neuroticism, and openness.
11	Psychoanalytic theory of personality	Sigmund Freud	This theory focuses on levels of awareness (consciousness), components of personality (id, ego, and superego), defense mechanisms, and psychosexual stages. The levels of consciousness are conscious, preconscious, and unconscious.
11	Neo-Freudian	Carl Jung	After his split from Freud, Jung employed what he called "active imagination" to explore his own spiritual unconscious and develop his own psychoanalytic theories on archetypes, the collective unconscious, and self-awareness.
8, 11	Learning theory of personality	B. F. Skinner	All behavior is learned through exposure to and interaction with the environment. Used by B. F. Skinner in his operant conditioning experiments.
11	Sociocultural perspective of personality	Lev Vygotsky	Social interactions with other people and the shared knowledge of a particular culture form individual personality. Culture teaches people what to think, how to think, and gives them the means to think. Initially, thought is external to the individual (the child), then becomes internalized as the individual grows and develops.

(Continued on next page)

(Continued from previous page)

CHAPTER	THEORY	THEORIST OR RESEARCHER	DEFINITION
12	Obedience to authority	Stanley Milgram	Psychologist Stanley Milgram was motivated to investigate whether normal people would obey the orders of an authority figure, even if they knew that they would harm others in the process. In his famous obedience experiment, 65 percent of participants obeyed the authority, despite the fact that they were asked to administer painful shocks (no shocks were administered).
12	Groupthink	Jerry Harvey	Groupthink is the social influence on group decision making. Sometimes a group can make a bad decision even with intelligent and well-meaning members of the group.
12	Contingency theories of leadership	Fred Fiedler	This theory states that both trait and situational factors contribute to leadership. Fiedler's model identifies two different leadership styles. One is the task-oriented leader who is concerned primarily with getting the job done. The other is the relationship-oriented leader who is more concerned with feelings and relationships in the group. The key idea is that the effectiveness of either the task-oriented or relationship-oriented leadership style depends on the situation the leader faces.
12	Theory X and Theory Y	Douglas McGregor	Theory X assumes that employees of an organization are inherently lazy and that management must tightly control an organization. Theory Y proposes that employees are inclined to become productive and the responsibility of management is to make it possible for people to achieve their best.
12	Contact hypothesis	Gordon Allport	Interaction between members of different groups will reduce intergroup prejudice. There are two contingencies in this theory. Both groups must be of equal status, and both must share a common goal.
12	Triangular theory of love	Robert Sternberg	Love consists of three elements: passion, intimacy, and commitment. Intimacy refers to the feelings of being close to and bonded with a partner. Commitment consists of two decisions: the short-term one that you love your partner and the long-term one to maintain that love and stay with your partner.

APPENDIX C

PSYCHOLOGY TIMELINE

19th century: The James-Lange Theory, formulated by William James, a psychologist and the founder of functional psychology, and Carl Lange, a physiologist, maintains that emotions are experienced only after perception of an event and physical reaction to the perception.

1860s: Gustav Fechner, a German psychologist, introduced a noninvasive way of measuring how brain activity responds to the environment.

1861: Paul Broca, a French physician, anatomist, and anthropologist, found an area of the left frontal lobe of the brain that is important for speech production.

1879: Wilhelm Wundt opened the first scientific laboratory in Leipzig, Germany. He wanted to discover the smallest unit of thought. Using a method he called introspection, volunteers were asked to verbally report every thought that passed through their minds when they were presented with a particular task. His approach to understanding the mind was known as structuralism.

1890: William James wrote the first psychology textbook. He is considered a pioneer in functionalism. He argued that knowledge about the mind could come not only from experimentation but also from the study of children, other animals, and the mentally ill.

1896: Sigmund Freud, a medical doctor and neurologist in Vienna, founded psychoanalysis. Its underlying assumption is that painful events have been hidden from people's awareness and once patients gain insight into these events, their symptoms will be relieved.

Early 1900s: Carl Jung, a Swiss psychiatrist and a favored student of Freud's, diverged from Freud's beliefs. Jung theorized that time and culture did little to change fears, behaviors, and thoughts. Jung believed that all humans possessed what he called a collective unconscious. Jung is considered the father of analytic psychology.

Early 1900s: Gestalt psychology gained more prominence. It proposes that in perception, the whole is different from the sum of the parts. This was a departure from structuralism, which hypothesizes that people perceived each element of an object separately and developed a sense of the world piece by piece.

1903: Ivan Pavlov, a Russian physiologist, published a study about conditioned reflexes. His experiments on digestion in dogs involved ringing a bell before each feeding. Soon the dogs began to salivate as soon as they heard the bell even before the food was presented. In 1904, he won the Nobel Prize for discovering the association between learning and conditioning.

1905: Edward Thorndike, an American scientist, published the law of effect. The law of effect posits that responses that are followed by a satisfying consequence will be linked to that situation and will more likely recur when the situation is encountered again.

1908: Alfred Binet, a French psychologist, developed an intelligence test known as the Binet test. It is now known as an IQ test.

1912: Psychologist Alfred Adler split from Freud's theoretical concepts. Adler believed that personality is not merely the result of biology but rather the result of a sense of inferiority, birth order, and parenting styles. During this time, he founded the Society of Individual Psychology.

1920s to 1960s: During this time period, psychology in the United States was heavily oriented toward behaviorism. Psychologists such as John Watson (1878–1958) and B. F. Skinner (1904–1990) explored the limits of the behaviorist approach in shaping behavior.

1920s: Walter Cannon, a physiologist, and Philip Bard, a graduate student of Cannon's, disagreed with the James-Lange Theory of Emotion. According to the Cannon-Bard Theory, a frightening experience causes both the emotion of fear and the physiological response of a faster heartbeat, but an increased heartbeat alone does not cause fear.

1920: John Watson, a behavioral psychologist, was interested in understanding fear responses. His experiment with Little Albert involved changing Albert's emotional associations with a white rat. Each time they presented the rat (the conditioned stimulus) to Albert, they also banged a large steel bar with a hammer. Eventually, the white rat sent Albert into a fearful state, and later his response was generalized to other furry animals and objects.

1921: Lewis Terman began a lifetime study on giftedness, following 1,500 schoolchildren for a 70-year period.

1922–1937: Karen Horney, a neo-Freudian psychoanalyst and psychiatrist, added a female voice to psychoanalytic theory. In her many papers, she argued that men and women are not as inherently different as Freud postulated and that the differences are due to society and culture rather than biology.

1932: The Tuskegee Study was conducted by the U.S. Public Health Service to monitor the effects of untreated syphilis. None of the participants were told the true nature of the study, the fact that they had syphilis, or that penicillin could cure it (when the drug became available). As a result, this study brought to the forefront the issue of conducting ethical research with human participants.

1938: Henry Murray, an American psychologist, defined achievement motivation as a basic need to strive for the accomplishment of goals. This may be expressed through the desire to learn and master skills, abilities, or ideas; be in control; or achieve goals.

1938: Electroconvulsive therapy (ECT) was introduced. ECT is a treatment method that employs an electric current between 70 and 150 volts to a patient's head to ease severe depression symptoms. It was a widely used form of treatment in the 1940s and 1950s.

1940s: With her mother, Katherine Briggs, Isabel Briggs Myers developed a personality inventory called the Myers-Briggs Type Indicator (MBTI). The MBTI seeks to identify the four dichotomies (favorite world, information, decisions, and structure) and the 16 features of personality that intertwine with these four dichotomies. It was first used in 1962.

1942: Psychologist Starke R. Hathaway and psychiatrist J. C. McKinley developed the Minnesota Multiphasic Personality Inventory (MMPI), now a widely used and recognized personality test and a clinical measure of mental illness. It was re-released as the MMPI-2 in 1989.

1943: Abraham Maslow, who studied human motivation, published the paper "A Theory of Human Motivation." His hierarchy of needs proposes that all humans must satisfy basic needs, such as the physiological need for food, water, and shelter, before they can realize their talents to the fullest.

1946: Edward Tolman, an American psychologist famous for his experiments on learning with rats in a maze, proposed that animals use more than simple stimulus-response or operant-reinforcer associations to learn about their environments.

1946: Using the new technology of computers and factor analysis, English psychologist Raymond Cattell developed the sixteen personality factors theory of personality. From this theory, Cattell developed the 16PF Personality Questionnaire, which is still in use today.

1947: The Nuremberg Trials were held after the barbarous practices of Nazi prison guards were made public. These trials resulted in the formation of the Nuremberg Code, a set of 10 guidelines that now serves as the foundation for the ethical treatment of human participants in research.

1947: B. F. Skinner, the father of behaviorism, returned to Harvard and remained there until his death in 1990. It was during this time that he focused much of his research on operant conditioning.

1948: Alfred Kinsey, a biologist, conducted a series of interviews to gather data about human sexuality. *Sexual Behavior in the Human Male* came out at this time, and later in 1953, *Sexual Behavior in the Human Female*. These books are commonly called the Kinsey Reports.

1949: Paul MacLean, an American physician and neuroscientist, developed a triune theory of the brain. According to his theory, three types of brain developed in the course of evolution: the reptilian brain, the limbic brain, and the neocortex.

1949: David Wechsler, an American psychologist, developed and published the original Wechsler Intelligence Scale for Children. Several versions of this scale have since been updated.

1950s: Many new psychopharmacological agents—drugs to treat psychological disorders—were discovered during this time.

1950s: Humanistic theory gained more prominence in psychology. The humanistic perspective values the integrity of each individual.

1950s: Noam Chomsky, an American linguist and cognitive scientist, began formulating a theory that all languages share a universal grammar, or common underlying structure.

1950s and 1960s: The deinstitutionalization movement—the process of discharging and reintegrating mental health inpatients into the community—was prevalent during this period.

1950: Erik Erikson, originally trained as a Freudian psychoanalyst, published his most well-known book, *Childhood and Society,* which highlights his theory of psychosocial stages of development. He argued that each stage includes a crisis that is resolved successfully or unsuccessfully.

1951: Carl Rogers, a humanistic psychologist, published *Client-Centered Therapy.* He argued that each individual has an internal core, or true self, that can become distorted when people attempt to gain the approval of others. He is viewed as the father of client-centered therapy.

1951: Bernice Neugarten, a preeminent authority on adult development, postulated that people respond to social clocks that are governed by cultural norms. Adults judged whether they were socially "on time" or "off time" based on cultural cues about age-appropriate behaviors.

1951: Solomon Asch, an American psychologist, became known for his famous compliance study in which a confederate gave the wrong answer and the majority of subjects conformed to the confederate's answer despite the fact that it was obviously wrong.

1952: In his book *The Structure of Human Personality,* Hans Eysenck theorized that human personality was comprised of variations of intelligence, neuroticism, introversion/extroversion, and psychoticism.

1952: The first edition of the *Diagnostic and Statistical Manual of Mental Disorders (DSM)* was published. It consisted of a uniform set of criteria for diagnosis of disorders. In its current version, the fourth edition revised, the *DSM* provides information, diagnosis criteria, and definitions for over 200 disorders in 17 categories. Diagnosis is based on a five-axis system that covers most of the biopsychosocial factors in an individual.

1953: The American Psychological Association established its first code of ethics.

1954: Gordon Allport, an American psychologist, played a prominent role in personality and social psychology. He argued that the world is too complicated for us to have a highly differentiated attitude about everything. Instead, we maximize our cognitive time and energy by developing elegant, accurate attitudes about some things while relying on sketchy beliefs for others. He also put forth the contact hypothesis, which proposes that interaction between members of different groups will reduce intergroup prejudice.

1955: David Wechsler developed and published the original Wechsler Adult Intelligence Scale. Versions of it have been updated since then.

1955: Albert Ellis was the founder of rational emotive behavior therapy (REBT), a cognitive behavioral therapeutic approach. His ABC model of activating event, belief, and consequence proposes that when faced with adversity, some people jump to negative beliefs, which cause feelings of distress (consequences).

1956: Jean Piaget, a Swiss biologist, developed the theory of cognitive development in the 1920s, but his theory was introduced in the United States in the 1950s by a Harvard psychologist named Jerome Bruner. Piaget postulated that children must accomplish the cognitive tasks of one stage before moving on to the next. His theory includes four stages: sensorimotor, preoperational, concrete operational, and formal operational.

1957: A case study was published on an individual only known by his initials, H.M, who suffered from epilepsy. In an effort to control his seizures, surgeons cut a part of H.M.'s brain called the hippocampus. By observing H.M.'s pattern of memory loss, psychologists learned more about the role of the hippocampus in the formation of new memories.

1957–1965: Gynecologists William Masters and Virginia Johnson studied the physiological responses of sexual arousal. They observed over 10,000 sexual acts and described a cycle of sexual response with four stages: excitement, plateau, orgasm, and resolution.

1958: Lawrence Kohlberg, an American psychologist, developed a foundational theory of human moral development. He posited a three-level, seven-stage theory of moral reasoning. The theory focuses on a morality based on justice.

1959: Frederick Herzberg, an American psychologist well known for work in business management, developed the two-factor theory and performed studies to improve understanding of employee motivation and attitudes. His book *The Motivation to Work* was published at this time.

1960s: Richard Lazarus, an American psychologist, gained prominence at this time for his work on emotions. He believed that people must first think about an experience in order to feel emotion. According to Lazarus, emotions occur through the process of conscious or unconscious cognitive appraisal, physiological arousal, and then emotional response and action.

1960: Douglas McGregor, an American psychologist, wrote *The Human Side of Enterprise*, which discussed his Theory X and Theory Y. Theory X proposes an assumption on the part of the manager that employees are inherently lazy and will avoid work whenever possible. On the other hand, Theory Y proposes that employees are not inherently lazy, but rather they have become passive as a result of socialization in organizations. According to Theory Y, every person has the potential to develop and assume responsibility and to work toward organizational goals.

1960: Biologist Jane Goodall arrived in Tanzania for observational studies of wild chimpanzees. By quietly watching the animals without disturbing them, she was able to document chimpanzee behaviors that had never before been seen by researchers. This laid the path for naturalistic observation.

1961: Albert Bandura, known for his social learning theory, focused much of his research attention on aggression and social learning, as evidenced by 1961's now-famous Bobo Doll experiment. The experiment showed that aggression to some extent is learned or modeled.

1961: David McClelland, an American social psychologist, becomes well known for his three needs theory. The theory, described in his book *The Achieving Society*, argues that human motivation is dominated by three needs: achievement, affiliation, and power.

1960 to 1970s: The Harvard Psilocybin Project was conducted, led by Dr. Timothy Leary, a psychologist. The project consisted of a series of experiments in which hallucinogenic psilocybin mushrooms were given to prisoners in an effort to reduce recidivism and to divinity students in an effort to induce profound religious states.

1962: Stanley Schachter and Jerome Singer developed the two-factor theory of emotion, which proposes that emotions develop from a physiological response and also from a cognitive label or thought that describes or defines the physical arousal.

1963: Stanley Milgram, an American psychologist at Yale University, published the results of his controversial study, now known as the Milgram Obedience studies, which investigated whether people would comply with the orders of an authority figure, even if they believed that their actions would harm others. This publication ignited fierce debate over the ethics of experimental research methods.

1967: Fred Fiedler was one of the first social psychologists to propose contingency models of leadership. His model identifies two leadership styles. One is the task-oriented leader who is concerned primarily with getting the job done. The other is the relationship-oriented leader who is more concerned with feelings and relationships in the group.

1968: Jane Elliott, a teacher in Ohio, performed a now-famous experiment about prejudice with her elementary school students, dividing them into two groups, blue-eyed people and brown-eyed people, and designating one group as special. Within a few hours, the favored group started treating the other group poorly.

1969: Charles Tart, an American psychologist known for his work in parapsychology, published his first book, *Altered States of Consciousness.* He is considered an expert on altered states of consciousness and his textbooks have contributed to modern psychology.

1969: Elisabeth Kübler-Ross, a Swiss psychiatrist, began to investigate how individuals cope with the knowledge of their own imminent death. She developed a stage theory to explain the coping process: denial, anger, bargaining, depression, and acceptance. Her now-famous book *On Death and Dying* was published in 1969.

1969: Martin Seligman's work on depression led him to develop the learned helplessness theory. The theory states that after experiencing an event that is perceived to be adverse, over time human beings and animals learn to behave helplessly even if there is the opportunity to change the circumstance. He is also the founder of the positive psychology movement, a complement to traditional psychology that focuses on well-being, making life more fulfilling, building a positive character, and helping groups and communities thrive.

1970s: Mary Ainsworth performed the strange situation experiment, which investigated attachment between infants and mothers in naturalistic and laboratory settings.

1971: Henri Tajfel, a British social psychologist known for his work in prejudice and intergroup relations, demonstrated that a group could form even in the absence of face-to-face contact between members. Members in the group would begin to identify themselves with their group, favoring their own members.

1974: Eleanor Maccoby, a developmental psychologist, published her most influential book, *The Psychology of Sex Differences*, which reviewed more than 1,600 studies about gender differences. She argued that parental and social norms are strong influences on gender, but biology is equally important.

1978: Paul Ekman and his colleagues developed the facial action coding system (FACS), a taxonomy of human expression classifications.

1979: J. J. Gibson, an American psychologist, pioneered an approach to perception called ecological perception. Instead of looking at stimuli, such as light, independently of their environment, the focus was on the stimuli as they occurred in the environment.

1980: Robert Zajonc, a social psychologist, disagreed with Lazarus's theory on emotions. Instead, he believed that emotions and cognition are separate processes and that emotional reactions may be faster than thought.

1981: David H. Hubel and Torsten Wiesel won the Nobel Prize for their research on the visual system. They found that certain cells in the visual system respond to very specific stimuli in the environment.

1982: Carol Gilligan published *In a Different Voice,* a book detailing a theory of moral reasoning that departed from Lawrence Kohlberg's moral development stage theory. She argued that girls and women make moral judgments based on caring for others.

1985: Robert J. Sternberg formulated his triarchic theory of multiple intelligence, which notes three distinct intelligences: componential, experiential, and practical.

1989: Robert Thayer, a psychologist, argued that moods involve both a physical arousal and the conscious elements of energy or tiredness and tension or calmness. His book *The Biopsychology of Mood and Arousal* was published at this time.

1990: The Big Five theory of personality is a merging of two theories: Cattell's sixteen personality factors theory and Eysenck's trait theory. Many researchers believed that Cattell's theory included too many personality traits and Eysenck's focused on too few, so the Big Five was born.

1999: Howard Gardner, an American developmental psychologist, became known for the concept of multiple intelligences. He theorized that intelligence consists of eight different types: linguistic intelligence, logical–mathematical intelligence, spatial intelligence, musical intelligence, bodily–kinesthetic intelligence, interpersonal intelligence, intrapersonal intelligence, and naturalistic intelligence.

2003: After 20 years, the Human Genome Project, which mapped the entire human genetic code, was completed. Although the mapping goal has been reached, analysis of the genome will continue for many years to come. The mapping of the genome has tremendous repercussions on the study of psychology.

APPENDIX D

BEING A CONSUMER OF RESEARCH

Research studies are designed and conducted to provide information in the fields of psychology, business, politics, medicine, and more. Psychologists conduct studies about relationships, attitudes, behaviors, and morals. Businesspeople conduct studies about what consumers like. Politicians conduct studies about how people are likely to vote.

Statistics are used to describe data and make generalizations about larger groups by examining a smaller subset group, referred to as a sample. The goal is to obtain a sample that represents a larger group.

Information can be measured and statistically analyzed through nominal, ordinal, interval, or ratio measurements.
- Nominal measurement describes by naming, such as by nationality or political affiliation. These data are nonnumeric. Numbers may be assigned to different groups, such as 1 for Democrat, 2 for Republican, and 3 for undecided, but these numbers cannot be used for meaningful calculations.
- Ordinal measurement sorts numerical data from small to large, such as arranging individuals by age, weight, or height.
- Interval measurement uses a range of expected values, such as temperature on a thermometer. Interval scales do not have a fixed zero. For example, temperatures can fall below zero.
- A ratio measurement, such as a grade on a test or time counted on a timer, has a fixed zero point. The type of measurement helps a researcher to decide what type of statistic to use. For example, it is not possible to take a mean of sex. A person is either genetically male or female, so there cannot be a mean of 1.4 for sex.

Samples and Populations

A population is a group of members who share at least one common characteristic. For instance, Americans, parents, students, minority groups, religious groups, and occupational groups are all considered populations. In a research study, a population is a large group about which some question is asked and an experiment is designed to answer. For instance, political research polls are used to find out how populations of voters feel about candidates and issues.

Because it is often impractical to test every member of a population, researchers select a subset of the larger population. This subset is called the sample. A sample must be representative of the larger population and must contain enough numbers to allow statistical analysis. In statistics, sample size is symbolized with the letter n.

Researchers use various sampling techniques to represent populations of interest. In random sampling, for example, everyone has an equal chance of being selected for the study. Simple or convenience sampling is another technique that includes the most accessible individuals available to the researcher. For instance, a researcher who wants to learn about the student body at a college (the population) sets up a table in a hallway and asks the first 50 people who walk by to fill out a questionnaire. This simple sample may or may not be representative of the entire student population.

Mean, Median, Mode

Statistics are used to interpret and understand large collections of data. Mean, median, and mode are three types of average computations that can be applied to sets of data.
- The mean is the sum of all the numbers in a data set added together and then divided by the total number of samples in the set. Mean is represented with the symbol $\bar{x}$.
- The median number is the one in the exact middle of an ordered data set.
- The mode or modes is the number or numbers that appear most often in a set of data.

Consider the following set of numbers: 1, 2, 4, 7, 7, 7, 7, 8, 9, 10, 12, 22, 23, 24, and 25. The mean, commonly called the average, is 11.2, which is the sum of all the numbers, 168, divided by the sample size or number of samples in the set, 15. The median is 8. The mode is 7. In a data set where no numbers repeat, there is no mode.

The range of the data set is the difference between the highest and lowest numbers; in this example data set, the range is 25 – 1, or 24.

Standard deviation is the degree of variability in a sample set, or how far the values fall from the mean. A low standard deviation indicates that most of the values in a set of data are close to the mean, while a high standard deviation indicates that the numbers spread across a larger range. A confidence interval is used to determine how reliable the results of a test are. Larger sample sizes yield more reliable statistical results.

In a research study, data are collected and entered into a list or computer program that can be used to organize and analyze the numbers. The numbers or data can be pictured with graphs, such as frequency distribution curves. A frequency distribution lists each value in the data set and how often it occurs. The most common frequency distribution is the bell-shaped (also called normal) curve.

Normal Curve

A normal curve graph is made by graphing each value in the data set as the result of a statistical equation called a Gaussian or probability density function. The normal curve, which is also called a Gaussian function distribution, describes the probability of obtaining a particular value within a range of numbers. Probability is a prediction of how often something will happen given the number of possibilities for the event to occur.

If something is guaranteed to happen, it has a probability of 1, or 100 percent. If there is no chance something will happen, it has a 0 percent probability. For example, the probability that you will roll a 4 any time you cast a six-sided die is 1 in 6 or a 16.67 percent chance.

Normal curves can describe many natural events and occurrences. For instance, frequency distributions for human height, weight, and IQ exhibit a normal curve, with most individuals falling into an average height, weight, or IQ, with extreme variations to either side. In a perfect normal curve, the mean, median, and mode all have the same value.

Reliability and Validity

Reliability and validity are related concepts that address if and how well a study answers the question it was designed to address. Reliability has to do with the precision of a measurement. Reliability describes the consistency of a set of measurements. In other words, a reliable test can be repeated. A test must be reliable in order to be valid; however, reliability is not a guarantee of validity. A very reliable test can be used to generate meaningless data.

Validity is the accuracy of a measurement, how well the test data answer the proposed question, or whether the test measured what it was designed to measure. Validity can be internal or external. Internal validity has to do with the design of the study and how carefully measurements are made. External validity is how well the results of a study can be applied to other cases or populations. Validity in testing can be applied to test whether your psychology course was designed well enough to help you learn the material. A valid test should reveal whether the students learned the material taught in the class. An equally reliable test could determine what the students had for breakfast, but that would not be a valid way of finding whether they had learned the class material.

80–20 Principle

The 80–20 principle, which is also called the Pareto principle, is a statistical rule derived from the work of Italian economist Vilfredo Pareto. The principle states that 20 percent of causes are responsible for 80 percent of consequences. In other words, 20 percent of effort yields 80 percent of results.

Pareto studied patterns of wealth and land distribution. He observed that 20 percent of the population owned 80 percent of the land. This predictable, imbalanced pattern was repeated consistently among different sets of data. For example, 80 percent of disruptions in a classroom are caused by 20 percent of the students. In business, 20 percent of customers are responsible for 80 percent of sales.

The actual numbers of each ratio may be different than 20 and 80 percent, but a pattern of imbalance remains constant in most samples. You probably socialize with only a small percentage of the people you know, for example, or wear only a few of the many pieces of clothing you own.

The Pareto principle was later restated in 1949 by George Zipf, a professor at Harvard University, who called it the principle of least effort. Zipf determined that people and resources organize themselves to reduce work.

In 1951, Joseph Juran applied the 80–20 rule to quality control at Western Electric Corporation. Juran coined the phrase "the vital few and the useful many" to describe the 80–20 rule. Juran, a management expert who has been called the father of quality, found that 20 percent of causes were responsible for 80 percent of quality defects and that overall quality could be improved dramatically by focusing on the relatively few sources of defects.

Author Richard Koch applied the 80–20 principle to daily life by suggesting that people can enjoy more time and less stress by focusing on the 20 percent of work, people, and activities that are most gratifying to them. He describes the "20 percent spike" as those strengths that yield the best results for your efforts and suggests that spending more time pursuing the areas that interest and excite you leads to a more successful and less stressful life.

REFERENCES

Koch, R. (1999). *The 80/20 principle: The secret to achieving more with less.* New York, NY: Crown.

Koch, R. (2004). *Living the 80/20 way: Work less, worry less, succeed more, enjoy more.* London, England: Nicholas Brealey Publishing.

GLOSSARY

0-9

8-circuit model of consciousness A theory developed by Timothy Leary that suggests the brain is composed of eight mini circuits that are each responsible for specific aspects of consciousness.

A

abilene paradox The tendency for a group to act in a way that is counter to the preferences of any single member of the group.

abnormal The thoughts and behaviors that stand outside of what is expected for a given society.

absolute threshold The smallest amount of stimulus energy necessary for an observer to detect a stimulus.

abulia Loss of motivation after brain injury.

accessibility The ease or speed with which attitudes can be retrieved from memory.

accommodation Piaget's term for the learner's process of adjusting mental frameworks to fit with observed reality.

accommodation The process by which a person modifies understanding of a concept to include newly acquired information or experiences.

achievement motivation The desire for learning, mastery, and achieving a high standard of performance.

acquisition The process of developing a conditioned response.

action potential A rapid rise and fall in the membrane potential of a cell.

actor-observer bias The tendency for people to attribute their actions to situational factors and the actions of others to the person's character.

actual-self It is how a person understands who they are without the social expectations and influences of those around them.

addiction A physiological and/or physical dependence on a substance.

adolescence The period of human development that bridges the physical and psychological gap between childhood and adulthood.

adrenal glands Glands located above the kidneys that release hormones in response to stress.

adulthood The developmental stage at which a human is functionally capable of sexual and emotional maturity, within which periods of growth and development continue to occur.

affect Emotions and motivations.

aggression Any behavior or action that involves the intention to harm someone.

alpha waves Brain waves that are slower than beta waves and occur as the body relaxes at the beginning of the non-REM sleep cycle.

altruism The provision of assistance to others, without any apparent reward for doing so.

amino acids The major excitatory and inhibitory neurotransmitters in the nervous system.

amnesia The inability to remember previously stored information, most often due to some form of damage to the brain.

amygdala Part of the brain that pairs emotion and memory; it is part of the limbic system.

amygdala Part of the brain that pairs emotion and memory; it is part of the limbic system.

anger A sympathetic nervous system arousal that occurs in response to perceived threats or harm.

anorexia nervosa Eating disorder associated with intentional starvation and extreme weight loss to a body weight of more than 15 percent below normal.

anterograde amnesia The inability to process information properly from short-term to long-term memory from the time of injury onward.

anterolateral system Sensory system in the body that carries information about pain and temperature.

antisocial behaviors Behaviors that cause harm to others.

appetite Psychological hunger that is motivated by emotional needs and the presence of appealing food.

archival research Research that uses materials collected in the past to investigate behavior or events that occurred in the past.

assimilation Piaget's term for the learner's process of incorporating new experiences into existing knowledge.

assimilation The process by which a person incorporates external stimuli or observations into a previously developed framework for understanding the world.

associative learning It is when people learn from making a connection between two events.

attitude A positive or negative evaluation of an object, event, idea, or person.

attractiveness heuristic Idea that an object that is visually impressive must be good.

attribution An inference about the underlying causes for one's own behavior, or the behavior of others.

attribution theory A description of the way in which people explain the causes of their own and other people's behavior.

authoritarian Parents who place high demands on their children and have a need for power and control in their relationships with their children.

authoritative Parents who have high demands for their children and also respect the children's individuality.

automatic thinking process Thinking that is nonconscious, unintentional, involuntary, and effortless.

autonomic nervous system A two-part, self-regulating system that controls the glands and internal organs.

autonomy versus self-doubt A stage of psychosocial development lasting from 18 months to three years of age; during this period, children explore their surroundings and their control over objects in their environment.

aversive conditioning A therapy in which the undesired behaviors are paired with an unpleasant stimulus designed to reduce or remove the unwanted behavior.

awareness The act of focusing on feelings, memories, thoughts, sensations, and environment.

axon hillock The part of the axon nearest to the cell body.

axons Structures emerging from the neuron that send electrochemical information to other cells.

B

baby-faced features Features that are characteristic of newborns or young children, such as large eyes, a small nose, round cheeks, smooth skin, and glossy hair; these features may convey an exaggerated sense of youthfulness, freshness, naïveté, and openness.

basal metabolic rate The amount of energy expended by the body in a resting state.

behavior A person's actions and how they respond to other people and events.

behavioral approaches to psychotherapy An approach that looks at observable behaviors and proposes that both normal and abnormal behaviors are learned.

behavioral perspective on mental illness A perspective that works with the abnormal behaviors themselves, as they present, without looking at the emotional content.

bell curve A graph that represents the normal distribution of data.

benign paroxysmal positional vertigo (BPPV) Disorder characterized by dizziness and loss of balance, which is caused by movement of the otoconia into sensitive portions of the ear canal.

beta waves Small, fast brain waves often associated with being awake or just beginning a sleep cycle.

bias The tendency to show favoritism to one side of an argument, or to a particular individual or group of individuals.

big five personality test A test to measure five broad domains or dimensions of personality.

binocular A stimulus that is perceived with two eyes.

biological theory of personality The assertion that personality is genetically determined.

biopsychosocial model of pain A model of pain that considers how psychological, social, cognitive, physiological, and behavioral factors contribute to pain.

biopsychosocial perspective A comprehensive perspective on mental illness that covers all aspects of an individual's life, including biological/medical components, emotional history, behaviors, and environmental circumstances.

brainstem Portion of the brain that connects it to the spinal cord.

bulimia nervosa Eating disorder associated with cycles of binge eating and purging through the use of laxatives, vomiting, or excessive exercise.

bystander effect The failure to offer help to someone who is obviously in need of assistance when other people are present.

C

cannon-bard theory of emotions The belief that emotions and physiological responses occur simultaneously.

case study An in-depth investigation of a single individual, a group of people, a business, or a phenomenon.

categorization The process of grouping objects (ideas, things, or people) into categories by virtue of their shared properties.

causal relationship A relationship in which one variable causes a change in another variable.

causation Demonstrates how one variable influences other variables.

central nervous system (CNS) The majority of the nervous system, including the brain and spinal cord.

central route to persuasion The process by which people rationally consider the arguments in an attempt at persuasive communication.

centration The cognitive inability to focus on more than one idea at a time.

cerebral cortex The upper part of the brain.

chemoreceptors Sensory receptors in the nose and mouth that respond to smells and tastes.

circadian rhythm The body's natural 24-hour internal clock, or sleep–wake cycle, that uses external and internal cues such as lightness and darkness to determine when the body should sleep and wake.

classical conditioning A form of therapy that acts to revise automatic processes by creating new automatic responses based on the introduction of a stimulus.

classical conditioning It is a type of learning that uses a stimulus to train the learner to perform a particular behavior at a particular time.

client-centered or person-centered therapy A psychotherapeutic approach that seeks to reintroduce clients to their own genuine experiences so they will practice unconditional acceptance and feel valued as people.

clinical hypnosis A form of psychotherapeutic treatment in which patients are placed in a trancelike state of consciousness that is different from the normal waking state.

cochlea Part of the inner ear that vibrates in response to sound.

cognition Thinking, attention, and processing and using information.

cognitive approaches Approaches to therapy that work to revise faulty or maladaptive thought processes that tend to elicit improper behavioral and emotional responses.

cognitive development The mental processes people use to make obser-

vations, solve problems, and communicate their ideas.

cognitive dissonance A feeling of internal discomfort that occurs when a person is aware of a conflict between two attitudes, or between an attitude and a behavior.

cognitive map A mental representation of an actual location or space.

cognitive neurology The study of the effects of nervous-system disorders on cognition.

cognitive process A process in which the recipient uses rational thinking to consider the arguments of a persuasive message.

cognitive psychology A field of psychology that investigates processes related to thinking, including memory, reasoning, and decision making.

collectivism The thought that people are integrated into and become part of a group as a whole and incorporate the collective goals of the group as their own.

collectivistic culture A culture in which the well-being of the group is valued over the autonomy of the individual.

color constancy The ability to sense the same color under different light levels and in different contexts.

common fate Psychological theory that things that are moving in the same direction appear to form a unit.

companionate love Feelings of intimacy and affection that are not accompanied by passion and physiological arousal.

competence versus inferiority A stage of psychosocial development lasting from age six to until puberty; during this period, children develop social and intellectual skills and become confident in their talents and competencies.

compliance The act of behaving in accordance with group or individual requests.

concrete operational stage A development stage from approximately age 7 through age 12 in which a child develops the ability to perform mental operations without visual cues.

conditioned response A learned response to a conditioned stimulus.

conditioned stimulus A stimulus that becomes associated with a particular response through learning.

cones Light-sensitive cells within the eye that sense color but are less light-sensitive than their counterparts, rods.

confederate An actor who participates in a psychological experiment who pretends to be a subject but is working for the researcher.

connectedness Psychological theory that things that appear physically connected appear to form a unit.

conscious mind A person's awareness of his or her own feelings, memories, thoughts, sensations, and environment.

consciousness An individual's awareness of his or her own feelings, memories, thoughts, sensations, and environment.

constructivism One of the main schools of learning theory; maintains that learning is a subjective, relative, and active process on the part of the learner.

contact hypothesis Hypothesis that interaction between members of different groups will reduce intergroup prejudice.

contingency theory of leadership The theory that both trait and situational factors contribute to leadership.

contrast effect A change in normal evaluation of an object based upon previous exposure to a similar object of greater or lesser value.

control condition This condition contrasts with the experimental condition and serves as a comparison for evaluating the effect of the treatment.

control group A group in which the participants do not receive the experimental stimulus or interventions.

convenience sample A nonprobability sampling method where participants are easily available to the researcher are recruited for a study.

cornea Clear outer membrane of the eye.

corpus callosum A bundle of neural fibers that connects the two halves of the brain.

correlation A process of measuring the direction and strength of the relationship between two variables.

correlational study A descriptive research method that investigates the relationship between two vari-

ables as they occur naturally, without manipulation by the experimenter.

correspondence bias The tendency to infer that a person's behavior corresponds to, or matches, their personality.

countertransference The therapist's response to the patient's transference, which may be useful in helping the patient to reenact earlier scenes and replay them in different ways.

couples therapy Therapy centered on conflicts between persons in a relationship with each other.

creativity The ability to create new and innovative ideas without help.

culture of honor A belief system in which men are expected to protect their reputation through physical aggression.

D

dark adaptation The process by which the eyes gradually adjust to darkness.

decay When information that has been encoded is lost or when information is improperly encoded initially.

deductive reasoning The use of general information and observations as a basis for drawing a more specific conclusion.

defense mechanisms Unconscious methods of working with anxiety issues.

deindividuation The process of losing one's sense of personal identity in a group.

deinstitutionalization The process of discharging and reintegrating mental health inpatients into the community.

delta sleep Deep sleep that occurs during the fourth stage of non-REM sleep and lasts about 30 minutes.

delta waves Slow, deep brain waves that mark the transition between light sleep and deep sleep during Stage III of non-REM sleep.

demographics Characteristics that are typical of a particular population, such as age, sex, income, and level of education.

dendrites Short structures that receive electrochemical information from other cells.

dependent variable The variable that is being measured in an experiment.

developmental psychology The branch of psychology that investigates how thoughts, feelings, and behaviors develop and change throughout the lifespan, from birth to death.

diagnosis Description of a pathological state, locating it within a range of norms and providing an assessment of its cause that may also assist in treating or curing the problem.

diagnostic and statistical manual of mental disorders (DSM) Published descriptive system for use in the diagnosis of, communication about, and standardization of treatment for psychological disorders.

dialectical behavior therapy A form of therapy that focuses on

self-acceptance regardless of circumstances.

dichotomies Pairs of opposite traits. Jung's four dichotomies are favorite world, information, decisions, and structure.

difference threshold The minimum difference required between two stimuli before an animal can detect that they are different.

discrimination Inappropriate and unjustified treatment of people based solely on their group membership.

discrimination The process that guides an organism to respond only to certain stimuli in certain situations.

discriminative stimulus A factor that determines the conditions under which a behavior is reinforced or not reinforced.

display rules Learned rules about appropriate displays of emotions.

disposition The personal traits that distinguish one person from another.

door-in-the-face technique The persuasive technique in which people are more likely to agree to a smaller request after having first rejected a larger request.

dorsal column–medial lemniscal system Sensory system in the body that carries information about touch and proprioception.

down syndrome An inherited condition caused when an extra chromosome 21 is transmitted during conception.

drive-reduction theory A theory of motivation suggesting that phys-

iological needs create an aroused state or drive that motivates behavior to reduce the need.

drug dependence A physical tolerance that is a result of a physiological process involving the liver and metabolism. This type of tolerance often results in increased use of drugs and sometimes overdose or death.

dysphoria The negative emotions of anxiety, sadness and depression, and anger.

E

ecological perception A theory that sees perception as an active process that is affected by the environment in which it occurs.

ego The area of the mind responsible for balancing the drives of the id with the ideals of the superego.

ego integrity versus despair A stage of psychosocial development in older adulthood that is marked by a person's integration of life experiences into a coherent whole.

elaboration likelihood model A model that proposes two ways in which persuasive communications can cause attitude change, through the central route to persuasion and the peripheral route to persuasion.

elaborative rehearsal Process in which information is attended to and organized and therefore is more likely to be transferred to long-term memory.

electroconvulsive therapy (ECT) A treatment method that delivers an electric current of between 70 and 150 volts to electrodes placed on a patient's head in order to ease severe depression symptoms.

embryo The third week after fertilization, when an embryo's heart is formed and beating.

emotion Aroused physiological response of the autonomic nervous system to which cognitive experiences and expressive behaviors contribute.

emotional intelligence The ability to recognize and categorize the feelings and emotions of others based on behaviors and other outward symptoms.

emotional stability The general degree of a person's steadiness in moving through life events; the likelihood that he or she will respond to challenges with equanimity.

empirical Relating to the direct observation and collection of data.

empiricists Scientists who believe that all knowledge comes from experience.

encoding The initial process of recording and identifying information.

endolymphatic fluid Fluid that moves inside the semicircular canals to signal rotation of the head to vestibular receptors.

endorphin A morphine-like substance produced by the body to reduce pain and create feeling of well-being.

epinephrine A hormone released by the adrenal gland to create the fight-or-flight reaction by accelerating the heartbeat, raising blood sugar, dilating pupils, and causing perspiration; also known as adrenaline.

episodic memory Memory of events that a person has experienced.

equilibration Piaget's term for self-regulating one's own knowledge and mentally reorganizing what is observed.

equilibration The concept that people want to bring their understandings of their environments into balance.

estrogen Female sex hormone that regulates ovulation and sexual receptivity.

ethics A branch of philosophy that considers questions of morality.

evolutionary psychologists Psychologists who investigate how the course of human evolution may have shaped contemporary human characteristics.

experimental condition This condition exposes participants to the treatment (to one version of the independent variable).

experimental group A group in which the participants are exposed to the experimental stimulus or intervention.

expertise A high degree of competency in a given field.

expertise heuristic Idea that expert approval makes something good.

explicit attitude An attitude that a person is aware of and can report.

explicit memories Information brought forth through conscious recall.

exposure therapy A form of therapy often used in fear or phobic situations to slowly expose an individual to the fear.

external attribution The inference that a person is behaving in a certain way because of an environmental or situational factor.

extinction The elimination of a conditioned response.

extrasensory perception The perception of external events without direct information from the senses.

extrovert A person who focuses thoughts and experiences outward, on other people and the world around him or her, and who tends to be outgoing and more social.

F

facial action coding system (FACS) A system that measures changes in facial activity according to 44 different action units (AU) that produce the variety of movements of facial muscles—such as those around the eyes, brows, nose, mouth, chin, dimples—and also head and eye positions and tilting.

facial affect program A set pattern of facial expressions in response to an emotion.

facial feedback hypothesis The theory that feedback from the facial muscles influences a person's experience of emotion.

facial recognition program A system that codifies various facial features and their expressive combinations, to be read as clues to the individual's emotional state.

familiarity heuristic Assumption that familiarity means something is good.

family therapy Therapy conducted with members of a family in which one or more members are having a problem, often an emotional or behavioral one.

fetal alcohol syndrome (FAS) An induced form of mental retardation that may occur when pregnant women drink during pregnancy.

fetus After the eighth week, the embryo is called a fetus, which is capable of spontaneous movement.

fight-or-flight response The first, or "alarm," stage of the sympathetic nervous system's GAS response to physical or psychological threats.

five-factor model of personality A merging of Cattell's 16 personality factors and Eysenck's trait theory, that focuses on extroversion, agreeableness, conscientiousness, neuroticism, and openness.

fixed-interval schedule A schedule of reinforcement in which the reinforcer is given after a set period of time has passed and a correct response has been given.

fixed-ratio schedule A schedule of reinforcement in which the reinforcer is given after a set number of correct behavioral responses.

focus groups Events at which a group of individuals who represent a target population are invited to meet and answer questions about new products and services.

foot-in-the-door technique The persuasive technique in which people are more likely to agree to a large request after they have agreed to smaller requests.

formal operational stage A development stage beginning around age 12 that continues throughout adulthood; during this stage people begin to use abstract thought.

fovea Central area within the eye where cones are prevalent.

free association A psychoanalytic technique in which patients say whatever occurs to them, or relate remembered dreams, after which the therapist works to find connections between such raw subconscious production and other presenting issues.

frustration-aggression theory The theory that frustration can contribute to aggressive behavior.

functionalism The school of psychology that studies the purpose of psychological processes.

G

gaba An inhibitory transmitter found throughout the brain. GABA malfunctions may be involved in seizure disorders, as the lack of inhibitory chemicals may lead to uncontrolled firing patterns.

gardner's multiple intelligences A theory that there are nine types of intelligences, including linguistic, logical–mathematical, spatial, musical, bodily–kinesthetic, interpersonal, intrapersonal, naturalistic, and existential.

gate control theory Theory that pain is mediated by a series of cells in the spinal cord.

gender identity Understanding and accepting oneself as male or female; typically, gender identity matches biological sex.

gender roles Behavioral patterns and expectations shared by a culture based on "maleness" and "femaleness."

general adaptation syndrome (GAS) The sympathetic nervous system's three-stage response to threats (alarm, resistance, exhaustion) caused by increased levels of epinephrine and norepinephrine.

generalization The idea that several related stimuli can potentially cause an organism to give a conditioned response.

generalized Expanded to the population.

generativity versus stagnation A stage of psychosocial development during which adults widen their focus to include the welfare of others—typically their families and communities.

genes The basic biological unit of heredity.

gestalt psychology Theory of psychology that suggests that an observer sees a whole image as different from the sum of its parts.

gifted and talented Children who are capable of high performance in general intellectual ability, specific academic aptitude, creative or productive thinking, leadership ability, or visual and performing arts.

gilligan's conventional stage of morality A stage of the ethic of care that is marked by a girl's belief that self-sacrifice is equivalent with goodness.

gilligan's postconventional stage of morality A stage of the ethic of care that is marked by a woman's ability to let go of a desire to be good through self-sacrifice to realizing that she, too, is a person of importance. This stage is reached when a woman adopts a belief in nonviolence toward others as well as toward herself.

gilligan's preconventional stage of morality A stage of the ethic of care in which an infant or young girl believes her primary goal is for individual survival at any cost.

glabrous skin Skin without hair.

glial cells Cells in the nervous system that do not directly send information to other cells.

good continuation Psychological theory suggesting that when points are connected in a way that forms a straight or smoothly curving line, they appear to follow the smoothest path.

grammar The dual set of rules used in a given language to promote consistency in application and meaning.

group Two or more people who interact with each other and whose needs and goals influence each other.

group therapy Therapy in which patients meet in a group to discuss issues or a given topic with a therapist or therapists.

groupthink The process in which groups of people make poor decisions despite the individual competence of group members.

H

haptic perception The process of identifying objects by touch.

harvard psilocybin project A series of experiments led by psychologist Timothy Leary exploring the effects of psilocybin mushrooms.

health psychology A science that investigates the relationship between an individual's beliefs and social environment, including genetics, family, culture, and individual differences, and his or her health.

heuristics Mental shortcuts that allow people to make rapid judgments.

hippocampus Area of the brain that deals with memory.

hippocampus Part of the brain implicated in memory; it is part of the limbic system.

hippocampus Part of the limbic system that helps transfer short-term memory to long-term memory.

homeostasis Regulation and maintenance of a balanced internal state.

horizontal–vertical illusion Optical illusion that leads observers to overestimate the length of a vertical line in comparison to a horizontal line.

human development The complete set of physical, cognitive, social, and emotional changes experienced by a person during the course of a lifetime.

humanistic psychology A holistic approach to understanding human psychology that is focused on meaning, values, spirituality, and self-actualization.

humanistic theory A theory that explains human behavior as based on the basic goodness of the person, rather than on more biologically or socially mechanistic models.

humanistic therapy An approach to psychotherapy proposing that abnormal behaviors occur in many cases as a result of feelings of alienation, depersonalization, loneliness, and failure to find meaning and fulfillment in life.

hunger The sensation of needing food.

hypersomnia A condition in which a person experiences frequent episodes of daytime sleepiness, or excessive or prolonged deep sleep at night.

hypnosis A method of accessing the unconscious mind by inducing a trance state resembling sleep.

hypothalamus A part of the brain that links the nervous system to the endocrine system and regulates body temperature, hunger, thirst, and sleep.

hypothalamus Complex structure within the brain that performs many regulatory and coordinating functions.

hypothalamus The pleasure center of the brain; it regulates the pituitary gland.

hypothesis A proposed explanation for an observation or scientific problem.

I

id Primitive sexual and aggressive energy that corresponds to the deepest part of the unconscious mind.

identity versus role confusion A stage of psychosocial development that begins in adolescence; during this period, people understand themselves in many dimensions and take on many roles in life.

implicit attitude An attitude that is involuntary, uncontrollable, and at times unconscious.

implicit memories Information brought to mind automatically, without intentional conscious recall.

incentive A positive or negative stimulus that motivates behavior.

independent variable The characteristic in an experiment that is manipulated or changed.

individualism An assertion that people strive to function as autonomous, unique people.

individualistic culture A culture that values the individual's ability to pursue his or her own goals free from the influence of others.

inductive reasoning The use of specific information and observations to infer a more general principle.

indulgent Parents who make few demands on their children, who therefore may not understand social rules but typically have high self-esteem and adequate friendships.

infantile amnesia The inability to remember early events in life; also called childhood amnesia.

ingroup A group to which one perceives oneself as belonging, toward whom one has positive biases.

initiative versus guilt A stage of psychosocial development lasting from age three to age six; during this period, children begin to develop mental and physical activities that develop self-confidence.

innate Inborn traits, characteristics, or tendencies.

insomnia A sleep disorder that causes difficulty falling asleep or staying asleep.

instinct and evolutionary theory A theory of motivation suggesting that human behaviors are a result of evolutionary adaptation.

instinct Species-specific, unlearned patterns of behavior.

institutional animal care and use committee (IACUC) A committee at a research institution that reviews the ethics and methodology of every experiment involving animals.

institutional review board (IRB) A committee at a research institution that reviews the ethics and methodology of all research involving human participants.

intelligence A person's capacity to understand, reason, and adapt to the world based on cultural norms.

interactionist approach Theory suggesting that language development is a combination of both biological and environmental circumstances.

interference theory Theory that proposes that information remains until other information comes along to crowd it out.

internal attribution The inference that a person is behaving in a certain way because of an internal disposition.

interval scales A scientific measurement tool with equal distances among the units on the scale.

intimacy versus isolation A stage of psychosocial development during which people learn to maintain intimate relationships.

introspection The process of looking inward and examining oneself and one's actions in order to understand oneself better.

introvert A person who focuses on inner thoughts and experiences; is probably quiet or even shy.

introvert/extrovert scale A measure of internal versus external emotional focus; a low score means the person is introverted and a high score means the person is extroverted.

J

James-Lange theory of emotion A theory stating that emotions result from an awareness of physiological responses and are experienced only after the perception of an event, and the physical reaction to the perception, have occurred.

K

k-complexes Brain waves that are less frequent than sleep spindles but have higher peaks.

kolb's experiential learning theory Theory of a four-step learning cycle consisting of

(1) concrete experience,
(2) abstract conceptualization,
(3) reflective observation, and
(4) active experimentation.

korsakoff syndrome The inability to form new memories, loss of memories already stored in long-term memory, inventing and repeating untrue stories, and having hallucinations.

L

latent learning Learning that occurs without being immediately expressed.

lateral thinking Thinking in a way that does not follow conventional patterns and normal methods.

law of effect The connection between a behavior and the behavior's outcome.

leader The person who exerts the most influence and power in a group.

learned helplessness The passive acceptance that bad things happen outside of the individual's control.

learning The process of making mental associations between ideas and concepts.

learning style Kolb's term for the learning skills that individuals tend to choose and develop over time.

learning style inventory (LSI) Kolb's test that determines which combination of learning skills an individual tends to use.

learning theory approach Theory suggesting that language development is based on nurture and repetition of observed behaviors.

learning theory of personality A theory opposing Freud's focus on pathology; it asserts that all behavior is learned through exposure to and interaction with the environment.

lens Clear structure in the eye that focuses images.

levels of analysis A variety of viewpoints from which researchers investigate a problem, such as biological, individual, group, community, and societal.

libido Pleasure-seeking energies of the id, generated by particular erogenous areas.

limbic system The parts of the brain that control emotions; the system includes the amygdala, hypothalamus, hippocampus, and pituitary gland.

linguistic-relativity hypothesis Language shapes how people view the world and ultimately is responsible for how people think.

longitudinal Data collected on the same group of individuals over an extended period of time with the benefit of examining changes over time.

loudness The amplitude of a sound, measured in decibels (dB). Humans have the capacity to hear sounds from 0 to 130 dB.

M

machiavellian Authoritarian and concerned with achieving ends, often at the expense of ethical principle.

mal de débarquement Disorder wherein a patient may feel dizziness and a feeling of rocking back and forth for a prolonged period following travel by boat or automobile.

manipulation Making an adjustment or change to an independent variable.

maslow's hierarchy of needs Basic needs for food, shelter, and clothing are primary personal motivators and self-actualization as the final goal for which humans may strive; higher needs cannot be satisfied until basic needs are met.

mastery goal A personal attempt to improve one's own performance for the purpose of learning and self-improvement.

mechanoreceptors Sensory receptors in the body that respond to tactile pressure and other tactile sensations.

medical perspective on mental illness A perspective that seeks to determine the root of issues based on physical symptoms and causes. It proposes that a physical examination of the individual will reveal physical abnormalities, injury, or imbalances that explain the mental illness.

meditation A form of altered consciousness that engages the brain in deep thought.

meissner's corpuscles Sensory receptors that respond to vibrations and slowly moving stimuli, such as taps on the skin.

melatonin A hormone released according to low light levels that causes increased sleepiness.

membrane potential The difference between the voltage of the interior and exterior portions of a cell.

menarche A young woman's first menstruation cycle; the start of menstruation.

menopause The period of transition during which a woman's menstrual cycle stops.

mental illness An issue that brings people mental or physical discomfort and causes them to perceive and behave outside of the norms for that culture.

mental retardation A condition whose diagnosis is based on a combination of low test scores and a person's inability to adapt to and understand his or her living environment.

mere exposure effect The phenomenon of developing a positive attitude toward a person or an object simply as a function of frequent exposure to the person or object.

merkel's disks Sensory receptors that respond to pressure and texture.

mind-body controversy The debate in psychology and philosophy about if and how the physical body and the mind are connected.

minnesota multiphasic personality inventory (MMPI) A personality test used as a clinical measure of mental illness, as a professional and career assessment instrument, to evaluate people seeking certain types of high-risk employment, and in some legal settings.

mob behavior The tendency for crowds to behave in more extreme ways than the people who compose them normally do.

model of inclusive fitness The proposal that people behave in an altruistic fashion to those with whom they share genes, a phenomenon known as kin selection.

monocular cues Visual cues that are perceived with one eye.

mood A broad outlook on life that is less intense than an emotion and less likely to be triggered by a specific event; it may last for an extended period of time.

moral anxiety A fear of violating one's own moral principles.

moro reflex An instinctive infantile reaction to a startle to throw open the arms and then pull the arms close to the body before relaxing.

morpheme The smallest unit of language that conveys meaning.

motivation A drive that causes behavior.

motivation-hygiene theory A theory that posits that factors linked to job satisfaction are different from factors linked to job dissatisfaction.

motor cortex The part of the cortex where movement is guided by information that it gets from the senses.

mucocutaneous skin Skin that contains mucous membranes.

myoclonic jerk The common sensation of the body jerking near the beginning of the non-REM sleep cycle.

mysticism The study of experiences that do not seem to have been perceived through known senses.

N

nativist approach Theory suggesting that language is an innate skill, a skill people are born with.

nativists Scientists who believe that people are born with certain knowledge and abilities.

naturalistic observation The observation and recording of behaviors in real-world environments.

negative correlation A correlation in which one variable goes up and the other variable goes down.

negative reinforcement It is when an unfavorable stimulus is removed following the desired behavior.

negative reinforcer Removal of an undesirable outcome that is dependent on previous behavior.

neo-freudians They are psychologists who downplayed Freud's emphasis on the role of sexuality in the unconscious mind, but furthered the cause of psychodynamic theory.

neurogenesis The brain's ability to produce new cells that can become part of its circuitry.

neurologist A physician who specializes in treating the nervous system.

neurology The study of disorders of the nervous system.

neuromodulators Neurotransmitters that act indirectly, altering the effect of other neurotransmitters by making their effects either short- or long-lived.

neuron A nerve cell; the smallest unit of the nervous system.

neuroplasticity The ability of neurons in the brain to change connections when given new information or stimulation.

neuroscience The study of the physiological aspects of psychology and behavior.

neurotic anxiety A feeling that occurs when the unconscious mind is concerned about losing control of the id's urges.

neuroticism A tendency to be less emotionally stable in general and more likely to suffer from phobias, obsessions, compulsions, and depression.

neurotransmitters The chemicals that are transmitted from one neuron to another.

nocioreceptors Sensory receptors in the body that respond to damage to the body, usually in the form of pain.

nonprobability sampling A category of sampling strategies where not everyone or every unit in the population under study has an equal chance of getting selected to participate in the study.

non–rapid eye movement (NREM) sleep A type of sleep, sometimes called quiet sleep, that has four stages and occurs before REM sleep.

norepinephrine A hormone similar to epinephrine that is released by the adrenal gland to create the fight-or-flight reaction by accelerating the heartbeat, raising blood sugar, dilating pupils, and causing perspiration.

normal The behaviors, attitudes, and approaches to life expected for a given society.

O

obedience Agreement to behave with the demands of an authority figure.

object permanence The understanding that an object remains in existence despite being out of sight.

observational learning Learning that occurs after an organism observes the behavior of another organism.

occlusion Visual cue that occurs when one object covers another, suggesting to the observer that the covered object is farther away than the covering object.

operant Any behavior that affects an organism's environment.

operant conditioning It is t therapeutic techniques that use positive and negative reinforcement to promote desired behavior, while discouraging undesirable behavior.

operant conditioning Learning in which future behaviors are affected by the consequences of current behaviors.

operant conditioning Therapeutic techniques that use positive and negative reinforcement to promote desired behavior while discouraging undesirable behavior.

optical illusion A perception that differs from reality.

organ of corti Part of the inner ear that contains sensory hair cells that change stimuli into electrical signals.

otoconia Calcium carbonate crystals encased in the otolith organs

whose movement signals to the brain the body's acceleration.

otolith organs Sensory structures (the **utricle** and **saccule**) in the inner ear, responsive to acceleration and gravity.

outgroup Those outside a group to which one belongs, toward whom one has negative biases.

outgroup homogeneity effect The tendency to think of ingroup members as unique people with diverse opinions and of outgroup members as less defined and more similar to each other.

P

pacinian corpuscles Sensory receptors in the body that respond to vibration and pressure.

paradoxical sleep Another term for REM sleep that refers to how the quick eye movements, increased respiration rate, and increased brain activity are contradictory to the relaxed voluntary muscles.

parasympathetic nervous system The part of the human nervous system responsible for calming the body; it controls the processes of "resting and digesting."

participant selection The process of choosing participants from a sample that represents the population of interest to the study.

passionate love An intense longing felt for another accompanied by physiological arousal.

perception The brain's process of transforming sensory signals into recognizable information.

perception The organization of the various inputs of sensation, which may involve understanding neural processing, understanding how to organize the physics of sensations, and understanding how to behave in response to these sensations, or a combination of all of those understandings.

perceptual organization A theory of perception that suggests that the whole that is perceived is different from the sum of its parts.

performance goal A goal that is assessed competitively in terms of how one performs relative to others.

performance-approach goals Trying to outperform others—for example, by getting good grades or running to win a race.

performance-avoidance goals Avoiding performing more poorly than other individuals—for example, desiring not to fail a class.

peripheral route to persuasion The process by which people are persuaded by peripheral heuristics and cues rather than rational arguments.

persistent vegetative state (PVS) An unconscious state in which an individual is in a deep coma. Until recently it was thought individuals who suffer from PVS are not able to communicate or react to external stimuli; recent research suggests that this state may not be completely unconscious.

personality A combination of behavioral, temperamental, emotional, and mental characteristics; a complex of individual experiences collectively referred to as "I" or "the self."

person-centered therapy A psychotherapeutic approach that seeks to reintroduce patients to their own genuine experiences so they will accept and be themselves through unconditional acceptance, understanding, and feeling valued as an individual.

persuasion Active, conscious attempt to change attitudes through a message.

phonemes The basic sounds used in language.

photoreceptor Cell that gathers light in the eye.

photoreceptors Sensory receptors in the eyes that respond to light waves.

physical space The region of comfort surrounding each person that dictates how close others should come.

pitch The frequency of a sound, which causes it to be perceived as "high" or "low."

pituitary gland The master endocrine gland that secretes hormones regulating growth, metabolism, thirst, temperature, and sexual behavior.

placebo effect Phenomenon in which a treatment that has no physiological effect reliably changes a symptom.

population The entire set of units, groups, or individuals with the characteristics that the researcher wishes to study.

positive correlation A correlation in which both variables change in the same direction.

positive psychology A psychological movement that focuses on mental health and positivity rather than mental illness.

positive reinforcement It is when a favorable stimulus is given following the desired behavior.

positive reinforcer A desirable outcome that is dependent on previous behavior.

positive self-talk The introduction into the ongoing dialogue with oneself of phrases and images that are encouraging and instructive, and block negative self-messages.

postsynaptic membrane The membrane of a neuron on the other side of the synapse.

preconscious mind The area of the mind that houses thoughts, memories, wishes, feelings, and knowledge that a person is not currently accessing but can easily retrieve if needed.

prefrontal lobotomy A form of psychosurgery in which parts of the frontal lobes are destroyed or removed.

prejudice A hostile or negative attitude toward a distinguishable group of people, based solely on their membership in that group.

prenatal development Human development from conception through birth.

preoperational stage The stage of development from age two and until approximately age seven that is marked by egocentrism and improved use of symbolic thought.

prestige The desire for recognition from others, including appreciation, attention, recognition, fame, and status.

private speech Vygotsky's term for instructions or guidance spoken to oneself while learning.

proactive interference When old information gets in the way of new information.

probability sampling A category of sampling methods where everyone or every unit in the population under study has an equal chance of getting selected to participate in the study.

proprioception The sensation of the positions of different parts of the body.

proprioceptors Sensory receptors in the body that respond to body position and related feedback.

prosocial behaviors Behaviors that tend to benefit others.

prospective memory The system of memory with which one creates the intention of doing something in the future.

proximity Geographical nearness.

psychoactive drugs A category of drugs that affect people psychologically. Examples include legal prescription drugs, such as alprazolam (Xanax), thioridazine (Mellaril), and haloperidol (Haldol), as well as illegal drugs, such as heroin, LSD, and ecstasy.

psychoanalysis Originated by Sigmund Freud, the clinical practice that attempts to bring an individual's unconscious conflicts into conscious awareness.

psychoanalytic perspective on mental illness A perspective holding that psychological disorders stem from unresolved childhood issues pertaining to sex drive and aggression. It deals with subconscious impulses and influences on conscious thought and behavior.

psychoanalytic theory of personality Freud's personality model, which focuses on levels of awareness or consciousness, components of personality, defense mechanisms, and psychosexual stages.

psychological phenomena Thoughts, behaviors, attitudes, emotions, or beliefs.

psychopharmacology The use of medications to treat psychological disorders.

psychosexual stages theory Freud's theory that early erogenous experiences influence personality growth and set the stage for later personality development and behavior.

psychosocial stages of development Erik Erikson's eight stages of psychological development; in Erikson's model, each stage includes a crisis that requires a resolution.

psychotherapy A general form of treatment that uses different approaches to work on psychological disorders through modifying behaviors and increasing self-understanding and acceptance.

psychoticism A tendency toward psychosis and psychotic behavior.

puberty The period of human sexual maturation.

punishment It is giving an unfavorable stimulus after the undesirable behavior.

pupil Gap in the center of the eye that light passes through.

Q

qualitative data Nonnumerical information, such as people rating their observations, interpretations, attitudes, or feelings.

quantitative data Numerical data.

R

random assignment A study design in which participants are assigned to experimental and control conditions by chance, minimizing preexisting differences among those assigned to the various groups.

randomization of subjects Random assignment of participants to either the experimental or the control group to ensure both groups are similar.

rapid-eye movement (REM) sleep A type of sleep that usually occurs about 90 minutes after falling asleep and is associated with fast eye movement, active brain waves, and relaxed muscles.

rational emotive behavior therapy (REBT) A cognitive behavioral therapeutic approach to coping with stress using an ABC model—activating event, belief, and consequence—based on the idea that adversity is an event or thought that causes distress due to irrational beliefs or judgments about the adversity.

rational emotive behavior therapy (REBT) A cognitive–behavioral therapeutic approach to coping with stress using an ABC model—activating event, belief, and consequence—based on the idea that negative thought patterns when facing adversity lead to negative feelings.

reality anxiety A feeling that occurs when a real event causes worry.

recapitulation theory A theory of motivation suggesting that the development of an individual organism repeats in an abbreviated way the evolutionary history of its species.

reciprocal helping The provision of aid to those not genetically related to oneself.

rehearsal The repetition of short-term information.

reinforcer An outcome dependent upon a previous behavior.

research ethics The obligation of researchers to treat participants with honesty, fairness, respect, and responsibility.

researcher bias The possibility that a researcher will influence the results of a study, either intentionally or unintentionally.

resting potential A membrane potential with a stable value.

retina Light-sensitive tissue within the eye.

retrieval The process of bringing up stored memories to a conscious level.

retroactive interference When new information interferes with the ability to keep older information.

retrograde amnesia The loss of information stored in long-term memory before the event that caused the amnesia.

retrospective memory Memories based on information that has already been presented.

reuptake The process by which neurons reabsorb neurotransmitters floating freely in the synapse.

rods Light-sensitive cells within the eye that are more sensitive than their counterparts, cones, but do not sense color.

rooting reflex An instinctive infantile reaction to a brush to the cheek to turn toward the touch and begin to suck.

ruffini endings Sensory receptors that respond to pressure and skin stretch.

rule of reciprocity The symmetrical idea that one is obligated to do something in return for a person who has done something for them.

S

sample A subset of the population.

scaffolding Simpler, step-by-step variations on a complex activity provided to a learner by an adult or expert.

scatterplot A graph that shows the association between two variables' positive or negative correlation.

schachter-singer two-factor theory of emotion Proposal that emotions develop from both a physiological response and a cognitive label or thought that describes or defines the physical arousal.

schedules of reinforcement Patterns of how reinforcers are given during operant conditioning.

schemas Mental structures that people use to organize their knowledge about the social world around themes or subjects and that influence the information people notice, think about, and remember.

scientific method A method of obtaining objective knowledge about the world through systematic, empirical, and replicable observations.

second force behavioral theory Any theory that presents behavior as a product of socialization as opposed to innate tendencies or inherited traits.

sedative-hypnotics Drugs such as alcohol, barbiturates, and minor tranquilizers that are addictive and often abused.

self-actualization It is the desire of a person to achieve his or her full potential.

self-concept It is how a person understands who they are within the framework of society and, or loved ones.

self-esteem A person's evaluation of his or her own self-worth.

self-esteem A person's opinion and assessment of his or her own worth.

self-perception theory Theory suggesting that attitudes are based on people's perception of how they behave toward an object or situation.

semantic memory Memory based on knowledge or information that you know but have not experienced.

semantics The rules used to produce specific meaning from morphemes, words, and sentences.

semicircular canals Bone tubes in the inner ear, arranged perpendicularly, that are responsive to rotation of the head.

sensation The processes by which your sense organs (eyes, ears, nose, mouth, and skin) detect external stimuli and transform them into signals that are transmitted to the brain.

sensation The way that physical energy affects the sensory receptors and organs.

sensorimotor The stage of development from birth to age two that is marked by using the senses to understand the environment.

sensory adaptation The process by which senses become less responsive to particular stimuli.

sensory conflict hypothesis A theory that proposes conflict between the separate inputs from two sensory systems as the cause of motion sickness.

serotonin A neurotransmitter.

set point A person's normal homeostatic body weight.

sex drive Sexual desire or motivation.

sexual response cycle Four stages of sexual response include excitement, plateau, orgasm, and resolution.

shaping A process by which a new behavior is learned through reinforcement of behaviors that are progressively more similar to the desired learned behavior.

short-term memory A temporary form of memory that interacts with long-term memory.

similarity–attraction hypothesis The theory that in friendships and intimate relationships, people are attracted to others with similar values and attitudes.

simple random sampling A probability sampling method where an individual is selected by chance.

situational theory of leadership The theory that a particular situation determines who will become a leader.

sixteen personality factors theory Cattell's theory of personality considering 16 pairs of traits, developed in response to Eysenck's scale.

sleep apnea A sleep disorder that is characterized by interrupted breathing during sleep.

sleep spindles Bursts of rapid, rhythmic brain waves that occur during Stage II sleep in which the heart rate decreases and the body temperature begins to lower.

snowball sampling A nonprobability sampling method where participants who meet the criteria of the study refer others.

social cognition The processes of perceiving and ascribing meaning to the presence of others.

social cognitive theory Bandura's idea that cognition affects learning.

social facilitation The tendency of an awareness of others to affect one's performance on a task.

social identity theory A social psychological theory that investigates how group membership affects a person's social identity.

social influence The influence of another's words, behavior, or mere presence on one's thoughts, feelings, and action; the phenomenon of being influenced by the presence of others.

social learning theory Bandura's theory that humans learn appropriate and inappropriate behaviors by participating in and observing social interactions with others.

social learning theory The theory that humans learn appropriate and inappropriate behaviors by participating in and observing social interactions with others.

social norms The implicit or explicit rules a group has for the behavior of its members.

social perception The processes by which humans make sense of their own and others' behavior.

social psychology The branch of psychology that investigates social relationships, from relationships between two individuals to group dynamics.

social role A schema related to expectations about how particular people are expected to behave.

social support A helping network made up of friendships, close relationships, and the larger communities in which people live.

sociocultural perspective of personality Vygotsky's belief that social interactions with other people and the shared knowledge of a particular culture form individual personality.

sociocultural perspective on mental illness A perspective proposing that normal and abnormal behaviors are the result of the interaction of the family, society, and culture a person is a part of.

somatosensory cortex Processes input from systems in the body that are sensitive to touch, including pain, pressure, and temperature.

somatosensory system The system incorporating sensory, motor, and cognitive functions.

space motion sickness Ailment experienced by space shuttle astronauts in the initial stages of space travel, characterized by dizziness, nausea, and vomiting.

spontaneous recovery The sudden reemergence of the conditioned response after a rest period.

stage model of memory A structural and functional model for memory describing three separate memory systems—sensory, short-term, and long-term memory—that operate in stages.

stereogram An image that uses shifting patterns to create the illusion of depth.

stereopsis An impression of depth that is perceived based on the slightly different position of the scene.

stereotype A generalization about a group of people in which certain traits are assigned to all members of the group without regard for its members' individuality.

stimulus A thing or event that causes a reaction, feeling, thought, or change in behavior; stimuli can be either internal or external.

stress A pattern of behavioral and physiological responses to events that matches or exceeds your ability to respond.

stress A physical response to threatening or emotional events.

structuralism The school of psychology that studies the structure of consciousness.

substantia gelatinosa (SG) cells Spinal cord cells that can either release or inhibit pain.

suckling reflex When a baby's lips are stimulated, the baby will instinctively make a sucking motion.

superego Higher ideals and standards of maturity and morality, as embodied by parents and society.

surveys Collections of questions used to gather information about participants.

sympathetic nervous system The part of the human nervous system responsible for activating the body, which triggers its fight-or-flight responses among others.

synapses Junctions between neurons characterized by a small gap over which neurotransmitters can flow.

synaptic vesicles Sacs of chemicals in the terminal button.

syntax Determines word order in a sentence.

T

tabula rasa A blank slate to be written upon; used to suggest the nature of an unformed person, uninfluenced by prior information or strong inner inclinations.

terminal bouton The part of the axon farthest away from the cell body.

testosterone Male sex hormone that regulates the growth of male sex organs and influences sex drive in males and human females.

testosterone Male sex hormone that regulates the growth of male sex organs and influences sex drive in males and human females.

thalamus The part of the brain that relays sensation and spatial sense to the cortex.

theory A systematic set of interrelated statements with the goal of explaining, understanding, or predicting some social or psychological phenomenon.

theory x versus theory y Two opposing theories of management: Theory X assumes that employees of an organization are inherently lazy and that management must tightly control an organization. Theory Y proposes that employees have the potential to become productive and that the responsibility of management is to make it possible for people to achieve their best.

thermoreceptors Sensory receptors in the body that respond to changes in temperature.

theta waves Brain waves that are slower than alpha and beta waves and occur during Stage I of non-REM sleep during the transition between being awake and asleep.

thinking The process of making mental associations between ideas for a specific goal or purpose.

third force theorists Those who believe that the constructs affecting personality development are more human, and thus more holistic, than previous models allowed for.

three needs theory A theory that human motivation is dominated by three needs: achievement, affiliation, and power.

trait A primary quality or inherited characteristic present in each person in varying degrees, a cluster of which make up the personality.

trait theory A personality theory based on the idea that personality is made up of three basic qualities or characteristic traits: introversion/extroversion, neuroticism, and psychoticism.

trait theory of leadership The theory that the qualities of the particular person in a leadership position shape a group's behavior.

transference In psychotherapy, when patients project feelings, thoughts, and behaviors characteristic of early formative relationships onto the therapist.

transhemispheric magnetic stimulation/transcranial magnetic stimulation (TMS) A form of brain imaging that interrupts current brain activity in a given location.

transmission (T) cells Spinal cord cells that transmit pain.

triangular theory of love Theory that states that love consists of three distinct ingredients: intimacy, passion, and commitment.

triarchic theory of intelligence A theory that people have three types of intelligence—analytical, creative, and practical.

trust versus mistrust A stage of psychosocial development lasting from birth through 18 months; during this period, a child develops an attachment to a caregiver.

U

unconditioned response A response that is reflexive, not learned.

unconditioned stimulus A stimulus that occurs naturally, eliciting a reflexive, or unconditioned, response in an organism.

unconscious mind The area of the mind that stores all the thoughts and knowledge that a person is not aware of.

unconsciousness An individual's lack of awareness of thoughts, memories, feelings, sensations, or environment.

uninvolved Parents who make few demands on children's behaviors and also reject their child's individuality, are generally neglectful, and place their own needs before those of children.

V

variable-interval schedule A schedule of reinforcement in which the reinforcer is given after varied periods of time have passed and a correct response is given.

variable-ratio schedule A schedule of reinforcement in which the reinforcer is given after a changing number of correct behavioral responses.

variables Measurable phenomena that have more than one value.

vertical thinking The thought process used in school for processing facts and thinking within the bounds of set criteria.

vertigo Sense of spinning or rotation while standing still.

vestibular sensory system A system of bony and membranous structures in the inner ear responsible for maintaining the body's sense of balance and orientation in space.

vestibulocollic reflex Vestibular reflex that works with the muscles of the neck to keep the head upright.

vestibulo-ocular reflex Vestibular reflex that keeps the vision steady while the head is in motion.

vestibulospinal reflex Vestibular reflex that works with the spine to stabilize the body as it moves.

visual drift illusion Optical illusion in which motion is incorrectly perceived in the periphery of the viewer's eye.

volunteer bias The possibility that sample populations may not truly represent a population of interest because people who volunteer for experiments may differ from the general population.

vygotsky's social development theory Learning theory that stresses the role of sociocultural context, particularly the presence of an expert companion, in a child's construction of knowledge.

Z

zone of proximal development Vygotsky's term for the difference between what a child can learn on his or her own and with an expert companion present.

zygote The new cell containing all the genetic material to create a new human being.

PHOTO CREDITS

Chapter 1 Opener, p. 2: © Kit Wai Chan (Fotolia); p. 4, top-left: © ktsdesign (Fotolia); p. 4, top-right: © Piotr Marcinski (Fotolia); p. 4, bottom-right: © Kenneth Sponsler (Fotolia); p. 5: © Deklofenak (Fotolia); p. 6: © Lisa F. Young (Fotolia); p. 7: © Rob (Fotolia).

Chapter 2 Opener, p. 20: © Stephen VanHorn (Fotolia); p. 21: © Galina Barskaya (Fotolia); p. 24: © Dmitry Naumov (Fotolia); p. 25, top: © Kitch Bain (Fotolia); p. 25, bottom: © James Peragine (Fotolia); p. 28: © diego cervo (Fotolia); p. 30: © Xuejun li (Fotolia); p. 32: U.S. Public Health Service; p. 33: © Brilt (Fotolia).

Chapter 3 Opener, p. 36: © rvvelde (Fotolia); p. 38: © ktsdesign (Fotolia); p. 41: © Monkey Business (Fotolia); p. 42: © Anita Potter (Fotolia); p. 43: © eveleen007 (Fotolia); p. 44: © Ilenia Pagliarini (Fotolia); p. 46, top: © picsfive (Fotolia); p. 46, bottom: © James Steidl (Fotolia); p. 47: © Luk Cox (Fotolia).

Chapter 4 Opener, p. 52: © Bobby Earle (Fotolia); p. 54: © Jan Rakic (Fotolia); p. 55: © LB3studios (Fotolia); p. 56: © Stocksnapper (Fotolia); p. 57: © Cristian Ciobanu (Fotolia); p. 59: © steve estvanik (Fotolia); p. 60: © olly (Fotolia); p. 61: © iofoto (Fotolia); p. 62: © Marc Dietrich (Fotolia); p. 63: © Kirill Zdorov (Fotolia); p. 64, top: © Jason Stitt (Fotolia); p. 64, bottom: © robertosch (Fotolia); p. 65: © Andres Rodriguez (Fotolia); p. 67: © Kzenon (Fotolia); p. 68: © diego cervo (Fotolia); p. 69: © Anita Potter (Fotolia); p. 70: © Aaron Amat (Fotolia); p. 71, top: © Karen Roach (Fotolia); p. 71, bottom: © Chariclo (Fotolia); p. 73: © tiero (Fotolia); p. 74: © Max Tactic (Fotolia).

Chapter 5 Opener, p. 80: © Argus (Fotolia); p. 82, top: © diego cervo (Fotolia); p. 82, bottom: © volff (Fotolia); p. 83 top-right: © araraadt (Fotolia); p. 83, middle: © Phase4Photography (Fotolia); p. 83, bottom-right: © Oleg Kozlov (Fotolia); p. 84: © David Davis (Fotolia); p. 85: © Lisa F. Young (Fotolia); p. 86: © Angelika Möthrath (Fotolia); p. 87: © stefanolunardi (Fotolia); p. 88: © Emir Jamak (Fotolia); p. 89: © Bert Folsom (Fotolia); p. 90: © James Steidl (Fotolia); p. 91: © deanm1974 (Fotolia).

Chapter 6 Opener, p. 94: © Pavel Losevsky (Fotolia); p. 96: © ktsdesign (Fotolia); p. 98: © Athanasia Nomikou (Fotolia); p. 99: © Arto (Fotolia); p. 100: © Monkey Business (Fotolia); p. 101: © Monkey Business; p. 102: © Anyka (Fotolia); p. 104, top: © Serhiy Kobyakov (Fotolia); p. 104, bottom: © Felix Mizioznikov (Fotolia); p. 105: © mangostock (Fotolia); p. 106: © Jaimie Duplass (Fotolia); p. 110: © Ralf Kraft (Fotolia); p. 111: © Monkey Business (Fotolia); p. 112: © YellowCrest (Fotolia); p. 113: © Yuri Arcurs (Fotolia).

Chapter 7 Opener, p. 118: © Yuri Arcurs (Fotolia); p. 120, top: © Andrzej Tokarski (Fotolia); p. 120, bottom: © Marek (Fotolia); p. 121: © Lisa Eastman (Fotolia); p. 123: © Fedels (Fotolia); p. 124: © Kasia Biel (Fotolia) l; p. 125: © vukas (Fotolia); p. 127: © Laurin Rinder (Fotolia); p. 128: © Anita Potter (Fotolia); p. 129: © M. Dykstra (Fotolia); p. 130: © pilarts (Fotolia); p. 132: © Noam (Fotolia); p. 133, top: © Alexander Raths (Fotolia); p. 133, bottom: © photoillustrator.eu (Fotolia); p. 134: © DURIS Guillaume (Fotolia); p. 136: © olly (Fotolia); p. 138: © Matty Symons (Fotolia); p. 139, top: © Dusaleev V. (Fotolia); p. 139, bottom: © Adam Borkowski (Fotolia); p. 140: © .shock (Fotolia); p. 142: © Tetiana Zbrodko (Fotolia).

Chapter 8 Opener, p. 146: © Robert Kneschke (Fotolia); p. 148: © mipan (Fotolia); p. 149: © Arcady (Fotolia); p. 153, top: © Konstantin Tavrov (Fotolia); p. 153, bottom: © Alex Bramwell (Fotolia); p 155, top: © cubephoto (Fotolia); p. 155, bottom: © gwimages (Fotolia); p. 156: ©Dmytro Konstantynov (Fotolia); p. 160: © Deklofenak (Fotolia).

Chapter 9 Opener, p. 164: © alex chernak (Fotolia); p. 165: © SeanPavonePhoto (Fotolia); p. 167, top: © loutocky (Fotolia); p. 167, bottom: © Anita Potter (Fotolia); p. 168: © Petro Feketa (Fotolia); p. 170: © Vladimir Wrangel (Fotolia); p. 171: © Jason Stitt (Fotolia); p. 172: © blanche (Fotolia); p. 173: © nyul (Fotolia); p. 175: © Yuri Arcurs (Fotolia).

REFERENCES

Chapter 1

Barker, S. (2007). *Psychology*. Malden, MA: Blackwell Publishing.

Bergman, M. S. (2010). The Oedipus Complex and psychoanalytic technique. *Psychoanalytic Inquiry*, 306(6), 535–540.

Hall, G. (2009). Watson: The thinking man's behaviourist. *British Journal of Psychology*, 100(1a), 185–187.

Harzem, P. (2004). Behaviorism for new psychology: What was wrong with behaviorism and what is wrong with it now. *Behavior & Philosophy*, 32(1), 5–12.

Hoffman, R. R., & Deffenbacher, K.A. (1991). A brief history of Applied Cognitive Psychology. *Applied Cognitive Psychology*, 6 (1), 1–48.

Leichsenring, F., Hiller, W., Weissberg, M., & Leibing, E. (2006). Cognitive-behavioral therapy and psychodynamic psychotherapy: techniques, efficacy, and indications. *American Journal of Psychotherapy*, 60(3), 233–259.

Macmillan, M. (2009). *Psychodynamic theories of the unconscious*. Retrieved from http://search.credoreference.com/content/entry/estcon/psychodynamic_theories_of_the_unconscious/0.

Matalon, N. (2011). The riddle of dreams. *Philosophical Psychology*, 24(4), 517–536.

McDonald, M., & Wearing, S. (2013). A reconceptualization of the self in humanistic psychology: Heidegger, Foucault and the sociocultural turn. *Journal of Phenomenological Psychology*, 44(1), 37–59.

McGuire, C., Rowland, T. (1966). *An introduction to Jean Piaget*. Texas University.

McLeod, S. A. (2009). *Jean Piaget*. Retrieved from http://simplypsychology.org/piaget.html.

Pieces of the mind, in conflict. (2004). *Secrets of Genius*, 29.

Rholetter, W. (2013). Operant conditioning. *Salem Press Encyclopedia*.

Rosenberg, M. (1965). *Society and the adolescent self-image*. Princeton, NJ: Princeton University Press.

Watson, J. B. (2009) Is thinking merely the action of language mechanisms? *British Journal of Psychology*, 100(1a), 169–180.

Zalenski, R. J., & Raspa, R. (2006). Maslow's hierarchy of needs: A framework in achieving human potential in hospice. *Journal of Palliative Medicine*, 9(5), 1120–1127.

Chapter 2

American Psychological Association. (2010). Ethical principles of psychologists and code of conduct, 2010 Amendments. Retrieved from http://www.apa.org/ethics

Benjamin, L. T., Jr., & Simpson, J. A. (2009). The power of the situation: The impact of Milgram's obedience studies on personality and social psychology. *American Psychologist*, 64 (1), 12–19.

Bottorff, J. L., McKeown, S., Carey, J., Haines, R., Okoli, C., Johnson, K. C., & Ptolemy, E. (2010). Young women's responses to smoking and breast cancer risk information. *Health Education Research*, 25(4), 668–677.

Centers for Disease Control and Prevention. (2009). *US public health service syphilis study at Tuskegee*. Retrieved from http://www.cdc.gov/tuskegee/timeline.htm

Elliot, A. J., Maier, M. A., Binser, M. J., Friedman, R., & Pekrun, R. (2009). The effect of red on avoidance behavior in achievement contexts. *Personality and Social Psychology Bulletin*, 35(3), 365–375.

Elliot, A. J., Maier, M. A., Moller, A. C., Friedman, R., & Meinhardt, J. (2007). Color and psychological functioning: The effect of red on performance attainment. *Journal of Experimental Psychology: General*, 136(1), 154–168.

Gazzaniga, M., Heatherton, T. & Halpern, D. (2010). *Psychological science*. New York: W. W. Norton.

Gosling, S. D., Rentfrow, P. J., & Swann, W. B., Jr. (2003). A very brief measure of the Big Five personality domains. *Journal of Research in Personality*, 37(6), 504–528.

Gravetter, F. J., & Forzano, L. (2009). *Research methods for the behavioral sciences*. Belmont, CA: Cengage.

Hendrick, J. L., & Switzer, J. R. (2007). Hands-free versus hand-held cell phone conversation on a braking response by young drivers. *Perceptual and Motor Skills*, 105(2), 514–522.

Louw, J. (1997). Regulating professional conduct. Part I: Codes of ethics of national psychology associations in South Africa. *South African Journal of Psychology*, 27, 183–188.

Miller, A. G., Collins, B. E., & Brief, D. E. (1995). Perspectives on obedience to authority: The legacy of the Milgram experiments. *Journal of Social Issues*, 51(3), 1–19.

Monette, D. R., Sullivan, T. J., & DeJong, C. R. (1998). Applied social research: Tool for the human services. Orlando, FL: Harcourt Brace and Company.

Nagy, T. F. (2011). A brief history and overview of the APA Ethics Code. In T. F. Nagy (Ed.), *Essential ethics for psychologists: A primer for understanding and mastering core issues* (pp. 29–48). Washington, DC: American Psychological Association.

Neuman, W. L. (2003). *Social research methods: Qualitative and quantitative approaches*. Boston: Pearson Education, Inc.

Scoville, W., & Milner, B. (1957). Loss of recent memory after bilateral hippocampal lesions. *Journal of Neurology, Neurosurgery & Psychiatry*, 20, 11–21.

Sulloway, F. J., & Zweigenhaft, R. L. (2010). Birth order and risk taking in athletics: A meta-analysis and study of major league baseball. *Personality and Social Psychology Review*, 14(4), 402–416.

University of Michigan Institute for Social Research. (2011). *Panel study of income dynamics*. Retrieved from http://psidonline.isr.umich.edu/

Chapter 3

Anderson, A. K., & Phelps, E. A. (2001). Lesions of the human amygdala impair enhanced perception of emotionally salient events. *Nature*, 411, 305–309.

Banissy, M. J., Sauter, D. A., Ward, J., Warren, J. E., Walsh, V., & Scott, S. K. (2010). Suppressing sensorimotor activity modulates the discrimination of auditory emotions but not speaker identity. *Journal of Neuroscience*, 30(41), 13552–13557.

Bor, J., Brunelin, J., Sappey-Marinier, D., Ibarrola, D., d'Amato, T., Suaud-Chagny, M. F., & Saoud, M. (2011). Thalamus abnormalities during working memory in schizophrenia. An FMRI study. *Schizophr Res.*, 125(1), 49–53.

Caine, R. N., & Caine, G. (1990). *Making Connections: Teaching and the Human Brain*. Nashville, TN: Incentive Publications.

Carpenter, S., & Huffman, K. (2013). *Visualizing psychology* (3rd ed.). Upper Saddle River, NJ: John Wiley & Sons.

Cavanagh, J. F., Cohen, M. X., & Allen, J. J. B. (2009). Prelude to and resolution of an error: EEG phase synchrony reveals cognitive control dynamics during action monitoring. *Journal of Neuroscience*, 29(1), 98–105.

Desimone, R. (1991). Face-selective cells in the temporal cortex of monkeys. *Journal of Cognitive Neuroscience*, 3(1), 1–8.

Egashira, N., Tanoue, A., Matsuda, T., Koushi, E., Harad, S., Takano, Y., … Fuiwara, M. (2007). Impaired social interaction and reduced anxiety-related behavior in vasopressin V1 a receptor knockout mice. *Behavioural Brain Research*, 178(1), 123–127.

Gholipour, B. (2014, February 3). A brain surgery decades ago is getting a new look and raising questions about memory. *Washington Post*.

Grohol, J. M. (2008, September 21). It's alright: Teens playing video games. Retrieved from http://psychcentral.com/blog/archives/2008/09/21/its-alright-teens-playing-video-games/

Gross, C. G., Rocha-Miranda, C. E., & Bender, D. B. (1972). Visual properties of neurons in inferotemporal cortex of the macaque. *Journal of Neurophysiology*, 35, 96–111.

Jonkman, L. M., Kenemans, J. L., Kemner, C., Verbaten, M. N., & van Engeland, J. (2004). Dipole source localization of event-related brain activity indicative of an early visual selective attention deficit in ADHD children. *Clinical Neurophysiology*, 115(7), 1537–1549.

Kilner, J. M., Neal, A., Weiskopf, N., Fristin, K. J., & Frith, C. D. (2009). Evidence of mirror neurons in human inferior frontal gyrus. *Journal of Neuroscience*, 29(32), 10153–10159.

Lagorio, C. (2006, June 14). This is your brain online: How video games, multitasking and blogging are shaping the GenTech brain. Retrieved from http://www.cbsnews.com/stories/2006/06/11/gentech/main1699513.shtml

Levin, H. S., Wilde, E. A., Chu, Z., Yallampalli, R., Hanten, G. R., Li, X., . . . Hunter, J. V. (2008). Diffusion tensor imaging in relation to cognitive and functional outcome of traumatic brain injury in children. *Journal of Head Trauma Rehabilitation*, 23(4), 197–208.

Ley, R. G., & Bryden, M. P. (1979). Hemispheric differences in processing emotions and faces. *Brain and Language*, 7(1), 127–138.

Macmillan, M. (2000). *An odd kind of fame: Stories of Phineas Gage*. MIT Press.

Macmillan, M., & Lena, M. L. (2010). Rehabilitating Phineas Gage. *Neuropsychological Rehabilitation*, 20(5), 641–58.

Maki, P. M., Zonderman, A. B., & Resnick, S. M. (2001). Enhanced verbal memory in nondemented elderly women receiving hormone-replacement therapy. *American Journal of Psychiatry*, 158, 227–233.

Murre, J. M., & Sturdy, D. P. (1995). The connectivity of the brain: Multi-level quantitative analysis. *Biological Cybernetics*, 73(6), 529–545.

Narr, K. L., Woods, R. P., Thompson, P. M., Szeszko, P., Robinson, D., Dimtcheva, T., …Bilder, R. M. (2007). Relationships between IQ and regional cortical gray matter thickness in healthy adults. *Cerebral Cortex*, 17(9), 2163–2171.

National Institutes of Health, U.S. Department of Health and Human Services. (2009). Stem cell basics. In *Stem Cell Information*. Bethesda, MD: Author.

Nestler, E. J. & Self, D. W. (2010). Neuropsychiatric aspects of ethanol and other chemical dependencies. In S. Yudofsky & R. E. Hales (Eds.), *Essentials of neuropsychiatry and behavioral neuroscience*. Arlington, VA: American Psychiatric Publishing.

Oberman, L. M., Hubbard, E. M., McCleery, J. P., Altschuler, E. L., Ramachandran, V. S., & Pineda, J. A. (2005). EEG evidence for mirror neuron dysfunction in autism spectrum disorders. *Cognitive Brain Research*, 24(2), 190–198.

Peters, & Jones, E. G. (1984). *Cerebral cortex*.

Ramachandran, V. S. (2006). Mirror neurons and imitation learning as the driving force behind the great leap forward in human evolution. Retrieved from http://www.edge.org/3rd_culture/ramachandran/ramachandran_p1.html

Reiss, A. L., Abrams, M. T., Singer, H. S., Ross, J. L., & Denckla, M. B. (1996). Brain development, gender and IQ in children: A volumetric imaging study. *Brain*, 119(5), 1763–1774.

Reuter-Lorenz, P., & Davidson, R. J. (1981). Differential contributions of the two cerebral hemispheres to the perception of happy and sad faces. *Neuropsychologia*, 19(4), 609–613.

Sergerie, K., Chochoi, C., & Armony, J. L. (2008). The role of the amygdala in emotional processing: A quantitative meta-analysis of functional neuroimaging studies. *Neuroscience and Biobehavioral Reviews*, 32(4), 811–830.

Soliman, F., Glatt, C. E., Bath, K. G., Levita, L., Jones, R. M., Pattwell, S. S., … Casey, B. J. (2010). A genetic variant

BDNF polymorphism alters extinction learning in both mouse and human. *Science, 327*(12), 863–866.

Sperry, R. W. (1964). The great cerebral commissure. *Scientific American, 210,* 42–52.

Sperry, R. W. (1968). Hemisphere disconnection and unity in conscious awareness. *American Psychologist, 23,* 723–33.

Sperry, R. W. (1970). Perception in the absence of neocortical commissures. In *Perception and its disorders* (Res. Publ. A.R.N.M.D., 48). New York: The Association for Research in Nervous and Mental Disease.

Squire, L. R., & Zola-Morgan, S. (1991). The medial temporal lobe memory system. *Science, 253*(5026), 1380–1386.

Swain, J. E., Lorberbaum, J. P., Kose, S., & Strathearn, L. (2007). Brain basis of early parent–infant interactions: Psychology, physiology, and in vivo functional neuroimaging studies. *Journal of Child Psychology and Psychiatry, 48*(3), 262–287.

Taub, E. (2004). Harnessing brain plasticity through behavioral techniques to produce new treatments in neurorehabilitation. *American Psychologist, 59*(8), 692–704.

Taub, E., Uswatte, G., King, D. K., Morris, D. M., Crago, J. E., & Chatterjee, A (2006). A placebo controlled trial of constraint-induced movement therapy for upper extremity after stroke. *Stroke, 37,* 1045–1049.

Toman, B. (2014). *Neuroregenerative medicine booklet.* Retrieved from http://www.mayo.edu/research/documents/neuroregenerative-medicine-booklet/doc-20092381

Tucker, D. M., & Williamson, P. A. (1984). Asymmetric neural control systems in human self-regulation. *Psychological Review, 91*(2), 182–215.

Weinstein, A., Brickner, O., Lerman, H., Greemland, M., Bloch, M., Lester, H....Freeman, N. (2008). Brain imaging study of the acute effects of THC on attention and motor coordination in regular users of marijuana. *Psychopharmacology, 196*(1), 119–131.

Wernicke K. (1995). The aphasia symptom-complex: A psychological study on an anatomical basis (1875). In *Paul Eling, reader in the history of aphasia: From sasi (Franz Gall to)* (pp. 69–89). Amsterdam: John Benjamins.

Wolf, U., Rapoport M. J., & Schweizer T. A. (2009). Evaluating the affective component of the cerebellar cognitive affective syndrome. *J. Neuropsychiatry Clin. Neurosci., 21*(3), 245–53.

Chapter 4

Agrawal, Y., Platz, E. A., & Niparko, J. K. (2008). Prevalence of hearing loss and differences by demographic characteristics among US adults: Data from the national health and nutrition examination survey, 1999–2004. *Archives of Internal Medicine, 168*(14), 1522–1530.

Angier, N. (2008, October 27). The unappreciated, holding our lives in balance. *The New York Times.* Retrieved from http://www.nytimes.com/

Angst, F., Verra, M. L., Lehmann, S., Brioschi, R., & Aeschlimann, A. (2009). Clinical effectiveness of an interdisciplinary pain management program compared with standard inpatient rehabilitation in chronic pain: A naturalistic, prospective controlled cohort study. *Journal of Rehabilitation Medicine, 41*(7), 569–575.

Askay, S. W., Patterson, D. R., Sharar, R., Mason, S., & Faber, B. (2009). Pain management in patients with burn injuries. *International Review of Psychiatry, 21*(6), 522–530.

Axelin, A., Salanterä, S., Kirjavainen, J., & Lehtonen, L. (2009). Oral glucose and parental holding preferable to opioid in pain management in preterm infants. *Clinical Journal of Pain, 25*(2), 138–145.

Beer, A. L., Hecke, A. H., & Greenlee, M. W. (2008). A motion illusion reveals mechanisms of perceptual stabilization. PLoS ONE, 3 (7), e2741. doi:10.1371/journal.pone.0002741

Benson, A.J. (1982). The vestibular sensory system. In H.B. Barlow & J.D. Mollon (Eds.), *The senses* (pp. 333–368). New York, NY: Cambridge University Press.

Bruce, C., Desimone, R., & Gross, C. G. (1981). Visual properties of neurons in a polysensory area in superior temporal sulcus of the macaque. *Journal of Neurophysiology, 46*(2), 369–384.

Buonomano, D. V., & Merzenich, M. M. (1998). Cortical plasticity: From synapses to maps. *Annual Review of Neuroscience, 21,* 149–186.

Chen, D., & Jones, J. H. (2000). Human olfactory communication of emotion. *Perceptual Motor Skills, 91,* 771–781.

Coakley, S., & Shelemay, K. (2002). Pain and its transformations: The interface of biology and culture. Cambridge, MA: Harvard University Press.

Davidhizar, R., & Giger, J. N. (2004). A review of the literature on care of clients in pain who are culturally diverse. *International Nursing Review, 51*(1), 47–55.

Elliott, D. B., Vale, A., Whitaker, D., & Buckley, J. G. (2009). Doesmy step look big in this? A visual illusion leads to safer stepping behavior. PLoS ONE, 4 (2), e4577. doi:10.1371/journal.pone.0004577

Feeney, E., O'Brien, S., Schannel, A., & Gibney, E. R. (2010). Genetic variation in taste perception: Does it have a role in healthy eating? *Proceedings of the Nutrition Society, 70*(1), 135–143. doi:10.1017/S0029665110003976

Fillingim, R. B., King, C. D., Ribeiro-Dasilva, M. C., Rahim-Williams, B., & Riley, J. L. III. (2009). Sex, gender, and pain: A review of recent clinical and experimental findings. *Journal of Pain, 10*(5), 447–485.

Gibson, E. J., Gibson, J. J., Smith, O. W., & Flock, H. (1959). Motion parallax as a determinant of perceived depth. *Journal of Experimental Psychology, 58*(1), 40–51.

Gibson, E., & Walk, R. D. (1960). The visual cliff. *Scientific American, 202,* 80–92.

Gläscher, J., Rudrauf, D., Colom, R., Paul, L. K., Tranel, D., Damasio, H., & Adolphs, R. (2010). Distributed neural system for general intelligence revealed by lesion mapping. *Proceedings of the National Academy of Science, 107*(10), 4705–4709.

Hain, T.C. (2011, May 12). Benign paroxysmal positional vertigo. Retrieved from http://www.dizziness-and-balance.com/disorders/bppv/bppv.html

Hain, T.C., & Helminski, J.O. (2007). Anatomy and physiology of the normal vestibular system. In S. Herdman (Ed.), *Vestibular rehabilitation* (3rd ed., pp. 2–18). San Francisco: Davis.

Heer, M., & Paloski W.H. (2006, October 30). Space motion sickness: incidence, etiology, and countermeasures. *Autonomic Neuroscience: Basic & Clinical,* 129(1–2), 77–79.

Highstein, S.M. (2004). Anatomy and physiology of the central and peripheral vestibular system: overview. In S.M. Highstein, R.R. Fay, & A.N. Popper (Eds.), *The Vestibular System* (pp. 1–10). New York, NY: Springer-Verlag.

Hummel, T., & Nordin, S. (2005). Olfactory disorders and their consequences for quality of life: A review. *Acta Oto-Laryngologica,* 125, 116–121.

Johnston, C. C., Rennick, J. E., Fillon, F., Campell-Yeo, M., Goulet, C., Bell, L., … Ranger, M. (2011). Maternal touch and talk for invasive procedures in infants and toddlers in the pediatric intensive care unit. *Journal of Pediatric Nursing.* Advance online publication. doi:10.1016/j.pedn.2010.12.016

Julesz, B. (1969). Foundations of cyclopean perception. *Journal of the Optical Society of America,* 59, 1544.

Kleeman, A. M., Kopietz, R., Albrecht, J., Schopf, V., Pollatos, O., Schreder, T., & Wiesmann, M. (2008). Investigation of breathing parameters during odor perception and olfactory imagery. *Chemical Senses,* 34(1), 1–9.

Kleiner, A. (2008). *The age of heretics: A history of the radical thinkers who reinvented corporate management.* New York, NY: Jossey-Bass.

Koffman, J., Morgan, M., Edmonds, P., Speck, P., & Higginson, I. J. (2008). Cultural meanings of pain: A qualitative study of black Caribbean and white British patients with advanced cancer. *Palliative Medicine,* 22(4), 350–359.

Kriegeskorte, N., Mur, M., Ruff, D. A., Kiani, R., Bodurka, J., Esteky, H., … Bandettini, P. A. (2008). Matching categorical object representations in inferior temporal cortex of man and monkey. *Neuron,* 60(6), 1126–41.

Lee, D. N., & Reddish, P. E. (1981). Plummeting gannets: A paradigm of ecological optics. *Nature,* 293, 293–294.

Nir, Y., & Tononi, G. (2010). Dreaming and the brain: From phenomonology to neurophysiology. *Trends in Cognitive Science,* 14(2), 88–100.

Pause, B. M., Hellmann, G., Goder, R., Aldenhoff, J. B., & Fersti, R. (2008). Increased processing speed for emotionally negative odors in schizophrenia. *International Journal of Psychophysiology,* 70(1), 16–22.

Rawson, N. E. (2003). Age-related changes in perception of flavor and aroma. *Generations,* 27(1), 20–26.

Schiff, W., & Oldak, R. (1990). Accuracy of judging time to arrival: Effects of modality, trajectory, and gender. *Journal of Experimental Psychology: Human Perception and Performance,* 16(2), 303–316.

Seubert, J., Kellermann, T., Loughead, J., Boers, F., Brensinger, C., Schneider, F., & Habel, Y. (2010). Processing of disgusted faces is facilitated by odor primes: A functional MRI study. *Neuroimage,* 53(2), 746–756.

Shepherd, G. M. (2007). The major senses: Sight, hearing, taste, smell, and touch. In F. E. Bloom and M. F. Beal (Eds.), *The Dana guide to brain health.* New York, NY: The Dana Foundation.

Sørensen, L. B., Moller, P., Flint, A., Martens, M., & Raben, A. (2003). Effect of sensory perception of food intake: A review of studies on humans. *International Journal of Obesity,* 27(10), 1152–1166.

Spangenber, E. R., Gerhmann, B., & Sprott, D. E. (2004). It's beginning to smell (and sound) a lot like Christmas: The interactive effects of ambient scent and music in a retail setting. *Journal of Business Research,* 58(11), 1583–1589.

Svoboda, E. (2007, June 12). When seasickness persists after a return to solid ground. *The New York Times.* Retrieved from http://www.nytimes.com/

Toomey, M. (2008). Update for nurse anesthetists part 4: Gender differences in pain: Does X = Y? *American Association of Nurse Anesthetists Journal,* 76(5), 355–359.

Vlaeyen, J. W. S., Crombez, G., & Goubert, L. (2007). The psychology of chronic pain and its management. *Physical Therapy Reviews,* 12, 179–188.

Winn, P. (Ed.). (2001). *Dictionary of biological psychology.* London: Routledge.

Yang, M., Clarke, A. M., & Crawley, J. (2009). Postnatal evidence against a primary role for the corpus callosum in mouse sociability. *European Journal of Neuroscience,* 28(8), 1663–1677.

Yeshurun, Y., Lapid, H., Dudai, U., & Sobil, N. (2009). The privileged brain representation of first olfactory associations. *Current Biology,* 19(21), 1869–1874.

Yeshrun, Y., & Soble, N. (2010). An odor is not worth a thousand words: From multidimensional odors to unidimensional odor objects. *Annual Review of Psychology,* 61, 219–241.

Chapter 5

Cleveland Clinic. (n.d.). *Sleep disorders in older child and teen.* Retrieved from http://my.clevelandclinic.org/documents/sleep_disorders_center/factsheets_collection.pdf

Domhoff, G. W. (2004). *Finding meaning in dreams: A quantitative approach.* Retrieved from http://psych.ucsc.edu/dreams/Library/fmid1.html

Domhoff, G. W. (n.d.). The "purpose" of dreams. Retrieved from http://psych.ucsc.edu/dreams/Library/purpose.html

Griffiths, R., Richards, W., Johnson, M., McCann, U., & Jesse, R. (2008). Mystical-type experiences occasioned by psilocybin mediate the attribution of personal meaning and spiritual significance 14 months later. *Journal of Psychopharmacology,* 22(6), 621–632.

Hall, R. (n.d.). Stages of sleep. Retrieved Psychology World website: http://web.mst.edu/~psyworld/sleep_stages.htm

Levy, N. (2006). *Consciousness and the persistent vegetative state.* Melbourne, AUS: University of Melbourne.

Lutz, A., Dunne, J. D., & Davidson, R. J. (2005). Meditation and the neuroscience of consciousness. In P. Zelazo, M. Moscovitz, & E. Thompson (Eds.), *Cambridge handbook of consciousness* (pp. 499–554). Retrieved from http://brainimaging.waisman.wisc.edu/~lutz/Meditation_Neuroscience_2005_AL_JDD_RJD_2.pdf

Marano, H. E. (2005, March 1). Why we dream. *Psychology Today*. Retrieved from http://www.psychologytoday.com/articles/200504/why-we-dream

Monti, M. M., Vanhaudenhuyse, A., Coleman, M. R., Boly, M., Pickard, J., Tshibanda, L., ... Laureys, S. (2010). Willful modulation of brain activity in disorders of consciousness. *New England Journal of Medicine, 362*, 579–589.

National Institute of General Medical Sciences. (2008, July). Circadian rhythms fact sheet. Retrieved from http://www.nigms.nih.gov/publications/factsheet_circadianrhythms.htm

National Institute of Neurological Disorders and Stroke. (2007, May 21). Brain basics: Understanding sleep: Sleep disorders. Retrieved from http://www.ninds.nih.gov/disorders/brain_basics/understanding_sleep.htm#back

Nicholson, C. (2006). Memory and consciousness: Consciousness to unconsciousness and back again. *Observer, 19*(8). Retrieved from http://www.psychologicalscience.org/observer/getArticle.cfm?id=2028

Owen, A., Coleman, M., Boly, M., Davis, M., Laureys, S., & Pickard, J. (2006). Detecting awareness in the vegetative state. *Science, 313*(5792), 1402.

Psychoanalysis—psychoanalytic theory of mind. (n.d.). Retrieved from http://science.jrank.org/pages/10900/Psychoanalysis-Psychoanalytic-Theory-Mind.html

Public Library of Science. (2008, August 27). Exploring the function of sleep. *ScienceDaily*. Retrieved from http://www.sciencedaily.com/releases/2008/08/080825203918.htm

Ryder, J. (2009, May 29). Is hypnosis really an altered state of consciousness? [Web log post]. *Psychology Today*. Retrieved from http://www.psychologytoday.com/blog/hypnosis-the-power-trance/200905/is-hypnosis-really-altered-state-consciousness

Singer, W. (2000). Phenomenal awareness and consciousness from a neurobiological perspective. In T. Metzinger (Ed.), *Neural correlates of consciousness: Empirical and conceptual questions* (pp. 121–138). Boston, MA: MIT Press.

Timothy Leary. (2004). In *Encyclopedia of world biography*. Retrieved from http://www.encyclopedia.com/doc/1G2-3404703777.html

Timothy Leary. (n.d.). Retrieved from http://www.timothyleary.us/

Weil, A. T. (n.d.). *Altered states of consciousness* (Drug Abuse Survey Project, Staff Paper No. 6). Retrieved from http://www.druglibrary.org/schaffer/library/studies/dwda/staff6.htm

Zhang, J. (2004). Memory process and the function of sleep. *Journal of Theoretics, 6*(6). Retrieved from http://www.journaloftheoretics.com/Articles/6-6/Zhang.pdf

Chapter 6

American Pregnancy Association. (2008, October). Using illegal street drugs during pregnancy. Retrieved from http://www.americanpregnancy.org/pregnancyhealth/illegaldrugs.html

Bretherton, I. (1992). The origins of attachment theory: John Bowlby and Mary Ainsworth. *Developmental Psychology, 28*, 759–775. Retrieved from http://www.psychology.sunysb.edu/attachment/online/inge_origins.pdf

Gerrig, R. J., & Zimbardo, P. G. (2009). *Psychology and life*. Boston, MA: Pearson.

Gilligan's *In a Different Voice*. (n.d.). Retrieved from http://www.stolaf.edu/people/huff/classes/handbook/Gilligan.html

Green, M., & Piel, J. A. (2002). *Theories of human development: A comparative approach*. Boston, MA: Allyn & Bacon.

Human Genome Project. (2008, September 16). Behavioral genetics. Retrieved from http://www.ornl.gov/sci/techresources/Human_Genome/elsi/behavior.shtml

Human Genome Project. (2010, December 31). Human genome project information. Retrieved from http://www.ornl.gov/sci/techresources/Human_Genome/home.shtml

Levinson, D. (1986). A conception of adult development. *The American Psychologist* 41(3), 3–13. Retrieved from http://www.imamu.edu.sa/topics/IT/IT%206/A%20Conception%20of%20Adult%20Development.pdf

Messer Zlatin, D. (1995). Life themes: A method to understand terminal illness. *OMEGA-Journal of Death and Dying, 3*(3), 189–206. Retrieved from http://baywood.metapress.com/app/home/contributionasp?referrer=parent&backto=issue,2,5;journal,123,245;linkingpublicationresults,1:300329,1

National Institutes of Mental Health. (2010, September 10). Teenage brain: A work in progress (Fact sheet). Retrieved from http://www.nimh.nih.gov/health/publications/teenage-brain-a-work-in-progress-fact-sheet/index.shtml

Palo Alto Medical Foundation. (2011). Puberty—Changes for females. Retrieved from http://www.pamf.org/teen/health/puberty/girlschanges.html

Palo Alto Medical Foundation. (2011). Puberty—Changes for males. Retrieved from http://www.pamf.org/teen/health/puberty/girlschanges.html

Perring, C. (n.d.). Kübler-Ross and other approaches. Retrieved from http://www.uky.edu/~cperring/kr.htm

Stevens, R. (2008). *Erik Erikson: Shaper of identity*. New York: Palgrave Macmillan

Chapter 7

Arnold, R., & Colburn, N. (2011, January 1). It's never too early. *School Library Journal, 57*, 20–28. Retrieved from http://www.schoollibraryjournal.com/slj/printissuecurrentissue/888330–427/its_never_too_early_parents.html.csp

Axmacher, N., Haupt, E., Cohen, M. X., Elger, C. E., & Fell, J. (2009). Interference of working memory load with long-term memory formation. *Cognitive Neuroscience, 29*, 1501–1513. doi: 10.1111/j.1460-9568.2009.06676.x

Best, J. (2009). Need to override your heuristic system? Better bring your deductive competence. *North American Journal of Psychology, 11*(3), 543–582.

Bhatti, A. A. (2009). Performance analysis and comparison of a minimum interconnections direct storage model with traditional neural bidirectional memories. *IET Nanobiotechnology, 3*(4), 81–102. doi: 10.1049/iet-nbt.2009.0002

Chamorro-Premuzic, T., & Furnham, A. (2004). A possible model for understanding the personality-intelligence interface. *British Journal of Psychology, 95*(Pt 2), 249–264.

Chandra, P. (2007). Review of language, mind, and brain: Some psychological and neurological constraints on theories of grammar. *Cognitive Systems Research, 8(1),* 53–56.

Chomsky, N. (1968). *Language and mind.* New York, NY: Harcourt Brace Jovanovich.

Daviglus, M. L., Bell, C. C., Berrettini, W., Bowen, P. E., Connolly, Jr., E. S., Cox, N. J., … Trevisan, M. (2010). National Institutes of Health state-of-the-science conference statement: Preventing **Alzheimer's disease** and cognitive decline. *Annals of Internal Medicine,* 153(3), 176–W.65.

Enchanted Mind. (2002). Creativity test. Retrieved from http://www.enchantedmind.com/html/creativity/iq_tests/creativity_test.html

Furnham, A. (2009). The validity of a new, self-report measure of multiple intelligence. *Current Psychology,* 28(4), 225–239. doi:10.1007/s12144-009-9064-z

Garand, D. (2009). Misunderstanding: A typology of performance. *Common Knowledge,* 15(3), 472–500. doi: 10.1215/0961754X-2009-024

Ikonomidou, C., Bittagau, P., Ishimaru, M. J., Wozniak, D. F., Koch, C., Genz, K., … Olney, J. W. (2000). Ethanol-induced apoptotic neurodegeneration and fetal alcohol syndrome. *Science* 2000, 287, 1056–1060.

Kearney, J. (2009). Rogerian principles and the writing classroom: A history of intention and (mis)interpretation. *Rhetoric Review,* 28(2), 167–184. doi: 10.1080/07350190902740034

Kennedy, D. P., Gläscher, J., Tyszka, J. M., & Adolphs, R. (2009). Personal space regulation by the human amygdala. *Nature Neuroscience,* 12, 1226–1227. doi: 10.1038/nn.2381

Koppel, J., & Goldberg, T. (2009). The genetics of episodic memory. *Cognitive Neuropsychiatry,* 14(4–5), 356–376. doi: 10.1080/13546800902990438

Kryukov, V. I. (2008). The role of the hippocampus in long-term memory: Is it memory storage or comparator? *Journal of Integrative Neuroscience,* 7(1), 117–184. doi: 10.1142/S021963520800171X

Kvavilashvili, L., & Fisher, L. (2007). Is time-based prospective remembering mediated by self-initiated rehearsals? Role of incidental cues, ongoing activity age, and motivation. *Journal of Experimental Psychology: General,* 136(1), 112–132.

Kvavilashvili, L., Kornbrot, D. E., Mash, V., Cockburn, J., & Milne, A. (2009). Differential effects of age on prospective and retrospective memory tasks in young, young-old, and old-old adults. *Memory,* 17(2), 180–196.

Lee, Y., & Silva, A. J. (2009). The molecular and cellular biology of enhanced cognition. *Nature Reviews: Neuroscience,* 10, 126–140. doi: 10.1080/09658210802194366

Loftus, E. F. (1997). Creating false memories. *Scientific American,* 277(3), 70–75. Retrieved from http://faculty.washington.edu/eloftus/Articles/sciam.htm

Oberauer, K. (2007). In search of the magic number. *Experimental Psychology,* 54, 245–246.

Ornat, S. L., & Gallo, P. (2004) Acquisition, learning, or development of language? Skinner's "verbal behavior" revisited. *Spanish Journal of Psychology,* 7(2),161–170.

Parker, A., Dagnall, N., & Coyle, A. M. (2007). Environmental context effects in conceptual explicit and implicit memory. *Memory,* 15(4), 423–434. doi: 10.1080/09658210701309834

Porter, S., & ten Brinke, L. (2010). The truth about lies: What works in detecting high-stakes deception? *Legal and Criminological Psychology,* 15(1), 57–75. doi: 10.1348/135532509X433151

Raica, D. A. (2009). Effect of action-oriented communication training on nurses' communication self efficacy. *Medsburg Nursing,* 18(6), 343–346, 360.

Simonton, D. K., & Song, A. V. (2009). Eminence, IQ, physical and mental health, and achievement domain: Cox's 282 geniuses revisited. *Psychological Science,* 20, 429–434. doi: 10.1111/j.1467-9280.2009.02313.x

Spada, M. M., Georgiou, G. A., & Wells, A. (2010). The relationship among metacognitions, attentional control, and state anxiety. *Cognitive Behaviour Therapy,* 39(1), 64–71.

Sporer, S. L., & Schwandt, B. (2006). Paraverbal indicators of deception: A meta-analytic synthesis. *Applied Cognitive Psychology,* 20(4), 421–446.

Sternberg, R. J. (2006). The nature of creativity. *Creativity Research Journal,* 18(1), 87–98.

Torrance, P. E. (2008). *Torrance Test of Creative Thinking.* Scholastic Testing Service. Retrieved from http://ststesting.com/ttctbro.pdf

Trebay, G. (2009, November 2). Testing her strong suit. *The New York Times.* Retrieved from http://www.nytimes.com

Tulving, E. (2002). Episodic memory: From mind to brain. *Annual Review of Psychology,* 53, 1–25.

Unsworth, N., Redick, T. S., Heitz, R. P., Broadway, J. M., & Engle, R. W. (2009). Complex working memory span tasks and higher-order cognition: A latent-variable analysis of the relationship between processing and storage. *Memory,* 17(6), 635–654. doi: 10.1080/09658210902998047.

Zhang, Q., He, X., & Zhang, J. (2007). A comparative study on the classification of basic color terms by undergraduates from Yi nationality, Bai nationality and Naxi nationality. Acta *Psychologica Sinica, 39(1),* 18–26.

Chapter 8

Cole, M., & Wertsch, J.V. Beyond the individual-social antimony in discussions of Piaget and Vygotsky. Retrieved from http://www.massey.ac.nz/~alock/virtual/colevyg.htm

Gallagher, J.M., & Reid, D.K. (1981). *The learning theory of Piaget and Inhelder.* Lincoln, NE: Authors Choice.

Gerrig, R. J., & Zimbardo, P. G. (2009). *Psychology and life* (19th ed.). Boston, MA: Allyn & Bacon.

Green, M., & Piel, J. A. (2002). *Theories of human development.* Boston, MA: Allyn & Bacon.

Kolb, D.A., Boyatzis, R.E., & Mainemelis, C. (2000). Experiential learning theory: Previous research and new directions. In R. J. Sternberg & L. F. Zhang (Eds.), *Perspectives on thinking, learning, and cognitive styles.* Mahwah, NJ: Lawrence Erlbaum.

Leonard, D.C. (2002). *Learning theories, A to Z.* Westport, CT: Greenwood Press.

Milbourn, G., Jr. (1996, November 17). Punishment in the workplace creates undesirable side effects. *Wichita Business Journal.* Retrieved from http://www.bizjournals.com/wichita/stories/1996/11/18/focus3.html

Pajares, F. (2004). Albert Bandura: Biographical sketch. Retrieved from http://www.des.emory.edu/mfp/bandurabio.html

Pritchard, A. (2009). *Ways of learning: learning theories and learning styles in the classroom.* New York, NY: Routledge.

Pritchard, A., & Woollard, J. (2010). *Psychology for the classroom: Constructivism and social learning.* New York, NY: Routledge.

Salen, K., & Zimmerman, E. (2003). *Rules of play: Game design fundamentals.* Cambridge, MA: MIT Press.

Sasso, N. (Producer & editor). (2009, December 8). A conversation with Eric Zimmerman [Audio podcast]. Interview by C. J. Pratt. *Another Castle.* Retrieved from http://gamedesignadvance.com/?page_id=1616

Shaffer, D.R. (2009). *Social and personality development* (6th ed.). Belmont, CA: Wadsworth, Cengage Learning.

Smith, L., & Tomlinson, P. (1997). *Piaget, Vygotsky and beyond: Future issues for developmental psychology and education.* New York, NY: Routledge.

Vargas, J. (2005). A brief biography of B. F. Skinner. Retrieved from http://www.bfskinner.org/BFSkinner/AboutSkinner.html

Chapter 9

Brodal, P. (2004). *The central nervous system: Structure and function* (3rd ed.). New York, NY: Oxford University Press.

Cannon, W. B. (1920). *Bodily changes in pain, hunger, fear and rage.* New York, NY: D. Appleton and Company.

Duenwald, M. (2005, January). The physiology of… facial expressions. *Discover Magazine.*

Ekman, P. (1972). Universals and cultural difference in facial expressions of emotion. In J. Cole (Ed.), *Nebraska symposium on motivation,* 1971 (Vol. 19, pp. 207–280). Lincoln, NE: University of Nebraska Press. Retrieved from http://www.paulekman.com/wp-content/uploads/2009/02/Universals-And-Cultural-Differences-In-Facial-Expressions-Of.pdf

Ekman, P. (1992). Are there basic emotions? *Psychological Review,* 99(3), 550–553.

Ekman, P. (2003). *Emotions revealed: Recognizing faces and feelings.* New York, NY: Henry Holt and Company.

Ekman, P. (2004). Emotional and conversational nonverbal signals. In J. M. Larrazabal & L. A. Perez (Eds.), *Language, knowledge, and representation* (pp. 39–50). The Netherlands: Klewer. Retrieved from http://www.paulekman.com/wp-content/uploads/2009/02/Emotional-And-Conversational-Nonverbal-Signals.pdf

Ekman, P., Friesen, W., & Hager, J. (2002). *Facial action coding system: The manual.* Salt Lake City, UT: A Human Face. Retrieved from http://face-and-emotion.com/dataface/facs/manual/TitlePage.html

Ellis, A. (2001). *Feeling better, getting better, staying better.* Atascadero, CA: Impact Publishers.

Ellis, A. (2001). *Overcoming destructive beliefs, feelings and behaviors: New directions for rational emotive behavior therapy.* Amherst, NY: Prometheus Books.

Emotional Intelligence Consortium. (n.d.). Emotional competence framework. Retrieved from http://www.eiconsortium.org/reports/emotional_competence_framework.html

Harrison, T. (1997). *Archibald Philip Bard: A biographical memoir.* Washington, DC: National Academies Press. Retrieved from http://www.nap.edu/readingroom.php?book=biomems&page=pbard.html

Hillstrom, K., & Hillstrom, L. C. (Eds.). (2011). Workplace anger. *Encyclopedia of Small Business.* Retrieved from http://www.enotes.com/small-business-encyclopedia/workplace-anger

Kendler, K. S., Halberstadt, L. J., Butera, F., Myers, J., Bouchard, T., & Ekman, P. (2008). The similarity of facial expressions in response to emotion-inducing films in reared-apart twins. *Psychological Medicine, 38,* 1475–1483.

Lange, C., & James, W. (1922). *The emotions.* Baltimore, MD: Williams and Wilkins Company.

Lewis, M., Haviland-Jones, J., & Barret, L. (2008). *Handbook of emotions.* New York, NY: Guilford Press.

Matsumoto, D. R. (2001). *The handbook of culture and psychology.* New York, NY: Oxford University Press.

Myers, D. (2005). *Exploring psychology.* New York, NY: Worth Publishing.

Plutchik, R. (2001). *The emotions.* New York, NY: University Press of America.

Schachter, S. (1964). The interaction of cognitive and physiological determinants of emotional state. In L. Berkowitz (Ed.), *Advances in experimental social psychology* (pp. 49–79). London, England: Academic Press.

Seligman, M. E. (1990). *Learned optimism.* New York, NY: Alfred A Knopf.

Seligman, M. E. (1995). *What you can change and what you can't.* New York, NY: Alfred A Knopf.

Seligman, M. E. (2002). *Authentic happiness.* New York, NY: Simon and Schuster.

Shimoff, M. (2008). *Happy for no reason.* New York, NY: Simon and Schuster.

Sibbald, B. (2003). Adrenaline junkies. *CMAJ,* 169(9), 942–943. Retrieved from http://www.canadianmedicaljournal.ca/cgi/reprint/169/9/942

Stone, F. (2003). Managing today's angry workforce. In *Business: The ultimate resource.* Cambridge, MA: Perseus Publishing.

Strack, F., Martin, L., & Stepper, S. (1988). Inhibiting and facilitating conditions of the human smile: A nonobtrusive test of the facial feedback hypothesis. *Journal of Personality and Social Psychology,* 54(5), 768–777.

Zajonc, R. B. (1984). On the primacy of affect. *American Psychologist,* 39(2), 117–123.

Chapter 10

Aanstoos, C., Serlin, I., & Greening, T. (2000). A history of division 32 (humanistic psychology) of the American Psychological Association. In D. Dewsbury (Ed.), *Unification through division: Histories of the divisions of the American Psychological Association* (Vol. V, pp.1–46). Washington, DC: American Psychological Association. Retrieved from http://www.apa.org/divisions/Div32/pdfs/history.pdf

Association for Humanistic Psychology. (2006). Five basic postulates of humanistic psychology. *Journal of Humanistic Psychology*, 46, 239. doi: 10.1177/002216780604600301

Association for Humanistic Psychology. (2010). Humanistic psychology overview. Retrieved from http://www.ahpweb.org/aboutahp/whatis.html

Baker, S. (2007, January 1). The sex hormone secrets. *Psychology Today*, 1–4. Retrieved from http://www.psychologytoday.com/articles/200612/the-sex-hormone-secrets

Baumeister, R. F., Catanese, K. R., & Vohs, K. D. (2001). Is there a gender difference in sex drive? Theoretical views, conceptual distinctions, and a review of relevant evidence. *Personality and Social Psychology Review*, 5(3), 242–273. Retrieved from https://www.csom.umn.edu/Assets/71520.pdf

Bovet, P. (2006). *The fighting instinct.* (J. Y. T. Greig, Trans.). Whitefish, MT: Kesslinger Publishing.

Brooks, G. (n.d.). Rehabilitation of mind, motivation, and identity after traumatic brain injury. Retrieved from http://www.northeastcenter.com/rehabilitation-of-mind-motovation-and-identity-after-traumatic-brain-injury.pdf

Carson, R. C., & Butcher, J. N. (1992). *Abnormal psychology and modern life* (9th ed.). New York, NY: Harper Collins.

Cooper, C. L., & Pervin, L. A. (1998). *Personality: Critical concepts in psychology.* New York, NY: Routledge.

Crain, W. (2005). *Theories of development: Concepts and applications* (5th ed.). Upper Saddle River, NJ: Pearson Prentice Hall.

Darwin, C. (2005). *The descent of man and selection in relation to sex.* In W. Crain, *Theories of development: Concepts and applications* (5th ed.). Upper Saddle River, NJ: Pearson Education. (Original work published 1871)

Darwin, C. (2005). *The origin of species.* In W. Crain, *Theories of development: Concepts and applications* (5th ed.). Upper Saddle River, NJ: Pearson Education. (Original work published 1859)

Garner, D. (2009, June 25). Books of the Times: Out of the bedroom, into the clinic. *The New York Times*, C28. Retrieved from http://www.nytimes.com/2009/06/26/books/26book.html

Graham, S., & Weiner, B. (1996). Theories and principles of motivation. In D. Berliner & R. Calfe (Eds.), *Handbook of educational psychology* (pp. 63–84). New York, NY: Macmillan.

Granacher, R. P. (2008). *Traumatic brain injury: Methods for clinical and forensic neuropsychiatric evaluation* (2nd ed.). Boca Raton, FL: CRC Press/Taylor and Francis Group.

Haines, J., & Neumark-Sztainer, D. (2006). Prevention of obesity and eating disorders: A consideration of shared risk factors. *Oxford Journal of Health Education Research*, 21(6), 770–782. Retrieved from: http://her.oxfordjournals.org/content/21/6/770.full

Harackiewicz, J. A., Barron, K. E., Pintrich, P. R., Elliot, A. J., & Thrash, T. M. (2002). Revision of achievement goal theory: Necessary and illuminating. *Journal of Educational Psychology*, 94(3), 638–645. doi: 10.1037//0022-0663.94.3.638

Hastak, S. M., Gorawara, P. S., & Mishra, N. K. (2005, September). Abulia: No will, no way. *Journal of the Association of Physicians of India*, 53, 814–818. Retrieved from http://www.japi.org/september2005/CR-814.pdf

Herzberg, F. (1987). One more time: How do you motivate employees? Cambridge, MA: *Harvard Business Review.* (Reprint, with commentary, of original article published January–February, 1968, pp. 88–96). Retrieved from http://www.facilitif.eu/user_files/file/herzburg_article.pdf

Herzberg, F., & Snyderman, B. B. (1959). *The motivation to work.* New York, NY: John Wiley and Sons.

Huitt, W. G. (2007). Maslow's hierarchy of needs. *Educational Psychology Interactive.* Valdosta, GA: Valdosta State University. Retrieved from http://www.edpsycinteractive.org/topics/regsys/maslow.html

Kinsey, A. C., Pomeroy, W. R., & Martin, C. E. (2003). Voices from the past: Sexual behavior in the human male. *American Journal of Public Health*, 93(6), 894–898. Retrieved from http://ajph.aphapublications.org/cgi/content/full/93/6/894

Lowe, M. R., & Levine, A. S. (2005). Eating motives and the controversy over dieting: Eating less than needed versus less than wanted. *Obesity Research*, 13(5), 797–806. Retrieved from http://lowelabs.com/publications/2005_Obesity_Research.pdf

Marx, K. (1970). *Introduction to a contribution to a critique of Hegel's Philosophy of Right.* (J. O'Malley, Trans.). Oxford, England: Oxford University Press. Retrieved from http://www.marxists.org/archive/marx/works/download/Marx_Critique_of_Hegels_Philosophy_of_Right.pdf (Original work published 1844).

Maslow, A. (1943). *A theory of human motivation* (Classics in the history of psychology). *Psychological Review*, 50, 370–396. Retrieved from: http://psychclassics.yorku.ca/Maslow/motivation.htm

Maslow, A. (1954, 1970). *Motivation and personality* (3rd ed.). New York, NY: Harper and Row.

Masters, W., & Johnson, V. (2010). *Human sexual response.* New York, NY: Ishi Press International.

McClelland, D. C. (2010). *The achieving society.* Eastford, CT: Martino Fine Books.

Money, J., Hampson, J. G., & Hampson, J. L. (1957). Imprinting and the establishment of gender role. *Archives of Neurology and Psychiatry*, 77, 333–336.

Myers, D. G. (2010). *Exploring psychology* (9th ed.). New York, NY: Worth Publishers.

National Institute of Neurological Disorders and Stroke. (2011). Traumatic brain injury information page. Retrieved from http://www.ninds.nih.gov/disorders/tbi/tbi.htm

Ogden, J. A. (2005). *Fractured minds: A case study approach to clinical neuropsychology.* New York, NY: Oxford University Press USA.

Polivy, J., & Herman, C. P. (2002). Causes of eating disorders. *Annual Review of Psychology*, 53(1), 187–213. Retrieved from http://comp.uark.edu/~nlwilli/polivy02.pdf

Powell, J. H., al-Adawi, S., Morgan, J., & Greenwood, R. J. (1996). Motivational deficits after brain injury: Effects of bromocriptine in 11 patients. *Journal of Neurology, Neurosurgery, and Psychiatry*, 60(4), 416–421. Retrieved from http://jnnp.bmj.com/content/60/4/416.full.pdf

Read, N. W. (1992, May). Role of gastrointestinal factors in hunger and satiety in man. *The Proceedings of the Nutrition Society, 51*(1), 7–11.

Reiss, S. (2004). Multifaceted nature of intrinsic motivation: The theory of sixteen basic desires. *Review of General Psychology, 8*(3), 179–193. doi: 10.1037/1089-2680.8.3.179

Seligman, M. E. P. (2002). *Authentic happiness: Using the new positive psychology to realize your potential for lasting fulfillment.* New York, NY: Free Press.

Simons, J. A., Irwin, D. B., & Drinnien, B. A. (1987). Maslow's hierarchy of needs. In W. G. Huitt (Ed.), *Psychology: The search for understanding* . New York, NY: West Publishing.

Ulrich, R. S. (1991). Effects of interior design on wellness: Theory and recent research. *Journal of Health Care Interior Design,* 97–109. Retrieved from http://www.majorhospitalfoundation.org/pdfs/Effects of Interior Design on Wellness.pdf

Weiner, B. (1985). An attributional theory of achievement motivation and emotion. *Psychological Review, 92*(4), 548–573. Retrieved from http://education.ucsb.edu/janeconoley/ed197/documents/weinerAnattributionaltheory.pdf

Wigfield, A., Eccles, J. S., Schiefele, U., Roeser, R. W., & Davis-Kean, P. (2006). Development of achievement motivation. In W. Damon & N. Eisenberg (Eds.), *Handbook of child psychology* (6th ed., Vol. 3, pp. 1–39). Hoboken, NJ: Wiley.

Chapter 11

Allport, G. (2008). *New World Encyclopedia.* Retrieved from http://www.newworldencyclopedia.org/entry/Gordon_Allport

Cattell, R. (2009). *The scientific analysis of personality.* Piscataway, NJ: Aldine Transaction.

Eysenck, H. J. (1997). *Dimensions of personality.* Piscataway, NJ: Transaction Publishers.

Francis, L. J., Lewis, C. A., & Ziebertz, H. G. (2006). The short-form revised Eysenck Personality Questionnaire (EPQ-S): A German edition. *Social Behavior and Personality, 34*(2), 197–204.

Hofstede, G. (n.d.). *Culture.* Retrieved from http://www.geerthofstede.nl/culture.aspx

John, O. P., Robins, R. W., & Pervin, L. A. (2008). *Handbook of personality: Theory and research* (3rd ed.). New York, NY: Guilford Press.

Kahn, M. (2002). *Basic Freud: Psychoanalytic thought for the 21st century.* New York, NY: Basic Books.

Library of Congress Public Affairs Office. (2010). Swiss psychiatrist Carl Jung's "Red Book" is focus of library exhibition opening June 17. Retrieved from http://www.loc.gov/today/pr/2010/10-052.html

MBTI Basics. (n.d.). *The Myers and Briggs Foundation.* Retrieved from http://www.myersbriggs.org/my-mbti-personality-type/mbti-basics/

McCarthy, J. (2005). Individualism and collectivism: What do they have to do with counseling? *Journal of Multicultural Counseling and Development, 33*(2), 108–117.

McCrae, R. R., & Allik, J. (2002). *The five-factor model of personality across cultures.* New York, NY: Springer.

Minnesota Multiphasic Personality Inventory-2 (MMPI-2). (2011). Product Detail. San Antonio, TX: Pearson Education. Retrieved from http://www.pearsonassessments.com/HAIWEB/Cultures/en-us/Productdetail.htm?Pid=MMPI-2

Oyserman, D., Coon, H. M., & Kemmelmeier, M. (2002). Rethinking individualism and collectivism: Evaluation of theoretical assumptions and meta-analyses. *Psychological Bulletin, 128*(1), 3–72.

Turner, F. J. (1996). *Social work treatment* (4th ed.). New York, NY: Free Press.

Voronov, M. & Singer, J. A. (2002). The myth of individualism-collectivism: A critical review. *The Journal of Social Psychology, 142*(4), 461–480.

Wrightsman, L. S. (1994). *Adult personality development* (Vol. 1, theories and concepts). Thousand Oaks, CA: Sage Publications.

Chapter 12

Allport, G. W. (2000). The nature of prejudice. In C. Stangor & C. Stangor (Eds.), *Stereotypes and prejudice: Essential readings* (pp. 20–48). Philadelphia, PA: Taylor & Francis Group.

Asch, S. (1951). Effects of group pressure upon the modification and distortion of judgments. In H. Guetzkow (Ed.), *Groups, leadership and men: Research in human relations* (pp. 177–190). Pittsburgh, PA: Carnegie Press.

Barelds, D. P. H., & Barelds-Dijkstra, P. (2007). Love at first sight or friends first? Ties among partner personality trait similarity, relationship onset, relationship quality, and love. *Journal of Social and Personal Relationships, 24*(4), 479–496. doi: 10.1177/0265407507079235

Baumeister, R. F., & Leary, M. R. (1995). The need to belong: Desire for interpersonal attachments as a fundamental human motivation. *Psychological Bulletin, 117*(3), 497–529. Retrieved from http://blog.lib.umn.edu/stei0301/sp_bbk/BandM%20Need%20to%20Belong.pdf

Beeler, C. K. (2010). Leader traits, skills, and behaviors. In M. D. Mumford (Ed.), *Leadership 101* (pp. 87–116). New York, NY: Springer Publishing.

Bem, D. J. (1967). Self-perception: An alternative interpretation of cognitive dissonance phenomena. *Psychological Review, 74*(3), 183–200. Retrieved from http://psycnet.apa.org/index.cfm?fa=buy.optionToBuy&id=1967-13584-001

Berkowitz, L. (1989). Frustration-aggression hypothesis: Examination and reformulation. *Psychological Bulletin, 106*(1), 59–73. Retrieved from http://robertmijas.com/blog/wp-content/uploads/2011/03/frustration-aggression.pdf, 0033-2909/89/$00.75

Berscheid, E. (2010). Love in the fourth dimension. *Annual Review of Psychology, 61,* 1–25.

Black, K., & Gold, D. (2008). Gender differences and socioeconomic status biases in judgments about blame in date rape scenarios. *Violence and Victims, 23*(1), 115–128.

Byrne, D. D. (1971). The ubiquitous relationship: Attitude similarity and attraction: A cross-cultural study. *Human Relations, 24*(3), 201–207.

Carstensen, L. L., Gottman, J. M., & Levenson, R. W. (1995). Emotional behavior in long-term marriage. *Psychology and Aging, 10(1)*, 140–149.

Cialdini, R. B., Vincent, J. E., Lewis, S. K., Catalan, J., Wheeler, D., & Darby, B. (1975). Reciprocal concessions procedure for inducing compliance: The door-in-the-face technique. *Journal of Personality and Social Psychology, 31(2)*, 206–215. Retrieved from http://www.psychology.uiowa.edu/Classes/31015sca/Cialdini%20Door%20in%20Face.pdf

Cunningham, M. R., Barbee, A. P., & Philhower, C. L. (2001). Dimensions of facial physical attractiveness: The intersection of biology and culture. In G. Rhodes & L. A. Zebrowitz (Eds.), *Facial attractiveness: Evolutionary, cognitive, and social perspectives* (pp. 193–238). London, UK: Ablex Publishing.

Dabbs, J. M., Carr, T. S., Frady, R. L., & Riad, J. K. (1995). Testosterone, crime, and misbehavior among 692 male prison inmates. *Personality and Individual Differences, 18(5)*, 627–633.

Darley, J. (2004). Social comparison motives in ongoing groups. In M. B. Brewer & M. Hewstone (Eds.), *Emotion and motivation* (pp. 281–297). Malden, UK: Blackwell Publishing.

Davidson, R. J., Putnam, K. M., & Larson, C. L. (2000). Dysfunction in the neural circuitry of emotion regulation—A possible prelude to violence. *Science, 289*(5479), 591–594.

Dollard, J., Doob, L., Miller, N., Mowrer, Q., & Sears, R. (1939). *Frustration and aggression.* New Haven, CT: Yale University Press.

Festinger, L. (1962). Cognitive dissonance. *Scientific American, 207*(4), 93–107.

Festinger, L., Schachter, S., & Back, K. (1950). *Social pressures in informal groups: A study of human factors in housing.* Oxford, England: Harper.

Fiedler, F. (1967). *A theory of leadership effectiveness.* New York, NY: McGraw-Hill.

Foley, L. A., Evancic, C., Karnik, K., King, J., & Parks, A. (1995). Date rape: Effects of race of assailant and victim and gender of subjects on perceptions. *Journal of Black Psychology, 21*, 6–18.

Freedman, J. L., & Fraser, S. C. (1966). Compliance without pressure: The foot-in-the-door technique. *Journal of Personality and Social Psychology, 4*(2), 195–202.

Friel, B. (2001). The Powell leadership doctrine. *Government Executive, 33*(7), 22–28.

Frontline. (1995–2011). A class divided. Retrieved from http://www.pbs.org/wgbh/pages/frontline/shows/divided/

Gibbons, F. X., Eggleston, T. J., & Benthin, A. C. (1997). Cognitive reactions to smoking relapse: The reciprocal relation between dissonance and self-esteem. *Journal of Personality and Social Psychology, 72*(1), 184–195.

Gottman, J. M., & Krokoff, L. J. (1989). The relationship between marital interaction and marital satisfaction: A longitudinal view. *Journal of Consulting and Clinical Psychology, 57*, 47–52.

Greenwald, A. G., Banaji, M. R., Rudman, L. A., Farnham, S. D., Nosek, B. A., & Mellott, D. S. (2002). A unified theory of implicit attitudes, stereotypes, self-esteem, and self-concept. *Psychological Review, 109*(1), 3–25. Retrieved from http://faculty.washington.edu/agg/pdf/UnifiedTheory.2002.pdf

Greenwald, A. G., McGhee, D. E., & Schwartz, J. K. (1998). Measuring individual differences in implicit cognition: The Implicit Association Test. *Journal of Personality and Social Psychology, 74*(6), 1464–1480. Retrieved from http://faculty.washington.edu/agg/pdf/Gwald_McGh_Schw_JPSP_1998.OCR.pdf

Harari, O. (2002). *The leadership secrets of Colin Powell.* New York, NY: McGraw-Hill Professional.

Harvey, J. B. (1988). The Abilene paradox: The management of agreement. *Organizational Dynamics, 17*(1), 17–34.

Heine, S. J., Foster, J. B., & Spina, R. (2009). Do birds of a feather universally flock together? Cultural variation in the similarity-attraction effect. *Asian Journal of Social Psychology, 12*(4), 247–258. doi: 10.1111/j.1467-839X.2009.01289.x

Hoffman, M. L. (1981). Is altruism part of human nature? *Journal of Personality and Social Psychology, 40*(1), 121–137. doi: 10.1037/0022-3514.40.1.121

Hovland, C. I., Janis, I. L., & Kelley, H. H. (1953). *Communication and persuasion.* New Haven, CT: Yale University Press.

Janis, I. L. (2007). Groupthink. In R. P. Vecchio (Ed.), *Leadership: Understanding the dynamics of power and influence in organizations* (2nd ed., pp. 157–169). Notre Dame, IN: University of Notre Dame Press.

Jones, E. E., & Nisbett, R. E. (1987). The actor and the observer: Divergent perceptions of the causes of behavior. In E. E. Jones, D. E. Kanouse, H. H. Kelley, R. E. Nisbett, S. Valins, & B. Weiner (Eds.), *Attribution: Perceiving the causes of behavior* (pp. 79–94). Hillsdale, NJ: Lawrence Erlbaum Associates.

King, E. B., Mendoza, S. A., Madera, J. M., Hebl, M. R., & Knight, J. L. (2006). What's in a name? A multiracial investigation of the role of occupational stereotypes in selection decisions. *Journal of Applied Social Psychology, 36*(5), 1145–1159. doi: 10.1111/j.0021-9029.2006.00035.x

Koss, M. P., & Cook, S. L. (2005). More data have accumulated supporting date and acquaintance rape as significant problems for women. In D. R. Loseke, R. J. Gelles, & M. M. Cavanaugh (Eds.), *Current controversies on family violence* (pp. 97–116). Thousand Oaks, CA: Sage Publishing.

Koss, M. P., Dinero, T. E., Seibel, C. A., & Cox, S. L. (1988). Stranger and acquaintance rape: Are there differences in the victim's experiences? *Psychology of Women Quarterly, 12*, 1–24.

Latané, B., & Darley, J. M. (1968). Group inhibition of bystander intervention in emergencies. *Journal of Personality and Social Psychology, 10*(3), 215–221.

Lewin, K. (1948). *Resolving social conflicts: Selected papers on group dynamics.* Oxford, England: Harper.

Manning, R., Levine, M., & Collins, A. (2007). The Kitty Genovese murder and the social psychology of helping: The parable of the 38 witnesses. *American Psychologist, 62*(6), 555–562.

McGregor, D. (2005). *The human side of enterprise.* New York, NY: McGraw-Hill. (Original work published 1960)

Miller, N. E., Mowrer, O. H., Doob, L. W., Dollard, J., & Sears, R. R. (1958). Frustration-aggression hypothesis. In C. L. Stacey & M. DeMartino (Eds.), *Understanding human motivation* (pp. 251–255). Cleveland, OH: Howard Allen Publishers.

Moorhead, G., Ference, R., & Neck, C. P. (1991). Group decision fiascoes continue: Space shuttle *Challenger* and a revised groupthink framework. *Human Relations, 44*(6), 531–550.

Moreland, R. L., & Beach, S. R. (1992). Exposure effects in the classroom: The development of affinity among students. *Journal of Experimental Social Psychology, 28*(3), 255–276.

Nisbett, R. E. (1993). Violence and US regional culture. *American Psychologist, 48*(4), 441–449.

Ostrom, T. M., & Sedikides, C. (1992). Out-group homogeneity effects in natural and minimal groups. *Psychological Bulletin, 112*(3), 536–552.

Petty, R. E. (1994). Two routes to persuasion: State of the art. In G. d'Ydewalle, P. Eelen, & P. Bertelson (Eds.), *International perspectives on psychological science: Vol. 2. The state of the art* (pp. 229–247). Hillsdale, NJ: Lawrence Erlbaum Associates.

Project Implicit. (n.d.). Retrieved from http://implicit.harvard.edu/implicit/research/

Selfhout, M., Denissen, J., Branje, S., & Meeus, W. (2009, June). In the eye of the beholder: Perceived, actual, and peer-rated similarity in personality, communication, and friendship intensity during the acquaintanceship process. *Journal of Personality and Social Psychology, 96*(6), 1152–1165.

Sternberg, R. J. (1986). A triangular theory of love. *Psychological Review, 93*(2), 119–135.

Tajfel, H., Billig, M. G., Bundy, R. P., & Flament, C. (1971). Social categorization and intergroup behavior. *European Journal of Social Psychology, 1*(2), 149–178. Online publication (2002) doi: 10.1002/ejsp.2420010202

Tajfel, H., & Turner, J. C. (2004). The social identity theory of intergroup behavior. In J. T. Jost & J. Sidanius (Eds.), *Political psychology: Key readings* (pp. 276–293). New York, NY: Psychology Press. (Original work published 1986)

Takooshian, H. (2009, March 11). The 1964 Kitty Genovese tragedy: Still a valuable parable. *PsycCRITIQUES, 54*(10), Article 2. Retrieved from http://psqtest.typepad.com/blogPostPDFs/200900817_psq_54-10_The1964KittyGenoveseTragedyStillAValuable Parable.pdf

Thompson, A. D., & Riggio, R. E. (2010). Introduction to special issue on defining and measuring character in leadership. *Consulting Psychology Journal: Practice and Research, 62*(4), 211–215.

Triplett, N. (2007). The dynamogenic factors in pacemaking and competition. In D. Smith & M. Bar-Eli (Eds.), *Essential readings in sport and exercise psychology* (pp. 2–12). Champaign, IL: Human Kinetics.

Vroom, V. H., & Jago, A. G. (2007). The role of the situation in leadership. *American Psychologist, 62*(1), 17–24.

Walster, E., Aronson, V., Abrahams, D., & Rottman, L. (1966). Importance of physical attractiveness in dating behavior. *Journal of Personality and Social Psychology, 4*(5), 508–516. Retrieved from http://www2.hawaii.edu/~elaineh/13.pdf

Wilder, D. A. (1984). Predictions of belief homogeneity and similarity following social categorization. *British Journal of Social Psychology, 23*(4), 323–333.

Wilder, D. A. (2001). Intergroup contact: The typical member and the exception to the rule. In M. A. Hogg & D. Abrams (Eds.), *Intergroup relations: Essential readings* (pp. 370–382). New York, NY: Psychology Press. (Original work published 1984, *Journal of Experimental Social Psychology, 20*(2), 177–194.) doi:10.1016/0022-1031(84)90019-2

Zajonc, R. B. (1965). Social facilitation. *Science, 149*(3681), 269–274.

Chapter 13

American Psychiatric Association. (2000). *Diagnostic and statistical manual of mental disorders* (4th ed., Text rev.). Washington, DC: American Psychiatric Publications.

American Psychiatric Association. (2013). *Diagnostic and statistical manual of mental disorders* (5th ed.). Arlington, VA: Author.

Bloom, J. D. (2010). The incarceration revolution: The abandonment of the seriously mental ill to our jails and prisons. *Journal of Law, Medicine and Ethics, 38*(4), 727–734. doi: 10.1111/j.1748-720X.2010.00526.x

Carr, D. (2008, April 20). Been up, been down. Now? Super. *The New York Times.* Retrieved from http://www.nytimes.com/2008/04/20/movies/20carr.html

Cheng, A. A. (2009). Psychoanalysis without symptoms. *Differences: A Journal of Feminist Cultural Studies, 20*(1), 87–101. doi: 10.1215/10407391-2008-017

Cortina, M. (2010). The future of psychodynamic psychotherapy. *Psychiatry, 73*(1), 43–56.

Doerfler, L. A., Moran, P. W., & Hannigan, K. E. (2010). Situations associated with admission to an acute care inpatient psychiatric unit. *Psychological Services, 7*(4), 254–265. doi: 10.1037/a0020642

Farb, N. A., Anderson, A. K., Mayberg, H., Bean, J., McKeon, D., & Segal, Z. V. (2010). Minding one's emotions: Mindfulness training alters the neural expression of sadness. *Emotion, 10*(1), 25–33. doi: 10.1037/a0017151

Haftgoli, N., Favrat, B., Verdon, F., Vaucher, P., Bischoff, T., Burnand, B., & Herzig, L. (2010). Patients presenting with somatic complaints in general practice: Depression, anxiety and somatoform disorders are frequent and associated with psychosocial stressors. *BMC Family Practice, 11*(67), 1–8. doi:10.1186/1471-2296-11-67

Mark, T. L. (2010). For what diagnoses are psychotropic medications being prescribed? *CNS Drugs, 24*(4), 319–326. doi: 10.2165/11533120-000000000-00000

McAllister, M. (2010). Solution focused nursing: A fitting model for mental health nurses working in a public health paradigm. *Contemporary Nurse, 34*(2), 149–157.

Miniussi, C., Cappa, S. F., Cohen, L. G., Floel, A., Fregni, F., Nitsche, M. A., … Walsh, V. (2008). Efficacy of repetitive transcranial magnetic stimulation/transcranial direct stimulation in cognitive neurorehabilitation. *Brain Stimulation, 1*(4), 26–36.

Morin, D., Cobigo, V., Rivard, M., & Levine, L. (2010). Intellectual disabilities and depression: How to adapt psychological assessment and intervention. *Canadian Psychology/Psychologie Canadienne,* 51(3), 185–193. doi: 10.1037/a0020184

Oyebode, F. (2006). History of psychiatry in West Africa. *International Review of Psychiatry,* 18(4), 319–325. doi: 10.1080/09540260600775397

Sanislow, C. A., Pine, D. S., Quinn, K. J., Kozack, M. J., Garvey, M. A., Heinssen, R. K., … Cuthbert, B. N. (2010). Developing constructs for psychopathology research: Research domain criteria. *Journal of Abnormal Psychology,* 119(4), 631–639. doi: 10.1037/a0020909

Schoevers, R. A., Van, H. L., Koppelmans, V., Kool, S., & Dekker, J. J. (2008). Managing the patient with co-morbid depression and an anxiety disorder. *Drugs,* 68(12), 1621–1634.

Shorter, E., & van Praag, H. M. (2010). Disease versus dimension in diagnosis. *The Canadian Journal of Psychiatry/Revue canadienne de psychiatrie,* 55(2), 59–64.

Snowden, A. (2009). Classification of schizophrenia, part 2: The nonsense of mental health illness. *British Journal of Nursing,* 18(20), 1228–1232.

Snyder, E. K. (2010). Psychiatric nursing: Nurse faulted, discharged patient without full mental health evaluation. *Legal Eagle Eye Newsletter for the Nursing Profession,* 18(7). Retrieved from http://www.nursinglaw.com/fullmentalhealth.pdf

Stanford, M. S. (2007). Demon or disorder: A survey of attitudes toward mental illness in the Christian church. *Mental Health, Religion and Culture,* 10(5), 445–449. doi: 10.1080/13674670600903049

Stern, S. (2009). Session frequency and the definition of psychoanalysis. *Psychoanalytic Dialogues,* 19, 639–655. doi: 10.1080/10481880903232058

INDEX

0-9

R

S

T

Notes

Notes

Notes

Notes

Notes

Notes

Notes

Notes

Notes

Notes

Notes

Notes